The DATA
Model for Teaching
Preschoolers with Autism

The DATA
Model for Teaching
Preschoolers with Autism

by

Ilene Schwartz, Ph.D., BCBA-D
University of Washington
Seattle

Julie Ashmun, M.Ed., BCBA
University of Washington
Seattle

Bonnie McBride, Ph.D., BCBA-D
University of Oklahoma Health Sciences Center
Oklahoma City

Crista Scott, M.Ed., BCBA
University of Washington
Seattle

and

Susan Sandall, Ph.D.
University of Washington
Seattle

·P A U L·H·
BROOKES
PUBLISHING Cº ®

Baltimore • London • Sydney

Paul H. Brookes Publishing Co.
Post Office Box 10624
Baltimore, Maryland 21285-0624
USA

www.brookespublishing.com

Typeset by Progressive Publishing Services, Emigsville, Pennsylvania.
Manufactured in the United States of America
by Sheridan Books, Chelsea, Michigan.

Cover image is © istockphoto/Christopher Futcher.

Library of Congress Cataloging-in-Publication Data
The Library of Congress has cataloged the print edition as follows:

Names: Schwartz, Ilene S.
Title: The DATA Model for teaching preschoolers with autism/by Ilene
  Schwartz, Ph.D., University of Washington, Julie Ashmun, M.Ed., University
  of Washington, Bonnie McBride, Ph.D., University of Oklahoma, Crista
  Scott, M.Ed., University of Washington, and Susan Sandall, Ph.D.,
  University of Washington.
Description: [First edition] I Baltimore : Paul H. Brookes Publishing Co.,
  [2016] I Includes bibliographical references and index.
Identifiers: LCCN 2016025989 (print) I ISBN 9781598573169 (Paper)
Subjects: LCSH: Autistic children—Education (Early childhood)—United
  States. I Children with disabilities—Education (Early childhood)—United
  States. I Behavioral assessment. I Mainstreaming in education—United
  States. I Inclusive education—United States. I Project DATA.
Classification: LCC LC4718. S356 2016 (print) I LCC LC4718 (ebook) I DDC
  371.94—dc23
LC record available at https://lccn.loc.gov/2016025989

British Library Cataloguing in Publication data are available from the British Library.

2020   2019   2018   2017   2016

10   9   8   7   6   5   4   3   2   1

Contents

About the Forms.. vi

About the Authors vii

Preface.. ix

Acknowledgments... xii

Section I: Fundamentals of the Project DATA Model

1   Introducing the DATA Model Approach...3

2   Characteristics of a High-Quality Inclusive Early Childhood
    Program for Children with Autism Spectrum Disorder 9

3   Basic Principles of Applied Behavior Analysis 19

4   Instructional Strategies to Facilitate Learning..................................29

5   Determining What to Teach 43

6   Writing and Using the Instructional Programs 51

7   Teaching Project DATA Style 69

8   Data-Based Decision Making 79

9   Collaborating with Families and Other Partners 95

10 Implementing Project DATA in Your Community 109

Section II: Project DATA Instructional Programs

I   Adaptive 118

II   Executive Functioning 166

III Cognitive...212

IV   Communication 264

V   Social...332

VI   Play 378

Glossary...415

References..419

Appendix

Appendix A: The DATA Model Skills Checklist 421

Appendix B: DATA Model Skills Checklist: Curriculum Crosswalk.................439

Appendix C: DATA Model Skills Checklist: Materials List 451

Appendix D: Frequently Asked Questions 455

Index 457

About the Forms

Purchasers of this book may download, print, and/or photocopy blank forms for educational use. These materials are included with the print book and are also available at **www.brookespublishing.com/schwartz/materials** for both print and e-book buyers.

About the Authors

Ilene Schwartz, Ph.D., BCBA-D, is Professor of Education at the University of Washington (UW) and the Director of the Haring Center for Research and Training in Inclusive Education at UW. She earned her Ph.D. in child and developmental psychology from the University of Kansas and is a Board Certified Behavior Analyst (BCBA-D). Ilene has an active research and professional training agenda with primary interests in the area of autism, inclusive education, and the sustainability of educational interventions. She has had consistent research funding from the U.S. Department of Education since 1990 and serves on a number of editorial review boards including the Topics in Early Childhood Special Education and the Journal of Early Intervention. Ilene is the director of Project DATA at the University of Washington and is currently involved in research projects examining the efficacy of the Project DATA model with toddlers and preschoolers with autism. Ilene is dedicated to building inclusive schools and societies and views inclusion as the celebration of diversity put into action. She is proud of what she and her colleagues have accomplished at the Haring Center, where research, training, and service are integrated to provide world-class early learning experiences to children with and without disabilities.

Julie Ashmun, M.Ed., BCBA, is Director of the Professional Development Unit at the University of Washington's Haring Center for Research and Training in Inclusive Education. She began working in preschool and child care centers in 1995, and since then has been a Project DATA teacher and coordinator, a professional development research assistant and trainer, and a family resource coordinator. Julie has a master's degree in education, with an emphasis in early childhood special education, and is a Board Certified Behavior Analyst (BCBA). Julie is interested in effective practices for professional development in education and adult learning. She also devotes her time to researching and working with children with neurodevelopmental delays, including autism, and working with families and educators. Julie's research focuses on assessment and intervention practices for inclusive school-based programs for children with disabilities, including autism spectrum disorders.

Bonnie McBride, Ph.D., BCBA-D, is Associate Professor of Pediatrics in the Department of Developmental and Behavioral Pediatrics at the University of Oklahoma Health Sciences Center. She has expertise in early childhood special education, early childhood education, and applied behavior analysis. She has a long history of using behavioral principles to work with children with autism spectrum disorder (ASD) and other disorders. She completed her doctoral work at the University of Washington where she was a teacher in the inclusive preschool and the first head teacher of Project DATA. Since moving to Oklahoma, Bonnie has been instrumental in increasing the availability of services to young children with ASD and their families. She has developed a statewide network to implement Project DATA for toddlers and preschoolers in Oklahoma. She has served as Principal Investigator for two randomized control trials of the Project DATA model funded by the Institute of Education Sciences (toddler and preschool).

Crista Scott, M.Ed., BCBA, taught for 8 years in early childhood special education. Most of that time was spent as a teacher in an inclusive preschool and coordinator for Project DATA at the University of Washington's Haring Center for Research and Training in Inclusive Education. Crista has a master's degree in education, with an emphasis in early childhood special education, and is a Board Certified

Behavior Analyst (BCBA). In addition to teaching in special education, Crista is interested in providing effective professional development activities. She was a product manager for the Office of Head Start's National Center on Quality Teaching and Learning, supporting the development and dissemination of professional development materials for educators in early learning. Crista supported an Institute of Education Sciences grant that investigated the use of self and in-person coaching strategies to increase the use of embedded teaching practices in early childhood special education classrooms. Currently, she is coordinating an evaluation project on the implementation of Filming Interactions to Nurture Development, a program that supports interactions between childcare providers and children in infant and toddler environments. This project is in partnership with Washington State's Department of Early Learning and the University of Oregon.

Susan Sandall, Ph.D., is Professor of Education at the University of Washington. Her scholarly interests are effective instructional practices for young children with disabilities in inclusive settings; the changing roles of teachers of young children with disabilities, their relationships with other providers, and the implications for personnel preparation; and effective approaches for professional development and knowledge utilization. Susan was Principal Investigator for the National Center on Quality Teaching & Learning, funded by the Office of Head Start, and continues this work through EarlyEdU. She serves on the Division for Early Childhood's (DEC) Commission on Recommended Practices and edits publications on DEC recommended practices. She is coauthor of *Building Blocks for Including and Teaching Preschoolers with Special Needs* (2000, 2008). Awards include the Mary McEvoy Service to the Field Award and the Merle B. Karnes Service to the Division Award from the Division of Early Childhood, Council for Exceptional Children.

Preface

While working at the University of Washington's (UW) Experimental Education Unit (EEU) in 1996, Ilene Schwartz and Bonnie McBride started receiving requests from parents for applied behavior analysis (ABA) services for their children with autism spectrum disorder (ASD). Some of the parents making these requests had children who were attending the inclusive preschool at the EEU; others had just heard that the people at the UW knew something about this "new" intervention that they had heard of—ABA. Many parents, in fact, came to the UW with a prescription from their primary care physician that had "40 hours of Lovaas" written out as if it was something that could be ordered up at a pharmacy. Before coming to the UW, both Bonnie and Ilene had worked in segregated, behavioral settings for children with ASD and were convinced that 40 hours a week of decontextualized discrete trial training was not the most appropriate way to meet the educational needs of preschool children with ASD. At the same time, however, they realized that 12 hours a week of inclusive preschool programming that their current program was providing was not meeting the unique needs of children with ASD either.

In an attempt to solve this problem (and with the assistance of a Project Demonstration grant from the U.S. Department of Education's Office of Special Education Programs), Project DATA (Developmentally Appropriate Treatment for Autism) was born in the fall of 1997. The purpose of the Project DATA model was, and continues to be, to develop, implement, evaluate, and disseminate a school based program for very young children with ASD that blended different theoretical approaches to meet individual needs. Although by training we are Board Certified Behavior Analysts, we are always open to learning from our colleagues and collaborating to develop intervention strategies that meet the needs of the diverse students on the autism spectrum. We were committed to developing a program that was effective, met the needs of consumers (e.g., parents and school district personnel), and was sustainable. Most important, we wanted to use what we had learned about inclusion, early childhood education, and new advancements in applied behavior analysis to create an intervention model that would help children and their families achieve meaningful outcomes, participate in their communities, and improve the overall quality of their lives.

For the past 18 years, we (along with hundreds of children, families, graduate students, and colleagues) have worked to define, evaluate, redefine, and disseminate the Project DATA model. We have provided training to school districts and community agencies in over 25 states and territories and a number of foreign countries. We have watched the toddlers and preschoolers who were our original participants grow up to become adults. Some of these young adults are off to college and living independent lives, and others still require a great deal of support. Many have jobs and all have taught us much about working with students with ASD and their families.

The purpose of this manual is to help teachers, applied behavior analysts, parents, and other educators implement the Project DATA model in their community. As we have worked with communities across the country and around the world, our team has learned that every community is going to make changes to the Project DATA model to help it fit into their existing values and beliefs. We hope that teams from different communities will embrace the values of the Project DATA model and work to implement it in a manner that is socially and ecologically valid in their own school and community settings. The values of the Project DATA model include

- Children with ASD are children *first*

- Children with ASD need to interact successfully with typically developing children everyday

- Student failure is instructional failure

These values guide every part of the model. They influence decisions about where and when instruction should occur, what types of skills should be taught, and the amount of staff training and coaching that is provided.

The fields of applied behavior analysis, education, and psychology have learned a lot about ASD since the Project DATA model started. We know that children with ASD benefit from high quality, inclusive, early intensive behavioral intervention programs (Strain, Schwartz, & Barton, 2011). The Project DATA model is an effective, sustainable strategy that professionals can use to implement such a program in their community.

HOW TO USE THIS MANUAL

There are many components that go into creating a high quality program for young children with ASD. The curriculum, that is, the skills and behaviors that are targeted for instruction, is one of the most essential components. The quality of an early intensive behavioral intervention (EIBI) program is only as good as the quality of the skills being taught. A core component of the Project DATA model is a quality of life influenced curriculum. That means that this model emphasizes skills that will help children participate independently in their families, schools, and communities. Our emphasis on a quality of life influenced curriculum is one of the primary components that distinguishes Project DATA from other EIBI programs, and therefore our assessment and curriculum are the centerpiece of this manual.

The DATA Model Skills Checklist and accompanying instructional programs are intended to be used in conjunction with a high quality early childhood curriculum. This reinforces our value that children with ASD are children first. We believe that a high quality curriculum is necessary, but not sufficient to provide the appropriate scope and sequence of instruction for children with ASD. It also explains why the DATA Model Skills Checklist is not a comprehensive assessment. It is not designed to be used as a stand-alone tool, but rather to augment existing early childhood curriculum-based assessments to provide a broad view of child behavior, including those behaviors and skills associated with the core deficits of ASD.

To create a comprehensive and individualized plan for a child with ASD using the Project DATA model, the educational team should compile information from at least three sources:

■ A comprehensive early childhood curriculum based assessment

■ The DATA Model Skills Checklist

■ The Project DATA Family Interview

Once those data are collected and compiled (see Chapter 5 for more details), the team should identify the high-priority skills and behaviors (ideally, these are the same behaviors included on the child's individualized family service plan or individualized education program). Then, using the instructional programs included in this manual, the team can begin to plan the intervention sessions. It is important to note that the programs included in this manual are a starting place. They will need to be modified to meet the needs of individual children. Some of these modifications may involve adding different sets of exemplars for programs to address children's interests (e.g., expressive identification), or adding programs that are idiosyncratic to the needs of the child and family. The tools included within this manual will help educators both revise existing programs and write new instructional programs as needed.

Writing the instructional program, however, is just the first step (see Chapter 6 for more details). With the instructional programs in hand, the team members are ready to plan instruction across the day. They need to decide which programs will be taught in a decontextualized manner sitting at the table working one on one with a teacher, which programs will be embedded into the ongoing activities and routines of the extended day program, and which programs will be targeted for maintenance and generalization in the inclusive preschool, at home and in other settings in the community. Decisions about data collection will also have to be made (see Chapter 8 for more details). How frequently will the team collect data? What types of data will the team collect? Who will summarize the data? And most importantly, how frequently will the team meet to review the data and make decisions about program modifications based on child performance?

Developing, implementing, and evaluating inclusive EIBI programs for students with ASD is a challenge. There are so many moving parts to these programs—assessment, curriculum, staff training, instructional practices, data-based decision making—that it can sometimes be difficult to keep them all straight. But, working with young children with ASD is an exhilarating and rewarding challenge. Like any undertaking, it is important to have the right tools. The Project DATA manual provides educational teams with the essential tools they need to implement high quality inclusive programming for young children with ASD.

Acknowledgments

Since 1997, the Project DATA staff have had the honor of working with hundreds of children, families, graduate students, staff members, school district administrators, and other colleagues who have helped us define and refine the meaning of developmentally appropriate treatment of autism. The Project DATA model came into existence because we had the privilege of working in an inclusive early childhood program that used applied behavior analysis to help children participate and learn. When we started to receive requests from parents for more intensive behavioral services for their children with autism spectrum disorder (ASD), we worked with our team to figure out a strategy to increase intensity, while not losing access to an inclusive learning community. The result was the Project DATA model, an endeavor that has been the anchor of my professional life for almost two decades.

This project has always been a team endeavor. We have learned so much from every child and family who has participated in Project DATA. Every graduate student who learned how to implement the Project DATA model helped us refine our training and coaching procedures. Every time we met with a school district administrator to explain the importance of these services, it helped us become better advocates for the model and for the children and families receiving the services. It is impossible for us to mention every collaborator individually, but there are some people that we would like to thank for their extraordinary support during this journey. A very special thank you to

- Chris Matsumoto, Principal of the Experimental Education Unit

- Ariane Gauvreau, Shane Miramontez, Kristen Morse Mengistu, Erin Greager, Jennifer Fung, Tara Godinho, Penny Williams, and Lorraine Symns, Project DATA head teachers

- Gusty Lee Boulware and Rina Marie Leon-Guerrero, part of the original Project DATA development team

- Megan Swanson, Program Coordinator

It has been a wonderful journey to watch the Project DATA model grow from an initial grant proposal into this manual. Thank you to everyone who has contributed along the way.

Fundamentals of the Project DATA Model

CHAPTER 1

Introducing the DATA Model Approach

The Experimental Education Unit at the University of Washington opened its doors to Project DATA (Developmentally Appropriate Treatment for Autism) in 1997, supported by a Model Demonstration Grant from the U.S. Department of Education's Office of Special Education and Rehabilitative Services. Project DATA combines the recommended practices from applied behavior analysis, early childhood special education, and early learning to form a program that recognizes the unique learning characteristics and support needs of children with autism spectrum disorder (ASD) and their families.

The DATA Model is built on the belief that children with ASD benefit from frequent, sustained interactions with their typically developing peers, as well as specialized and intensive instruction designed to address the primary deficit areas of ASD. The DATA Model was designed to help school districts meet the needs of young children with ASD and their families in ways that are effective, sustainable, and acceptable to all parties.

This manual describes the Project DATA model, as well as the philosophy on which it is based, the research on the model, and the evidence-based instructional strategies it uses. This manual also provides some tips on how to implement the DATA Model in individual schools and communities.

CORE BELIEFS OF THE PROJECT DATA MODEL

The DATA Model is built on two core beliefs. The foremost belief is that children with ASD are children first. This belief is easy to understand but often difficult to implement. It means that children with ASD should be afforded the same opportunities to play, learn, and have fun as they would if they were typically developing. It means that teachers and other project staff should ensure that every child with ASD experiences a moment of joy every day at school. The goal is to teach the children skills and behaviors that will enable them to interact successfully and within the same activities and settings as other children their age. It also means that the project will not hold them to standards or impose instructional strategies that are not age- and developmentally appropriate—such as working one-on-one with an adult in a small clinic room for many hours a day or working on discrete skills that do not help children interact with and participate in their family and community. Enacting the belief that "children with ASD are children first" requires teachers to work with children with ASD in environments where typically developing children spend time (e.g., preschools, homes, playgrounds) and target behaviors that will enhance interactions between children with and without ASD. Project DATA staff members have high standards for all children and appreciate that children work hard (they are in school for at least 20 hours per week) to learn the skills and behaviors that will help them participate and succeed in the elementary school general education environment.

The DATA Model is an inclusive approach to working with children with ASD. Children with ASD in this program spend time playing and learning with their typically developing peers from the very first day of school. Inclusion is not just a philosophy or a placement decision, but a guiding principle that informs what is taught, how staff teach, where instruction is provided, and how success is defined. Viewing children with ASD as children first requires staff to identify meaningful child outcomes—not just test scores or school placement—but outcomes that have impact on the long-term quality of life for the child and family. This belief permeates every component of Project DATA.

The second core belief of the DATA Model is that student failure is instructional failure. This is related to data collection and data-based decision making. Instructional problems exist when children are not making adequate or timely progress. An instructional strategy may be considered an "evidence-based" strategy because of the number of times it has been replicated in the research literature. It is not an effective intervention for a specific child, however, unless the data for that child show meaningful progress toward important educational outcomes. This commitment to recognizing student failure as instructional failure reminds staff to continuously monitor student performance data to determine the success of every instructional program. When programs are not "working," staff systematically review the type, intensity, location of the instruction, issues of motivation and reinforcement potency, and the myriad contextual variables that influence instructional effectiveness to determine how the instructional programming can be improved.

Research Support for the DATA Model

One of the founding goals for Project DATA was to create a program that provided effective educational services for young children with ASD, would be acceptable to the consumers of the program, and would be sustainable. In an attempt to achieve these desired outcomes, three broad evaluation questions were addressed:

- Did children achieve important developmental gains?

- Were parents satisfied with the program?

- Were other consumers satisfied with the program?

Evidence suggests that Project DATA has been successful in making meaningful changes to children's behavior with a program that is acceptable to parents and other consumers. When asked about Project DATA, one parent explained:

> Project DATA is a million little things done right every day to help my child succeed, and let me tell you, those things add up!

The majority of evidence about the success of the DATA Model comes in the form of information about child outcomes. One measure of this success is children's educational placement after they leave Project DATA. Approximately 58% of children with ASD who participated in Project DATA for at least 1 year leave preschool and enter inclusive kindergarten programs (Schwartz & Davis, 2006). These placement data are encouraging and compare positively with outcomes of other early intensive behavior intervention programs. School placement data, however, are not always a clear indicator of child performance, since placement decisions are often influenced by school district policies, advocacy, and the availability of programming in the neighborhoods in which children live, but they are one of many types of information that are meaningful to consumers (e.g., parents and school district personnel).

Although the school placement data are promising, more substantial support for the DATA Model comes from a retrospective record review conducted on 69 program participants (Schwartz, Thomas, McBride, & Sandall, 2013). Pre- and postdata were reviewed for 69 preschoolers who participated in Project DATA for at least 1 year. The measures used in the evaluation were

■ Childhood Autism Rating Scale (CARS; Schopler et al., 1998), a rating scale to measure autism symptomology

■ The Peabody Picture Vocabulary Test, 3rd edition (PPVT-III; Dunn & Dunn, 1997), a test of receptive vocabulary

■ Assessment, Evaluation, and Programming System, 2nd edition (AEPS; Bricker et al., 2002). A comprehensive curriculum-based measure for children birth to 6 years. The AEPS has subscales in the domains of fine motor, gross motor, adaptive, cognitive, social communication, and social.

■ Preschool and Kindergarten Behavior Scale, 2nd edition (PKBS-2; Merrell, 2003). The PKBS has a social skills scale with three subdomains: social cooperation, social interaction, and social independence. It also has a problem behavior scale with two subdomains: externalizing problems and internalizing problems.

All of these measures were administered to children in Project DATA at the beginning and end of the program. To determine the effectiveness of the Project DATA model paired-sample t tests were run on the average score for each measure described above. The results of the pre- and posttest analysis indicated that there were statistically significant differences at the $p < .01$ level on all of the measures except the PKBS Problem Behavior Scales. The findings suggest that children who participated in Project DATA demonstrated statistically significant changes in the

■ Amount of autism symptomology that they demonstrated (i.e., CARS)

■ Size of their receptive vocabularies (i.e., PPVT)

■ Number of age appropriate skills that they demonstrated in the developmental domains of fine motor, gross motor, social, cognitive, social communication, communication, and adaptive (i.e., AEPS)

■ Amount of appropriate social skills that they demonstrated (i.e., PKBS).

The only measure that did not demonstrate statistically significant change was the problem behavior subscale of the PKBS. Interestingly, on this rating scale, the children in Project DATA, on average, scored in the same range as typically developing children. Although there was a small decrease in the amount of problem behavior reported over the time spent in Project DATA, the change was not statistically significant.

The final evaluation question examines the acceptability of Project DATA by consumers other than parents (e.g., school districts). Since beginning Project DATA in 1997, the University of Washington project staff have conducted trainings in a large number of states and helped numerous school districts and community agencies implement this model. Most importantly, the original school district, with whom we partnered in 1997, is still a partner and the two organizations continue to work together to provide effective, acceptable, and sustainable programs to all students with ASD and their families.

Five Core Components of Project DATA

With those two core beliefs as a bedrock, the Project DATA model was developed to include five core components, as shown below in Figure 1.1. The five core components are

■ Integrated early childhood experience

■ Extended, intensive instruction

■ Technical and social support for families

■ Collaboration and coordination among all providers working with the child and family

■ Quality of life influenced curriculum

The Integrated Early Childhood Experience   The integrated early childhood experience component is at the center of the DATA model. This reinforces the belief that children with ASD are children first and confirms the staff's intention to ensure that every child in the program has frequent and regularly scheduled opportunities to interact successfully with typically developing peers. These words are selected intentionally. This component is not described as *enrollment* in a program with typically developing peers; rather emphasis is placed on the opportunities to successfully promote interaction. Experience and more than 50 years of research demonstrate that merely putting children with disabilities in a classroom with typically developing children without specialized instruction and support will result in children with and without disabilities who are placed in a room together, but not interacting. This is particularly true of ASD, with its primary deficits in the areas of social and communication skills. (See Allen [1972] for one of the first published reports of systematically integrated preschool classrooms.)

Project DATA requires that, from their first day in an early childhood program, children with ASD have access to a high-quality early childhood program that combines the principles of developmentally appropriate practice (Bredekamp & Copple, 1997) with specialized instruction and support to help children with special needs achieve their individual learning objectives. The details of implementing this type of inclusive classroom are described in *Building Blocks for Teaching Preschoolers with Special Needs* (Sandall & Schwartz, 2008). This component is described in detail in Chapter 2.

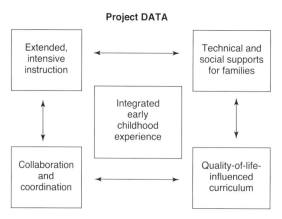

Figure 1.1.   Project DATA model. (From Schwartz, I.S., Sandall, S.R., McBride, B.J., & Boulware, G.L. *Topics in Early Childhood Special Education* [*24*, 3] pp. 156–168, copyright © 2004 by Hammill Institute on Disabilities Reprinted by Permission of SAGE Publications, Inc.)

The other four components surround and support the child's participation in the Integrated Early Childhood Experience. Just as scaffolding supports new construction, the other four components support the growth of independence. Like scaffolding supporting new construction, the idea of the other four components is to support the growth of independence, not to interfere with it. When this "job" is completed, the teaching team should be able to remove the scaffolding and reap the benefits of the "construction" of new skills, in new environments, with new people.

Extended, Intensive Instruction The extended, inclusive instruction component ensures that children in Project DATA receive sufficient instruction to meet their learning needs. The issue of "dosage" or number of hours of programming is often the focal point of discussions surrounding early intensive behavioral interventions (EIBI) for children with ASD (Strain, Schwartz, & Barton, 2011). Dosage and intensity, however, are parts of a complex equation that cannot be defined by the number of hours of services that children provide. Issues of engagement, curriculum, and child progress must also be considered when discussing the appropriate intensity of programming for children with ASD. In most public school-funded developmental preschools children with ASD receive 10–12 hours of services per week and this amount and type of programming is often inadequate to help children make meaningful progress towards meeting educational goals. That level of service is clearly insufficient. But Project DATA staff were not, and still are not, convinced that children need 40 hours per week of educational intervention. Based on the research then available (Dawson & Osterling, 1997), Project DATA staff adopted a goal that children should receive 20–25 hours of school-based intervention each week. A subsequent report by the National Research Council (2001) supports this level.

Children spend about half of the 20–25 hours in a high-quality, integrated program, and during the rest of the time, they receive intensive instruction that is provided one-to-one or in small groups, depending on the needs of the child. The purpose of this component is to provide individualized instruction, using the behavioral instructional strategies best matched to what is being taught, to meet the needs of every child. This component is described in detail in Chapters 4 and 5.

Technical and Social Support for Families Project DATA's second supporting component is technical and social support for families. Raising a child with ASD creates special support needs, including accurate and timely information about diagnosis, treatment options, and behavioral strategies. Families experience everyday situations with children who may not react in the ways parents or others expect. They also face increased needs for social support because parents of children with ASD experience even more stress than parents of children with other types of disabilities (Smith, Hong, Seltzer, Greenberg, Almeida, & Bishop, 2010).

In Project DATA, family support is provided through two primary activities: home visits and parent education/support events. Every family receives a monthly home visit both to support the parents in responding to issues at home and to carry through with gains achieved at school. Classroom teachers plan and provide the visits; families control the agenda, location, and timing of them. This way the visits cover the issues that are most important to the family. For example, if parents want help with the bedtime routine, then the home visit occurs at bedtime. If grocery shopping is the issue, then the teacher accompanies the family to the supermarket. And if attending religious school is causing problems for the family, then the "home visit" may consist of a visit to the religious school class and a training session for those teachers.

In addition to home visits, families are strongly encouraged to participate in the parent education and support events. These events occur about six times per year and are usually held at school in the evening with childcare provided. They consist of a formal presentation based on a topic of interest (e.g., toilet training, challenging behavior) followed by informal time for parents to talk to each other. This component is discussed in detail in Chapter 9.

Collaboration and Coordination The third support component of Project DATA is **collaboration and coordination** across services. In addition to the regular collaboration between the child's preschool and Project DATA staff, this component includes others whom the family perceives to be members of the child's team. Nearly every family participating in Project DATA receives some family-negotiated services for their children. Family-negotiated services include any therapeutic services that are not part of a child's individualized education program (IEP). These services may include private speech therapy, behavioral programming, or hippotherapy (i.e., horseback riding therapy). In Project DATA, the goal is to bring everyone who is working with the child and family around the table (or virtual table) annually for a meeting. The purpose of this meeting is not to plan or even to agree on an approach to treatment but to create relationships so that all team members can communicate, problem-solve, or support the family in a seamless and effective manner. This component is described in detail in Chapter 9.

Quality-of-Life Influenced Curriculum The final supporting component of the Project DATA model is the **quality-of-life-influenced curriculum**. This component of the model was inspired by the late Ted Carr (Carr, 2007), who suggested that quality of life is the appropriate dependent measure when evaluating positive behavior support and intervention programs. When planning curriculum for children in Project DATA, teachers need to be cognizant both of what they are choosing to teach and what they are *not* choosing to teach. Project DATA chooses to teach skills that help children be more independent, be more successful in inclusive school and community settings, and interact more successfully with their families and friends. This component is described in detail in Chapters 3 and 5.

These five components make up Project DATA—a technical but not dogmatic approach to providing EIBI for children with ASD. The Project DATA model has been demonstrated to be effective and sustainable. This manual can help teaching teams understand Project DATA and then implement the model in their home, school, or community.

SUMMARY

Project DATA is a comprehensive, school-based program to meet the needs of young children with ASD and their families. The Project DATA program is based on two important beliefs:

1. Children with ASD are children first.

2. Student failure is instructional failure.

Using these beliefs as our guide, the Project DATA developed, evaluated, and disseminated a program that blends approaches to meet the unique needs of children with ASD. Practices from applied behavior analysis, early childhood special education, and early learning are blended into a program that is responsive to the needs of children and families, effective at teaching the skills that they need to be successful at school and in the community, acceptable to consumers, and sustainable in public school settings. This manual provides the steps for teams to follow to implement Project DATA in their school and community.

CHAPTER 2

Characteristics of a High-Quality Inclusive Early Childhood Program for Children with Autism Spectrum Disorder

As introduced in Chapter 1, the core component of the DATA model is participation in a high-quality, inclusive early childhood program. The purpose of this chapter is to provide an overview of what needs to be in place so that children with ASD can participate and thrive in an inclusive preschool program. To benefit from an inclusive program, children need to participate in the activities, interact with their peers, and engage with the materials. Participation across valued activities, rituals, and routines that occur across the school day and environment is key to learning. Inclusion does not just mean physical integration. Inclusion is about belonging and being a member of a group (e.g., classroom). Inclusion means that children with disabilities are full members of the classroom community and that they are able to interact successfully with typically developing peers across all activities and environments of the school day. To accomplish this, the children with ASD and their teachers and peers, must receive the education, support, and coaching they need to be successful. How much support is enough? How much training is enough? There is only one way to answer those questions—look at child behavior. When the needs of all the children are being met, the right level of coaching and support is being provided.

When thinking about the characteristics of high-quality early childhood programs for children with ASD, it is advantageous to harken back to one of the guiding principles of Project DATA: children with ASD are children first. This means that to create a high-quality program for children with ASD, Project DATA teams have to start with a high-quality program for all children. An early learning program that meets the quality standard for all young children will be the cornerstone of the Project DATA model, and modifications, instructional supports, and additional assistance can be added to that cornerstone as needed by individual children. In general, a high-quality early childhood program is one that meets the needs of individual students, is developmentally and individually appropriate, respects children's cultural and linguistic diversity, and uses evidence-based strategies to facilitate learning and development. Some necessary components of a developmentally appropriate learning environment include

- Engaging interactions

- A responsive and predictable environment

- Many opportunities to respond and participate

- Teaching that is matched to the child and activity

- Developmentally appropriate materials, activities, and interactions

- Safe and hygienic practices

- ▨ Appropriate levels of child guidance
- ▨ Meaningful involvement of families

This chapter will refer to *Building Blocks for Teaching Preschoolers with Special Needs, Second Edition* (Sandall & Schwartz, 2008) as a guidebook for creating such an inclusive early childhood program. The Building Blocks Framework provides a comprehensive guide to help early childhood programs meet the needs of children with disabilities. It also contains basic information about key components of high-quality early childhood programs and important child outcomes. The purpose of this chapter is to focus on how a program that is already successful in including some children with disabilities can make changes to facilitate the success and full inclusion of children with ASD. This chapter will highlight

- ▨ The core deficits of ASD and how they may provide challenges for working with children in inclusive programs

- ▨ How to use strategies from the Building Blocks Approach to support children with ASD in inclusive programs

- ▨ Key strategies for addressing challenging behavior in inclusive programs.

CORE DEFICITS OF AUTISM SPECTRUM DISORDER AND INCLUSION

The prevalence of ASD has increased dramatically in the past few decades (the Centers for Disease Control and Prevention currently estimates prevalence at 1 in 68 [2011]). As the number of children with ASD increases, so does the amount known about how to provide effective early intervention to children with ASD and their families. ASD is a spectrum disorder, meaning that children diagnosed with this disability vary in what symptoms appear, how these symptoms manifest, and how children with this disorder respond to intervention. It means that there is no "typical" profile of a child with ASD. As many family members and professionals say, "When you meet one child with ASD, you have met one child with ASD." Although there may be a range in ability and severity of children with ASD, the most current definition of ASD identifies two core areas of deficit:

1. Persistent deficits in communication and social interaction that occur across different settings

2. Restricted, repetitive patterns of behavior, interests, or activities

These symptoms must have been present early in life (i.e., before age three), result in significant impairment in functioning, and not be better explained by cognitive disability or global developmental delay (APA, 2013).

Given the dynamic and very language-based approaches of most early learning programs, the core deficits of ASD may create specific challenges for including children with ASD in these environments. Early childhood programs are noisy, lively environments, full of changing social and communicative demands. Even in the most well-structured early learning environments, activities, materials, and expectations can change multiple times across the day and perhaps hundreds of times across 1 month. Adults often think of high-quality early childhood programs as those with children spending long periods of time working on child-initiated projects, playing outdoors with their friends, and sitting with their peers listening to books being read. Yet, many children with ASD do not initiate age appropriate activities, may be unwilling to interact with new materials, often do not initiate or respond to peers, and may not have the language skills or social knowledge to participate in a group activity. Given these challenges, some parents and advocates may think that a busy early childhood program is not the best place for a child with ASD. Project DATA teachers believe that it is exactly the right place for a child with ASD. Children with ASD have primary deficits in social-communicative behaviors. They need to spend time with children who demonstrate appropriate social-communicative and play behaviors and receive the appropriate types of instruction and support to interact with and learn from their peers.

BUILDING BLOCKS FOR INCLUDING CHILDREN WITH AUTISM SPECTRUM DISORDER

The key to helping children with ASD succeed in inclusive settings is to ensure that the environment is designed to facilitate their success. The staff must be trained and know how, when, and where to provide support; appropriate goals must be selected; and intentional instruction must be provided with sufficient intensity across activities to ensure that children achieve valued outcomes. The Building Blocks Framework (Sandall & Schwartz, 2008) provides many strategies that can be used to provide that support, but three particular tactics are especially important in supporting children with ASD in inclusive settings. The first of these is a well-designed classroom environment that

- Fosters independence and feelings of competence

- Encourages staff efficiency

- Decreases challenging behavior by making it easier to engage in appropriate behavior

- Facilitates appropriate social interactions among children

- Increases predictability, opportunities for initiation, and communication

Environments should be orderly, inviting, and attractive. In other words, a well-designed classroom environment is one that provides children with an adequate amount of support to play, learn, and have fun. A well-designed classroom environment should also support interactions between peers, provide children with space and opportunity for quiet time, and have well-trained teachers available to provide appropriate levels of guidance. More information about designing classroom environments can be found at the National Center for Quality Teaching and Learning in Head Start website (http://eclkc.ohs.acf.hhs.gov/hslc/tta-system/teaching/practice/engage).

For children with ASD, however, the environment may require special features that provide more explicit support than typically developing children may need. This does not mean that learning environments for children with ASD need to look sterile or clinical. It means that teachers need to be intentional when they design these environments, when they add extra features to the environments (e.g., schedules, visual supports), and when they teach children how to use the features that are embedded in the environment.

A well-designed classroom should include a physical environment with different activity areas that have clear, physical, and visual boundaries. For example, the area in which blocks should be used should be clear based on the classroom furniture, floor covering, and visual support (e.g., pictures, symbols, examples of block structures). Areas should be designed so that every child can be seen at all times and there are spaces for children to work and play independently, in small groups, and to gather as a community. The furniture and barriers (e.g., bookshelves) should create spaces that are comfortable and lend themselves to the intended purpose. For example, the writing area should include child-sized work tables and chairs, as well as interesting writing materials with visual supports of ideas or models of what could be written or drawn for the children with ASD.

Materials should be well-organized, easily accessible, and in good working order. Providing a wide variety of materials in every classroom helps to promote engagement, and there should be materials and activities that enable every child in the classroom to be independent on some activities and to be challenged cognitively on some activities. Include materials that incorporate child interests. For children with ASD these high interest materials should be incorporated across different areas of the classroom (e.g., in the block area, the reading area, the art area). Materials and activities in the classroom should also reflect the priorities of the classroom team. For example, if teaching children to interact with their peers is important, then materials should promote social initiations and cooperative play. If independent play is important, then there should be materials and space available for every child to have access to toys that they know how to use appropriately and the opportunity to use those toys. If teaching fine motor skills is a value, then opportunities to interact with writing materials, modeling clay, and scissors should be available to children every day.

When designing environments for children with ASD, it is helpful to make all elements of the environment as structured and clear as possible. This extends to the physical, temporal, and social environments. This does not mean that the environment needs to be overly simple or bare, rather it needs to be well-designed. Materials need to have an assigned place, they need to be kept in that place, and ideally that place should be labeled using words and symbols or pictures.

A final suggestion in designing environments that facilitate participation and learning for children with ASD is to use visual supports in an intentional manner. In many programs for children with ASD, visual supports adorn every surface of the classroom. Although visual supports can be helpful, they are not the solution; they are merely one teaching tool that is available to the team. Like all instruction, visual supports must be selected carefully with a goal in mind. Visual supports can be used to help children learn the schedule, learn specific tasks, provide warnings for classroom transitions, communicate with teachers and peers, ask for a break, and remember the classroom rules. Visual supports, however, do not teach. They are tools that teachers can use to provide instruction in a manner that has been shown to be very effective with young children with ASD.

The guiding questions when designing classrooms for young children should be

▦ Does the classroom help the child know what to do?

▦ Does the classroom help the child be more independent?

▦ Does the classroom provide the child with space to play with peers, to work with teachers, and to have some independent time?

All strategies described above—classroom schedules, visual supports, well-arranged classrooms, interesting materials—can help achieve that goal.

The second strategy from Building Blocks that is extremely helpful when including children with ASD in a preschool classroom is using an activity matrix to make sure that instruction is planned and implemented across all environments (Schwartz, Sandall, & Gauvreau, 2013). An activity matrix is a form that combines a classroom schedule with a list of a child's learning objectives. This form serves as a guide to help classroom staff determine when and where instruction will occur. It also helps teams plan what level of staff support is needed across different activities, what materials are needed, and how to group children to ensure that all children's needs can be met. Many teachers report that one advantage of using an activity matrix is that it allows them to create a visual representation of all the IEP goals that their children are working on. In other words, it creates an IEP-at-a-glance. It provides teachers a convenient opportunity to look at all of the active IEP goals a child is working on at any one time. This way the teacher can ensure that all of the goals are being addressed and that data are being collected regularly to determine if the instructional strategies being used are effective.

An activity matrix can be constructed in many ways. The function of the matrix is more important than what the actual form looks like, so it is important to find a format that works best for the teaching team. Basically, an activity matrix is a table that lists the classroom schedule down the left hand column and lists every domain in which a child has a goal across the top (see Figure 2.1). The idea is to fill in the matrix so that every active goal on the child's IEP is assigned to a specific activity. When a goal is assigned to a specific activity, the team is making a commitment to ensure that specially designed instruction on a specific goal will take place during that time, and data will be collected to evaluate instructional effectiveness. Issues to consider when assigning instructional goals to classroom activities include

■ Child strengths and need for support

■ The fit between the instructional goal and the scheduled classroom activity

■ Overall schedule of the day to ensure that active and passive activities are alternated

■ Staffing

	Communication	Social	Adaptive/ independence	Motor
Arrival/dismissal		Greeting teacher	Hanging up backpack	
Circle time	Imitating actions Answering questions	Greeting peers		
Small group	Increasing vocabulary Sequencing		Increasing time on task	Drawing
Free choice	Commenting Labeling emotions	Cooperative play Emotional regulation		
Snack	Conversation with peers		Eating a variety of food Leaving nonpreferred food on plate	
Outdoor play			Putting on coat Hanging up coat	Jumping Using playground equipment Catching
Shared reading	Answering questions about story	Attending to different speakers		

Figure 2.1. Sample activity matrix.

The third Building Blocks strategy is embedded learning opportunities (ELO). ELOs are episodes of embedded instruction that occur within ongoing classroom activities and routines (Sandall & Schwartz, 2008). Embedded instruction is a key component of creating effective inclusive settings; however, it is essential that embedded instruction be planned. Embedded instruction is the use of short, intentional teaching episodes that are inserted into ongoing classroom activities to increase children's opportunities to practice targeted skills and behaviors with support and feedback. Teachers will say that they address objectives all day long by embedding instruction across settings. However, when data is collected to see how often instruction occurs and how effective that instruction is, teachers are surprised by the paucity of actual instruction and learning that is taking place. Embedded instruction must be intentional instruction and using an activity matrix can help teams plan more carefully, ensure that necessary materials are available, and ensure that data are collected to determine if the instruction being provided is effective. An activity matrix does not specify which type of instructional strategies will be used, it simply indicates when instruction will occur. The embedded teaching episodes can focus on a child's IEP goals or on helping the child access the current classroom curriculum. Like all intentional instruction, ELOs require teachers to

▨ Clarify the learning objective.

▨ Use an activity matrix to select activities or classroom routines where instruction can successfully be embedded.

▨ Design the instructional interaction, including how data will be collected.

▨ Implement the instruction as planned.

▨ Give clear instructions.

▨ Let the child respond.

▨ Provide feedback, either a reinforcer for a correct response or error correction.

▨ Analyze the effectiveness of the instruction.

ELO and other types of naturalistic instruction are most effective when they can utilize natural reinforcers. Like all reinforcers (see Chapter 3 for a more detailed discussion of reinforcement and other behavioral principles), natural reinforcers are items or activities that, when presented contingent on a desired behavior, increase the likelihood of that behavior happening again. A natural reinforcer is one that is part of an ongoing activity. For example, if a child is on a swing and asks for a push, the reinforcer is getting pushed. The child learns that when he or she asks for a push, he or she receives one. If the child wants a toy that is high on a shelf and he or she gets the attention of a teacher and points, the reinforcer is access to the preferred and requested toy. Natural reinforcers are very powerful because the child is communicating what they want.

One of the goals of ELOs is to provide short instructional interactions embedded in activities that are motivating to the child and have multiple natural reinforcers (see some examples of ELOs in Table 2.1). ELOs do not remove the child from the ongoing activity. In this approach, teachers and related service staff bring specialized instruction to the child and the activity the child has chosen, rather than bringing the child to the location and the activity that the teacher has chosen to conduct a lesson. Therefore, ELOs need to be short so that they do not interfere with the natural flow of activities and potentially hinder the naturally reinforcing properties of the activity. One of the challenges of using ELOs—or any type of embedded or naturalistic instruction—is that it may be difficult to provide

Table 2.1. Targeted behavior: Increasing vocabulary

Context	Teacher behavior	Child response	Consequence/ natural reinforcer
Small group art project	Children are working on collages of different shapes, teacher holds up a diamond (targeted vocabulary word) and says to child, "What is this shape?"	Child points and says, "Diamond."	Teacher responds, "You are right. This is a yellow diamond," and gives the child the shape for his collage.
Free choice	Children are playing at the water table. A child reaches for a funnel (a targeted vocabulary word), and the teacher blocks his access and says, "What do you want?"	Funnel	Teacher responds by handing the child the funnel and saying, "I like to pour the water into a funnel."

the number of trials or opportunities to respond that children with ASD require in order to learn. One of the strengths of the Project DATA model is that it combines embedded instruction with more traditional sessions of intensive and explicit instruction. Both are necessary to help children with ASD learn new skills and use those new skills in a generalized way.

ADDRESSING CHALLENGING BEHAVIOR IN INCLUSIVE PROGRAMS

Challenging behaviors happen. Having a procedure for how to deal with challenging behaviors is an essential part of any program when working with young children, especially young children with ASD. The first step in putting a procedure in place in an inclusive early childhood program is education for the adults. It is imperative that all of the adults in the program understand that challenging behavior is communicative behavior. This means that behavior serves a function for children and, when developing plans to eliminate the challenging behavior, it is essential that the teacher or caregiver understand what the child is trying to communicate. In other words, what function does the behavior serve for the child? For example, when a child throws a puzzle at a teacher who has asked them to do the same puzzle many, many times, the child may be saying, "No, thank you. I do not want to do this puzzle," or the child may be attempting to *avoid* the task. If a child cries when a teacher walks away or attends to another child, the child may be saying, "Pay attention to me," or attempting to *obtain* the teacher's attention. The majority of challenging behavior is motivated by these two functions—attempts to obtain something (e.g., attention, something tangible) or attempts to avoid something.

An effective and developmentally appropriate plan to decrease challenging behavior will teach the child to achieve the function, that is, communicate their message, in a socially appropriate way. These plans will include strategies to teach children to use appropriate behaviors (e.g., asking using words, symbols, or gestures) to obtain what they want or to avoid or modify things they do not want. In other words, the goal is to decrease the challenging behavior, *and* increase the child's ability to communicate what they want or need and advocate for themselves.

The very best way to address challenging behaviors is to prevent them. Teachers can prevent challenging behaviors by ensuring that the environment is set up to support and teach appropriate behaviors that enable children to be more in control of their own situation (e.g., requesting, appropriate strategies to protest, asking for help). Positive behavior intervention and support (PBIS) and other tiered approaches (e.g., Dunlap, Wilson, Strain, & Lee, 2013; Hemmeter & Fox, 2009) are designed with prevention as their first block or tier. PBIS is a proactive and comprehensive approach to dealing with challenging behavior. This approach views challenging behavior as communicative behavior and acknowledges that understanding what motivates and maintains a challenging behavior is the first step in eliminating the behavior. PBIS focuses on working with teachers to create supportive school climates and teaching children appropriate alternative behaviors they can use to achieve the same function as the challenging behavior (e.g., what is an appropriate strategy to ask the teacher for attention or to tell him or her that you do not want to do the same puzzle again?). The idea behind these approaches is that if universal strategies (i.e., strategies that apply to all children) are put into place in all early learning programs, the majority of challenging behaviors can be avoided. These strategies include

■ Following a well-designed classroom schedule

■ Clear classroom expectations and rules

■ Positive child–teacher interactions

■ Contingent reinforcement for appropriate child behaviors

■ A well-planned physical environment

■ Opportunities for children to make choices

When challenging behaviors do occur, it is important that classroom teams respond quickly and appropriately. It is essential that challenging behaviors are not inadvertently reinforced. For example, a child who is whining in the checkout aisle of a grocery store and is quieted down with a candy bar will learn quickly that whining and crying serves the function of obtaining preferred sweets. Teams need to work quickly to

■ Brainstorm about the challenging behavior and collect appropriate assessment information

■ Teach appropriate replacement behaviors and, if necessary, implement a consequence so that the challenging behavior is not being reinforced

■ Embed these interventions across all the environments in which the child spends time.

■ Fade the extra support as the rate of challenging behavior decreases

Additionally, teams need to continue to evaluate their efforts by collecting and analyzing data to ensure that the intervention that they developed is implemented with fidelity and is effective (Gauvreau & Schwartz, 2013).

SUMMARY

Participation in a high-quality, inclusive early education program is the core component of the Project DATA model. Through this participation children with ASD have the opportunity to interact successfully every day with their typically developing peers. Since ASD is primarily a social-communicative disorder, opportunities to practice and learn social and communicative skills with appropriate models is essential for children and helpful to adults (both parents and teachers) so that they observe ongoing examples of age and culturally appropriate behavior. The dynamic nature of inclusive preschool environments can sometimes be a challenge for young children with ASD. These environments are often loud, and have high levels of verbal demands, as well as changing schedules and activities. Children with ASD can be successful in inclusive classrooms when provided with appropriate levels of structure and support. Other children in the environment will also benefit from some of the universal supports that are often most helpful (e.g., schedules, well-designed environments, high rate of positive teacher feedback from the teacher). Although challenging behaviors are problematic, when teachers employ preventive strategies and present appropriate alternatives, children with ASD can thrive in inclusive early learning programs.

CHAPTER 3

Basic Principles of Applied Behavior Analysis

Applied behavior analysis (ABA) is the study of using behavioral principles to change socially important behaviors. Baer, Wolf, and Risley (1968) noted that the *Applied* in ABA refers to behaviors and settings that are "socially important rather than convenient for study" (p. 92). Since the 1970s, ABA has been the treatment of choice for students with ASD. Hundreds of peer-reviewed articles, books, and treatment manuals describe programs and intervention strategies based on ABA that have been demonstrated to be effective to teach appropriate behaviors and decrease the inappropriate behaviors of children, adolescents, and adults with ASD (Wong et al., 2015). Because Project DATA is based on ABA, a rudimentary understanding of ABA and basic behavioral principles is indispensable in order to truly understand the DATA model and implement it with fidelity.

Applied behavior analysis involves creating teaching and living environments that support appropriate behavior and discourage inappropriate behavior. This is done by arranging antecedents (i.e., a stimulus or environmental change that occurs *before* the target behavior) and consequences (i.e., a stimulus or environmental change that occurs *after* the target behavior) to promote appropriate behavior. This three-term contingency, antecedent-behavior-consequence (also referred to as stimulus-response-stimulus), can be said to be the primary building block of ABA. Another defining characteristic of ABA is that behavior analysts study behavior that is observable and available for measurement. Behavior analysts operationally define behaviors in detail so that everyone working with a child can agree whether or not a behavior occurred. This emphasis on careful definition, measurement, and analysis of data is key to effective instruction for children with ASD and will be addressed in Chapter 8.

When thinking about ABA and behavioral principles, the idea of changing consequences is usually the first strategy that comes to mind. Consequences are only one part of the equation, and in fact they are the part of the equation over which interventionists have the least control. Behavior analysts also carefully attend to what happens before the target behavior, the antecedent. The most sustainable behavior change occurs by changing antecedents. It is also easier to change the antecedents in most classroom settings than it is to change the consequences. Changing the antecedents can set a child up for success, helping them gain access to naturally occurring reinforcers in the environment (e.g., participating in fun activities). This chapter provides a basic review of behavioral principles. For readers who want a more thorough grounding in ABA and the science of behavior there are many good texts available (e.g., Alberto & Troutman, 2012; Cooper, Heron, & Heward, 2007; Mayer, Sulzer-Azaroff, & Wallace, 2014).

CHANGING ANTECEDENTS

Antecedents are stimuli (i.e., some aspect of the physical or social environment) that set the stage for a behavior to occur. For example, if a teacher asks a student a question and the student answers, the question was the antecedent. If an alarm clock rings and its owner gets out of bed, the ringing of the alarm was the antecedent to the behavior of getting out of bed. Antecedents can be verbal, environmental, or internal (e.g., hunger). They can occur naturally (e.g., rain is an antecedent for opening an umbrella or pulling up the hood on a jacket) or they can be planned (e.g., setting the alarm on a fitness tracker to alert the wearer after he or she has sat still for 60 minutes). Changing antecedents is an effective strategy to promote appropriate behavior and decrease or prevent challenging behavior. Although there are many ways one can manipulate or change antecedents, four strategies are emphasized in Project DATA:

▦ Increase the clarity of expectations through improved instructions and prompts.

▦ Improve the clarity of the environment.

▦ Improve the quality of the environment.

▦ Control access to preferred activities to increase the salience of potential reinforcers.

Increase the Clarity of Expectations Through Improved Instructions and Prompts

Instructions are simple and direct types of antecedents (more information about instructions and prompts is provided in Chapter 4). Instruction can be verbal, written, gestural, or environmental. Instructions signal to a child that he or she is expected to perform a behavior. They also signal that a reinforcer is available if they demonstrate that behavior. Instructions always precede a child's response. When an instruction has been reliably paired over time with a reinforcer (presented to a child upon a correct response), it is understood that the instruction signals the availability of a reinforcer. That special type of instruction is called a discriminative stimulus (S^D). Using good instructions can help clarify expectations. Good instructions should

▦ Tell students to engage in observable behavior (e.g., "put the block down" rather than "think about what you are doing")

▦ Meet the students at the appropriate language level (i.e., use very simple language for beginning learners and become more complex over time)

▦ Be positive (e.g., "do this" rather than "stop that")

▦ Provide children with the opportunity to respond (i.e., wait at least 5 seconds for the child to respond)

▦ Set children up for success

Prompts are another component of changing antecedents and are paired with instructions. Like instructions, prompts occur before a child's response and they are the only part of the instructional framework called a discrete trial (more information about this in Chapter 4) that is optional and that must be removed or faded out. A prompt occurs either at the same time or shortly after an instruction. The purpose of a prompt is to provide additional information to the child about the instruction. A prompt provides a cue or a hint. For example, if the teacher asks the child to point to the green block and then points to the green block before the child responds, the pointing is a prompt. The teacher is providing the child with a hint, so that they can respond correctly and so that the teacher can provide a reinforcer for the correct behavior. Although prompts can be helpful in teaching new skills and clarifying expectations, it is very important that prompts are removed or faded as quickly as possible so that children do not become prompt dependent. Good prompts should

▪ Yield the correct response (i.e., If a teacher provides a prompt and the child answers incorrectly, it was not a good prompt.)

▪ Use the least amount of intrusion possible to yield the correct response

▪ Occur during or after the instruction and before the child's response

▪ Be removed or faded systematically

Improve the Clarity of the Environment

One of the most widely used strategies for changing antecedents is to make the environment easier to understand. This includes many types of environmental arrangements that both simplify and explain expectations. For example, a simple list that includes all of the chores a child must do before they can watch a movie on their tablet is a type of environmental arrangement that simplifies the environment. Providing the child with a placemat with outlines where the plate, napkin, cup, and silverware should be placed is another example of improving the clarity of the environment. Three strategies most frequently used to simplify the environment are

▪ Visual supports

▪ Schedules

▪ Arranging the environment to reduce clutter and improve function

Visual Supports Using visual supports with children with ASD is a popular evidence-based strategy. This strategy has become so popular that visual supports are often overused. The goal of visual supports is to help a child be more independent. Visual supports are a type of prompt but are often less intrusive than an adult needing to be present to provide support. Remember, the goal of prompts is to remove them. The same is true with visual supports. In some cases, visual supports will not be faded out (e.g., anyone who uses a list-making app on a smart phone is using a visual support). In those cases, the goal is to make the visual support as age appropriate as possible and ensure the person using the visual supports has control of it (i.e., is responsible for carrying it, setting it up, and has input to its contents).

Visual supports can take many different forms and serve many different functions. A timer can be used to help students know how long they have to stay in a certain area of free choice. A "first-then" board can be used to let a student know that first he or she has to work with the teacher on a nonpreferred task before he or she gets to choose the next activity. A list of symbols by the front door of the house labeled "Don't Forget" can help a child remember to pick up his or her backpack and coat. A book displaying different items of clothing on each page can help a child dress without adult support. These are just a few examples of the hundreds of visual supports that have been created for children in Project DATA. All of these visual supports share the following features:

▪ They are created to address a specific need.

▪ The purpose of the visual support is to help the child be more independent at a specific time of day or in completing a specific task.

▪ Children are taught how to use the visual support.

As children became more independent using the visual support, efforts are made to either fade out the visual support or to ensure that it is age appropriate and controlled by the child.

Schedules   Schedules are a special class of visual supports. Schedules organize activities or routines that need to be accomplished in either a certain order or within a certain amount of time. Schedules help both teachers and students understand routines and expectations. Teachers can develop schedules for groups of children (e.g., classroom schedules) or an individual (e.g., an activity schedule outlining what an individual child is expected to do during free choice). The purpose of schedules is to help children be more independent. In other words, not every child with ASD needs an individualized schedule. Some children can get enough information from the classroom schedule. The purpose of using a schedule as an antecedent manipulation is to provide the child with extra support as needed. For example, some children may need the daily schedule taped to the table where they sit. Others may benefit from the schedule depicted by symbols on a ring that is attached to their belt loop. Still others may benefit from a schedule on a high tech device such as a tablet or phone. Schedules need to be portable, they need to be understandable to the child and the team (including the family), and they need to be designed to help the child be more independent.

Arranging the Environment to Reduce Clutter and Improve Function   Another common strategy to improve the clarity of the environment is to ensure that the environment is arranged in a thoughtful and functional manner. In other words, a place for everything and everything in its place. A well-organized environment where materials are located in logical and consistent places, where materials work, and where materials are labeled is an important component of changing antecedents to create environments that promote better outcomes for children with ASD. It is important to note that a well-organized environment does not necessarily mean a sterile environment. Teachers in Project DATA classrooms display children's work, family pictures children bring in from home, and decorate the classrooms like high-quality preschool classrooms. It is essential, however, that children have an environment in which to work and play that is consistent, safe, uncluttered, and in good working order.

Improve the Quality of the Environment

Techniques to improve the quality of an environment can include enriching the environment, increasing the rate of reinforcement, and decreasing the demands. Each of these strategies could help to decrease challenging behaviors and provide more opportunities for appropriate behaviors to occur. Improvements in the quality of the environment can be simple, temporary, and tailored to individual preferences. For example, decreases in demands may be put into place when a parent calls the school staff to tell them that their child did not sleep the night before. Lack of sleep is a physiological setting event that may increase the likelihood of challenging behavior. In this instance, a simple change of antecedent to help prevent challenging behavior is to decrease demands by shortening instructional sessions, using easier tasks, and requiring the child earn fewer tokens for every break. The next day, after the child has gotten a good night's sleep, the rate of demands returns to normal. A benefit of addressing this type of issue by changing antecedents is that teachers are being proactive to prevent challenging behavior, rather than having to be reactive.

Some examples of other strategies to improve the quality of the environment include

▨   Enrich the environment

▨   Add new materials

▨   Rotate materials

- Teach children new ways to use materials
- Increase choices in work activities (e.g., "Do you want to work on coloring or sorting?")
- Embed child preferences
- Increase activity level (e.g., dancing, running, climbing, riding a bike)
- Increase the rate of reinforcement
- Increase the rate of descriptive praise
- Make preferred activities and materials contingent
- Embed instruction in motivating activities
- Listen to child voice and preferences
- Teach children to give their peers compliments
- Decrease demands
- Be responsive to child behavior; always end instructional sessions on a success
- Be flexible, willing to shorten a session before challenging behavior occurs
- Intersperse difficult tasks with easy tasks (e.g., acquisition tasks with maintenance tasks)
- Alternate active tasks with passive tasks
- Make sure the child is comfortable (e.g., has a chair that fits; not too hot; not thirsty)

Control Access to Preferred Activities to Increase the Salience of Potential Reinforcers

Reinforcers come in all shapes and sizes. Reinforcers are individual; something that serves as a reinforcer for one child may not serve as a reinforcer for another. The effectiveness of a reinforcer may vary over time. Something that was functioning as a reinforcer in the morning may not function as a reinforcer in the afternoon for the same child. Reinforcers are defined by their function. In other words, something is only a reinforcer if, when it is presented contingent upon a target behavior, the likelihood of that behavior occurring increases. Because reinforcers are defined functionally, it is important to consider the potency or salience of different reinforcers. The potency of reinforcers changes over time and can be influenced by a number of environmental features that are referred to as setting events. These setting events can include

- External environment (e.g., being sprayed by water may function as a reinforcer when children are playing with water on a hot summer day and may be aversive at other times)
- Internal states (e.g., when hungry, food is more reinforcing)
- Recent history (e.g., Even if popcorn is Sophie's favorite food, she may not be motivated to work for it if she just ate a large bowl of it.)
- Access (e.g., If Lily likes to look through magazines and she has a stack sitting next to her bed, she may not be very motivated to do extra work to access the same stack of magazines.)

Controlling access to preferred materials or activities is an effective strategy to increase the value of selected reinforcers. For example, if a child loves ice cream, his or her parents could limit access to ice cream to the end of the day contingent on a behavior that they are working on (e.g., no toilet accidents = ice cream at the end of the day; homework done = ice cream). This works equally well with nonfood related reinforcers. If a child likes to play with a tablet or other specific toy, access to that toy can be limited to work sessions or other times controlled by the parent. The important issue here is that limiting access to a highly preferred potential reinforcer is not depriving the child of opportunities to play and interact. It is simply controlling access to a very preferred item or activity to harness its reinforcing value to help the child learn valued skills and behaviors more quickly.

Changing Consequences

Often, when thinking about applied behavior analysis, teachers assume that changing consequences is the only action to take. Changing consequences is one strategy to affect behavior, but it is important to remember that consequences are about future behavior. A teacher provides reinforcement contingent on a target behavior to increase the likelihood that the behavior will occur again *in the future*. Changing antecedents is about current behavior; changing consequences is about future behavior.

A consequence is a stimulus that occurs after a target behavior. There are two primary types of consequences: reinforcement and punishment. In the simplest terms, reinforcement increases the likelihood of a behavior happening again and punishment decreases the likelihood of a behavior happening again. When discussing consequences, it is important to consider the effect the consequence has on behavior to determine what type of consequence it is. Unlike other approaches to teaching and learning, ABA is less interested in what an adult intended and more interested in the effect the adult behavior had on the target behavior. Consider the example below in which consequences led to something different than the teacher intended.

Molly is a 3-year-old girl with ASD who was fully included in a preschool program. She loved playing with modeling clay and all types of craft activities. She did not, however, like to work in groups and she certainly did not like to share her craft materials with her peers. Every time the teacher distributed baskets of tools to use with the modeling clay, Molly would begin to engage in mildly challenging behavior, grabbing materials from her peers and screeching. The teacher would remove Molly from the small group and give her a basket of tools and some clay to play with by herself. As soon as Molly had her own craft materials, the challenging behavior stopped and she was fully engaged with the clay, often making comments to her teachers and peers about the items she was creating.

Consider the difference between the lesson that the teacher was trying to teach, the intended consequence, and the lesson that was actually taught. The teacher was trying to discourage or punish the challenging behavior by not allowing Molly to work with her peers. What actually happened, however, is that the teacher reinforced the challenging behavior by giving Molly her own craft materials. This example illustrates why it is important to look at the actual behavior and the effect that a consequence has on behavior when determining if a consequence is producing the intended outcome.

Positive reinforcement is the consequence most often used in ABA and it may be the most important of all behavioral principles. Positive reinforcement is the presentation of a stimulus (e.g., toy, cookie, activity, descriptive praise) contingent on a target behavior that results in an increased likelihood of that behavior happening again. Positive reinforcement occurs all day, in every setting. All people learn through positive reinforcement, but what functions as a reinforcer is individual and can change over time. In the example above, being able to work with craft materials by herself was the reinforcer for Molly's inappropriate behavior. Some children may love to play outside and the opportunity to play outside may function as a reinforcer. Other children may not like to go outside, but having time to draw would be a reinforcer. Some children are willing to work hard for "screen time" with an iPad or computer; others are not interested in technology but will work hard to jump on a trampoline. For a few children, it may be difficult to find activities that are reinforcing, but perhaps there are certain foods that could function as a reinforcer. Both appropriate and inappropriate behaviors can be reinforced. Some examples of positive reinforcement are shown in Table 3.1.

As shown in the examples in Table 3.1, positive reinforcement occurs in every setting in which a child spends time. It can be intentional (e.g., teaching a child to request something by pointing at it), part of a very natural interaction (e.g., picking up a baby when he or she lifts his or her arms), or unintentional (e.g., providing more time to play when the child engages in an inappropriate behavior). What all of these examples have in common is that an adult adds a stimulus (e.g., an activity, praise, or a tangible item) contingent on a target behavior and that behavior is more likely to occur in the future. The important point to remember about positive reinforcement is that a stimulus is added and the behavior increases. Another important feature of reinforcement is that what the adult intended is not important. What is important is the effect the consequence has on the child's behavior.

In contrast with that is negative reinforcement. Negative reinforcement also increases the likelihood of a behavior happening again. But, in negative reinforcement, rather than adding a preferred stimulus, an aversive or nonpreferred stimulus is removed. For example, if Joe is struggling to carry heavy boxes of books to his office and asks a passing colleague, "Can you help me?" and he or she takes one of his boxes, his request for help is negatively reinforced. The aversive stimulus (carrying heavy boxes) is removed and Joe will be more

Table 3.1. Examples of positive reinforcement

Description	Target behavior	Reinforcer
A baby lifts her arms up to her father, and her father picks her up and smiles and talks to her.	Baby lifting her arms when father is present	Being picked up and social interaction
A teacher and child are looking at a picture book. The teacher stops and says to the child, "What do you see on the page?" When the child responds by naming one of the pictures, the teacher responds by saying, "You are right, that is a big lion," and allows the child to turn the page.	Picture labeling	Letting the child turn the page, continuing the interaction, and descriptive praise
At snack time, the teacher has grapes and cheese on a tray in front of him. A child points to the cheese and the teacher puts a piece of cheese on his plate and says, "You said you want cheese."	Requesting preferred items by pointing	Presentation of preferred food, descriptive praise
In preschool it is time to clean up from free play and get ready for storytime. Timmy, a 4-year-old boy with ASD, does not like storytime, and he does not want to stop playing with the trains. When the teacher says it is time to clean up, Timmy starts to cry. The teacher says, "You may have 5 more minutes with the trains, and then join us at circle."	Crying to avoid nonpreferred activities (e.g., putting the trains away and joining the class at circle time)	More time to play with the trains and avoiding the nonpreferred activity

likely to ask for help again in the future. Another example of negative reinforcement is often observed in supermarkets. A child is whining and asking for candy. The caregiver says "no" a few times and finally gives in and says, "OK, have some candy." The behavior of the caregiver is negatively reinforced. The child stops whining (i.e., removes the negative stimulus) and the caregiver is more likely to give the child candy in the future when he or she whines. Interestingly, this is also an example of positive reinforcement. The child's behavior (i.e., whining) is positively reinforced and the likelihood that the child will whine the next time he or she is taken shopping increases.

Negative reinforcement is used less frequently than positive reinforcement, but it is one of the four basic types of consequences that occur in ABA (see Table 3.2). It is used regularly when dealing with challenging behaviors. A common intervention for children who demonstrate challenging behaviors during difficult or nonpreferred activities is to teach those children to ask for a break or for assistance. That intervention is based on negative reinforcement. By providing a short break to the child upon the child's request, the child gets to escape the difficult task. This is an example of negative reinforcement at work. When a child gets to take a break from a nonpreferred activity, the behavior of asking to take a break is being negatively reinforced. Like positive reinforcement, negative reinforcement increases behavior. The difference is that negative reinforcement removes an aversive stimulus (e.g., carrying a heavy box, completing a nonpreferred task) contingent on the target behavior.

How frequently and consistently a behavior receives reinforcement has an impact on learning. When and why reinforcers are provided is called the schedule of reinforcement. Reinforcement is usually either provided on a continuous schedule or an intermittent schedule. Behavior that is reinforced on a continuous schedule is reinforced every time it occurs. Continuous reinforcement schedules are most often used in the very early stages of instruction. For example, if teaching a child to point to request items, the instructor wants to reinforce that behavior (i.e., provide the item the child is pointing to) every time it occurs. Although continuous reinforcement is very powerful in teaching new behaviors, it is not very effective in teaching durable or strong behaviors.

Intermittent reinforcement establishes strong behaviors (see Table 3.3). Behavior that is reinforced using an intermittent reinforcement schedule receives reinforcement only some of the time it occurs. This can be on a highly regular schedule (e.g., every third time a behavior occurs), or on a variable schedule (e.g., on average, every third time a behavior

Table 3.2. Understanding basic consequences

	Increase behavior	Decrease behavior
Add a stimulus	Positive reinforcement S^{R+}	Positive punishment
	Example: Zipping up a jacket for a child who is struggling with his or her zipper and says, "Help me, please."	*Example: A child is flipping on and off the light switch and the parent says, "No," in a firm voice. The verbal reprimand is functioning as the punisher for the self-stimulatory behavior.*
Remove a stimulus	Negative reinforcement S^{R-} (removal of an aversive stimulus contingent on the target behavior)	Negative punishment sometimes called response cost (removal of a preferred stimulus contingent on an inappropriate behavior)
	Example: A child asks to leave a room that is very noisy and the teacher says, "Yes." The behavior of avoiding the noise (an aversive stimulus) by using language is being reinforced.	*Example: A child is watching a movie on a tablet and hits a child who sits down next to him or her. The teacher removes the tablet. Removal of the tablet functions as a punisher for the hitting.*

Table 3.3. Examples of intermittent reinforcement schedules in everyday activities

Raising one's hand in class	No child gets called on every time he or she raises his or her hand. It happens intermittently and randomly. Of course, if you stop calling on him or her altogether, or don't call on him or her enough, he or she will stop raising his or her hand.
Starting an old car	If you have an old car that starts sporadically, you will keep turning the key in the ignition over and over until the car starts. You are on a *variable* reinforcement schedule. You know it will start eventually. Compare this to a new car. If you have a brand-new car and it doesn't start, you will stop trying very quickly. This is because you are on a *continuous* reinforcement schedule.
Gambling	A slot machine is the ultimate example of a variable reinforcement schedule. You don't get money back every time you play. You get it back intermittently and randomly—just often enough to keep you playing.
Asking for candy in the check-out aisle	A child and his or her father are checking out with groceries at the supermarket. The child points to candy and says, "Want it." The father says, "No, you can have some fruit when we get home." The child asks repeatedly and the father repeatedly says, "No." During these requests, the child escalates from pointing and asking nicely to whining and crying. After about 10 requests (and many other shoppers looking at the father), the father finally says, "Fine, pick out the candy you want." Both positive and negative reinforcement are in play here. The child's inappropriate behavior (e.g., crying, whining) is positively reinforced. The father's behavior is negatively reinforced when the child stops crying and whining when given the candy.

occurs—the behavior might be reinforced twice in a row then occur five more times before it is reinforced again). The reinforcement that occurs in natural environments is more likely to be intermittent reinforcement. Intermittent reinforcement creates extremely strong and durable behaviors, behaviors that are more difficult to change through extinction (i.e., not reinforcing behaviors that have previously been reinforced), or planned ignoring.

The next type of basic consequence is punishment. The technical definition of punishment is when a stimulus is presented or removed contingent on a target behavior, the likelihood of that behavior occurring in the future decreases. Although in common usage, punishment is viewed as something quite aversive and unpleasant, this consequence is used more often than one might think. For example, a player on a sports team is late for practice and the coach tells him or her to run a lap before joining practice. Charles is late for a bus trip to a museum, and the bus leaves without him, causing Charles to miss the trip; that is also an example of punishment. Sometimes implementing a natural consequence functions as punishment. For example, if a child spills his or her water at snack and has to wipe it up, the process of wiping it up functions as a punisher, decreasing the likelihood that the child will spill their drink again.

The examples above, where a negative consequence is added, are often referred to as positive punishment. When a positive stimulus is removed, rather than added, contingent upon a behavior the teaching team wants to decrease, it is called negative punishment. An example of negative punishment, sometimes called response cost, would be if a child is watching a movie on a tablet and hits a child who sits down next to him or her to join in watching. Contingent on hitting, the tablet is removed. This type of punishment is used more frequently in classroom and early learning settings.

Although punishment can be effective in some situations, it is not used as frequently as reinforcement for a number of reasons. First, it is not as effective as reinforcement. Reinforcement teaches new behavior. Punishment does not. Punishment can suppress inappropriate behaviors providing a window during which new, appropriate behaviors can be taught, but punishment alone does not teach alternative solutions to challenging behaviors. For instance, in the example with the athlete who is late to practice, running the lap may motivate the athlete to be on time; but if the underlying problem with tardiness is due to organizational issues or the ability to tell time, punishing late arrivals is not going to do anything to help solve the problem. Second, people satiate to punishment. A teacher can start to use a simple reprimand as a punisher for a child in a classroom, but if the teacher continues to do that and does not teach an appropriate alternative, the reprimand will lose its effectiveness. This may lead the teacher to scolding, or something more inappropriate. The tendency for the intensity of punishment to increase is a noteworthy argument against the use of punishment. Finally, and perhaps most important, there is a societal tentativeness about the use of punishment. The first ethical responsibility for all people in the helping professions is to do no harm. Although punishment, when used correctly is not harmful and can be an important teaching tool, there are many stories of this behavioral strategy being misused and, therefore, it should be avoided when possible.

SUMMARY

ABA is the application of behavioral principles to teach socially important behaviors and outcomes. There are few issues that are more socially important than the education of young children. ABA has been used to teach children with ASD since the 1970s, and there are hundreds of peer-reviewed articles demonstrating the effectiveness of behavioral intervention strategies. The three-term contingency, antecedent-behavior-consequence (sometimes referred to as stimulus-response-stimulus), is the primary foundation of ABA. Behavioral teaching strategies, therefore, are developed by either changing the antecedents in the three-term contingency or by changing the consequences. The most commonly used (and perhaps the most powerful) behavioral principle is reinforcement. Positive reinforcement is the presentation of a stimulus (e.g., toy, cookie, activity, descriptive praise) contingent on a target behavior that results in an increased likelihood of that behavior happening again. Negative reinforcement also increases the likelihood of a behavior happening again, but rather than presenting a positive stimulus, it removes a negative or aversive stimulus. Punishment decreases the likelihood of a behavior happening again but for ethical and practical reasons we use it infrequently. Changing antecedents is an effective strategy for teaching appropriate behavior and preventing the occurrence of challenging behavior.

CHAPTER 4

Instructional Strategies to Facilitate Learning

The purpose of this chapter is to describe the primary instructional practices used in Project DATA. These practices are used because there is strong evidence demonstrating their effectiveness in teaching children with ASD and because of their adaptability across settings and content. To be an effective teacher, it is necessary to know how to implement a variety of instructional strategies, but it is even more important to know how to select which instructional strategy should be used in a specific context to teach a specific skill to a specific child. Selecting instructional strategies is just one of the many steps involved in providing a high-quality instructional program. Project DATA teaching staff need to be sure that the instructional strategies they select

- Are used to teach skills that are important to the child and valued by the family
- Are implemented with high fidelity by all staff
- Are taught to all staff, and staff are provided with adequate coaching to implement them correctly
- Are implemented in an environment that is designed to promote learning
- Are evaluated regularly with data on child progress

The instructional practices used in Project DATA are based on the principles of ABA. ABA practitioners study behavior and its relationship to the environment. Therefore, the teaching strategies focus on arranging the environment to promote and support learning. This means that teachers implementing the DATA model change antecedents (what happens before the behavior) and consequences (what happens after the behavior) to improve the likelihood of appropriate behavior and decrease the likelihood of challenging or inappropriate behavior.

DISCRETE TRIALS

The basic instructional unit used in Project DATA is the discrete trial. A discrete trial is an instructional framework with a "distinct onset and offset and a discrete intertrial interval" (Koegel, Russo, & Rincover, 1977, p. 200). This type of instructional framework enables teachers to break complex tasks into distinct and discrete units. These units can be taught explicitly, with the intensity needed by each child to learn the targeted skills. A discrete trial consists of five components, four required and one optional:

- Instruction
- Prompts (this component is optional)
- Child's response
- Consequence
- Intertrial interval (see Figure 4.1)

A discrete trial has the following components:

Figure 4.1. Discrete trial.

It is important to note, however, that the definition of a discrete trial does not state where the instruction should occur, how long it should last, or the materials that should be used. Project DATA does *not* define discrete trial teaching as something that is done with a child with ASD and an adult sitting at a table in an isolated setting using boring instructional materials. Discrete trial training is a method of organizing instructional interactions, which can be used to teach a variety of skills, in a variety of settings, to people with a variety of abilities. Discrete trials can be implemented at a work table, on the playground, or at the snack table. They can be implemented during activities initiated by the teacher or embedded into activities selected by the child. The details of how each component of a discrete trial is organized and implemented can vary dramatically based upon the needs of the child, the skill being taught, and the teaching objective selected (see Figure 4.2).

Component 1: The Instruction

The first component of a discrete trial is instruction. The instruction tells the child what they are supposed to do. Instructions can be verbal or nonverbal, and they can be simple or complex, but they need to clearly delineate the expectations of the teacher in this specific teaching episode. When starting instruction with a child, teachers should begin with simple one-step instructions. As the child learns more skills, teachers can increase the length and complexity of the instructions to prepare the child to be successful in a wide variety of learning environments.

> ▨ Skills are broken down into very small parts.
>
> ▨ Clear instructions are provided.
>
> ▨ Prompting is provided as necessary to promote correct responding.
>
> ▨ Each subskill is taught to mastery before moving on.
>
> ▨ Concentrated teaching of the skill is provided.
>
> ▨ The instructional interaction is always initiated by the teacher.
>
> ▨ A response by the child is always required.

Figure 4.2. Distinctive features of a discrete trial.

Before a teacher gives instruction, it is important to ensure that the child is ready. A child demonstrates readiness when he or she is attending to the adult and the materials, and is in the area where instruction will take place. The child does not need to be seated. Good instruction can take place standing up, while walking, or while on a swing; however, the child should be oriented to the adult and attending to the materials that will be used in the instructional interaction.

Although many people use the terms *instruction* and S^D as synonyms, that is not technically correct. S^D is the abbreviation for the behavioral term *discriminative stimulus*. An S^D is a special type of instruction that indicates reinforcement is available for the behavior being requested. For example, when a teacher tells a child to stand up, and the child complies, the teacher provides a positive reinforcer contingent on the behavior of standing up. Remember, a positive reinforcer is a consequence that increases the likelihood of a behavior happening again. The goal is for children to be able to discriminate when it is appropriate to demonstrate certain behaviors and when it is not. For example, children are taught to stand up when the teacher asks them to, when the bell rings, or when the teacher calls a child to the front of the room to take a turn. Ideally, children should not stand up indiscriminately during snack, circle, or individual work time. If a child does stand up frequently when they are not supposed to (i.e., when there is not positive reinforcement available for that behavior), it may be said that the child is demonstrating a challenging behavior called "out of seat." Understanding what an S^D is and is not helps teachers select instructions carefully. Teachers must be clear in what they ask children to do, consider the consequences for what is being taught, and consider how the skills they are teaching will extend beyond the classroom or extended-day program setting into home and community settings, and the influence these skills will have on children's overall quality of life.

There are several guidelines for giving high-quality instructions:

■ Keep instruction simple and concise.

　■ To help the child focus on the relevant instruction, avoid extraneous information. Teachers should say, "Throw the ball," not, "OK, whose turn is it? You need to throw me the ball." As the child progresses, the instructional language should gradually begin to approximate the type of language that would be used with typically developing children of the same age, including indirect instructions, as well as the type of language teachers often use in schools.

■ Ensure that the child is paying attention before providing instruction.

　■ The child should be oriented toward the teacher and instructional materials.

■ Tell children what to do; do not ask them.

　■ In this type of teaching arrangement, children's responses are not optional. Do not ask the child if they want to engage in a behavior; tell them to do so. For example, if a teacher says, "Are you ready to put your toys away?" a correct response from the child might be, "No." If the child answers no to that question (note that it was not an instruction), then the teacher should say, "OK, you can play for 2 more minutes." If an adult wants the child to put their toys away, then they should say, "It is time to clean up." Modeling the appropriate behavior by helping them put their toys away is a great way to teach children to follow directions.

■ The behavior that a teacher asks the child to perform must be observable.

　■ Do not ask a child to "think about what you are doing." It is not possible to tell if the child is following the instruction or not. Teachers should tell the child exactly what they want done; for example, "Pick up your pencil" or "Walk in the hallway."

▓ Keep instructions positive.

  ▓ Tell the child what to do rather than what not to do. For example, a teacher might say, "Put your hands in your pockets," rather than, "Stop flapping your hands."

▓ Give the child time to respond (at least 3 to 5 seconds).

  ▓ Teachers often give an instruction and immediately repeat the instruction or add a prompt. Teachers need to give the child enough time to process an instruction before stepping in with a prompt.

▓ Once an instruction is given, teachers must ensure the children follow through with that instruction.

  ▓ Children need to learn that when a teacher gives an instruction, it is necessary to follow it. Teachers must be ready to provide assistance to the child, if necessary, to help them follow the direction, and, of course, to provide positive reinforcement when they do follow the direction.

Children learn by doing, and the goal of instruction is to provide multiple opportunities to respond. Providing clear instructions helps children be more successful and independent.

Component 2: The Prompt (If Necessary)

A prompt is any assistance given to the student before the student responds to an instruction. Prompts are related to and supplement the instruction. A good prompt provides the least amount of support necessary to facilitate a correct response. There are two primary types of prompts: response prompts and stimulus prompts. Response prompts provide information to the child to enhance their response (e.g., a teacher pointing to a picture to show a child the correct response). Stimulus prompts change some characteristic of the stimulus to facilitate the correct response (e.g., enlarge the font size of the card with the correct response in a letter naming activity). This manual discusses response prompts. A more detailed discussion of both response and stimulus prompts can be found in Cooper, Heron, and Heward (2007).

Prompts are an important part of the instructional toolbox. It is important to remember, however, that prompts are a temporary addition to help children learn new skills and behaviors. Prompting is similar to what theorists outside of behavior analysis call scaffolding. The idea of scaffolding provides a wonderful metaphor for prompting. In the same way that scaffolding is an unsightly temporary structure installed during a construction project and then removed when the project is finished, prompting is used to teach new skills but removed when children are independent. Scaffolding, like prompting, is necessary to yield the beautiful finished project, but the project is not finished as long as the scaffolding is still attached. No one would want to live in a house that was still surrounded by scaffolding, and teachers do not want to teach behaviors that are still dependent on adult prompting. Therefore, all prompts that are added must be removed. The process of removing prompts is called *prompt fading.*

Prompt fading is one of the most difficult parts of the discrete trial. While it is easy to add prompts, it may be challenging to remove them. Not removing prompts, or using more prompts than necessary, creates learners who are over reliant on prompts, or prompt dependent. When working with young children, it is important to be diligent in prompt fading so that learners do not become prompt dependent. There are two primary strategies for prompt fading: increasing the amount of time between the instruction and the prompt and decreasing the intensity or salience of the prompt.

Increasing the amount of time between the instruction and prompt is a type of prompt fading called time delay. In this strategy, teachers begin by providing the prompt (e.g., point to the correct response in a discrimination task) at the same time as the instruction. This is called a *zero-second delay*. When children are successful with this level of delay, teachers systematically increase the time between the instruction and the prompt. For example, in a 3-second delay, the teacher gives the instruction, "Show me purple," and then waits 3 seconds to provide the child with an opportunity to respond independently. If, after the wait time, the child has not responded, the teacher provides the prompt. If the child responds correctly before the prompt, (i.e., beats the prompt) the teacher provides positive reinforcement. If the child has responded incorrectly, then the teacher provides an error correction (see the section below). The logic of the time-delay prompt-fading procedure is to teach children to beat the prompt through the use of differential reinforcement. Children receive a more powerful reinforcer if they answer correctly and independently (i.e., before the prompt is provided). *It is important to remember that a prompt must come before the child's response. If it comes after the child's response, it is a consequence.*

Decreasing the intensity or salience of a prompt is a type of prompt-fading strategy called *most-to-least prompting* or graduated *guidance*. The logic of this type of prompt fading is that the teacher provides the most intrusive prompt necessary (e.g., hand-over-hand guidance) to ensure that the child makes the correct response. After the child is responding correctly with one level of prompting, teachers decrease the intensity or type of prompting. For example, in this type of prompt-fading sequence, the type of physical assistance provided may proceed from hand-over-hand prompting to guiding a child's response with a tap to his elbow, a tap on his shoulder, or using a point prompt. Although the path differs, in both time delay and most-to-least prompting the desired outcome is the same—independent child performance.

Types of Prompts

▪ Physical. A physical prompt is any type of physical support or guidance a teacher provides to help a child complete the response. Examples of physical prompts include hand-over-hand directing the child to point to the correct response, helping the child grip his or her pants and pull them up, providing support to the child's elbow to help him or her pour juice, and lifting a child's leg to help him or her climb up a climbing toy on the playground.

▪ Visual. A visual prompt is any sign, cue, or signal that a teacher provides to supplement an instruction or routine. These may include

  ▪ A schedule during free time indicating where a child needs to play

  ▪ Pointing to a correct response

  ▪ A carpet square during circle time indicating where a child is supposed to sit

  ▪ A sheet over the sensory table during center time indicating that the sensory table in not available

  ▪ A line on the classroom floor indicating where children need to stand to line up

▪ Modeling. Modeling is a special subtype of visual prompt. A model is when a teacher provides a sample of the behavior that the child is expected to perform to supplement other forms of instruction. For example, if the teacher says, "Clap your hands," and also claps his or her hands, the teacher's hand clapping is a prompt. The instruction is verbal; the teacher is providing extra information to the child when he or she claps his or her hands.

▩ Verbal. A verbal prompt is when the teacher provides extra information to the child after the instruction but before the child's response. It is not just repeating the instruction; this is usually considered bad instruction. Remember, a prompt adds information for the child. For example, if the child and teacher are looking at a picture of a lion in a book and the teacher points to the picture and says, "What is that?" if the child does not respond, the teacher may add the verbal prompt "lion."

Guidelines for Using Prompts

▩ Prompts are a powerful instructional tool and must be used intentionally.

▩ Prompts occur *before* the child's response.

▩ Prompts must be faded systematically.

▩ A prompt is only successful if it yields the correct response.

▩ Use prompts judiciously (i.e., be wary of combining different kinds of prompts because they will all need to be faded).

Component 3: The Child Response

An essential part of a discrete trial is allowing time for the child to respond. Since the goal of teaching is improving children's independent responding, it is important to provide children with the opportunity to show what they know. Minimally, teachers should provide children 5 to 10 seconds to respond. Some children may need a little bit more time; however, it would be very unusual to provide a child more than 15 seconds to respond. A student's response is what he or she does after an instruction. The next component of a discrete trial, the consequence, is based on the child's response. Project DATA teaching teams track four types of child responses:

▩ *Independent correct*: responds correctly with no prompts

▩ *Prompted correct*: responds correctly with a prompt

▩ *Error*: responds incorrectly, with or without a prompt

▩ *No response*: does not respond, with or without a prompt

Examples of Child Responses   The teacher tells the child, "Show me the red crayon." The child might

▩ Point to the red crayon on her own: *Independent correct*

▩ Point to the red crayon with the teacher giving a hand-over-hand prompt: *Prompted correct*

▩ Point to the blue crayon: *Error*

▩ Engage in self-stimulatory behavior: *No response*

Component 4: The Consequence

Children learn by doing. They also learn from the consequences that their behaviors produce. When their behaviors yield positive consequences, they are more likely to engage in those behaviors again. That is an example of positive reinforcement in action. When they engage in behaviors that create aversive or undesired consequences, they are less likely to engage in those behaviors again.

A consequence is the teacher's way of providing feedback to the child. When a child responds correctly, teachers should acknowledge that correct response with some type of reinforcement (e.g., praise, smile, access to a tangible item). When the student responds with an error or no response, teachers will want to provide some type of feedback that the response was incorrect and what response they were looking for (e.g., looking away, a simple correction). Positive reinforcement is the most powerful evidence-based strategy in the instructional toolbox. It is important to use it frequently, correctly, and contingently to help children with ASD be as successful and independent as possible.

There are several guidelines teachers should follow when using positive reinforcement:

▧ Conduct frequent preference/reinforcer assessments to ensure that effective reinforcers have been identified.

▧ Deliver reinforcers immediately after the target response.

▧ Deliver reinforcers contingent upon the desired behavior.

▧ Vary the reinforcers.

▧ Always pair tangible reinforcers with social praise.

▧ Collect child performance data to demonstrate that the stimulus being used is functioning as a reinforcer (a stimulus, even a highly preferred stimulus, is only a reinforcer if it increases the likelihood of the behavior to happen again).

▧ Consider the schedule of reinforcement being used. Use continuous reinforcement (CRF) when teaching a new skill; decrease the frequency of the reinforcement provided (i.e., thin the reinforcement schedule) as children acquire the skills.

If a child responds to a teacher's instruction incorrectly, it is very important to correct the error. The most important idea to remember about error correction is that it is an instructional tool. It is a neutral consequence. It is not negative, and it should never be viewed or presented as aversive. Teachers should use an error correction to let the student know that they were incorrect by ending the trial with a neutral "no," "hands down," or otherwise indicate that the child should get ready for another instruction. Project DATA uses the following error correction procedure:

▧ Child makes an error; teacher says "no" in a neutral voice and withholds reinforcement.

▧ Teacher models the correct response.

▧ Teacher repeats the trial with a prompt to ensure the child responds correctly.

▧ Teacher reinforces the prompted correct response.

▧ Teacher repeats the trial to provide the child with an opportunity to demonstrate the behavior independently.

For example,

▧ The task is receptive vocabulary, selecting the appropriate picture from an array of three cards.

▧ The teacher says, "Touch the pencil," and the child points to the wrong picture.

▧ The teacher says, "No, hands down."

▨ The teacher says, "This is a pencil," while pointing to the picture of a pencil.

▨ The teacher says, "Touch the pencil," and physically prompt the child to touch the picture of the pencil. Teacher provides social praise for the child's response.

▨ The teacher says, "Touch the pencil," and the child touches the pencil. Teacher provides social praise and other positive reinforcement for correct response.

One of the guiding principles of Project DATA is that child failure is instructional failure. If a child is making numerous errors, the teacher needs to investigate the instruction that is being provided to determine

▨ Is instruction being provided with fidelity?

▨ Are salient reinforcers being used?

▨ Is instruction being provided at the appropriate intensity?

▨ Is the correct level of prompting being used?

▨ What changes need to be made to the instructional program?

▨ What changes need to be made to the context of instruction?

Component 5: Intertrial Interval

The final component of a discrete trial is the intertrial interval. The intertrial interval is a brief period of time between the end of one trial and the beginning of the next. This interval reminds the teacher that each discrete trial is a finite teaching episode. This brief pause, usually lasting between 2 and 5 seconds, highlights the idea that each trial is complete and does not run into the next instructional episode.

RECOMMENDED PRACTICES IN USING DISCRETE TRIALS

Discrete trials are one method for organizing and delivering instructional interactions. Discrete trials do not provide information about what should be taught, what materials should be used, or where instruction should occur. In the 40 years that applied behavior analysts have been using discrete trials to work with children with autism and related disorders, practitioners in this field have learned much about how to make the explicit instruction in discrete trials as effective as possible. These strategies make instructional sessions more fun, engaging, and, therefore, more successful. In Project DATA, discrete trial teaching sessions always include the following recommended practices:

▨ Alternate acquisition and maintenance trials. In order to maintain motivation and increase the effectiveness of instruction, teachers implementing the DATA model do not present massed trials of any task. Rather, they present approximately three trials of an acquisition task, followed by two or three trials of a maintenance task, followed by three trials of another acquisition task. Using this pattern provides multiple trials of all current programs, but does so in a manner that has been shown to increase engagement.

▨ Use natural reinforcers when possible. Natural reinforcers are those that are inherent to a task (e.g., using crayons to teach coloring and providing access to a different crayon contingent on naming the color).

■ Use interesting materials. Materials that appear in the child's natural home and school environment, reference the child's preferences, and are culturally relevant.

■ Pay attention to pacing. Instructional sessions should move along at a brisk pace. Materials should be prepared before the session begins and children should not have to wait for teachers to get organized.

■ Pay attention to the reinforcement schedule. The schedule of reinforcement is a description of the contingencies that are in place. In other words, how frequently and for which behaviors will children receive social praise, tokens, access to tangibles, or other types of reinforcers? It is essential to effective programming that teachers use a robust enough schedule to promote acquisition, fluency, generalization, and maintenance, but that the schedule is thinned (i.e., reinforcement is provided less frequently) as quickly as possible to promote durable and robust levels of responding.

■ Conduct frequent preference assessments. The purpose of a preference assessment is to identify activities and objects (e.g., toys, food) that have a high likelihood to function as a reinforcer. Reinforcers can only be identified functionally. An object is only a reinforcer if it increases the likelihood of a behavior happening again when it is presented contingently on the occurrence of a target behavior. Figure 4.3 provides a data collection sheet for a forced choice preference assessment. Using this strategy, the child is presented with three objects or activities and told to "take what you want." The child makes a choice and has the opportunity to play with or enjoy his or her selection. This process is repeated with at least two more sets of three objects or activities. The objects the child selects are marked as preferred on the data collection sheet. Finally, the three preferred items are presented, and the child is asked to choose one. The item selected is marked as the highly preferred item. Preference assessments should be conducted frequently—at least weekly—and any time members of the team believe that the potency of the reinforcement available is interfering with child progress.

Naturalistic Teaching Strategies

One of the defining characteristics of the Project DATA approach to teaching is that, regardless of where a teaching interaction occurs, it is intentional and of high quality. There is a class of teaching strategies known as naturalistic teaching strategies. Some people may assume that, because these teaching strategies are embedded into the ongoing activities and routines of the classroom and community settings, they require less planning or are less formal than discrete trial teaching. This is not true. Incidental teaching (one of the most well-researched naturalistic teaching strategies) is not accidental teaching. It is intentional, linked to valued child outcomes, and although the child may initiate the teaching episode, the adult conducts the actual instruction. Sometimes discrete trial teaching and naturalistic instruction are viewed as very different practices. They are not. Clear, explicit instruction is at the core of both. Both require the teacher to close the instructional loop—that is, provide an instruction to the child and then provide a consequence based on the child's response. The quality and intentionality of the instruction is not different; the context of the instruction is the primary difference.

A number of effective instructional strategies can be easily embedded into the preschool day. As a group, these strategies are often referred to as naturalistic strategies. All of these strategies require teachers to follow the child's lead to determine what he or she is interested in, ask the child to engage in some social or communicative behavior, and then provide the child with feedback about his or her response related to the ongoing activity (e.g., open the lid to a jar if a child asks for assistance). Most important, these strategies are

Preference Assessment

Child: _____ Date initiated: _____ Date completed: _____

Use the preference assessment to identify preferred items and activities that may be used as reinforcers. To complete the preference assessment, do the following:

1. Gather at least 10 items or activities (such as drawing) that may be of interest to the child. Consider parent input, age of child, sensory needs, and so forth, and record each item below.

2. Place 2–4 items in front of the child. If the child has not seen the item before, you may consider allowing him to manipulate the item for a few seconds.

3. Once the child chooses an item, allow him or her to play with it for a few seconds while you check the item as "preferred" on the list. Place that preferred item aside. Continue until you have several items set aside as "preferred."

4. Place 2–4 "preferred" items in front of the child.

5. Once the child chooses an item from the preferred set, allow him to play with it for a few seconds while you mark the item as "highly preferred." Continue until you have a few items set aside as highly preferred.

Item/activity	Nonpreferred	Preferred	Highly preferred
1.			
2.			
3.			
4.			
5.			
6.			
7.			
8.			
9.			
10.			
11.			
12.			
13.			
14.			
15.			

Figure 4.3. Preference assessment.

used in brief instructional episodes or bouts that do not interfere with the ongoing activity that served as a context for the instruction. Additionally, these strategies all share some common characteristics:

1. Used during ongoing activities and interactions

2. Repeated and brief interactions between adult and child

3. Responsive to children's behavior

4. Provide children feedback and naturally occurring consequences

5. Require purposeful planning on part of teacher

Different naturalistic instructional strategies vary in the amount of support and independence that they provide to the child (Schwartz, 1987). The most often used naturalistic instructional strategies are presented below, ranging from the one that provides the most support to the one that allows for the most child independence:

▪ Choice making: This strategy provides the most support to the child. The adult initiates this instructional interaction by following the child's lead. Then the adult provides two options to the child and asks the child to make a choice. The adult provides prompting as necessary to facilitate a correct response and provides the natural consequence of providing access to the item the child chooses. When introducing children to this technique, it is helpful to give a choice between preferred and nonpreferred items. These choices are often quite contrived. As children improve their ability to make choices, it is good to provide more realistic choices that occur in the classroom.

  ▪ The teacher is playing with Wendy at the sensory table. This is the first day she has used choice making with Wendy. Wendy enjoys using different types of tools to dig in the sand. Currently, the teacher has all the digging utensils. She holds up the blue shovel (Wendy's favorite) and a ball and says, "Do you want the shovel or the ball?" Wendy points to the shovel and the teacher hands it to her and says, "You are digging in the sand with the blue shovel."

▪ Model–question: This strategy is outstanding for building vocabulary and is sometimes referred to as the mand-model procedure in the research literature. When using this procedure, adults follow the child's lead to identify an instructional opportunity (model), then they ask the child to label or describe the target of the interaction (mand). If the child needs more support, the adult models the correct response. The interaction is brief and ends with the adult providing access to the targeted item or activity.

  ▪ The teacher is working on new vocabulary words with Xavier in the context of the block area. She shows him a triangle-shaped block. She does not believe that he knows the name of the shape and says, "This block is a triangle" (model); "What shape is it?" (mand). Xavier says, "Triangle," and she gives him the block and says, "You are right. A triangle has three sides." Later in the week after Xavier has had practice with this new word, she holds up the triangle and says, "What shape?" (mand). The teacher says, "You are right. It is a triangle," and gives him the block.

▪ Time delay: This strategy is best used to facilitate spontaneous responding. In this procedure, the adult follows the child's lead to identify an item or activity of interest. Then the adult blocks the child's access to the object while maintaining eye contact with the child for 5 to 10 seconds. When the child requests the object or activity, he or she receives access to it. Adults use prompting as necessary to keep the interaction brief and successful.

▪ The teacher and Zandy are standing at the door to go outside for recess. The teacher has her hand on the doorknob and looks expectantly at Zandy. Zandy says, "Open," and the teacher opens the doors and says, "Let's open the door and go to recess."

▪ Incidental teaching: This is the strategy that provides the most independence for the child and is the only strategy that is child-initiated. An incidental teaching episode begins when a child makes an initiation and the adult asks the child to expand his utterance. The adult uses prompting as necessary to keep the interaction brief and successful and provides access to the targeted item or activity after the child makes the requested expansion.

▪ Yosef is playing with trucks in the block area but notices that the bridge he likes to play with is not with the other blocks and trucks. He looks up and sees that his teacher has put it up on a shelf that is out of his reach. He taps his teacher's arm and points to the bridge. The teacher says, "What?" (asking for an expansion of his utterance), and Yosef replies, "I want bridge." The teacher hands it to him and says, "Here is the bridge for your trucks."

Shaping

Shaping is an important tool in the instructional toolbox of every adult working with children with ASD. Shaping is the process of reinforcing successive approximations of the behavior as it moves toward the desired form of the behavior. For example, if a teacher wants a child to play at the sensory table for 5 minutes, and currently they stay at the sensory table for 30 seconds, the teacher will shape that behavior by reinforcing longer and longer episodes of appropriate play. In other words, the teacher begins providing reinforcement for staying at the sensory table for 30 seconds; once the child is doing that consistently, the teacher requires that the child play at the sensory table for 45 seconds before providing reinforcement, then 60 seconds. It may take a while, but shaping is an excellent strategy to teach improved accuracy and duration of behaviors. Shaping requires patience and careful measurement and tracking of the desired behavior. However, with persistence, shaping is an effective way to teach a wide variety of skills and behaviors.

Chaining

Whereas shaping is the process of refining a specific behavior, chaining is the process of linking steps of a task or a skill into a unified whole. For example, when teaching a child to brush their teeth, the adult will chain the steps of the task analysis together into a fluent and functional behavior. Most often teachers use backward chaining, where the last step of the task analysis is taught first. This means that the instructor would prompt the child through the entire task analysis and then focus on teaching them to do the final step of the chain (e.g., wiping their mouth on the towel) independently. Backward chaining has been found to be more efficient when working with young children with ASD.

Decontextualized versus Embedded Teaching

The Project DATA approach to teaching believes that the distinction between naturalistic and discrete trial teaching is a false dichotomy. Discrete trial teaching conducted while sitting at a table in a classroom is "decontextualized teaching." It is decontextualized because the context in which the skill being taught is not the context in which the child will use the skill in a natural and functional manner. Teaching that occurs at a snack table or while the child is at play is often embedded because program teams are using explicit instruction to teach the child a valuable skill in the context in which the skill naturally occurs. This discussion will continue with examples of embedded and decontextualized teaching in Chapter 7.

SUMMARY

This chapter describes the basic instructional strategies used in Project DATA. Discrete trials, naturalistic instructional strategies, shaping, and chaining are all effective instructional tools, but like any tools they are effective only if teachers know how to use them and if they apply the correct tool in the correct situation. As teachers gain confidence and competence in using these instructional tools, an important challenge is to match these tools both to the student's needs and to the skills and behaviors that they are teaching. One of the basic concepts of applied behavior analysis is parsimony. The idea of being thrifty or frugal can be helpful when thinking about instructional strategies. Start with the most simple and straightforward approach and let the data determine the next steps. More about selecting and using instructional strategies is provided in Chapter 7.

CHAPTER 5

Determining What to Teach

Knowing what to teach children with ASD is as important as knowing how to teach. Any instructional interaction is only as strong as the target goal. If teachers use high-quality, evidence-based instructional strategies to teach skills that are not functional, culturally relevant, and developmentally appropriate, children may learn many skills, but the overall quality of the program will still be poor. Children often exit programs that lack coordinated curricular planning with a number of disjointed, discrete skills that do not enable the child to function more independently at school and in community settings and do not improve the overall quality of life for the child and his or her family. Since one of the guiding principles of Project DATA is a quality-of-life influenced curriculum, determining what to teach is an important part of the intervention process. This means that the curriculum planning focuses on selecting skills that are

- Functional (if the child cannot do them, someone will have to do them for the child)

- Individualized

- Valued by the family

- Related to increasing the child's independence at school, home, and in the community

- Culturally relevant

- Developmentally appropriate

The first step in determining what to teach is to assess the child's current level of performance. This means that teachers need to determine which skills and behaviors the child can demonstrate independently, what level of support is required for the child to demonstrate other skills, and which skills the child can demonstrate across different settings and with different people. This is not a straightforward process. In addition to having a list of skills that the child has learned, teachers need to know

- The settings in which the child can demonstrate the skills (e.g., school, home, Grandma's house)

- The support that the child may need to demonstrate the skill (e.g., visual schedule, an adult in close proximity)

- The fluency with which the child completes the skills (i.e., can the child complete the skills with enough speed and accuracy for this skill to be useful?)

Teachers also need to know which skills are valued by family members and which skills will help the child participate more independently in all the settings in which the child spends time (e.g., their integrated early childhood program, home, Sunday School, Grandma's house).

Assessments can be used to collect all of this information. Assessment is the process of gathering information for the purpose of making decisions. Assessment of young children, including those with ASD, can take many forms and serve many purposes. In the areas of early childhood education and applied behavior analysis, assessments are used in many ways. For example, assessments can be used to do the following:

■ Conduct a screening to determine if a child may be at risk for a disability and need additional assessment

■ Determine the presence of a disability and provide a diagnosis

■ Determine how the child's behavior compares on average, to other children who are the same age

■ Determine what is motivating and maintaining a challenging behavior to determine the function that a challenging behavior serves for the child

For more details about assessment in early childhood special education refer to Grisham-Brown and Pretti-Frontczak (2011) or McLean, Hemmeter, and Snyder (2014). The focus of this chapter is the DATA Model Skills Checklist, an assessment designed for program planning. This assessment is used in conjunction with comprehensive early childhood assessments in Project DATA to develop individualized curricular plans for every child. These plans use information from comprehensive early childhood assessments (e.g., AEPS) and the autism-focused DATA Model Skills Checklist to ensure that all the relevant skills that need to be addressed are included in a child's curricular plan. Finally, strategies for including information from teachers, parents, and other caregivers in the assessment process will be discussed. Information from these key informants will enable the school team to create a program that will help the child learn, generalize, and maintain skills that will help the child be successful across environments and truly improve the quality of their life and the lives of their families.

ASSESSMENT IN EARLY CHILDHOOD CLASSROOMS

Austin was diagnosed with ASD at 30 months and had been receiving home-based services from the publicly funded early intervention provider in his town. The day after his third birthday, Austin began attending an inclusive preschool and extended day program at his neighborhood school, which was implementing Project DATA. The first 2 weeks of the program were spent getting to know Austin, helping him learn the classroom routine, developing a relationship with him, and collecting assessment information. Teachers talked to his parents and asked them to complete a parent interview (see Chapter 9). They also completed two curriculum-referenced assessments—one designed to collect information across all developmental domains and the DATA Model Skills Checklist, designed to address the core areas of programming for children with ASD. In order to collect the information, his teachers observed Austin in his preschool classroom interacting with typically developing peers, at recess, in extended day and at home. Finally, to round out their knowledge about Austin's strengths and areas of need, they completed some direct testing in the classroom. Now the teachers are trying to figure out how to analyze the information that they have and which skills to prioritize as they develop Austin's program of instruction.

Providing high-quality instruction for children begins with assessing their learning needs. Once children qualify for special education and are enrolled in an inclusive preschool classroom, the program planning part of the assessment process begins. The most effective tools for program planning are curriculum-referenced assessments. A curriculum-referenced assessment evaluates a child's abilities in the context of a predetermined sequence of curriculum objectives. Commonly used curriculum-referenced assessments for young children include *Teaching Strategies GOLD*, *The Carolina Curriculum for Preschoolers with Special Needs*, *The Assessment, Evaluation and Programming System*, and *Hawaii Early Learning Profile (HELP)*. The information for these assessments can be collected in classroom, home, and community contexts. They encourage educators and family members to work together to gather the information necessary to create a thorough portrait of the child's behavioral profile. Curriculum-referenced assessments also allow for monitoring progress over the course of the school year. The outcomes of the curriculum-referenced assessment will guide a teacher in developing daily learning targets for all children, including those who have individual family service plan/IEPs.

Although many comprehensive curriculum-referenced assessments provide a picture of child behavior, often this level of assessment is not sufficient for children with ASD. While these assessments provide a broad picture of child development across developmental domains, they may not provide a deep look into areas that are core deficits for children with ASD. For example, imitation is a skill that many children with ASD need to work on in preschool. Most assessments for preschool children have one or two items about imitation. This does not provide detailed enough information for program planning for children with ASD. Teaching teams need to know more about their imitation skills since they are related to the core deficits of the disorder and a foundation for learning in the context of a preschool classroom. Rather than simply assessing the presence or absence of imitation skills, in order to adequately plan a program for a young child with ASD teachers might want to know the following:

■ Can the child imitate actions with objects?

■ Can the child imitate gross motor movements?

■ Can the child imitate sounds and words?

■ Can the child imitate a teacher during circle time?

■ Can the child imitate while sitting across from a teacher?

■ Can the child imitate his peers while playing?

DATA Model Skills Checklist

The DATA Model Skills Checklist has been developed and refined in order to gather more detailed information about behaviors related to positive outcomes and improved quality of life for children with ASD. It is a curriculum-referenced assessment that addresses areas of particular need for children with ASD (e.g., core deficit areas and areas related to success at school, home, and in the community). The DATA Model Skills Checklist is designed to supplement other curriculum-referenced assessments. It is not a stand-alone assessment; rather, it is designed to provide more in-depth information on the specific programming needs of children with ASD.

A complete version of the DATA Model Skills Checklist can be found in Appendix A. Below is a description of items that would be found in each domain area.

■ The *Adaptive* section concentrates on skills such as appropriate meal-time behaviors, independent personal hygiene, school skills (e.g., managing materials, making transitions, participating in a group activity), self-advocacy (e.g., asking for a break when needed), and behaviors that interfere with participation and learning.

■ *Executive Functioning* addresses a child's ability to be flexible (e.g., relinquishing a toy to a peer), to self-regulate, to persist at a task, to problem-solve with adults and peers and to label, demonstrate, and identify different emotions.

■ The *Cognitive* section focuses on imitation skills, matching, categorizing, sequencing, and early literacy skills.

■ *Communication* addresses following directions, responding, initiating, and receptive and expressive vocabulary.

■ The *Social* section of the DATA Model Skills Checklist focuses on joint attention, pragmatic rules, and interactions with others.

■ Finally, the *Play* section addresses play fundamentals (e.g., appropriate interactions with toys), independent play, and interactive play.

Many of these skills will be found on other curriculum-referenced assessments. However, the skills are not explored in the same detail as they are in the DATA Model Skills Checklist. To understand how the DATA Model Skills Checklist compares to two widely used curriculum-referenced assessments, refer to the assessment crosswalk displayed in the Appendix. This document cross-references the items on the DATA Model Skills Checklist with those on the AEPS.

Implementing the DATA Model Skills Checklist   The DATA Model Skills Checklist is designed to supplement a curriculum-referenced assessment that addresses multiple domains of child development. Both of these assessments should be completed within the first few weeks of a child entering a Project DATA program and should be redone every time a new IFSP/IEP or program plan is written for the child. Teachers can gather information from multiple informants and strategies (e.g., from parent interviews, observation across the school day and contexts, and direct testing situations) to complete this assessment. The goal is to complete the most comprehensive and accurate portrait of the child's behavior across settings. It is very important to remember that the purpose of the DATA Model Skills Checklist is to assess levels of independent child behavior. Since many children with ASD have an uneven behavior profile it is important to assess all the items on the checklist.

The DATA Model Skills Checklist is scored with a 0, 1, 2 scoring key. Guidelines for the scoring, along with a sample item from each domain are shown in Figure 5.1.

General Guidelines for Completing the DATA Model Skills Checklist   Before completing the DATA Model Skills Checklist, it is important to have the materials ready for the assessment, including items for a reinforcer assessment. The materials list for completing the assessment can be found in Appendix C. Some items on this list include identical pictures for matching, sequenced picture cards, cause and effect toys, and toys related to a play theme. To gather items for a reinforcer assessment, Project DATA teachers ask the child's preschool teacher and parents to identify the child's preferences, as well as observe the child in the home or classroom. Project DATA teachers then gather these items prior to assessment to determine the child's strongest preferences, or reinforcers.

The DATA Model Skills Checklist is usually completed within four to six extended day sessions and one or two classroom observations. During the first session of the assessment, the primary goal is to establish a positive relationship with the child and determine the child's preferences. These preferences are used to maintain interest and motivation during the assessment but are not used as reinforcers for correct assessment responses. Some children with ASD have clear preferences, so the reinforcer assessment may not take long to complete. Other children with ASD may have a variety of preference items and activities,

Directions:

1. Several items are directly tested; others are observed and scored during classroom routines and activities. Adult instructions are provided for items to be directly tested. Scoring is as follows:

   2 = Consistently/always meets criterion

   1 = Inconsistently/sometimes meets criterion

   0 = Does not/never meets criterion

2. After completing the checklist, put a * next to items that are priorities for learning.

A. Adaptive			
1. **Mealtime**	**Scoring**	**Comments**	*
1.4 Remains at table during meals *Child remains at table until he or she asks to leave, adult excuses child, or the natural end of the mealtime.*	0 1 2		

B. Executive functioning			
1. **Flexibility**	**Scoring**	**Comments**	*
1.2 Accepts interruptions or unexpected change *Child may verbally or nonverbally, appropriately express displeasure with change but is able to accept change/interruptions and move on*	0 1 2		

C. Cognitive			
1. **Imitation**	**Scoring**	**Comments**	*
1.5 Imitates multistep sequences *Imitates multistep actions or phrases while following along with teacher in a group setting (e.g., repeat-after-me songs or rhymes, action songs).*	0 1 2		

D. Communication			
3. **Initiating**	**Scoring**	**Comments**	*
3.5 Requests the end of an activity *Child will ask to be "all done" or "finished" after working with an activity.*	0 1 2		

E. Social			
1. **Joint attention**	**Scoring**	**Comments**	*
1.5 Initiates gaze to establish joint attention *For example, looks at a child crying and then looks at adult*	0 1 2		

F. Play			
1. **Play fundamentals**	**Scoring**	**Comments**	*
1.2 Uses play materials appropriately *Child acts on objects using functionally or socially appropriate actions. Functionally or socially appropriate actions are those for which the object was intended or designed (e.g., child holds play telephone to ear, puts comb to head and attempts to comb hair, puts glasses on eyes).*	0 1 2		

Figure 5.1. Selected items from the DATA Model Skills Checklist.

and these preferences may change daily. For these children, a reinforcer assessment may need to be completed during each extended day session. Other general guidelines for completing the DATA Model Skills Checklist include the following:

▪ Complete all domains and all items of the checklist.

▪ Testing and observation can begin on any domain of the checklist.

▪ Use naturally occurring opportunities (e.g., snack) to assess skills as much as possible.

▪ Moving between domains on the assessment may prevent challenging behaviors from occurring as the child will not be overloaded with tasks from one domain or tasks that are too difficult (e.g., intersperse movement tasks with those that require the child to sit at the work table).

▪ Vary assessment tasks with preferred and maintenance tasks to promote better engagement and affect.

▪ Use the same high quality child interaction strategies used in teaching when conducting the direct testing portion of the assessment (e.g., give frequent breaks, alternate hard and easy items, make the child-teacher interactions positive).

▪ Reinforce child behavior and attention during testing sessions.

▪ Keep the testing sessions fun.

Remember the goal of an assessment is to get an accurate picture of the child's abilities. The testing situation should be designed to promote the child's best behavior, using environmental design strategies, pacing strategies, and positive reinforcement to help the child be as successful as possible and to make the experience positive.

Translating Assessment Information into a Program of Instruction

Once the assessments are complete, the teacher will analyze the data and work with the information from all of the assessments, including the DATA Model Skills Checklist, the child's current IFSP/IEP, and input from the family to determine priority learning goals for each child in the classroom. The instruction provided should be part of a linked system so the team will be in constant motion during the process of teaching, gathering information, evaluating that information and then adjusting teaching accordingly.

Determining which skills to teach is influenced by assessment information and the Project DATA program philosophy. Instruction should begin with skills that are rated a "1" on the DATA Model Skills Checklist. A skill with a rating of a "1" means that the child can demonstrate the skill some of the time. Starting with those skills will help the child and the instructional team experience success quickly. Of all the skills that are rated "1," the team should select those skills and behaviors that will have the biggest impact on the quality of life for the child and family. Staff members also want to ensure that children have a comprehensive program, so skills from a variety of domains should be included in a child's instructional program. That means that as program staff begin to determine the content of a child's program of instruction, it is necessary to consider which skills will help that child:

▪ More independent

▪ Happier

▪ Able to participate in activities at school, community, and home

▓ Able to develop relationships

▓ Successful in activities that are important to the child and family

▓ A functional communicator

Priority should be given to instructional programs that will help children be independent across settings and be able to participate more fully in activities in their inclusive preschool, home, and community settings. Every child must have a functional communication system. Having a functional communication system means that the child has a standard method (e.g., standard gesture, AAC, or speech) of expressing his wants and needs and protesting in an appropriate way. Children who can control their environment through functional communication (i.e., asking for what they want or telling people what they do not want) are less likely to engage in challenging behaviors.

When selecting skills to target for instruction, the first thing to do is look at core skill areas. It's important to ensure that the child can demonstrate independent performance of these most basic skills:

▓ Requesting

▓ Imitation (e.g., objects, large motor)

▓ Matching

▓ Joint attention

▓ Following directions

▓ Building vocabulary

▓ Functional toy play

▓ Staying on task for increasing lengths of time

▓ The beginning steps in self-advocacy (e.g., asking for a break, protesting in an appropriate manner)

Teachers can determine children's repertoire of these basic skills by examining the results of the DATA Model Skills Checklist. When determining the skills to address, teachers should review the results of the DATA Model Skills Checklist and make a list of the skills on which the child scored a 1. The team should prioritize those skills based on the child's IFSP/IEP, family preferences, and the impact the skills will have on the child's quality of life (i.e., independence, access to less restrictive environments). It's also important to consider the range of skills across domains. Ideally children should have a program of instruction that addresses areas of need from across different domains. Now that the skills to address have been selected, the next step is to write instructional programs and begin teaching. More about programs and program writing is provided in Chapter 6.

One of the most frequently asked questions is how many instructional programs are kept open for a child at any one time. There is no simple answer to that complex question. The number of programs that are open at any one time depends on the child's needs, the instructional setting, program design, and many other factors. One way to answer that question is to have as many programs as necessary to help the child continue to make progress toward meaningful educational outcomes. That answer, although it fits with Project DATA philosophy, is often not helpful in real-life situations. In general, teachers working with Project DATA have a minimum of five and usually not more than 10 programs open for every child at any one time. It is important to remember, however, that the goal is to move children through programs as quickly as possible and to write new programs as soon as a child meets criteria on their current program. Since child performance data is collected daily, progress on current programs is monitored frequently and accurately, moving children through stages of learning quickly and efficiently. The instructional team must be nimble in their data-based decision making and make changes to current instructional programs or add new instructional programs as needed. Data collection and data-based decision making is discussed in Chapter 8. Writing, adapting, and using instructional programs are discussed in Chapter 6.

After completing the AEPS and the DATA Model Skills Checklist, Austin's teachers determined that he had good rudimentary imitation skills and functional play skills. However, he required intensive instruction on the other 4 basic skills: requesting, joint attention, following directions, and building vocabulary. To round out his program of instruction, based on assessment information and parent priorities teachers added programs for the following:

■ *Toilet training (Adaptive 2.1)*

■ *Participates in a group activity for at least 5 minutes (Adaptive 3.9)*

■ *Verbal imitation (Cognitive 1.4)*

■ *Matches identical pictures (Cognitive 2.2)*

■ *Follows one-step directions (Communication 1.1)*

■ *Uses gestures to initiate (Communication 3.1)*

■ *Identifies at least 50 common nouns (Communication 4.1)*

■ *References communicative partner (Social 1.1)*

■ *Turn taking with peers (Social 3.3)*

■ *Completes a play sequence (Play 1.5)*

His parents are very excited about the skills that are being addressed and his teachers are ready to get going!

SUMMARY

A high-quality assessment is the cornerstone of any good program for a child with ASD. A high-quality assessment provides information about the child's strengths and areas of need, preferences, and family priorities and beliefs. A high-quality assessment also provides information across development domains and, for children with ASD, a deep look into the areas of development most frequently affected by the core deficits of ASD. When conducting assessments for children with ASD it is helpful to combine strategies used to collect information. The strategies most often used in Project DATA are observation, direct testing, and interviews with parents and other caregivers. Once the data from the assessments are collected, the child's instructional team needs to translate the results into educational programs. This is done by integrating information from the assessments with parents' priorities and program philosophy. Together, this information will guide the instructional team's decision about where to begin instruction, ensuring that the programs selected will help the child make progress towards meaningful outcomes that will result in an improved quality of life for the child and their family.

CHAPTER 6

Writing and Using the Instructional Programs

Identifying the skills to teach is just the first step in effective programming for children with ASD. Ensuring that instructional programs are written in a manner that uses effective instructional strategies, integrates authentic opportunities for teaching and learning, and incorporates strategies to facilitate generalization and maintenance is key. The goal of an instructional program is to ensure that each child receives the most efficient and effective instruction. Part of that efficiency is the assurance that all members of the team are implementing instruction in a consistent manner. Instructional programs should be as simple and straightforward as possible. Parsimony is an important attitude that influences our practice in applied behavior analysis and should also influence our instructional programs. Parsimony means frugality. High-quality instructional programs are parsimonious with the time and effort required to write and implement them. When thinking about writing programs for children with ASD, the idea of parsimony means using the simplest approach possible to accomplish a goal. In other words, when writing instructional programs, sometimes less is more.

This chapter describes the process used to develop instructional programs. It also provides guidance in writing lesson plans that facilitate instruction in both discrete and embedded instructional situations. Samples of instructional programs are included from every domain on the DATA Model Skills Checklist, as well as a sample lesson plan used in Project DATA to provide models of what instructional programs can look like. Finally, information is provided about how to organize children's assessments, programs, and other information to make them easily accessible.

WRITING INSTRUCTIONAL PROGRAMS

Once the assessment is complete and the lead teacher has worked with the educational team, including the child's parents, to determine priority learning goals, an instructional program must be written for every goal that is going to be addressed. Remember, this work is part of a linked system so a child's program is a work in progress. As they teach, Project DATA instructors gather information on the child's learning, evaluate that information and then adjust teaching accordingly. The purpose of an instructional program is to describe

- What is being taught

- The steps of the skill or behavior being taught

- Example sets to teach the target skills

- Mastery criterion for how the instructional team will know when the child has learned the skill

- How generalization and maintenance will be facilitated

It is very important to write an instructional program for every skill and behavior being taught. Having an instructional program ensures consistency and makes communication across all members of the educational team easier. When instructional programs are used in a classroom, staff members are more likely to

▦ Use the same set of directions when teaching a specific skill

▦ Use consistent prompting strategies

▦ Use the same set of materials for teaching

▦ Program for generalization and maintenance

▦ Collect reliable data across instructors

▦ Teach with increased fidelity

Project DATA instructional programs have three main components: a behavioral objective, a mastery criterion, and a task analysis or teaching sequence. The behavioral objective identifies what will be taught. The mastery criterion describes how much and what types of behavior the child needs to demonstrate to confirm that teaching is successful and complete. The task analysis or teaching sequence describes the steps to follow to teach the behavioral objective.

Writing a Behavioral Objective

The first step in writing any instructional program is to describe the intended outcome of instruction. That is, what will the child be able to do when the instruction is completed? The behavioral objective is a tool to define what the program team wants to teach. A behavioral objective answers the *who*, *what*, and *when* questions about teaching:

▦ Who is learning?

▦ What is being taught?

▦ Under what conditions will the learner be able to demonstrate the behavior?

▦ When will the program team know that the child has learned the behavior (i.e., mastery)?

Some examples of behavioral objectives include

▦ Adaptive 1.4—When called to a meal, and with a plate of food on the table and at least one other person sitting at the table, Dahlia will stay seated at the table for at least 10 minutes for 3 consecutive days.

▦ Cognitive 1.2—When presented with a nonverbal model and an instruction to imitate (e.g., "Do what I do," "Do this"), Gavin will imitate the teacher's action with 90% accuracy across three consecutive sessions.

▦ Play 2.1—When asked to "go play" or presented with an array of toys or materials that Betty knows how to use, Betty will play (i.e., engage appropriately with the toys with no more than 15 seconds in a row of unengaged time) for 5 minutes with no comments or prompts from adults.

▦ Social 3.7—In a small group activity where a peer needs assistance (e.g., cannot open a bag from his lunch, does not have the appropriate materials to complete an activity), Drew will ask the child if he needs help and if the peer answers, "Yes," Drew will provide the appropriate amount and type of assistance four out of five opportunities.

▦ Communication 3.6—While looking at a book with an adult, Sophie will initiate at least one comment per page for a total of 10 comments per reading session, using at least 5 different books.

The objectives above describe different learners (e.g., Dahlia, Gavin, Betty, Drew, Sophie) who are learning a variety of different skills and behaviors (e.g., sitting at the table with their family for a meal, nonverbal imitation, playing independently, providing help to a peer, and making comments). The objectives also describe some *conditions* that should be in place for the child to demonstrate the behavior (e.g., When teaching Dahlia to sit at the table for a meal, the conditions include that at least one other person needs to be at the table; when teaching Betty to play independently, the condition is that she knows how to use the toys that are available). Finally, all of the objectives include *mastery criteria* that are specific to the behavior being taught. Some use simple percent correct (e.g., nonverbal imitation—when an adult performs an action and says, "Do this," "Copy me," or "Do what I'm doing," the child will imitate the adult's large motor movement with 80% accuracy), while others have a more complicated data collection system that include a two-part response (e.g., carrying out a solution to a problem—When a problem arises, the child will carry out a solution suggested or will negotiate or compromise with a peer to solve a problem across four of five opportunities that occur during free play).

There is no one best format for behavioral objectives as long the information needed to write and implement an instructional program is provided. Many school districts now use computer programs to assist in writing IEP objectives (e.g., IEP Online), and it is acceptable to vary the form of the objective to meet the requirements of the instructional system. The key to writing good objectives is to determine the range of behaviors being addressed and types of data collected based on the needs of the child and priorities of the family, not the capabilities of a computer program. Writing a behavioral objective is a little like picking out a destination on a map. It provides information about the desired destination, but it does not map out the journey (that is done by the teaching sequence). Like planning for any good trip, however, picking an interesting (and in this case important and functional) destination is an important first step.

Selecting Appropriate Mastery Criteria

The mastery criteria set in a behavioral objective determines the type of data that will be collected during instruction and how well a child needs to complete the skill in order to move on to the next step in the instructional process. The criteria for many skills that are taught in EIBI programs are written in "percent correct" format. In fact, the criteria of 80% correct across 3 days is ubiquitous in special education and EIBI. While that criterion may be appropriate for some skills and some learners, it may not be appropriate for others, and could actually be considered silly or dangerous. For example, how can a child count to 10 or cross the street with 80% accuracy? Do adults really want children to be toilet trained with 80% accuracy? It is essential to match the type of data (e.g., frequency [how many], rate [how many in a specified amount of time], or duration [how long does it last]), with a criterion that makes sense in the life of the child and family. For example, when writing an objective for toilet training, the mastery criterion may be zero accidents for 3 days in a row, when being reminded to use the toilet every 30 minutes. When the child achieves that goal, it may be increased to zero accidents for 3 days in a row, when being reminded to use the toilet every 45 minutes. A meal-time goal may focus less on number of bites eaten and more on length of time sitting at the table (if that is the family's priority). For example, an appropriate dinner time goal for many families may be "given quiet toys to play with and other family members sitting at the table, Ava will stay at the dinner table for 10 minutes."

One of the guiding principles of Project DATA is that family priorities influence the selection of behavioral objectives since we use a quality-of-life influenced curriculum. When determining criteria, the instructional team should always keep the family's specific priorities in mind because the intended outcome of the child's target skill or behavior will vary in situations outside of school (e.g., home, child care, community). For example, if staying at the dinner table is a priority for Dahlia's family, how long does she need to stay at the table for them to be satisfied with the change in her behavior? Is it acceptable for her to have quiet toys or books to occupy her time at the table? Don Baer, one of the patriarchs of applied behavior analysis, often said, "You know you have changed a behavior enough when the person who originally complained about the behavior stops complaining." In other words, staying at the table for 10 minutes may be appropriate for Ava's family, but not for Dahlia's family. The job of a behavior analyst is not to determine what behaviors are important, but to help children and families achieve behaviors that they identify as the most important and valuable to them.

Another way to set appropriate criteria for target behaviors is to observe typically developing children in similar situations. For example, if the target objective was "Accepts being told 'No' without becoming upset/angry" (Executive Function 1.3), it would be helpful to know what typically developing children do when told "No." Is it appropriate to negotiate? To stomp their foot and say, "Darn it?" To say, "Maybe next time?" These decisions should be informed by parent feedback and considered in the context of the environments where the child with ASD spends time.

When writing instructional programs, it is important to consider the four stages of learning:

1. Acquisition

2. Fluency

3. Generalization

4. Maintenance

These stages of learning must be incorporated into the instructional planning process and generalization criteria should be set for all programs (Bailey & Wolery, 1992).

Acquisition is learning the characteristics and features of the task. For example, when teaching a simple color discrimination, a child has acquired this skill when he or she can point to the color that the teacher has named 80% of the time, when the desired object is presented with two distractors. Often this type of instruction occurs with a limited set of materials, in limited environments, and in very controlled settings. Although it is technically correct at this point in the teaching and learning sequence to say that the child can demonstrate that he or she knows the name of different colors, he or she cannot yet use this skill in a functional manner or in a manner that helps to improve the quality of his or her life.

Fluency is the ability to use the skill at a normal speed or at a certain speed combined with sufficient endurance to make it useful. For example, if a child has learned all the steps of putting on his shoes and socks, but it takes him 5 minutes to put on each shoe and sock, that skill is not functional, because parents and teachers are not going to let him spend that much time just putting on shoes and socks. He needs to learn how to complete the task in a timely manner—that is, in a time that is similar to that of typical peers or that his instructional team agrees is a reasonable personal goal.

Generalization is the ability to demonstrate a skill or behavior across settings, materials, and people that are different from how and where the skill was taught; and to maintain these changes over time. For skills to influence a child and family's quality of life, the child needs to be able to demonstrate their new skills and behaviors in multiple settings. For example, it is nice that Dahlia has learned to sit at the table for lunch at school, but for the skill to impact her quality of life, she needs to be able to sit at the table with her mother for breakfast, sit at the table with her entire family when they go to a restaurant, and sit at the table with her cousins at her grandmother's house.

Finally, maintenance is the ability to generalize newly acquired skills over time. Building on the example above, if Dahlia does not go to her grandmother's house for a month, is she still able to demonstrate her improved mealtime behavior? The ability to maintain skills and behaviors over time is what leads to important, durable behavior change.

There are no firm guidelines about writing generalization and maintenance criteria, but as a rule these criteria include goals for demonstrating the behavior across a certain number of people (e.g., three different teachers, or three teachers and a parent), settings (e.g., in preschool, on the playground, while waiting in line for the bus), and with different materials. When writing these criteria consider how data will be collected. For example, when writing a criterion that includes demonstrating the behavior at home, program staff may need to rely on parent reporting rather than direct observation.

Developing the Teaching Sequence or Task Analysis

If the behavioral objective is the destination teachers want to reach in their instructional journey, then the teaching sequence (sometimes called a task analysis) is the path used to get there. The teaching sequence describes the series of steps that must be taught to reach the desired instructional goal. There are multiple types of teaching sequences that vary based on the type of task being taught. All of the different types, however, share the common characteristic of identifying the subtasks necessary to complete a specific behavior or skill. These teaching sequences provide the teacher with the set of behaviors that must be taught for children to achieve the behavioral objective.

A traditional task analysis is used to teach multiple steps of a complex behavior. Although task analyses are often thought to be effective only in teaching self-care skills (e.g., brushing teeth, dressing) this process of breaking down a complex skill into simple, discrete tasks can be very helpful when teaching other types of behaviors (e.g., having a conversation, helping a peer, completing a worksheet). A skill sequence is used when teaching skills that require a gradual progression of discriminating between more examples of the same concept class (e.g., identifying colors or shapes). A skill sequence can also be used when instruction involves changing the conditions under which a child must demonstrate the target behavior (e.g., decreasing the frequency of prompts to the toilet, increasing the length of time during which a child is expected to play independently).

Although these two types of teaching sequences may look different (see Figures 6.1 and 6.2 for complete examples of teaching sequences), the same general process is used to develop them. Five steps are used to develop both of these teaching sequences:

1. Specify the target behavior (this has already been accomplished by writing the behavioral objective).

2. Consider if the skill is appropriate and important for the target child (this has already been done by conducting assessments such as the DATA Model Skills Checklist).

3. Identify the steps of the skill and put them into a sequence.

4. Determine the sequence of the skills to be taught.

5. Begin teaching, collecting data, and using the data to make instructional decisions based on the child's progress.

Project DATA outlines the behavioral objective, the criteria for acquisition and maintenance, and the teaching sequence on the instructional program sheet (see Figures 6.1 and 6.2 for completed examples of instructional program sheets and Figure 6.3 for a blank version). It is useful to have all of this information on a single piece of paper when planning instruction and reviewing child progress. This instructional program sheet is used to develop lesson plans (see below) and to track instruction.

INSTRUCTIONAL PROGRAM SHEET: Adaptive

Mealtime: *Drinks from an Open Cup—Example*

Child:_____ Date initiated: _____ Date completed: _____

Objective: In the presence of an open cup with liquid and told "Drink some _____" or "Take a drink," or when thirsty, the child holds the cup, drinks from the cup, and places the cup back on the surface.

Mastery criterion:
- 90% or higher correct responding for each set
- Minimum of 10 opportunities per day
- 2 consecutive teaching days
- No spilling

Generalization:
People: At least two adults
Settings: At least two settings
Materials: At least three different cups

Things to consider: May also teach sitting at the table and/or eating skills

Task analysis
1. Puts hands on cup
2. Picks up cup
3. Brings cup to mouth
4. Tilts cup toward mouth
5. Sips
6. Takes cup away from mouth, turning upright
7. Puts cup on table
8. Releases cup

PROGRAMMING LOG

	Acquisition		Generalization		Maintenance	
	Start date	End date	Start date	End date	Date/data	Date/data
1	2/12/14	2/25/14				
2	2/25/14	3/7/14				
3	3/7/14	3/20/14				
4	3/20/14	4/4/14	4/4/14	4/25/14	5/15/14; 100%	6/15/14; 100%

Figure 6.1. Sample instructional program sheet—Task analysis.

INSTRUCTIONAL PROGRAM SHEET: Communication

Comprehension and Expression of Words and Sentences: *Identifies Attributes—Receptive*

Child:_____ Date initiated: _____ Date completed: _____

Objective: When presented with materials that are varied by size, shape, or color and asked to identify one of them receptively based on its size, shape, or color (e.g., "show me the big ball," "find blue," or "put it with circles"), the child identifies an item or an item in a picture based on the size, shape, or color by pointing to, tapping, or putting it with the correct item.

Mastery criterion:
- 90% or higher correct response for each set
- Minimum of 10 opportunities per day
- 2 consecutive teaching days
- Identifies at least four sizes, six shapes, and six colors

Generalization:
People: At least two adults
Settings: At least two settings
Materials: Across a variety of pictures/objects for each attribute

Things to consider: Materials for child to choose from must be varied across one attribute only (e.g., all materials are triangles, varying only by color; all blocks are orange squares, varying only by size). Consider having child sort by attribute before receptively identifying the items by attribute.

Teaching sequence
1. Identifies items by at least two different sizes (e.g., big, little)
2. Identifies items by at least two other sizes (e.g., huge, medium)
3. Identifies items by at least three shapes (e.g., circle, square, triangle)
4. Identifies items by at least three shapes (e.g., oval, rectangle, diamond)
5. Identifies items by at least three colors (e.g., blue, red, yellow)
6. Identifies items by at least three colors (e.g., purple, orange, green)

PROGRAMMING LOG

	Acquisition		Generalization		Maintenance	
	Start date	End date	Start date	End date	Date/data	Date/data
1						
2						
3						
4						
5						
6						

Figure 6.2. Sample instructional program sheet—Skill sequence.

INSTRUCTIONAL PROGRAM SHEET:

Subdomain: _____ *Skill:* _____

Child:_____ Date initiated:_____ Date completed: _____

Objective:

Mastery criterion:

▪

▪

▪

Generalization:
People:
Settings:
Materials:

Things to consider:

Teaching sequence or task analysis
1.
2.
3.
4.

PROGRAMMING LOG

	Acquisition		Generalization		Maintenance	
	Start date	End date	Start date	End date	Date/data	Date/data
1						
2						
3						
4						

Figure 6.3. Blank program sheet and lesson plan form.

LESSON PLAN:

Subdomain: _____   *Skill:* _____

Settings and materials	
Decontextualized	**Embedded**

Teaching
What direction or cue will you give?
How will you prompt the child's response?
Circle type of prompt(s) used:
Physical   Visual
Modeling   Verbal
Other: _____
Circle prompt fading procedure used:
Time Delay   Most to Least
Graduated Guidance
Other: _____
What is the child's response?
What reinforcers are you using?

Sets

1. _____

_____

_____

_____

2. _____

_____

_____

_____

3. _____

_____

_____

_____

4. _____

_____

_____

_____

5. _____

_____

_____

_____

USING INSTRUCTIONAL PROGRAMS TO GUIDE LESSON PLANNING AND TEACHING

Once the educational team has decided which skills and behaviors to teach, they must determine when, where, and how they will be taught. Project DATA emphasizes that the teaching loop called a discrete trial (see Chapter 4) is the core of every instructional interaction. This loop consists of five steps:

1. Instruction

2. Prompt (if necessary)

3. Child's response

4. Consequence

5. Intertrial interval

The context of teaching is not prescribed by a discrete trial, and this type of instruction can be used in very structured settings (e.g., sitting at a work table) or unstructured settings (e.g., playing in the water at a sensory table). Teachers in Project DATA differentiate this as decontextualized teaching (teaching used in very structured settings) and embedded instruction (teaching used in unstructured settings). The primary difference between decontextualized and embedded teaching is the setting in which the instruction takes place, not the instructional strategies used. For example, teaching color identification using decontextualized instruction may take place at a work table using plastic bears of different colors. These same materials may be used in the block area (assuming that blocks are a preferred activity for the target child) to teach color identification using embedded instruction.

In general, most children benefit from both types of instruction. Therefore, instructional plans are developed for both decontextualized and embedded instruction using the lesson plan form (see Figure 6.4). This form is completed for every program the child is working on and is used to communicate with staff and families, and to plan the instructional day for the child (see Chapter 7).

The lesson plan form is divided into three parts: settings and materials, teaching strategies to be used, and the instructional sets or teaching sequences to be addressed. The lesson plan form requires teachers to answer the following questions about when, where, and how instruction will occur:

1. What *materials* will be used?

    a. This must be answered for decontextualized and embedded instruction

2. What is the *setting* of the instruction?

    a. This must be answered for decontextualized and embedded instruction

3. What *direction or cue* will the teacher provide?

    a. What will the teacher say or do (e.g., arrange the environment) to signal to the child that a response is required?

4. How will the teacher *prompt* the child's response if necessary?

    a. Visual, gestural, physical, verbal

    b. How will prompts be faded?

5. What is the *target response*?

LESSON PLAN: Adaptive

Mealtime: *Drinks from an Open Cup—Example*

Settings and materials	
Decontextualized	**Embedded**
Work at table: Child preferred small cup with preferred liquid	Snack and mealtimes. Same cups and liquids as served to peers

Teaching
What direction or cue will you give?
Cup is present "Take a drink" "Drink some"
How will you prompt the child's response?
Circle type of prompt(s) used:
(Physical)   Visual Modeling   Verbal Other: _____
Circle prompt fading procedure used:
Time Delay   (Most to Least) Graduated Guidance Other: _____
What is the child's response?
Independent response on each step or part of the task
What reinforcers are you using?
Preferred liquid and cups are used initially in decontextualized setting and pair with behavior-specific praise
What is the correction procedure?
Start the task sequence over, with the direction, and then use the least intrusive prompt throughout the sequence unless the child demonstrates mastery of one of the steps in the sequence.

How will you collect data? *(circle answer)*	
(Percentage correct)	Frequency
Duration	Permanent Product
(Other) percentage correct for each step of the task	

Sets

Teach using backward chaining:

1. Teach steps 7 and 8

2. Teach steps 5 and 6

3. Teach steps 3 and 4

4. Teach steps 1 and 2

Figure 6.4. Sample lesson plan.

6. What *consequences* are being used?

    a. How will correct responses be reinforced?

    b. What is the correction procedure for incorrect responses?

7. How will you *collect data*?

8. What steps of the *skill sequence* are being addressed?

How to Organize Instructional Information

All of the instructional information for every child in Project DATA should be stored in an individual instructional binder. These binders are living documents and should be used daily to record and review child data, record interactions with the families, and record notes from instructional planning meetings. Student binders look different across programs, but should include the following (see Figures 6.5 through 6.8 for examples of some of these forms):

▦ Child information sheet—Programs should use the same form for the Project DATA portion of the day that are used for the rest of the program. These forms will vary across programs, but should include information like the following:

    ▦ Child name, address, phone number

    ▦ Best contact information for parents

    ▦ Names of siblings and other important family members

    ▦ Names of pets

    ▦ Medical information (e.g., allergies)

    ▦ Dietary restrictions

▦ Behavior information sheet

    ▦ Information about challenging behaviors (including intervention plans)

    ▦ Information about how the child communicates

    ▦ Preferred activities

    ▦ Reinforcers

▦ Assessment information

    ▦ The DATA Model Skills Checklist

    ▦ Reinforcer assessment

    ▦ Parent contact log

    ▦ Phone log

    ▦ Home visit log

▦ Meeting notes

    ▦ Notes from team meetings

    ▦ Notes from data review meetings

Child's name:_____   Month/year: _____

Use the binder cover sheet to track monthly updates of the child's programming sets. To complete this form, do the following:

1. Fill in the title for each instructional programming sheet in the left column. For example, write "Imitates Actions with Objects."

2. Fill in the current set for that program in the right column. For example, write "Set 3."

Program	Set

Figure 6.5. Binder cover.

DAILY PROGRAM CHECKLIST

Student: _____

The program checklist is a daily tracking form used to address programming and maintenance goals throughout the week at school. To complete this form, do the following:

1. Fill in the date for instruction in the top row. Be sure to include the year.

2. Write all current and maintenance programming goals in the left column, and place a checkmark in the box next to the current or maintenance goal addressed on the date listed at the top. Be sure to only place a checkmark if enough opportunities for that goal were addressed during the teaching session. The number of opportunities is designated in the instructional program sheet.

Date:														
Current programs														
Maintenance														

Figure 6.6. Daily program checklist.

MAINTENANCE AND GENERALIZATION TRACKING FORM

Child: _____

Use the maintenance and generalization tracking form to track maintenance and check for generalization for all programming goals that the child has mastered. To complete this form, do the following:

1. When the child reaches mastery criterion on an instructional program, write the name of the programming goal in the left column under "Program," and the date of completion under the "Date Completed" column.
2. After generalization data are taken, fill in the date and the data taken in the "Generalization" column.
3. When maintenance data are completed, fill in the date and the data taken in one of the boxes provided under the "Maintenance Check" column.

Program	Date completed	Generalization Date/data	Maintenance check Date/data	Date/data
		1)	1)	2)
		2)	3)	4)

Figure 6.7. Maintenance and generalization tracking form.

INDIVIDUAL PROGRAM REVIEW SHEET

Child: _____

Staff member: _____   Classroom teacher: _____

Use the program review sheet to review current programming, analyze data, and make data-based decisions. Both the lead teacher/behavior analyst and the assisting staff member (i.e., para educator or instructional assistant) working directly with the child should fill out this form. To complete this form, do the following:

1. Before meeting with the classroom teacher/behavior analyst, fill in the "date," "program name," "current level" "current set," and "supports/prompts needed" columns.

2. With the classroom teacher/behavior analyst, review this information and fill in the last column "changes to make" based on the child's current performance.

Date	Program	Current level	Current set	Supports/ prompts needed	Changes to make

Additional Notes:

Figure 6.8.   Individual program review sheet.

■ Instructional program information. For each instructional program there should be

  ■ Instructional program sheet

  ■ Lesson plan form

  ■ Graph of child performance data

■ Data sheets

SUMMARY

Behavioral objectives, instructional programs, and lesson plans are tools that help teachers figure out and communicate three essential questions:

1. What is being taught? (i.e., target skill)

2. How is the target skill or behavior being taught? (i.e., lesson plans to target desired skill)

3. How will they know when the child has acquired the skill? (i.e., mastery criteria, behavioral mastery)

The answers to these three questions guide what is being taught and can influence the fidelity with which the lessons are implemented. Lessons implemented with high fidelity improve learning outcomes in children.

CHAPTER 7

Teaching Project DATA Style

Project DATA is a technical, but not dogmatic, approach to using applied behavior analysis to teach children with ASD. Project DATA teachers use applied behavior analysis strategies with high fidelity, but apply these strategies in a manner that enables them to stay true to the core beliefs of the program. These beliefs include

- Children with ASD are children first.

- Children with ASD have opportunities, from day one of intervention, to interact successfully with typically developing children.

- The integrated early childhood experience is the child's primary educational program. The purpose of the extended, intensive instruction and other components of the Project DATA model are to help the child participate and succeed in preschool, home, community, and other valued activities.

- Intensive instruction does not have to be decontextualized instruction. Embedded instruction is essential in promoting positive outcomes.

- The primary outcome variable for Project DATA is improved quality of life for children with ASD and their families.

The purpose of this chapter is to describe how to put all of the instructional components of Project DATA together for an individual child. The chapter explains how to implement the extended, intensive instruction component of the model and provides strategies to increase the quality of instruction provided in these settings. This chapter also discusses the relationship between the instruction provided to students in the intensive and inclusive components of the program, as well as how to match specific instructional strategies to settings, target behaviors, and learner characteristics.

WHAT DEFINES TEACHING PROJECT DATA STYLE?

What makes Teaching Project DATA Style different? First, Project DATA teachers acknowledge that there is no one right way to teach all children with ASD. Teaching—especially teaching children with ASD—is a process, not a formula. Teaching Project DATA Style requires adults (e.g., teachers, parents, therapists) to work together to solve instructional problems in a manner that helps children be as independent and successful as possible. *Rather than saying there is one right way to teach a specific skill, Project DATA teachers believe that the right way to teach any skill is by using instructional strategies that incorporate behavioral principles, build on child interests, and use child progress monitoring data to demonstrate that the child is learning.*

Within this broad framework, three components of instruction are essential to Project DATA:

1. Viewing discrete trial teaching on a continuum from decontextualized to embedded instruction

2. Reliance on visual supports to teach a range of behaviors

3. Selecting instructional targets that are related to improving quality of life as the primary outcome

These components guide instruction in Project DATA, and especially in the extended, intensive instructional part of the day, in a manner that differentiates Project DATA from other programs designed to work with young children with ASD.

One of the distinctive features of Project DATA is how discrete trials are viewed within the overall context of instruction. *A discrete trial is just a way of framing an instructional interaction and there is nothing in the description of discrete trials that suggests that this instructional strategy should only be used in quiet settings, with children sitting at work tables.* Project DATA staff believe that the steps of a discrete trial are at the core of *every* instructional interaction. The difference between what is often called naturalistic instruction and what is often referred to as discrete trial training is the location and materials that are used; however, the actual components of the instruction are the same. Consider the following two examples. In both vignettes, teachers are using discrete trials to teach a child to point to familiar objects. In Vignette 1, Drew is receiving instruction in a decontextualized manner. In Vignette 2, Rosalie is receiving instruction on the same program, but her instruction is embedded in a play activity.

Vignette 1: Drew is new to Project DATA and preschool and is just starting to work on identifying common household items. Set one of his program includes the following items: fork, cup, spoon, napkin, and bowl. During individualized instructional time Drew and his teacher are sitting at a small table. She has materials and her data sheet at her side. Drew is sitting at the table putting stickers on a piece of paper, one of his favorite things to do. The teacher begins and says, "Drew, my turn," and extends her hand. Drew hands her his paper and stickers. The teacher says, "Thank you. You are ready for work." The teacher displays three objects (i.e., cup, napkin, and bowl) on the table. The teacher says, "Point to bowl." Drew does so, and the teacher gives him a high-five and says, "You are correct. That is a bowl." She marks his response on her data sheet, rearranges the items on the table, and says, "Point to napkin." Drew responds with the correct answer and the teacher responds, "You are a superstar. Great job." She records his response, rearranges the items, and says, "Show me the cup," intentionally changing the instruction from "point to" to "show me" as part of her effort to program for generalization. Once again, Drew is correct and the teacher records his response and provides verbal praise. Then, she provides him with an instruction to complete a maintenance task—that is, a task that Drew has already demonstrated that he can complete with 80% accuracy across three sessions. For Drew, the maintenance task today is nonverbal imitation (e.g., "Do this," while the teacher claps her hands). This is one of Drew's favorite tasks and he is quite good at it. She continues this, rearranging items, praising correct responses, alternating acquisition and maintenance tasks for 4–5 minutes. After that time, she hands Drew his stickers and paper and says, "Super job. You have earned a break."

Vignette 2: Rosalie is also learning to identify fork, cup, spoon, napkin, and bowl. She loves to play in the house keeping area of the classroom so her teachers are embedding instruction on this program during dramatic play. Rosalie and her peers are washing dishes in the house area when the teacher comments on their play, then holds up a cup and a spoon in front of her, and says, "Point to the cup." Rosalie responds correctly and the teacher gives Rosalie the cup saying, "This cup is dirty. Can you wash it?" Then the teacher records Rosalie's response, interacts with other children for 1–2 minutes, then returns to Rosalie who is now setting the table with her friends. The teacher holds up a napkin and a fork and says, "Show me napkin." Rosalie responds correctly. The teacher gives her the napkin and asks, "What are you cooking over here?" then records her data. The teacher continues to embed discrete trials into the play activity until she gets 10–15 trials or Rosalie moves on to another activity.

In Project DATA, discrete trials are used in decontextualized and embedded instruction. Decontextualized instruction most often takes place at a table in a one-on-one teaching format. This instruction is teacher directed, but every attempt is made to make the instructional setting fun and inviting. Even in decontextualized instruction, many strategies (e.g., child's interests, natural reinforcers, and alternate acquisition and maintenance) are used to keep the child engaged and motivated. Decontextualized teaching sessions are started by teachers and ended by teachers. Although teachers attempt to keep children highly motivated in the activity, these sessions look like traditional, teacher-led, intensive instruction. Embedded instruction takes place during the activities and routines that are part of every classroom experience. Embedded instruction occurs while sitting on the floor playing with blocks, walking down the hallway to the playground, and at the snack table. Embedded instruction is planned and intentional. Although children's responses to embedded discrete trials are obligatory, children can end an embedded instructional session by changing activities. For example, in the vignette above, if Rosalie left the house keeping area, instruction on common household items would end; embedded instruction on a different objective, appropriate to her new activity, would begin based on the activity that Rosalie chose and what objective the teacher had planned to embed in the new activity. A distinguishing feature of embedded instruction is that the teacher *plans* multiple teaching opportunities across the daily routines and activities. All children receive decontextualized and embedded instruction every day. The ratio of the type of instruction depends on what skills the child is learning, what stage of learning they are currently addressing (i.e., acquisition, fluency, generalization, or maintenance), and the child's learning history.

Using visual supports is another distinctive feature of Project DATA. Visual supports are evident in every part of instruction in Project DATA. They are used to teach appropriate behaviors, teach children to be more independent, teach self-management, teach children to make choices, and teach children to advocate for themselves (Gauvreau & Schwartz, 2013). The common theme across all of these examples is the word *teach*. Teaching children, and the adults with whom they share environments, how to use visual supports is key. Visual supports can be extremely helpful when created, implemented, and faded appropriately. The key to all visual support use is that it makes the child more independent.

Since improved quality of life is our primary outcome variable, the target skills and behaviors must be inextricably linked to helping children participate independently in valued activities, rituals, and routines (Billingsley, Gallucci, Peck, Schwartz, & Staub, 1996). This means that children in Project DATA spend more time working on social, play, and independence skills than on discrete cognitive or preacademic skills.

Extended, Intensive Instruction

One of the core components of Project DATA is an extended instructional day (also referred to as extended day). The model of an extended instructional day was developed so that school districts could build onto their existing preschool programs for children with disabilities or universal preschool programs. Project DATA strongly recommends that children with ASD spend a minimum of 20 hours per week at school engaged in developmentally appropriate learning environments. Hours alone do not indicate the intensity or appropriateness of a program for children with ASD, but hours are an essential part of the equation. Other components of the intensity equation are the quality of the instruction, the match between what is being taught and what the child needs to learn, opportunities to interact successfully with typically developing children, and the use of data-based decision making. The mix of an inclusive classroom experience and intensive instruction through an extended day program are an effective, acceptable, sustainable, and developmentally appropriate way to meet the needs of young children with ASD. In the Project DATA model that has existed at the University of Washington since 1997, children spend approximately 11.25 hours per week in an inclusive preschool program and 11.25 hours per week in an extended day program. The inclusive preschool program is described in Chapter 2. The extended day program will be described below.

Goal The goal of the extended day instructional component of Project DATA is to prepare the child to participate more fully and learn more successfully in the inclusive classroom. The research on early intervention for children with ASD is clear. Programs need to be comprehensive, intensive, and use effective instructional strategies. Although there is no exact formula to determine the right amount of individualized versus group instruction, or opportunities to interact with typically developing children needed to achieve the most promising outcomes for children with ASD, programs must evaluate child outcome data and modify the program as necessary to meet individual needs. Every Project DATA-inspired program should design a model that meets their local institutional needs (e.g., school district or early intervention center) and the needs of their children and families.

The Project DATA philosophy is that children with ASD need to spend as much instructional time as possible with typically developing peers. For most children with ASD, the instruction provided in a high-quality early childhood environment is necessary, but not sufficient to achieve optimal outcomes. Extra, intensive instruction provides children with ASD an opportunity to receive focused instruction on specific skill deficits (e.g., social communication skills), which often make participation in the inclusive classroom more challenging. Learning these skills in a segregated setting (e.g., the extended day part of the program) is an important first step, but skills are not considered to be functional until the children can demonstrate those skills appropriately and independently in the inclusive classroom and other settings (e.g., home) in which they spend time.

Staffing and Class Composition The extended, instructional component of Project DATA is solely comprised of children with ASD. The extended day part of the program is an essential component of the child's educational program, but it is not the child's primary classroom placement. The child's primary placement is in an inclusive preschool classroom. The extended instruction provided during this component is viewed like a related service similar to speech therapy or occupational therapy.

Although the number of children receiving extended instruction at the same time varies from year to year, the staffing ratio remains the same. The basic staffing ratio is one adult to two children. More adults may be added if necessary to meet the needs of the children, but there should never be less than a one-to-two ratio. The ratio is determined by the needs of the children in the program. If many children need one-to-one instruction for the majority of the extended, instructional time, then staff members are added. If, however, many of the children in the group benefit from working in small groups, that is how instruction is provided. All children have some time during the day to practice their skills in small instructional groups, and all children have some time to work individually with an adult.

Even though the staff in the extended, instructional part of the day ranges between one-to-one and one-to-two, children are not assigned one-to-one instructional assistants. When discussing the staffing needs of a group of children, teachers do not say, "Betty needs a one-to-one instructional assistant"; rather the program staff may say, "The amount of support that Betty needs to be successful in our classroom requires an additional staff member in the classroom." This difference is not purely semantic. In the first example, one adult is assigned to Betty and that adult may actually interfere with Betty's opportunities to interact with peers or participate in classroom activities. In the second example, the program staff are emphasizing the role of instruction and adult support to help children participate, learn, and succeed. The staff are also emphasizing that the child is part of the classroom culture and that all adults who work in the classroom have a shared responsibility for helping her be successful. This more flexible staffing pattern also allows Betty to be independent during some activities, yet still provide extra support when necessary.

The extended, instructional component is conducted by dedicated Project DATA staff. At the original Project DATA classroom at the University of Washington (UW), the extended instructional day is led by a certified special education teacher with specialized training in applied behavior analysis and working with children with ASD. The rest of her team is made up of instructional assistants. At UW, teachers have two half-day sessions of Project DATA, comprising a 1.0 full-time equivalent (FTE) position. Some of the larger districts that have implemented Project DATA have also adopted this staffing model. In other districts, teachers are assigned to teach a half-day section of preschool and a half-day section of the intensive, extended instruction. Although this works in some districts, many teachers find this type of arrangement difficult to sustain (see Chapter 10 for a discussion about implementing Project DATA in individual districts).

Schedule Children in Project DATA attend a half-day preschool program 5 days a week. In addition, they participate in an extended instructional day program for at least 10 hours per week. This program may be offered 3 to 5 days per week. Currently at UW, children attend preschool 5 days per week and extended instruction for 3 days. One UW partner district provides preschool and extended day 4 days per week for the children with ASD in their schools. There is not one right way to arrange the schedule. Many variables including transportation, space, and the preschool schedule will influence the best time to offer extended day programming. Sample schedules for children attending Project DATA are shown in Figure 7.1.

Since time alone does not provide any information about the intensity or appropriateness of a program, the time within the extended day program must be carefully scheduled to ensure that the child is learning as much as possible. Therefore, children need to be actively engaged with adults, peers, or age appropriate materials for the vast majority of the day. Although there is an overall group schedule, this time is viewed more like an extended tutoring program than a classroom, so within the scheduled activity, children are working on whatever is most important for them. In the extended day program every moment is also viewed as instructional time. For example, if the schedule says "recess," that means that children are learning how to interact with their peers on the playground and use the playground equipment appropriately. If the schedule says "lunch," children may be learning to sit at the table during a meal, point to request food, or try a wider variety of food items. A typical afternoon extended day schedule is shown in Figure 7.2.

Physical Environment Just like designing any instructional environment, the first step in designing the environment for the extended day program is to consider the function of that space. The primary function of the extended day program is to provide intensive instruction to individuals or small groups of children, with some need for free choice, group activities, and meals. Therefore, the classroom must be designed to accomplish that function.

Drew's preschool/DATA schedule

	Monday	Tuesday	Wednesday	Thursday	Friday
Morning	Preschool with teacher Emily	Preschool with teacher Emily	Preschool with teacher Emily	Preschool with teacher Emily	Preschool with teacher Emily
Afternoon	DATA extended instructional day with teacher Lorraine		DATA extended instructional day with teacher Lorraine	DATA extended instructional day with teacher Lorraine	

Rosalie's preschool/DATA schedule

	Monday	Tuesday	Wednesday	Thursday	Friday
Morning		DATA extended instructional day with teacher Erin	DATA extended instructional day with teacher Erin		DATA extended instructional day with teacher Erin
Afternoon	Preschool with teacher Emily	Preschool with teacher Emily	Preschool with teacher Emily	Preschool with teacher Emily	Preschool with teacher Emily

Figure 7.1. Project DATA weekly schedule.

Rosalie's afternoon DATA schedule

Time	Activity	Scheduled tasks/programs/activities
11:00 a.m.	Transition from preschool	
11:10 a.m.	Recess	
11:40 a.m.	Lunch	
12:10 p.m.	Free choice	
12:30 p.m.	Table work	
1:30 p.m.	Small group project (e.g., art, game, story time)	
1:50 p.m.	Snack	
2:10 p.m.	Table work	
2:45 p.m.	Prepare to go home	

Figure 7.2. Project DATA daily schedule.

The extended day classroom is arranged with a number of comfortable teaching spaces that accommodate two children and one teacher. Most of these spaces are work tables that line the perimeter of the classroom. Because of the amount of explicit instruction that takes place at these tables, there must be space for instructional materials, toys, other reinforcers, and data sheets. Most of the materials are stored in portable plastic bins. These bins can be easily switched out when different children are in the extended day classroom (i.e., morning class and afternoon class). Some of this individual instruction takes place at tables, while some may take place while sitting on the floor playing with toys. Therefore, open space to play, with interesting and age-appropriate toys, is also essential for individual instructional time.

In addition to space for individual instruction, there are tables that can be used for meals and small group activities (e.g., art activities, board games). Like in other early learning environments, it is ideal to locate these tables near a sink and on floors that can be easily cleaned.

The Project DATA extended day classrooms differ from many instructional environments for children with ASD because they look more like typical preschool classrooms than clinical settings. Although there are lots of data sheets, instructional materials, visual supports, sensory reinforcers (e.g., swings), and even some edible reinforcers, there are lots of toys, pictures, and children's work displayed on the walls. These environments are designed to help children learn to participate and flourish in typical early learning settings, therefore elements of physical design from early learning environments are incorporated into the extended day classroom. Children need to learn to work in groups with other children and participate in activities that happen in classrooms elsewhere in our school and in the community. Therefore, the extended day program provides children with opportunities to practice these types of activities with instructional support. Children learn to be successful eating lunch with their peers, playing board games (and sometimes lose), and managing their own materials, as well as learn basic communication, social, and adaptive skills that are more often associated with ASD-focused curricula.

Instructional Grouping   One of the most difficult questions to answer when setting up an extended day program is, "What is the appropriate size of the instructional group?" Although some programs for young children with ASD provide all of their instruction one-to-one, this is not always practical, sustainable, necessary, or even beneficial. One way to answer this question is to look at the data, that is, to answer the question empirically: The best size instructional group is the one in which the child makes the most progress. Another strategy is to answer it pragmatically: What group size does the program staffing allow? In Project DATA, the staffing ratio is always at least one adult to two children. If some children in the program need more intense support, then more staff are added. Some children, however, make very good progress working in groups of two or three. It is important to address the question of instructional grouping by looking at child progress rather than getting caught up in rhetoric or philosophy. Some children who are working on advanced social skills and conversations benefit from being in groups with other children. When a child is learning to have conversations with peers, one-on-one instruction is actually a barrier to their progress. Groups are determined based on children who have similar types of programs, similar likes and interests, and who may be developing a friendship. The size of a group in which a child works also changes during the day and length of time he or she participates in Project DATA. Most children spend part of their day working one-on-one with a teacher but may work in a group of two or three on an art project and may sit at a lunch table with five children and three teachers.

Having instructional groups with more than one child also means that teachers need to be prepared to work with more than one child at a time. There are two primary strategies for working with two children with ASD at the same time in the extended day program—sequential instruction and concurrent instruction. Both of these strategies are used in Project DATA.

Sequential instruction involves working with one child, while the other child in the group is engaged in either independent work or free choice time. For example, Muriel has just completed 5 minutes of discrete trial training and is given toys that she likes and knows how to engage with in an appropriate manner; meanwhile, the teacher works individually with Barbara. The teacher may alternate instruction this way for the majority of the table work period.

Concurrent instruction involves working with both children at the same time. Children may be working on the same task and be taught to answer teacher questions chorally, or they may be working on different tasks with the teacher alternating trials between children.

In most cases, teachers use a combination of the sequential and concurrent approaches to group instruction. For example, a teacher may begin the table work session by doing some concurrent instruction on maintenance skills such as two-part nonverbal imitation. That may lead into giving children each a turn to "be the leader" in the imitation trials, which addresses peer imitation (Social 3.3). The teacher then makes the transition to sequential imitation by giving one child a *play schedule* to follow (Play 2.1), while conducting one-to-one instruction with the other child. This may go on for 30 minutes, alternating between children every 5 to 6 minutes, until the entire group takes a break outside for a few minutes. When they come back inside, the children sit on the floor with the teacher and play with blocks and farm animals. They move to the table to play a board game and then make the transition back into sequential instruction for the rest of the table work period.

Selecting Instructional Strategies Data-based decision making guides all instruction in Project DATA. Teachers begin the process by looking at the instructional problem they want to solve. Then the instructional team reviews the research literature and collections of evidence-based practices (Wong et al., 2015) for potential instructional strategies that may be effective to address the instructional problem. The team considers the activities and contexts in which they will be teaching the skill and the real life situations in which the child will need to use the skill. They also consider what is known about the child's learning history and experience with other objectives. Finally, the team makes a choice about the instructional strategy to use. Teachers implement the instruction, collect data, and review the data frequently to ensure the child is making progress. Programs are then changed as needed based on the data.

How Do Staff Communicate Across the Classroom and Extended Day?

Ensuring that staff members across all components of the child's day are on the same page is an ongoing challenge and concern. Getting the adults to implement programs correctly and consistently has long been cited as one of the challenges in inclusive education, and in Project DATA, there are so many different staff members (e.g., classroom staff, speech language pathologists and other related service staff, extended day staff) interacting with a child during the week that this challenge may be heightened.

The Project DATA approach to working with staff is not all that different than the approach taken when working with children. Project DATA values assume

▪ All staff members are people first and need to be treated with kindness and respect, even if we differ in philosophy or opinions.

Child: _____   Date: _____

DATA teacher(s):_____

Current Instructional Programs

Program/set	Current skill level/comments	How can the classroom/home help?

Completed Instructional Programs

Program/sets	How can you help with generalization?

Special information (new words, skills, reinforcers, challenges)

Figure 7.3.   News from Project DATA.

■ Communication is vital to collaboration. Although there is no one right way to interact or communicate with staff members, all team members are responsible for finding effective communication strategies that will enhance the program for the children and families. The best way to interact is in a way that yields the desired outcomes.

■ Visual supports are important.

■ Reinforcement works.

With those strategies in mind, the Project DATA staff members work hard to collaborate with the lead teachers in the children's inclusive preschool classroom, keeping in mind that the preschool classroom is considered the child's primary placement. It is extremely important for all members of the team, including the family, to be clear about this. The head teacher of the preschool classroom is the child's primary teacher. The Project DATA staff members are related service providers. This clarification of roles is extremely helpful in enhancing collaboration and seamless implementation of programming. Project DATA staff attend the classroom team meetings at least monthly, and more often if time permits. Project DATA staff also work with the classroom teachers to write the child's IEP and attend the IEP meeting. Like other related service staff, Project DATA staff provide input into the IEP process, but do not lead the IEP process. Project DATA staff also share frequent updates with the classroom teachers. An example of a form used to share information between classroom teams is shown below in Figure 7.3. The purpose of these updates is to facilitate communication among the staff and to ensure consistent programming.

SUMMARY

Teaching Project DATA Style means that classroom staff use the very best instructional strategies to teach children with ASD across all parts of their school day. Instruction takes place in the inclusive preschool program, in the extended day program that only enrolls children with ASD, on the playground, and in the hallways. All of this instruction is data-based, meaning that child progress data is collected on every objective and reviewed frequently. All program decisions (e.g., what is taught, instructional strategies used, how much instruction is provided, and size of instructional groups) are based on the data. If children are making adequate progress toward meaningful educational outcomes, then the program team is providing appropriate instruction. If not, components of the instructional program are modified until child performance improves. Ensuring meaningful outcomes for students is the goal of teaching Project DATA Style.

CHAPTER 8

Data-Based Decision Making

Collecting data on student performance is an essential component of teaching. Teachers who collect and use child performance data are better able to provide the type of individualized instruction necessary to help children learn in an efficient manner (Greenwood, Delquadri, & Hall, 1984; Sandall, Schwartz, & LaCroix, 2004). What are data and how does the instructional decision-making process use that data to make it a useful part of the data-based education? The Project DATA definition of data is information (most often about child behavior or child performance on instructional programs) that can be used to answer interesting and important questions about learning. For example

- If program teams are interested in knowing whether or not a child is having success with the toilet-training program, they need to collect data about the number of toilet accidents.

- If program teams are interested in knowing whether or not a child is becoming more successful at playing with peers at school, they need to collect data on the amount of time the child spends playing with his peers and the number of times teachers provide directions or feedback during this play.

- If program teams are interested in knowing whether or not a child can imitate an adult's behavior in a structured teaching situation, they need to collect data on the percent of trials during which the child imitates the adult's model.

- However, if program teams are interested in knowing why a child is aggressive in preschool and not in extended day, they will have to collect data about the number and types of aggressive behaviors, but also about the teacher behavior, environment, antecedents, and consequences that occur in preschool and in extended day. These data will help the teams not just understand the frequency of the aggressive behavior, but gather information about the function of the behavior—that is, what is motivating and maintaining challenging behavior.

Collecting the data is only the first step in using data-based decision making. Once the data are collected, they must be summarized (e.g., graphed) and analyzed. Then the instruction team needs to decide the next step in the child's program based on the data. The purpose of this chapter is to describe types of data that can be collected to describe different aspects of child behavior, suggest strategies to summarize and graph the data, and describe how data are used to make instructional decisions.

WHY COLLECT DATA?

A simple, but not very interesting, answer to the question, "Why collect data?" is that it is required by law. As part of providing free, appropriate public education to children with disabilities, special education personnel need to demonstrate that children are making meaningful progress toward important educational outcomes. A more interesting answer to the question is that collecting data enables teachers to more accurately measure child progress and evaluate the effectiveness and adequacy of their educational programming. In other words, data collection is a key component of any high-quality educational program because it enables teachers to evaluate what is working and what is not working. With that knowledge, teachers can modify programs to truly meet the needs of individual children.

Data are taken to

▩ Monitor progress

▩ Evaluate a child's programming (i.e., how the child is progressing)

▩ Communicate with others about the child's performance

▩ Identify phases of learning: mastery, generalization, and maintenance

▩ Maintain compliance with federal and state mandates

All data are not created equal. The quality of the data-based decision making process that is conducted in any program is only as good as the accessible, raw material. In data-based decision making, the raw materials are the data. Good data are reliable and valid. Reliable data are precise data, meaning that everyone who observes a behavior records it the same way. Valid data are accurate data, meaning teams can actually measure what they want to measure (e.g., If teams are interested in knowing about children's friendships, what data can they collect that actually measures the number or reciprocity of friendships?). The best data are those that provide the team with information they need to answer a question. Matching the type of data collected with the question being asked (i.e., instructional objective) is one key to an effective data collection system. Another is developing a data collection system that makes sense to the classroom staff, is efficient, and is sustainable.

TYPES OF DATA

Different types of data allow teachers to collect information about different dimensions of behavior. For example, frequency data reveals how often a behavior occurs. Frequency data are very useful to track challenging behavior or correct responses. These data can be converted easily to percent-correct data—one of the most frequently used metrics to track child responses. Duration data counts how long a behavior lasts. Duration data can be very useful when teaching a child to engage in tasks independently and can help answer questions like, "How long can Tyrone play independently?" For some behaviors, the team may want to collect multiple types of data. For example, when trying to decrease tantrums, it is helpful to know how often tantrums occur and how long they last. There is no one right way to collect data and no best type of data to collect. The best data are those that help the team answer questions. Good data are collected regularly, reliably, and analyzed soon after they are collected. Some of the most frequently used types of data are described below. More detailed descriptions of data collection methods can be found in many texts about applied behavior analysis (e.g., Alberto & Troutman, 2012; Cooper, Heron, & Heward, 2007).

▩ **Frequency.** Frequency data records how often a behavior occurs. Frequency data are often used to count the occurrence of challenging behaviors, social initiations, correct responses, and many other types of data. Frequency counts are best used for behaviors that have a discrete beginning and end. Frequency counts are one of the most versatile and easy ways to collect data. Frequency data can also be converted into percent-correct data. Percent-correct data are among the most commonly used strategies to report child progress.

▩ **Duration.** Duration data records how long a behavior lasts. Duration data are used when trying to increase or decrease the length of a behavior. Duration data are useful when teaching students to work independently, to get dressed more quickly, or to increase the amount of time they spend playing with other children. Duration data are useful when teaching children endurance with a newly acquired skill. For example, when teaching a child to participate in a group activity, duration data will help demonstrate how long the child is participating in an instructional group, and those data can be compared to the benchmark for that behavior set by the typically developing children in the same classroom.

■ **Rate.** Rate data assess the frequency of a behavior during a specified period of time. Rate is an excellent measure when the behavior of interest occurs during periods of different length (e.g., number of social initiations during free play). It is also a useful metric when the goal of a behavior is to increase the fluency of a behavior. Fluency is one of the four aspects of learning (i.e., acquisition, fluency, generalization, and maintenance) (Wolery, Bailey, & Sugai, 1988). It is especially important to consider the fluency of a behavior when considering the durability of the behavior and how useful that behavior is for children in real-life situations. For example, if a child takes 10 minutes to put on his or her shoes, that is not really a useful skill. The child needs to become fluent (i.e., faster) with that skill before it will help to improve the quality of their life.

■ **Level of Independence.** The goal for most skills and behaviors taught to young children is for the children to be able to engage in the behavior independently (i.e., without adult assistance). Level of independence data are collected using rating scales that indicate how much, and sometimes what type, of adult assistance is provided. These rating scales often range from 1 to 4, with 1 indicating full physical prompting and 4 indicating independent performance. These types of data are especially useful when teaching self-help skills, play skills, and adaptive behaviors in the classroom (e.g., getting ready for lunch, making transitions between activities).

■ **Permanent Product.** Permanent product data are useful when engaging in the target behavior creates an artifact that can be saved and compared to previous artifacts to document progress. An example of a behavior for which permanent product data is a parsimonious choice is "writing your name" or any handwriting goal. Rather than developing a rating scale to define improvement in handwriting, teachers can save a weekly sample of work and compare it to previous work to document progress.

■ **Time Sampling.** The data collection methods described above are examples of event recording. When using event recording, the observer records every instance of a behavior that occurs during a specific data collection period. In other words, the occurrence of the target behavior is the cue for data collection to occur. In time sampling, data collection is cued by the passage of time. For example, rather than recording each time a child makes a social initiation (i.e., frequency count), when using time sampling you would indicate whether or not a social initiation occurred during your observation interval (e.g., 10 seconds). Time sampling procedures are very useful for behaviors that are difficult to count (e.g., high rates of self-stimulatory behavior) or when you want to record data on the same behavior for many children at the same time (e.g., engagement during a classroom activity). One of the most useful types of time sampling data collection for teachers is a momentary sample. Using a momentary time sample is like collecting a series of snapshots of a target behavior. The first step to using a momentary time sample is to divide your observation period into time intervals. For example, a 45-minute free-play period could be divided into 1-minute intervals, the 6-hour school day could be divided into 15-minute intervals, or a 10-minute small-group activity could be divided into 10-second intervals. As each interval is signaled by a stop watch or other timing device, the observer indicates whether or not the behavior occurred at the *instant* of the signal. Another type of time sampling technique is the interval recording technique. This technique is similar to momentary time sampling, but instead of recording whether or not the behavior occurs at one instant, the behavior is recorded if it occurs anytime during the interval. Time sampling techniques yield data on the percent of intervals during which the behavior occurred.

CREATING, SELECTING, AND USING DATA SHEETS

There is no set rule for what data sheets should look like. The best data sheet is used regularly to collect information that is useful in determining how a child is progressing in their instructional programs. That said, there are some tips for developing data sheets. Every data sheet should include a place for

■ The child's name

■ The instructor's name

■ The date (including the year)

■ The target behavior

■ Comments (this section is important for teachers to record comments about student performance, including stimuli that were working well as reinforcers, issues regarding motivation, and specific parts of the task that seemed problematic.)

Some other issues to consider when developing data sheets include

■ **Where will the data sheet be used?** Is it being used for decontextualized, intensive teaching that is conducted at the table? Is it being used for embedded instruction? Is it being used for both? The form of the data sheet needs to match the function for which it is intended, and it must fit into the daily routine of classroom activities.

■ **Are the data sheets organized by day or activity?** Some teachers like to create a data sheet that has all the programs for a child across the day. This means that a child has a new data sheet every day, but only has one data sheet for the entire day. Other teachers like to have a different data sheet for every program. This means that one child will have multiple data sheets that will be used across many days. In both cases, the data from the data sheets will need to be transferred to graphs or other charts being used to analyze the data.

■ **What will the data sheets look like?** Some teachers like to use data sheets produced on 8.5x11-inch paper kept on clipboards. Some teachers like to use data sheets on small index cards that they attach to their waistbands with retractable key chains. Still others like to wear carpenter aprons when they work and stash their data sheets and pencils in the oversized pockets of the aprons.

■ **Do the data sheets make sense to the classroom staff?** This may be the most important question of all. The best data sheet is one that is used by staff members on a regular basis. The head teacher must provide training and ongoing coaching on data collection. Staff members need to understand why data collection is important and how the information they are collecting is used. Staff members must understand that data collection is not a task that they do in addition to teaching, rather it is an essential part of teaching. It is helpful to get input from the staff members who are collecting data about what they do and do not like about data sheets. In Project DATA, staff are encouraged to make modifications to the data sheet, if it improves their ability to collect data reliably.

The section below contains some data sheets frequently used in Project DATA. All of these data sheets can be used in both embedded and decontextualized instruction. They can either be used as-is or adapted to meet the needs of students and the program. Remember, the best data sheet is one that is used a lot! Therefore it is helpful to let the instructional assistants—the people actually collecting the data—have some input on which data sheets will be used. For more information about creating and using data sheets, as well as a collection of over 50 different types of data sheets, see *Show Me the DATA* (Leon-Guerreo, Matsumoto, & Martin, 2011).

Trials Daily Data Sheet

This is one of the most basic data sheets (Figure 8.1). It is extremely useful when teaching skills with discrete steps or discrimination tasks. This sheet is best used for one skill or behavior at a time and can be used across instructional settings. For example, if teaching pointing to request, this data sheet could be used at snack and at free choice. The information from this data sheet should be transferred onto graphs in the child's binder at the end of every instructional day.

Trials Daily Data Sheet with Graphing

This data sheet is a variation of the massed trial data sheet (Figure 8.2). An advantage of this data sheet is that it can be used as a combination data sheet and graph. To use this data sheet, the teacher begins recording child responses in the first column, in the box with the 1. This indicates that it is the first instructional trial of the day on this specific task. If the child gets a correct response, the 1 is circled, if not, an X is made in the box (see the key at the bottom of the data sheet). Once all 10 trials are completed, the number correct is counted and the square with the corresponding number is colored in. The data for that day is then graphed. For example, on the first day of instruction on nonverbal imitation, the child had four correct trials and six incorrect trials; at the end of the day, the teacher would color in the 4. On day two of instruction, the child has five correct trials, the teacher colors in the 5. On day three of instruction with seven correct answers, the teacher colors in the 7. On one piece of paper the team can see the actual performance data and a graph of those data.

Daily Data Sheet

This data sheet is more appropriate for teachers who want to put many different instructional programs on one data sheet (Figure 8.3). Each box on this sheet can contain data from a different objective. Unlike the two data sheets described above, this sheet would only be used for one day, then data would be transcribed onto the graphs in the child's binder.

Task Analysis Daily Data Sheet

This data sheet is useful when collecting data on programs that are chains of behaviors or that use a task analysis for instruction (e.g., handwashing, getting reading to go home) (Figure 8.4). For these tasks, each step of the behavioral chain or task analysis is written on a line under the skill set heading and then data can be collected for multiple days on this day sheet. Like with other data sheets, this information will need to be transferred to the child's binder.

TRIALS DAILY DATA SHEET

Student:_____   Teacher:_____   Year:_____

Program:_____

Date	Level of prompt	Trials										Total	% Correct
		1	2	3	4	5	6	7	8	9	10	/	
		1	2	3	4	5	6	7	8	9	10	/	
		1	2	3	4	5	6	7	8	9	10	/	
		1	2	3	4	5	6	7	8	9	10	/	
		1	2	3	4	5	6	7	8	9	10	/	
		1	2	3	4	5	6	7	8	9	10	/	
		1	2	3	4	5	6	7	8	9	10	/	
		1	2	3	4	5	6	7	8	9	10	/	
		1	2	3	4	5	6	7	8	9	10	/	
		1	2	3	4	5	6	7	8	9	10	/	
		1	2	3	4	5	6	7	8	9	10	/	
		1	2	3	4	5	6	7	8	9	10	/	
		1	2	3	4	5	6	7	8	9	10	/	
		1	2	3	4	5	6	7	8	9	10	/	
		1	2	3	4	5	6	7	8	9	10	/	
		1	2	3	4	5	6	7	8	9	10	/	
		1	2	3	4	5	6	7	8	9	10	/	
		1	2	3	4	5	6	7	8	9	10	/	
		1	2	3	4	5	6	7	8	9	10	/	
		1	2	3	4	5	6	7	8	9	10	/	
		1	2	3	4	5	6	7	8	9	10	/	
		1	2	3	4	5	6	7	8	9	10	/	
		1	2	3	4	5	6	7	8	9	10	/	
		1	2	3	4	5	6	7	8	9	10	/	
		1	2	3	4	5	6	7	8	9	10	/	
		1	2	3	4	5	6	7	8	9	10	/	
		1	2	3	4	5	6	7	8	9	10	/	
		1	2	3	4	5	6	7	8	9	10	/	
		1	2	3	4	5	6	7	8	9	10	/	
		1	2	3	4	5	6	7	8	9	10	/	
		1	2	3	4	5	6	7	8	9	10	/	
		1	2	3	4	5	6	7	8	9	10	/	

Level of prompt:

FP = Full prompt

PP = Partial prompt

G = Gestural prompt

V = Verbal prompt

P = Picture prompt

Trials:

Circle correct responses

Cross out (X) incorrect responses

Figure 8.1.   Trials daily data sheet.

TRIALS DAILY DATA SHEET WITH GRAPHING

Student:_____   Teacher:_____   Year:_____

Program:_____

Date:																			
Program changes:	10	10	10	10	10	10	10	10	10	10	10	10	10	10	10	10	10	10	10
1.	9	9	9	9	9	9	9	9	9	9	9	9	9	9	9	9	9	9	9
	8	8	8	8	8	8	8	8	8	8	8	8	8	8	8	8	8	8	8
2.	7	7	7	7	7	7	7	7	7	7	7	7	7	7	7	7	7	7	7
	6	6	6	6	6	6	6	6	6	6	6	6	6	6	6	6	6	6	6
3.	5	5	5	5	5	5	5	5	5	5	5	5	5	5	5	5	5	5	5
	4	4	4	4	4	4	4	4	4	4	4	4	4	4	4	4	4	4	4
4.	3	3	3	3	3	3	3	3	3	3	3	3	3	3	3	3	3	3	3
	2	2	2	2	2	2	2	2	2	2	2	2	2	2	2	2	2	2	2
5.	1	1	1	1	1	1	1	1	1	1	1	1	1	1	1	1	1	1	1
Total correct responses:																			

Program:_____

Date:																			
Program changes:	10	10	10	10	10	10	10	10	10	10	10	10	10	10	10	10	10	10	10
1.	9	9	9	9	9	9	9	9	9	9	9	9	9	9	9	9	9	9	9
	8	8	8	8	8	8	8	8	8	8	8	8	8	8	8	8	8	8	8
2.	7	7	7	7	7	7	7	7	7	7	7	7	7	7	7	7	7	7	7
	6	6	6	6	6	6	6	6	6	6	6	6	6	6	6	6	6	6	6
3.	5	5	5	5	5	5	5	5	5	5	5	5	5	5	5	5	5	5	5
	4	4	4	4	4	4	4	4	4	4	4	4	4	4	4	4	4	4	4
4.	3	3	3	3	3	3	3	3	3	3	3	3	3	3	3	3	3	3	3
	2	2	2	2	2	2	2	2	2	2	2	2	2	2	2	2	2	2	2
5.	1	1	1	1	1	1	1	1	1	1	1	1	1	1	1	1	1	1	1
Total correct responses:																			

Program:_____

Date:																			
Program changes:	10	10	10	10	10	10	10	10	10	10	10	10	10	10	10	10	10	10	10
1.	9	9	9	9	9	9	9	9	9	9	9	9	9	9	9	9	9	9	9
	8	8	8	8	8	8	8	8	8	8	8	8	8	8	8	8	8	8	8
2.	7	7	7	7	7	7	7	7	7	7	7	7	7	7	7	7	7	7	7
	6	6	6	6	6	6	6	6	6	6	6	6	6	6	6	6	6	6	6
3.	5	5	5	5	5	5	5	5	5	5	5	5	5	5	5	5	5	5	5
	4	4	4	4	4	4	4	4	4	4	4	4	4	4	4	4	4	4	4
4.	3	3	3	3	3	3	3	3	3	3	3	3	3	3	3	3	3	3	3
	2	2	2	2	2	2	2	2	2	2	2	2	2	2	2	2	2	2	2
5.	1	1	1	1	1	1	1	1	1	1	1	1	1	1	1	1	1	1	1
Total correct responses:																			

Circle correct responses.

Cross out (X) incorrect responses.

Fill in the square of the total number of correct responses each day.

Figure 8.2.   Trials daily data sheet with graphing.

Child's name:_____   Date:_____

Program:_____

	Stimulus	Response
1		
2		
3		
4		
5		
6		
7		
8		
9		
10		
Percentage correct:		

Program:_____

	Stimulus	Response
1		
2		
3		
4		
5		
6		
7		
8		
9		
10		
Percentage correct:		

Program:_____

	Stimulus	Response
1		
2		
3		
4		
5		
6		
7		
8		
9		
10		
Percentage correct:		

Program:_____

	Stimulus	Response
1		
2		
3		
4		
5		
6		
7		
8		
9		
10		
Percentage correct:		

Program:_____

	Stimulus	Response
1		
2		
3		
4		
5		
6		
7		
8		
9		
10		
Percentage correct:		

Program:_____

	Stimulus	Response
1		
2		
3		
4		
5		
6		
7		
8		
9		
10		
Percentage correct:		

Program:_____

	Stimulus	Response
1		
2		
3		
4		
5		
6		
7		
8		
9		
10		
Percentage correct:		

Program:_____

	Stimulus	Response
1		
2		
3		
4		
5		
6		
7		
8		
9		
10		
Percentage correct:		

Program:_____

	Stimulus	Response
1		
2		
3		
4		
5		
6		
7		
8		
9		
10		
Percentage correct:		

Response Key:

FP = Full prompt

PP = Partial prompt   **V** = Verbal prompt   **+** = Correct

G = Gestural prompt   **P** = Picture prompt   **--** = Incorrect

Figure 8.3.   Daily data sheet.

Child's name:_____

Program:_____ Date:_____

	Step	Response				% Correct
1						
2						
3						
4						
5						
6						
7						
8						
9						
10						
All steps percentage correct:						

Program:_____ Date:_____

	Step	Response				% Correct
1						
2						
3						
4						
5						
6						
7						
8						
9						
10						
All steps percentage correct:						

Program:_____ Date:_____

	Step	Response				% Correct
1						
2						
3						
4						
5						
6						
7						
8						
9						
10						
All steps percentage correct:						

Program:_____ Date:_____

	Step	Response				% Correct
1						
2						
3						
4						
5						
6						
7						
8						
9						
10						
All steps percentage correct:						

Program:_____ Date:_____

	Step	Response				% Correct
1						
2						
3						
4						
5						
6						
7						
8						
9						
10						
All steps percentage correct:						

Program:_____ Date:_____

	Step	Response				% Correct
1						
2						
3						
4						
5						
6						
7						
8						
9						
10						
All steps percentage correct:						

Response Key:

FP = Full prompt

PP = Partial prompt   **V** = Verbal prompt   **+** = Correct

G = Gestural prompt   **P** = Picture prompt   **--** = Incorrect

Figure 8.4.   Task analysis daily data sheet.

Child's name:_____   Year:_____

Program:_____

Stimulus	Date				
Percentage correct:					

Program:_____

Stimulus	Date				
Percentage correct:					

Program:_____

Stimulus	Date				
Percentage correct:					

Program:_____

Stimulus	Date				
Percentage correct:					

Program:_____

Stimulus	Date				
Percentage correct:					

Program:_____

Stimulus	Date				
Percentage correct:					

Response Key:

FP = Full prompt

PP = Partial prompt   **V** = Verbal prompt   **+** = Correct

G = Gestural prompt   **P** = Picture prompt   **--** = Incorrect

Figure 8.5.   Weekly data sheet.

Weekly Data Sheet

This is a variation of the daily data sheet and is designed to be used with different types of instructional programs for 1 week at a time (Figure 8.5). Like with other data sheets, this information will need to be transferred to the child's binder.

SUMMARIZING CHILD PERFORMANCE DATA

One of the primary reasons to collect data is to provide information to the instructional team, including the parents, to discuss and assess child performance. In order to make the data useful as a tool in these discussions, it must be summarized so that everyone can see it. The best way to do that is to graph the data, one graph per target objective. These graphs are updated daily.

The graphs used in Project DATA are standard line graphs and all forms of data (e.g., frequency, duration, rate, and time sample) can be displayed on these graphs. The vertical line (i.e., the y-axis) is the ordinate; the horizontal line (i.e., x-axis) is the abscissa. The scale used to measure the behavior (e.g., percent correct or number of aggressive behaviors) is shown on the ordinate; time (e.g., days or instructional sessions) is shown on the abscissa. Since Project DATA follows the public school calendar, staff use graph paper with dates, including school holidays, already filled out (see Figures 8.6 and 8.7). This consistency across the formats of graphs makes it easier to compare child progress on different programs, looking across different graphs. It is also useful to look at changes in child behavior before or after school breaks. Data on the graph are indicated with a symbol, usually a dot, and different behaviors can be displayed in the same graph using different symbols (e.g., initiations to teachers and initiations to peers). Data points within conditions are connected with a solid line. Changes in conditions, such as introducing a new set of instructional materials or changing the behavior plan, are indicated with a dotted vertical line. This is called a phase change line. All conditions are labeled. Figure 8.8 displays a sample graph.

Although graphical display is the most common way to summarize child performance data, this approach does not work for every team. Some teams prefer to display data on calendars, tables, or matrices. The desired outcome is that the data the team collects should be displayed and used to make decisions about child performance. Programs should use whatever display methods work best for the team.

MAKING DATA-BASED DECISIONS

The reason for data collection is to gather the information needed to engage in data-based decision making. This means that information about child performance is used to make decisions about the instruction that the child is receiving. Based on the child's performance data, the instructional team decides to continue the program as is, to modify the instructional program, or to discontinue the program.

Data are graphed daily and the teacher working with the child should review progress data daily. If staff have any questions or concerns they should discuss them with the head teacher immediately. The head teacher should meet with every staff member weekly or every other week (if the staff member has worked on the project for at least 1 year) to review the child's progress. The head teacher and staff member should look at every graph and make notes about how to proceed. The results of these meetings should be logged in the child's notebook on the individual program review sheet (see Figure 6.8).

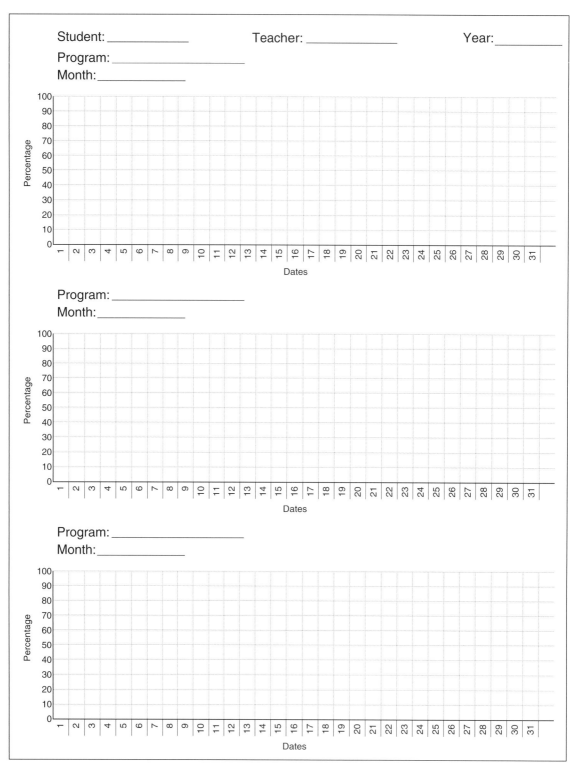

Figure 8.6. Monthly graph with percentages.

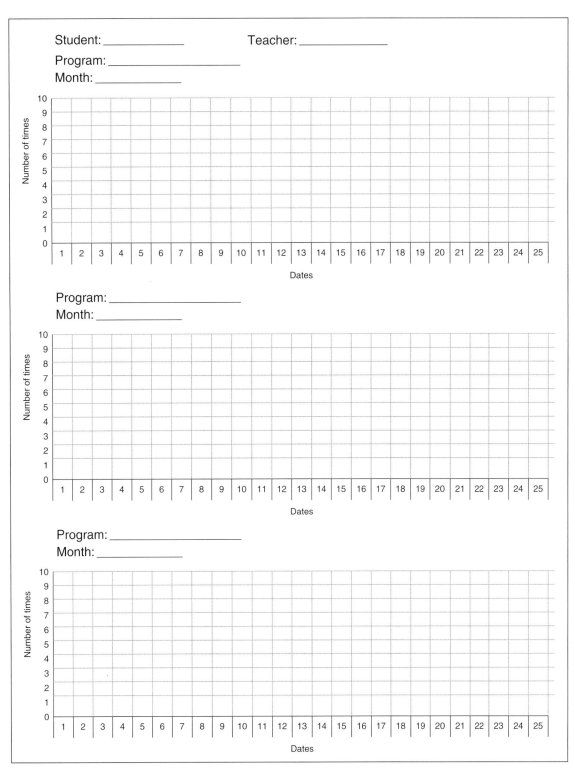

Figure 8.7. Monthly graph with frequency.

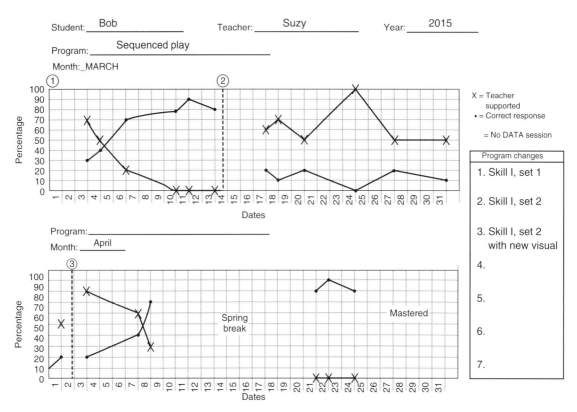

Figure 8.8. Percentage graph example.

During these data review meetings, the teachers are looking at the data to determine what they reveal about child progress. In general there are four main patterns that appear in the data:

1. The child is making steady progress, the program is working, and instruction should continue as is.

2. The child is not making progress, the data are flat. The task is too difficult and the program—either the objective or the teaching strategy—should be modified.

3. The child's performance is variable. This may be due to many issues. The program may be too easy, there may be a compliance problem, the child may know some of the exemplars used in instruction, but not all of them, or staff may not be implementing the intervention with fidelity. More investigation is needed.

4. The child has met criteria and is ready to move on to a new set, a new program, and generalization and maintenance checks.

When making instructional modifications, it is important to make sure there are enough data points (at least five) to draw a conclusion about child progress. Once a decision is made to modify the program, the changes must be noted in the child's notebook and staff need to be told (and trained if necessary) about the changes. Sufficient time (five to ten instructional sessions) must be allowed to see if the change is effective before making other changes to the program. Using data-based decision rules is a bit of a dance. Teachers need to be responsive to changes (or lack of changes) in child data, but not change conditions too quickly. It is also important to consider other factors that may be affecting child learning (e.g., medical conditions, the fidelity of the instruction, or motivation) when examining child performance data.

SUMMARY

Data are information that can be used to answer interesting questions. Child performance data helps educators answer an interesting and important question: Are children learning what they are being taught? The type of child performance data collected depends on the type of behavior that you are teaching. Collecting child performance data is an essential part of teaching. Collecting data, however, is only the first step in using these data to guide instruction. Once the data are collected, they need to be summarized. One of the most universal methods of data summary is graphing. After the data are graphed they need to be analyzed frequently. This analysis should be done by someone who knows the specific child, has expertise in teaching children with autism, and understands behavioral principles. In the Project DATA model, this analysis is done by the staff member working with the child on a daily basis (e.g., paraprofessional) and the head teacher. In general, there are four main patterns that appear in the data: steady progress, no progress, variable performance, and criteria met. Based on the results of the data inspection, changes need to be made to the instructional program, changes need to be documented in the child's notebook, and staff need to be alerted to the revised programs.

CHAPTER 9

Collaborating with Families and Other Partners

Children with ASD are children first. That means, like other children, they are surrounded by family members, caregivers, teachers, and friends who contribute to their growth, development, and well-being. Including members of the child's family and extended community in planning and implementing an educational program is a priority for Project DATA. Even if children spend 25 hours per week at school, they spend 143 hours per week at home and in the community. Children with ASD will be more successful when family members, child care providers, and other important people in their life understand and support what children are learning at school *and* when the school team understands the priorities, beliefs, and needs of the family. This chapter describes the Project DATA approach to

- Providing technical and social support to families

- Working collaboratively with other providers

- Supporting transitions across programs

PROVIDING TECHNICAL AND SOCIAL SUPPORT TO FAMILIES

Families are made up of a diverse group of individuals that include parents, siblings, grandparents, aunts, uncles, cousins, guardians, extended family, and friends. Some family members may be living together under one roof; others may have more than one household where the child with ASD spends time. In Project DATA, parents identify who makes up their family, and teachers include that group of people in planning and family support events. It is important to consider each family member because they each have strengths to contribute and needs to address. This family systems approach considers that all family members are interrelated and that each family is a unique social system. Like all children, children with ASD are parts of families; families, like children, are not defined by ASD.

Although families are not defined by the presence of a child with ASD, it would be naïve not to acknowledge the impact that having a child or a sibling with ASD has on family life. Parents of children with ASD report extreme levels of chronic stress (Smith, Greenberg, & Seltzer, 2012). Parents of children with ASD report spending up to 2 hours per day more than the parents of typically developing children on basic caregiving responsibilities and that the need for basic caregiving and supervision continues long beyond that required by typically developing children. The need for family support extends far beyond parents. Other family members, especially siblings, benefit from clear information (i.e., technical support) and the opportunity to share their experiences with others who are also living with a brother or sister with ASD or a related disability (Meyer & Vadasy, 2007).

Families may have a number of difficulties meeting the demands associated with raising a child with ASD due to the child's uneven intellectual abilities, lack of communication skills and social responsiveness, and pervasive challenging behaviors. Project DATA offers extensive family education and support services to address these demands and challenges. The goal of Project DATA services is to empower parents of young children with ASD by providing experiences that enhance their knowledge, ability, and confidence to effectively address their children's behavior and skill development. Project DATA makes a distinction between "technical support" and "social support" when describing the services provided to the families of children with ASD. Technical support addresses the specialized information needs that family members of children with ASD have. These may include

■ Basic information about ASD

■ Information about different treatment options

■ Assistance in understanding research findings

■ Strategies to teach children basic self-care, play, and social interaction skills

■ Strategies to improve the quality of community outings

■ Strategies for addressing challenging behavior at home and in the community

■ Ideas of how to talk to family members about ASD

Social support helps family members connect to networks of other families of children with ASD or related disabilities so they can begin to develop a supportive social network.

Technical Support

Project DATA staff members offer formal technical support to families through parent education classes and home or center visits. Teachers offer informal technical support to families when they visit the classroom, contact the classroom staff with questions via email or phone, and through classroom newsletters. The parents of children entering Project DATA are encouraged to attend a three-part course on the basics of applied behavior analysis, teaching children at home, and managing challenging behavior. *Steps to Independence* (Baker & Brightman, 2003) is used as a text for this series. In addition, Project DATA parent education meetings are offered on topics suggested by parents, and have included

■ Embedding instruction into family guided routines

■ Effectively addressing challenging behaviors: positive support strategies

■ Teaching communication skills

■ Teaching self-help skills including toilet training, eating, sleeping, and dressing

■ Evaluating alternative therapies

■ Play dates: fostering social relationships

■ Emotional regulation

■ Creating visual supports and social stories

■ Creating an effective IEP

Over the years Project DATA staff have offered parent education classes in a number of different configurations, including monthly classes, a short series of weekly classes, and weekend classes. Although programs need to offer parent education classes in a manner that meets the needs of their families, the following guidelines are helpful for all parent education classes:

■ Each meeting during the series is 1½ hours

■ Evening and morning sessions are offered to meet different work and school schedules

■ Childcare for the child with ASD and their siblings is provided

The format of a parent education meeting includes interactive topic discussion with some lecture material. The meetings are led by Project DATA staff with many guest speakers from the community. During the meetings, parents are encouraged to ask questions and share stories, similar to a support group format. By providing two different meeting times, the groups are smaller in size and can be arranged around a large table or in a circle to promote interaction among the caregivers. A variety of caregivers attend the meetings, including parents, grandparents, aunts or uncles, and primary child care providers, such as a nanny. The first hour of the meeting is dedicated to the chosen topic and led by Project DATA staff. The final half-hour of the meeting is a more informal exchange led by parents with staff participating as needed.

As part of a child's participation in the Project DATA program, families are strongly encouraged to attend parent education classes either at the early childhood center or in the community. Parents are asked to attend at least six hours of educational meetings each year. These meetings may include Project DATA classes, community workshops, support groups, and conferences. The rationale for encouraging parents to remain involved in parent education activities is that parents continually report the need for information about parenting their child with autism. The goal is not to have families dependent on the Project DATA parent education activities, but to have them find parent education and support activities in the community that they enjoy and that they find helpful.

The second component of the parent support program is home visits. Although these are referred to as home visits, staff members meet with families at their most preferred location, which can include the child's home, a child care center, a grandparent's home, at the school, or in the community (e.g., park, grocery store, church, library). Home visits are scheduled monthly, last 2 hours, and have family-controlled agendas. This means that the parents determine what topics will be addressed and whether the visits include parent coaching, outings in the community, or collaboration with other members of the child's team.

During the first home visit, the Project DATA parent interview is used to gather information about family priorities, goals, concerns, and dreams for their child. Information gleaned from this interview determines at least five family goals for the year. These annual goals are addressed during the visits using the Project DATA family interview form (see Figure 9.1). As family priorities shift throughout the year, adjustments are made accordingly. A majority of the goals focus on

■ Teaching new skills to the child

■ Generalization of current skills

■ Sibling interactions

■ Decreasing or eliminating challenging behaviors

■ Promoting independence

■ Successful behavior in the community, such as going to the grocery store, hair salon, or religious gatherings

■ Identifying available resources in the community

During these visits, parents are encouraged to invite extended family members and others they believe are important in providing support and assistance to their family and child.

PROJECT DATA: Family Interview Survey

Child's name:_____

Parent/caregiver being interviewed:_____

Interviewer:_____

Use the questions on this interview as a guide to get to know the child's family or caregivers. This is a flexible interview and does not need to be completed in order—rather ask questions and follow the lead of those being interviewed. You may find that some questions are answered without being asked. Finally, this can and should be used in conjunction with any other parent/caregiver questionnaire that is used in your program.

Activities and interactions
1. Tell me about (child's name).
2. What are (child's name)'s strengths?
3. What makes (him or her) happy?
4. What makes (child's name) sad? How do you comfort (him or her)?
5. How do you think (he or she) learns best?

Figure 9.1. Family interview survey.

6. How do you teach (child's name) new skills?

7. Do you ever have difficulty interacting with (child's name)? What makes it easy or hard?

8. What activities do you like to do with (child's name) to feel emotionally connected to him or her?

9. When (child's name) exhibits behaviors that you find challenging, what helps and doesn't help in these situations?

10. What does your child like to play with? How do you play with (child's name)?

11. How do you communicate with (child's name)?

12. Do you have favorite activities or rituals that you like to do with (child's name)?

(continued)

PROJECT DATA: Family Interview Survey

Routines			

Ask parent/caregiver if he/she finds the following times to be *Not stressful, Somewhat stressful,* or *Very stressful*? (If helpful, place a cue card with responses in front of parent/caregiver). As appropriate, ask the parent or caregiver to elaborate.

	Not stressful	Somewhat stressful	Very stressful
1. Bathing (child's name)	( )	( )	( )
2. Toileting (diapering) (child's name)	( )	( )	( )
3. Driving with (child's name)	( )	( )	( )
4. Mealtimes with (child's name)	( )	( )	( )
5. (Child's name)'s bedtime routines	( )	( )	( )
6. (Child's name)'s sleeping	( )	( )	( )
7. Playing with (child's name)	( )	( )	( )

Figure 9.1. *(continued)*

	Not stressful	Somewhat stressful	Very stressful
8. Communicating with (child's name)	( )	( )	( )
9. Keeping (child's name) occupied	( )	( )	( )
10. Visiting friends/relatives with (child's name)	( )	( )	( )
11. Having friends/relatives visit when (child's name) is present	( )	( )	( )
12. Transitions with (child's name) (e.g. home to car, car to home, playtime to mealtime)	( )	( )	( )
13. Going on vacation with (child's name)	( )	( )	( )
14. Running errands/outings with (child's name)	( )	( )	( )

(continued)

PROJECT DATA: Family Interview Survey

Information for coordinating services
1. Tell me about the current services your child and/or family are receiving related to your child's special needs.
2. What else you would like to tell me about your child?
3. Of the things we have discussed, what are the priorities for you and/or your family?
4. What is the best way for us to communicate with you? _____ Text _____ Email _____ Phone calls (please specify your preferred phone number)
5. Where would you like to have home visits take place? _____ Our home _____ Center _____ Other (please specify)

Figure 9.1. (*continued*)

During a home visit, the staff member takes notes and provides additional information about what the child is doing in his or her preschool classroom and Project DATA classroom. They typically review notes from the last home visit, which includes family goals, and address any new or relevant topics that arise. See Figure 9.2 for an example of the Project DATA "Home Visit Notes" on which the staff member takes notes and shares information.

A final component of technical support is to provide families with information about service options, current autism research, workshops, and community activities. This information is provided during home visits, parent education meetings, on a bulletin board outside the Project DATA classroom, and with an e-mail mailing list for current and past Project DATA families. This e-mail group is offered to all families and it gives them an opportunity to communicate with other parents and for staff members to pass on information regarding resources and workshops or conferences. If families choose not to join this e-mail group or do not have an e-mail account, or need the materials in a language other than English, the lead teacher or home visit staff member is accountable for providing the information to these families. Hard copies of flyers are sent home in children's backpacks and usually accompanied with a phone call or discussed during a home visit.

In addition to these opportunities to pass along information, a parent library of books, videos, and manuals is available. The Project DATA library is updated every 6 months to keep current with literature regarding ASD. Parents are asked to sign out books and return them in a timely manner (e.g., 2 weeks). In addition to adult reading, books for siblings and friends of children with ASD are provided.

Social Support

Based on feedback from parents, support groups for parents and other caregivers that are separate from parent education (i.e., technical support) activities are also offered at the center. Parents value both technical and social support activities and each type of support helps parents become and remain confident and competent parents to their children with ASD. School-based parent support groups are led monthly by the school social worker. A female social worker also offers groups for mothers only, and a male social worker leads support groups for fathers. These specialized support groups are offered quarterly. In addition to offering support groups, families are provided with information about other support groups in the community. Families are encouraged to find a support group or other support network that meets their needs, wherever that group may be. For some families this support network may be in the community, associated with a cultural or faith-based organization, or online. If families prefer to participate in the school-sponsored support groups, they are encouraged to transition to a community-based support group before their child transitions to elementary school. That way, parents are established in a new community of support prior to their child's transition to a new school (see more information about transition support below). The goal is for all families to feel part of a group that listens to them and can help them address issues that are important to them and their family.

In addition to traditional support groups, Project DATA offers many other activities for families. Families are invited to a number of activities during the school year in which they are encouraged to meet each other and establish informal supports. The goal of these activities is to help families establish a normalized relationship with the school community; to encourage parents to get involved, meet other families, and develop a support network that may extend long beyond the preschool years. These activities include

■ Open house

■ Ice cream socials

HOME VISIT NOTES

Child: _____ Date: _____ Time: _____

Who was at the visit? _____

Update from school

Preschool

DATA

Follow-up from last visit

Figure 9.2. Home visit notes.

Today's topics

Resources requested/tasks to do

Follow-up with school

Other news from home/comments

- School carnival with games appropriate for children of all abilities

- Informal coffees

- Work parties for school-related events

- Class picnics

Working Collaboratively with Other Providers

One of the core components of Project DATA is collaboration and coordination across all providers. The intent is to ensure that all professionals working with the child and family come together at least once per year. The purpose of this meeting is not to plan, rather to meet as a team to build relationships that will allow seamless communication, services, and problem solving for everyone working with the child.

Who attends these meetings? Project DATA staff work with the family to create an inclusive list of participants, including all providers of "family-negotiated services." A family-negotiated service is any type of therapeutic service that the school district does not pay for. It can include speech therapy, nutrition services, occupational therapy, child care, hippotherapy (i.e., horseback-riding therapy), or private behavior therapy. It is very important to emphasize that the purpose of this meeting is not planning, especially since some family-negotiated services may be theoretically inconsistent (e.g., behavioral services, sensory integration, floor time). The purpose of these meetings is to develop collegial relationships, share information about the types of services being provided, and exchange ideas; in other words, to attempt to create a seamless community of providers for the family. These relationships can be very helpful if a child or family encounters a crisis or the child develops a new challenging behavior. If this happens providers should be able to talk to each other to inquire if they are seeing the same behaviors and to brainstorm about potential solutions. This seamless approach to teaming supports the family, enabling their providers to talk together rather than requiring the family to choreograph all of the information sharing.

Supporting Transitions

Transitions are often difficult for children and families. They can be especially difficult if your child is rigid, has difficulty making friends, communicating his or her needs, and following directions—all common behavioral characteristics of children with ASD. Transitions require families and children to change their routines, adapt to new rules, meet new people, and learn new ways to do things. The purpose of the transition support in Project DATA is to

- Identify skills needed in the new environment and help the child learn them

- Help the staff in the new school program (i.e., the receiving staff) learn about the child's strengths and areas of need

- Help the family support the child in the new school

- Help the family find new sources of support to meet their needs.

To identify skills needed in the new environment, an environmental assessment is conducted comparing the two settings. Some skills are quite obvious, for example when a child makes the transition to kindergarten, they are often required to carry their lunch through the cafeteria on a tray, a daunting task if you have never carried anything on a tray. Other skills may not be as obvious, for example having to manage your own materials (e.g., keeping pencils, crayons, paper in your desk) or learning to use the play equipment on a new playground or operating the sinks in a new bathroom. Once the skills that need to be learned are identified, they can be embedded into the classroom routine. For example, if a child will need to carry their lunch on a cafeteria tray, a teacher can begin by asking that child to carry some pencils to their table on a tray, then some crackers, and finally perhaps put multiple items on the tray. Teaching these skills does not require the preschool teacher to spend a great deal of time addressing them, rather embed opportunities for practice and feedback so that children can enter their new classrooms with some experience and confidence demonstrating the new skills.

Helping the receiving school (the child's new school) staff gain an accurate picture of the child's strengths and areas of need can help promote a smooth transition. Project DATA staff encourage the receiving teacher to come and visit before the end of the school year, but that is often not possible. If staff from the receiving school cannot visit before the end of the school year, Project DATA staff make videos showing students at their best—demonstrating their best academic, social, behavioral, independence, and play skills. The goal of these videos is to enable the receiving teachers to see the children at their very best to ensure that their new teachers have high expectations and have appropriate levels of support in place. Finally, Project DATA staff prepare extensive transition reports detailing children's skills, behavior plans, and support needs. Copies of any visual supports that the child uses are also included in the transition plan so that the new teachers can have them in place for the children from day one in the new setting.

Helping families support their child in a new school can help make a transition less stressful for the child and his or her parents. When parents and children graduate from Project DATA, parents should feel confident as advocates for their children, and understand the importance of working as a member of a team. Parents of young children with ASD entering elementary school are entering a long (potentially 16-year) relationship with the school district. A primary goal of the Project DATA parent support and education is to help families learn to advocate for their children's needs, yet do so in a positive, collaborative manner.

Finally, as children make a transition to a new school, parents are encouraged to leave the security of Project DATA and make their own transition to new sources of technical and social support. As much as the Project DATA staff enjoy interacting with the families, it is important for them to find new support networks based in their community. Often these resources come from community advocacy organizations, public schools, or spiritual communities; but as families connect with more sustainable forms of social support, Project DATA fades out their involvement. Staff do, however, continue to follow the progress of children and families, are available to answer questions as children progress in school, and will visit the children's new classrooms if invited by the new teacher.

SUMMARY

Many people have said that it takes a village to raise a child, and when raising a child with ASD, this proverb has renewed resonance. Raising a child with ASD presents families with many informational and support needs. The Project DATA model makes a distinction between technical support, the need for information about topics related to ASD—such as effective teaching techniques and evaluating intervention options; and social support, the need to feel connected to others who share and understand your experience. In Project DATA, staff work with families to provide both technical and social support through parent education programming, home visits, and support groups. Annual meetings of all the service providers working with that family help families receive seamless support across services. This includes the school team (including Project DATA staff) and professionals providing any family-negotiated services. The purpose of these meetings is to create a community of professionals to support the child and family, not to plan programming. Finally, since transitions are a challenging time for both children and families, part of the family support program is to help families plan and implement successful transitions for their children. This includes identifying and teaching skills that their children will need to be successful in the next environment, communicating with new school staff, and helping families find sources of social support that will be sustainable once the child makes a transition to the new program.

CHAPTER 10

Implementing Project DATA in Your Community

Implementing Project DATA is a community effort. To implement the model with integrity and fidelity, communities need to identify the partners who can provide access to and funding for the inclusive early childhood experience, the intensive instruction component, and family support and education. In addition, every program that implements the Project DATA model must tailor the program to make it fit into its own community. This chapter discusses how different communities may implement the essential components of the model to meet the needs of children with ASD and families, and describes the staff training experiences that are necessary to establish and maintain the integrity of the program in the course of staff changes.

IDENTIFYING PARTNERS

The Project DATA model was designed to be implemented in a public school setting. The rationale for this decision is that public schools are required to provide free, appropriate education to all young children with disabilities, including children with ASD. The goal of Project DATA is to help public schools provide this education in a manner that is effective, sustainable, and acceptable to consumers. Public elementary schools, however, are just one of many types of programs that can either house Project DATA or be a key partner in a multiagency implementation of Project DATA. The appropriate partners for implementing Project DATA are those agencies who

- Are tasked with providing appropriate educational and therapeutic services to young children with ASD

- Have access to a high-quality early childhood program that includes typically developing children

- Are committed to using evidence to make decisions about educational and therapeutic services for children with ASD

- Are committed to including families in the educational process

- Are willing to work together

In addition to public schools, other key partners may include Head Start, state-run universal preschool programs, other community preschools, mental health or behavioral health centers, and local colleges or universities (especially those that may run an early childhood education program or an applied behavior analysis program). Identifying the appropriate partners is just one of the ways that communities tailor Project DATA to meet local needs, priorities, and values.

Getting Started

Once the community partners are identified, it is important to identify the agency that will take the lead on this project and a person who will be the team leader. The team leader will be responsible for initiating meetings, creating agendas, and making sure that the project is implemented in a timely manner. When selecting the team leader, consider who on the team has dedicated time to spend on this project and has the authority (or easy access to the people who do have that authority) to make decisions about program changes and resources (e.g., fiscal, staff, space) to implement those changes.

One of the most challenging aspects for many school districts in implementing Project DATA is to find access to a high-quality inclusive early childhood program. If this challenge is present in the community, it is a good place to start the planning. Rather than beginning from scratch to build an inclusive program, it is often easier and more sustainable in the long run to build partnerships with existing programs that provide high-quality early learning experiences for typically developing children. These programs differ in every community and may include, but are certainly not limited to

▨ Head Start

▨ Universal preschool programs

▨ State prekindergarten programs

▨ Child care (e.g., private programs, Boys and Girls Clubs)

Some school districts choose to run their own inclusive programs by either braiding together existing district-run programs (e.g., Head Start and developmental preschool) or by charging tuition for typically developing children attending the program. *The Preschool Inclusion Toolbox: How to Build and Lead a High Quality Program* by Barton and Smith (2015) is a wonderful resource for programs wanting information about running an inclusive preschool program. Additional information designed for program administrators, including information about U.S. Department of Education rules and regulations can be found online at www.pyramidplus.org/resources/tech_assist.

Another part of implementing Project DATA is to decide on the schedule. In many school districts, developmental preschools and inclusive programs meet 4 days per week. These districts often choose to run the extended day program on all 4 days. In other districts, the developmental preschools or inclusive programs meet 5 days per week. In these districts, the extended day component can be run 3 days per week for 4 hours per session, or all 5 days with a shorter session each day. There is no one right way to arrange the schedule. The goal is to create a schedule that provides children with at least 20 hours per week at school, approximately half of which is in an inclusive environment and half in an arrangement to provide extended, intensive instruction. At the same time, the schedule needs to be feasible, sustainable, and most importantly able to be supported by the school infrastructure (e.g., there is available transportation).

Staffing (including issues of ratio, training, supervision, and qualifications) is another stumbling block for many programs. Since beginning Project DATA in 1997, the implementation team has observed almost every possible constellation of staffing in school districts around the country implementing Project DATA. This section provides guidelines for different positions in Project DATA and their concomitant qualifications and responsibilities.

Project DATA Head Teacher   The head teacher should have a special education certificate, training in ABA, and experience working with young children with ASD. Ideally, the head teacher would also be a Board Certified Behavior Analyst (BCBA). The head teacher is responsible for training and supervising all of the classroom assistants. He or she is also responsible for writing the instructional programs for all of the students and meeting with the classroom assistants regularly to ensure that the programs are updated, based on the child performance data, at least twice per month. He or she is also responsible for conducting monthly home visits and coordinating with the children's teachers from their inclusive program. In some programs, the head teacher works with children during the extended day portion of the day; in others, he or she spends that time coaching the staff, working with families, conducting assessments, and writing and updating instructional programs. In some smaller programs, the head teacher role is only a half-time assignment. In these districts the teacher may run an inclusive preschool classroom in the morning or have another assignment at the school. It is always preferable to have head teachers assigned to Project DATA on a full-time basis.

Classroom Assistant   The classroom assistant should have a college degree and experience working with young children with disabilities. Experience with ABA is preferred but not required because all Project DATA staff members should receive training in using behavioral teaching strategies before they begin working with the children and coaching on these strategies throughout their employment. The classroom assistants work directly with the children, providing instruction during the extended day part of the program. They are responsible for implementing the instructional programs, collecting data, graphing the data, and working with the head teacher to update the instructional programs based on those data. As stated in Chapter 7, the minimum staffing ratio during the extended day component of the program is one staff member to two children. If, however, more staff members are needed to provide the level of support and instruction required by the children, those staff members are added.

Coordinator/Administrator   The program administrator is responsible for coordinating admission, transportation, IEP meetings, and all of the other details required to run a school program. This could be the existing school principal or early childhood coordinator. It would be ideal if this person could also be a support for the head teacher, providing guidance and mentoring in needed areas (e.g., staff supervision, challenging behaviors). If the administrator does not have this expertise, the program should consider contracting with a behavior specialist who can provide that coaching and mentoring to the head teacher.

IMPLEMENTING WITH FIDELITY

An implementation checklist is provided in Figure 10.1. The purpose of this checklist is to provide a clear picture of the distinctive features of Project DATA across the five different components of the program. All of the elements in the checklist are described in earlier chapters in this manual. This checklist can be used in three primary ways:

▧   Program planning

▧   Evaluating program quality

▧   Evaluating sustainability

PROJECT DATA: Implementation Checklist

Program: _____

Date of observation: _____ Name of observer: _____

Program total: _____

In order to be considered to be implementing Project DATA with fidelity, programs must show sufficient (rating of a 2) evidence on 15 of 18 program characteristics, including the five items in italics.

Are the following program elements observable or clearly documented?

1. High-quality early childhood program	Scoring		
a. *Typical peers available for at least half the time*	0	1	2
b. Age appropriate materials and activities	0	1	2
c. Adequate level of reinforcement	0	1	2
d. Adequate level of engagement	0	1	2
e. Environment is appropriate for children with autism	0	1	2
f. Activity matrix is used to plan instruction	0	1	2
2. Extended, explicit instruction			
a. *Children are in program at least 20 hours per week*	0	1	2
b. Children receive instruction in core deficit areas across settings	0	1	2
c. Data collected on all active objectives	0	1	2
d. Data are graphed or summarized appropriately	0	1	2
3. Family support			
a. Home visits occur (or are offered) monthly	0	1	2
b. *Parent education programs occur at least quarterly*	0	1	2
c. Program staff are in contact with families	0	1	2
4. Collaboration and coordination			
a. *Staff members in classroom and extended day program communicate regularly*	0	1	2
b. Staff members communicate with providers of family-negotiated services per family permission and request	0	1	2
c. Program staff work with family and receiving program to plan appropriate transition	0	1	2
5. Quality-of-life influenced curriculum			
a. Families are involved in selecting objectives	0	1	2
b. *Generalization and maintenance are assessed for all objectives*	0	1	2

Key: 0 = No evidence

1 = Some, but not sufficient, evidence

2 = Sufficient evidence

Comments:

Figure 10.1 Project DATA implementation checklist.

Program Planning

As a planning tool, the implementation checklist can be used as a needs assessment, an assignment list, and a to-do list. It provides a list of what program elements must be put in place that can be helpful when beginning discussions with district and program personnel about adopting the Project DATA model. It also provides a concise list of every element that must be addressed when building the program or when merging existing resources to implement Project DATA. It is also useful as a tool to help consider the range of people who should be on your planning team. The team needs to have members who represent the types of services that will be provided and have the skills to work together to build this new program.

In the planning phase it is essential to have representatives on the team who can address the issues of finances, space, and transportation. Other difficult questions that will need to be addressed during the planning phase include

- How does Project DATA fit into the program site's overall program mission, values, and philosophy?
    - Which children will be included in Project DATA?
    - Will children only be included if they have a medical diagnosis of ASD? If so, is the district paying for that diagnostic evaluation or providing it on site?
    - Will children with an educational determination of ASD be included?
    - What is the district policy about providing the ASD label to young children?
- Do children who are at risk for ASD qualify for the program?
    - Do all children who have ASD or are at risk for ASD qualify for the program or are there other criteria (e.g., IEP referral)?
    - Do children who have developmental disabilities and could benefit from this program, but are not suspected to have ASD, qualify for the program?
    - What are the desired qualifications for the head teacher and classroom assistants?
    - How will this fit into the person's caseload?
    - What constitutes a 1.0 FTE?
    - Who will serve as the coordinator?
    - Who will provide the training and on-going coaching?
- Who in the district or program has the expertise to be the intellectual lead for this program?
    - Is there a need to contract with external experts to provide training and ongoing coaching?
    - Who can provide back-up support to behavior staff?

There is no one right answer to these questions, but it is important to decide how each program will address these issues. To see how the Project DATA program at the University of Washington addresses these questions, see the FAQ in Appendix D.

Evaluating Program Quality

Once the program begins, the implementation checklist can be used as a self-assessment. The self-assessment process should be conducted every 3 months until appropriate levels of implementation fidelity are achieved. If a program has appropriate levels of administrative and technical support, it is reasonable to expect that fidelity can be reached in 1 year.

When conducting the self-assessment, it is helpful to consider the procedural fidelity measure as a type of linked assessment. It can be used in a similar manner as when planning instructional programs for children. The areas in which the assessment suggests that program improvements are needed, are the areas of growth, or targeted objectives. Viewing the self-assessment information that way helps keep the project improvement activities grounded in data-based decision making. That is, do the data (in this case the score on the implementation checklist) suggest that program staff are making progress toward achieving the goal of implementing Project DATA? If the data are showing growth, continue. If the data are not showing growth or are showing growth at a very limited rate, then program staff members need to change their behavior to achieve the stated goal.

Evaluating Sustainability

Once the program has achieved fidelity (15 of the 18 items, including the 5 key items in italics) on the implementation checklist, the frequency of self-assessment should be decreased, and it should be completed once or twice a year. More importantly, the purpose of the self-assessment will change. Rather than working to achieve the goal of program fidelity, the goal shifts toward maintenance and sustainability. In many ways, this is even more difficult than program implementation. When implementing a new program, there is often excitement about the new program, additional resources, and special attention paid to the new program. Existing programs must be maintained, while sometimes still implementing new innovations in another part of the overall program. It is incumbent on leaders to help staff stay motivated, interested, and up-to-date so that they can maintain the quality of the existing program. The data from the implementation checklist can help identify areas in which staff members may need additional guidance or coaching, or where policies may have to be adapted to maintain the quality of the existing program. Some questions or issues that may need to be considered in maintaining the quality of Project DATA implementation include

▨ Are the children making progress?

▨ Are parents satisfied with the program?

▨ How are new staff brought on board, trained, and socialized into the philosophy of Project DATA and your program overall?

▨ Does Project DATA continue to be a good match with the overall program mission, values, and philosophies?

▨ What continuing education could be provided to Project DATA staff (e.g., workshops on social skills interventions or using technology with children with ASD)?

▨ What professional coaching could be provided to Project DATA staff to improve their practices?

▨ Are the correct people on the team? Do new staff need to be hired or does the program leadership need to consider reassigning staff?

▨ Is the current staffing pattern working for the staff members, program, and families?

▨ Are there consistent items on the implementation checklist that are also scored low? If so, what is the program doing to improve in these areas?

▨ Does the program leadership need to hire consultants to work with the classroom or administrative staff to improve any areas of the program?

SUMMARY

Project DATA has been shown to be an effective, sustainable program. The original Project DATA classroom opened in 1997 and is still in operation. Districts in more than 23 other states and territories have also implemented this program. It is important to remember that the process of implementing Project DATA in a specific community is not merely a direct replication of what is conveyed in this manual. Authentic and sustainable implementation requires that adopters identify the distinctive features of the new program and identify how they will fit into the values, beliefs, and philosophy of each community and program. The best replications of Project DATA are those that implement the core and tailor the rest to meet local community standards and needs. Some important considerations to facilitate the success of any adoption and implementation, including Project DATA is to insure that

- The proposed model is a match with the mission, values, and philosophy of the program
- Participants have a voice throughout the process
- The right people are on the team
- The resources needed for implementation are secured
- Enough time is provided for the planning, implementation, and maintenance of the new program
- Evaluate programmatic efforts and make changes based on those data

SECTION II

Project DATA
Instructional Programs

I. ADAPTIVE 118
   Mealtime 118
   Personal Hygiene 128
   School Skills 134
   Self-Advocacy 152

II. EXECUTIVE FUNCTIONING 166
   Flexibility 166
   Self-Regulation 178
   Persistence, Organization, and Time Management 186
   Problem Solving 194
   Emotional Knowledge 202

III. COGNITIVE 212
   Imitation 212
   Matching and Categorizing 224
   Sequencing 240
   Emergent Literacy 248
   Emergent Math 260

IV. COMMUNICATION 264
   Following Directions 264
   Responding 274
   Initiating 284
   Comprehension and Expression of Words and Sentences . . 300

V. SOCIAL 332
   Joint Attention 332
   Pragmatic Rules 346
   Interaction with Peers 360

VI. PLAY 378
   Play Fundamentals 378
   Independent Play 392
   Interactive Play 400

INSTRUCTIONAL PROGRAM SHEET: Mealtime

Drinks from an Open Cup

Child: _____ Date initiated: _____ Date completed: _____

Objective: In the presence of an open cup with liquid and told "Drink some _____" or "Take a drink," or when thirsty, the child holds the cup, drinks from the cup, and places the cup back on the surface.

Mastery criterion:
- 90% or higher correct responding for each set
- Minimum of 10 opportunities per day
- 2 consecutive teaching days
- No spilling

Generalization:
People: At least two adults
Settings: At least two settings
Materials: At least three different cups

Things to consider: May also teach sitting at the table or eating skills

Task analysis	Teaching sequence
1. Puts hands on cup	1. Teach two steps of task analysis
2. Picks up cup	2. Teach next two steps of task analysis
3. Brings cup to mouth	3. Teach next two steps of task analysis
4. Tilts cup toward mouth	4. Teach next two steps of task analysis
5. Sips	
6. Takes cup away from mouth, turning upright	
7. Puts cup on table	
8. Releases cup	

PROGRAMMING LOG

	Acquisition		Generalization		Maintenance	
	Start date	End date	Start date	End date	Date/data	Date/data
1						
2						
3						
4						

LESSON PLAN: Mealtime

Drinks from an Open Cup

Settings and materials	
Decontextualized	**Embedded**

Teaching
What direction or cue will you give?
How will you prompt the child's response?
Circle type of prompt(s) used:
Physical   Visual Modeling   Verbal Other: _____
Circle prompt fading procedure used:
Time delay   Most to least Graduated guidance Other: _____
What is the child's response?
What reinforcers are you using?
What is the correction procedure?
How will you collect data? *(circle answer)*
Percentage correct   Frequency Duration   Permanent product Other: _____

Sets

1. _____
   _____
   _____
   _____

2. _____
   _____
   _____
   _____

3. _____
   _____
   _____
   _____

4. _____
   _____
   _____

5. _____
   _____
   _____
   _____

INSTRUCTIONAL PROGRAM SHEET: Mealtime

Drinks from an Open Cup—Example

Child: _____   Date initiated: _____   Date completed: _____

Objective: In the presence of an open cup with liquid and told "Drink some _____" or "Take a drink," or when thirsty, the child holds the cup, drinks from the cup and places the cup back on the surface.

Mastery criterion:
- 90% or higher correct responding for each set
- Minimum of 10 opportunities per day
- 2 consecutive teaching days
- No spilling

Generalization:
People: At least two adults
Settings: At least two settings
Materials: At least three different cups

Things to consider: May also teach sitting at the table and eating skills

Task analysis	Teaching sequence
1. Puts hands on cup	1. Teach two steps of task analysis
2. Picks up cup	2. Teach next two steps of task analysis
3. Brings cup to mouth	3. Teach next two steps of task analysis
4. Tilts cup toward mouth	4. Teach next two steps of task analysis
5. Sips	
6. Takes cup away from mouth, turning upright	
7. Puts cup on table	
8. Releases cup	

PROGRAMMING LOG

	Acquisition		Generalization		Maintenance	
	Start date	End date	Start date	End date	Date/data	Date/data
1	2/12/14	2/25/14				
2	2/25/14	3/7/14				
3	3/7/14	3/20/14				
4	3/20/14	4/4/14	4/4/14	4/25/14	5/15/14; 100%	6/15/14; 100%

LESSON PLAN: Mealtime

Drinks from an Open Cup—Example

Settings and materials	
Decontextualized	**Embedded**
Work at table: Child preferred small cup with preferred liquid	Snack and mealtimes. Same cups and liquids as served to peers

Teaching
What direction or cue will you give?
Cup is present "Take a drink" "Drink some"
How will you prompt the child's response?
Circle type of prompt(s) used:
(Physical)   Visual Modeling   Verbal Other: _____
Circle prompt fading procedure used:
Time delay   (Most to least) Graduated guidance Other: _____
What is the child's response?
Independent response on each step or part of the task
What reinforcers are you using?
Preferred liquid and cups are used initially in decontextualized setting and pair with behavior-specific praise
What is the correction procedure?
Start the task sequence over, with the direction, then use the least intrusive prompt throughout the sequence unless the child demonstrates mastery of one of the steps in the sequence.
How will you collect data? *(circle answer)*
(Percentage correct)   Frequency Duration   Permanent product (Other:) percentage correct for each step of the task

Sets
Teach using backward chaining:
1.   Teach steps 7 and 8
2.   Teach steps 5 and 6
3.   Teach steps 3 and 4
4.   Teach steps 1 and 2

INSTRUCTIONAL PROGRAM SHEET: Mealtime

Eats with a Spoon or Fork

Child: _____ Date initiated: _____ Date completed: _____

Objective: When presented with food that requires a fork or spoon for use, and told "Time to eat" or when the child is hungry, he or she initiates and uses a fork or spoon by spearing food or scooping.

Mastery criterion:
- 90% or higher correct responding for each set
- Minimum of 10 opportunities per day
- 2 consecutive teaching days
- Little or no spilling, as age appropriate

Generalization:
People: At least two adults
Settings: At least two settings
Materials: At least two different spoons or forks

Things to consider: Movement of bringing fork or spoon to mouth and back down should be controlled and slow. Serve easy to scoop and spear food when teaching this skill (e.g., applesauce, pudding, cut up soft fruit).

Task analysis	Teaching sequence
1. Grasps spoon or fork	1. Teach two steps of task analysis
2. Scoops or spears food with spoon or fork	2. Teach next two steps of task analysis
3. Brings spoon or fork to mouth	3. Teach next two steps of task analysis
4. Puts spoon or fork in mouth and takes bite	4. Teach next two steps of task analysis
5. Takes spoon or fork from mouth	
6. Puts spoon or fork on table, plate, or bowl	

PROGRAMMING LOG

	Acquisition		Generalization		Maintenance	
	Start date	End date	Start date	End date	Date/data	Date/data
1						
2						
3						

The DATA Model for Teaching Preschoolers with Autism by Ilene Schwartz, Julie Ashmun, Bonnie McBride, Crista Scott, and Susan Sandall. Copyright © 2017 by Paul H. Brookes Publishing Co., Inc. All rights reserved.

LESSON PLAN: Mealtime

Eats with a Spoon/Fork

Settings and materials	
Decontextualized	**Embedded**

Teaching
What direction or cue will you give?
How will you prompt the child's response?
Circle type of prompt(s) used:
Physical   Visual
Modeling   Verbal
Other: _____
Circle prompt fading procedure used:
Time delay   Most to least
Graduated guidance
Other: _____
What is the child's response?
What reinforcers are you using?
What is the correction procedure?
How will you collect data? *(circle answer)*
Percentage correct   Frequency
Duration   Permanent product
Other: _____

Sets

1. _____
   _____
   _____
   _____

2. _____
   _____
   _____
   _____

3. _____
   _____
   _____
   _____

4. _____
   _____
   _____

5. _____
   _____
   _____
   _____

INSTRUCTIONAL PROGRAM SHEET: Mealtime

Eats a Variety of Food

Child: _____ Date initiated: _____ Date completed: _____

Objective: When presented with foods not currently in child's repertoire and told, "Time to eat," Child eats the foods.

Mastery criterion:
- Eats _____ new foods (this number depends on team decision)
- Eats three bites of each new food
- At least 2 days for each food

Generalization:
People: At least two adults
Settings: At least two settings
Materials: At least three different meals (breakfast, lunch, and dinner)

Things to consider: Consider extra exposure to food (e.g., do cooking projects, play with food in sensory table). Consider family preferences when choosing foods to introduce.

Teaching sequence
1. Bowl of new food is near child's plate for mealtime
2. Food is on child's plate for at least 5 seconds
3. Food is on child's plate for at least 10 seconds
4. Child tolerates food on plate for an indefinite amount of time
5. Child touches food with finger
6. Child holds food in hand
7. Child touches food to lips
8. Child touches food to tongue
9. Child licks food
10. Child takes a small bite of food
11. Child takes a regular size bite of food
12. Child chews and swallows more than one bite
13. Child eats the food provided

Adapted from Ogata, Beth, & Lucas, Betty. (1999). *Autism, Nutrition, and Picky Eating.* In Yang, Yuchi, Lucas, Betty, & Feucht, Sharon (Eds.). *Nutritional Interventions for Children with Special Health Care Needs.* (3rd ed.) (pp. 272–273). Seattle, WA: Washington State Department of Health.

PROGRAMMING LOG

	Acquisition		Generalization		Maintenance	
	Start date	End date	Start date	End date	Date/data	Date/data
1						
2						
3						
4						

LESSON PLAN: Mealtime

Eats a Variety of Food

Settings and materials	
Decontextualized	**Embedded**

Teaching
What direction or cue will you give?
How will you prompt the child's response?
Circle type of prompt(s) used:
Physical · · · · · · · · Visual Modeling · · · · · · · Verbal Other: _____
Circle prompt fading procedure used:
Time delay · · · · · · Most to least Graduated guidance Other: _____
What is the child's response?
What reinforcers are you using?
What is the correction procedure?
How will you collect data? *(circle answer)*
Percentage correct · · · · Frequency Duration · · · · · · Permanent product Other: _____

Sets

1. _____
   _____
   _____
   _____

2. _____
   _____
   _____
   _____

3. _____
   _____
   _____
   _____

4. _____
   _____
   _____
   _____

5. _____
   _____
   _____
   _____

INSTRUCTIONAL PROGRAM SHEET: Mealtime

Remains at the Table During Meals

Child: _____ Date initiated: _____ Date completed: _____

Objective: During snack or lunch at school, the child remains with the group at the table until the child asks to leave, adult excuses child, or until the natural end of the meal.

Mastery criterion:
- Remains at the table for the duration of the meal, asks to leave or is excused
- Three consecutive meals
- At least 2 days

Generalization:
People: At least two adults
Settings: At least two settings
Materials: At least three different meals (e.g., breakfast, lunch, dinner)

Things to consider: May also teach eating skills. Materials may be brought to the table, such as a book, to keep child occupied or as a point of reference for mutual sharing.

Teaching sequence
1. Considering child's baseline, remains at the table for an additional period of time (e.g., 15 seconds to 1 minute)
2. Child asks to be excused (e.g., "All done." "Can I be excused?")
3. Remains at the table, doubling the amount of time from the first set, may ask to be excused or told the meal time is all done
4. Double the amount of time from previous set
5. Consider sitting for entire duration or meal

PROGRAMMING LOG

	Acquisition		Generalization		Maintenance	
	Start date	End date	Start date	End date	Date/data	Date/data
1						
2						
3						
4						
5						

The DATA Model for Teaching Preschoolers with Autism by Ilene Schwartz, Julie Ashmun, Bonnie McBride, Crista Scott, and Susan Sandall. Copyright © 2017 by Paul H. Brookes Publishing Co., Inc. All rights reserved.

LESSON PLAN: Mealtime

Remains at the Table During Meals

Settings and materials	
Decontextualized	**Embedded**

Teaching
What direction or cue will you give?
How will you prompt the child's response?
Circle type of prompt(s) used:
Physical   Visual
Modeling   Verbal
Other: _____
Circle prompt fading procedure used:
Time delay   Most to least
Graduated guidance
Other: _____
What is the child's response?
What reinforcers are you using?
What is the correction procedure?
How will you collect data? *(circle answer)*
Percentage correct   Frequency
Duration   Permanent product
Other: _____

Sets

1. _____
   _____
   _____
   _____

2. _____
   _____
   _____
   _____

3. _____
   _____
   _____
   _____

4. _____
   _____
   _____

5. _____
   _____
   _____
   _____

INSTRUCTIONAL PROGRAM SHEET: Personal Hygiene

Toilet Trained—Urine

Child: _____ Date initiated: _____ Date completed: _____

Objective: When the child feels the need to urinate, he or she tells an adult or walks into the bathroom and completes the toileting routine (taking care of clothing, wiping, and flushing).

Mastery criterion:
- No accidents
- At least 1 school week
- Completes routine—adult may provide some assistance for clothing and occasional reminders are acceptable, as developmentally appropriate

Generalization:
People: At least two adults
Settings: At least two settings
Materials: At least two bathrooms
Time: No accidents for at least 2 weeks
Determining readiness (recommendations only, not required, but helpful to have before toilet training):
- Should not begin before chronological age of 18 months to 2 years
- Can follow simple directions
- Can sit on chair for 5 minutes
- Can wait at least 1.5 hours between elimination times (important to look at fluid intake)
- Child acts differently or seems to notice when diapers are wet or soiled

Things to consider: Take baseline data to indicate how frequently child wets diaper. Consider beginning toileting schedule every 20–30 minutes and then increasing schedule in 15-minute increments as child is successful. Child may need successful trips walking into a bathroom before learning the routine, considering the sensory stimulation in a bathroom. Consider giving the child access to more fluids, to increase the likelihood that he or she will need to urinate.

Task analysis	Teaching sequence
1. Enters bathroom or stall	1. Teach two steps of task analysis
2. Pulls down pants and underwear	2. Teach next two steps of task analysis
3. Sits on toilet	3. Teach next two steps of task analysis
4. Eliminates in the toilet	4. Teach next two steps of task analysis
5. Uses toilet paper	5. Teach next two steps of task analysis
6. Stands up	
7. Pulls pants and underwear back up	
8. Flushes the toilet	
9. Washes hands	
10. Dries hands	

PROGRAMMING LOG

	Acquisition		Generalization		Maintenance	
	Start date	End date	Start date	End date	Date/data	Date/data
1						
2						
3						
4						
5						

LESSON PLAN: Personal Hygiene

Toilet Trained—Urine

Settings and materials	
Decontextualized	**Embedded**

Teaching

What direction or cue will you give?

How will you prompt the child's response?

Circle type of prompt(s) used:

Physical	Visual
Modeling	Verbal

Other: _____

Circle prompt fading procedure used:

Time delay	Most to least
Graduated guidance	

Other: _____

What is the child's response?

What reinforcers are you using?

What is the correction procedure?

How will you collect data? *(circle answer)*

Percentage correct	Frequency
Duration	Permanent product

Other: _____

Sets

1. _____

2. _____

3. _____

4. _____

5. _____

INSTRUCTIONAL PROGRAM SHEET: Personal Hygiene

Toilet Trained—Bowel

Child: _____ Date initiated: _____ Date completed: _____

Objective: When the child feels the need for a bowel movement, he or she tells an adult or walks into the bathroom and completes the toileting routine (taking care of clothing, wiping, and flushing).

Mastery criterion:
- No accidents
- At least 1 school week
- Completes routine, but may need some assistance with wiping. Adult may provide some assistance for clothing and occasional reminders are acceptable, as developmentally appropriate.

Generalization:
People: At least two adults
Settings: At least two settings
Materials: At least two different bathrooms
Time: No accidents for at least 2 weeks
Determining readiness (recommendations only, not required, but helpful to have before toilet training):
- Should not begin before chronological age of 18 months to 2 years.
- Can follow simple directions
- Can sit in chair for 5 minutes
- Child acts differently or seems to notice when diapers are soiled.

Things to consider: Take baseline data to indicate how frequently and when child has a bowel movement. Child may need successful trips walking into a bathroom before learning the routine, considering the sensory stimulation in a bathroom.

Task analysis	Teaching sequence
1. Enters bathroom or stall	1. Teach two steps of task analysis
2. Pulls down pants and underwear	2. Teach next two steps of task analysis
3. Sits on toilet	3. Teach next two steps of task analysis
4. Eliminates in the toilet	4. Teach next two steps of task analysis
5. Uses toilet paper	5. Teach next two steps of task analysis
6. Stands up	
7. Pulls pants and underwear back up	
8. Flushes the toilet	
9. Washes hands	
10. Dries hands	

PROGRAMMING LOG

	Acquisition		Generalization		Maintenance	
	Start date	End date	Start date	End date	Date/data	Date/data
1						
2						
3						
4						
5						

The DATA Model for Teaching Preschoolers with Autism by Ilene Schwartz, Julie Ashmun, Bonnie McBride, Crista Scott, and Susan Sandall. Copyright © 2017 by Paul H. Brookes Publishing Co., Inc. All rights reserved.

LESSON PLAN: Personal Hygiene

Toilet Trained—Bowel

Settings and materials	
Decontextualized	**Embedded**

Teaching

What direction or cue will you give?

How will you prompt the child's response?

Circle type of prompt(s) used:

Physical   Visual

Modeling   Verbal

Other: _____

Circle prompt fading procedure used:

Time delay   Most to least

Graduated guidance

Other: _____

What is the child's response?

What reinforcers are you using?

What is the correction procedure?

How will you collect data? *(circle answer)*

Percentage correct   Frequency

Duration   Permanent product

Other: _____

Sets

1. _____

2. _____

3. _____

4. _____

5. _____

INSTRUCTIONAL PROGRAM SHEET: Personal Hygiene

Washes Hands

Child: _____   Date initiated: _____   Date completed: _____

Objective: When child's hands are dirty or when an adult says, "It's time to wash your hands," the child washes and dries hands.

Mastery criterion:
- 80% or higher correct responding for each set
- Minimum of five opportunities per day
- 3 consecutive teaching days

Generalization:
People: At least two adults
Settings: At least two settings
Materials: At least two sinks

Things to consider: Child may be affected by the temperature of the water, the force of the water, and the type of sink it is (turn on water vs. a touchless sink).

Task analysis	Teaching sequence
1. Turns on water or puts hands under faucet to activate water 2. Puts soap on hands 3. Lathers hands 4. Rinses soap off hands 5. Turns off water, or if touchless, skip this step 6. Gets towel or puts hands under blower 7. Dries hands 8. Throws away towel, if using towels	1. Teach two steps of task analysis 2. Teach next two steps of task analysis 3. Teach next two steps of task analysis 4. Teach next two steps of task analysis

PROGRAMMING LOG

	Acquisition		Generalization		Maintenance	
	Start date	End date	Start date	End date	Date/data	Date/data
1						
2						
3						
4						

LESSON PLAN: Personal Hygiene

Washes Hands

Settings and materials	
Decontextualized	**Embedded**

Teaching
What direction or cue will you give?
How will you prompt the child's response?
Circle type of prompt(s) used:
Physical   Visual Modeling   Verbal Other: _____
Circle prompt fading procedure used:
Time delay   Most to least Graduated guidance Other: _____
What is the child's response?
What reinforcers are you using?
What is the correction procedure?
How will you collect data? *(circle answer)*
Percentage correct   Frequency Duration   Permanent product Other: _____

Sets

1. _____
   _____
   _____
   _____

2. _____
   _____
   _____
   _____

3. _____
   _____
   _____
   _____

4. _____
   _____
   _____
   _____

5. _____
   _____
   _____
   _____

INSTRUCTIONAL PROGRAM SHEET: School Skills

Manages Personal Belongings

Child: _____ Date initiated: _____ Date completed: _____

Objective: When given a direction to get his or her materials (e.g., lunchbox, backpack, coat) or during a transition in the schedule, the child gets and puts away personal belongings needed for the activity.

Mastery criterion:
- 80% or higher correct response for each set
- Minimum of five opportunities per day
- 2 consecutive teaching days
- Minimum of three different personal belongings

Generalization:
People: At least two adults
Settings: At least two settings
Materials: Across a variety of personal belongings

Things to consider: Child may follow a direction such as "put your coat away" or "go get your backpack," or child may learn to follow the classroom routines and not need a direct instruction. Managing personal belongings may include a task analysis that is unique to the action or belonging.

Teaching sequence
1. Manages one personal belonging
2. Manages two personal belongings simultaneously (e.g., coat and backpack)
3. Manages three personal belongings, simultaneously if appropriate (e.g., coat, backpack, and lunchbox)

PROGRAMMING LOG

	Acquisition		Generalization		Maintenance	
	Start date	End date	Start date	End date	Date/data	Date/data
1						
2						
3						

The DATA Model for Teaching Preschoolers with Autism by Ilene Schwartz, Julie Ashmun, Bonnie McBride, Crista Scott, and Susan Sandall. Copyright © 2017 by Paul H. Brookes Publishing Co., Inc. All rights reserved.

LESSON PLAN: School Skills

Manages Personal Belongings

Settings and materials	
Decontextualized	**Embedded**

Teaching
What direction or cue will you give?
How will you prompt the child's response?
Circle type of prompt(s) used:
Physical   Visual
Modeling   Verbal
Other: _____
Circle prompt fading procedure used:
Time delay   Most to least
Graduated guidance
Other: _____
What is the child's response?
What reinforcers are you using?
What is the correction procedure?
How will you collect data? *(circle answer)*
Percentage correct   Frequency
Duration   Permanent product
Other: _____

Sets

1. _____

2. _____

3. _____

4. _____

5. _____

INSTRUCTIONAL PROGRAM SHEET: School Skills

Uses Classroom Materials

Child: _____   Date initiated: _____   Date completed: _____

Objective: During classroom activities, the child uses classroom materials such as markers and scissors as intended.

Mastery criterion:
- 80% or higher correct responding for each set
- Minimum of five opportunities per day
- 3 consecutive teaching days
- Five different classroom materials

Generalization:
People: At least two adults
Settings: At least two settings
Materials: Across a variety of materials

Things to consider: Types of materials may include: markers, crayons, pencils, scissors, glue, folders, paints, paint brushes, sensory table, play dough, and chairs. Consider developmentally appropriate use of materials. For example, if the child is 2-years-old, he or she may only scribble on paper with markers; however, if the child is 4-years-old, he or she may be drawing shapes with the markers.

Teaching sequence
1. Uses one classroom material
2. Uses another classroom material
3. Uses at least three different classroom materials
4. Uses at least four different classroom materials
5. Uses at least five different classroom materials

PROGRAMMING LOG

	Acquisition		Generalization		Maintenance	
	Start date	End date	Start date	End date	Date/data	Date/data
1						
2						
3						
4						
5						

LESSON PLAN: School Skills

Uses Classroom Materials

Settings and materials	
Decontextualized	**Embedded**

Teaching
What direction or cue will you give?
How will you prompt the child's response?
Circle type of prompt(s) used:
Physical   Visual
Modeling   Verbal
Other: _____
Circle prompt fading procedure used:
Time delay   Most to least
Graduated guidance
Other: _____
What is the child's response?
What reinforcers are you using?
What is the correction procedure?
How will you collect data? *(circle answer)*
Percentage correct   Frequency
Duration   Permanent product
Other: _____

Sets

1. _____

   _____

   _____

   _____

2. _____

   _____

   _____

   _____

3. _____

   _____

   _____

   _____

4. _____

   _____

   _____

   _____

5. _____

   _____

   _____

   _____

INSTRUCTIONAL PROGRAM SHEET: School Skills

Completes Transitions Between Activities

Child: _____   Date initiated: _____   Date completed: _____

Objective: When an activity is finished, child cleans up if needed, gets materials for next activity, and lines up and remains with group completing the transition.

Mastery criterion:
- 80% or higher correct response for each set
- Minimum of five opportunities per day
- 3 consecutive teaching days

Generalization:
People: At least two adults
Settings: At least two settings
Materials: Across transitions for preferred and not preferred activities

Things to consider: A transition may include stopping the activity, cleaning up materials, and getting materials for the next activity. Consider teaching this skill while teaching emotional regulation.

Teaching sequence
1. Transitions from a less preferred activity to a more preferred activity
2. Transitions from two different less preferred activities
3. Transitions from one preferred activity to another preferred activity
4. Transitions from at least four different activities, both preferred and not preferred
5. Transitions from at least five different activities, both preferred and not preferred

PROGRAMMING LOG

	Acquisition		Generalization		Maintenance	
	Start date	End date	Start date	End date	Date/data	Date/data
1						
2						
3						
4						

LESSON PLAN: School Skills

Completes Transitions Between Activities

Settings and materials	
Decontextualized	**Embedded**

Teaching
What direction or cue will you give?
How will you prompt the child's response?
Circle type of prompt(s) used:
Physical   Visual
Modeling   Verbal
Other: _____
Circle prompt fading procedure used:
Time delay   Most to least
Graduated guidance
Other: _____
What is the child's response?
What reinforcers are you using?
What is the correction procedure?
How will you collect data? *(circle answer)*
Percentage correct   Frequency
Duration   Permanent product
Other: _____

Sets

1. _____

   _____

   _____

   _____

2. _____

   _____

   _____

   _____

3. _____

   _____

   _____

   _____

4. _____

   _____

   _____

   _____

5. _____

   _____

   _____

   _____

INSTRUCTIONAL PROGRAM SHEET: School Skills

Walks with Peers Across School Settings

Child: _____ Date initiated: _____ Date completed: _____

Objective: During transitions outside of the classroom but within the school grounds, the child follows the group direction and stays with the large or small group, walking next to or in line with peers.

Mastery criterion:
- 80% or higher correct response for each set
- Minimum of five opportunities per day
- 3 consecutive teaching days

Generalization:
People: At least two adults and four peers
Settings: All school settings available for walking with the group
Materials: Across transitions for preferred and not preferred activities

Things to consider: Consider teaching child to follow directions, such as "Walk with me," "Wait," and "Stop" as prerequisite skills. Independently walking with the group does not include an environmental support such as a rope for children to hold or holding hands.

Teaching sequence
1. Walks from less preferred activities to a more preferred activity
2. Walks from at least one preferred activity to a less preferred activity
3. Walks from at least three different activities, both preferred and not preferred
4. Walks from at least four different activities, both preferred and not preferred

PROGRAMMING LOG

	Acquisition		Generalization		Maintenance	
	Start date	End date	Start date	End date	Date/data	Date/data
1						
2						
3						
4						

LESSON PLAN: School Skills

Walks with Peers Across School Settings

Settings and materials	
Decontextualized	**Embedded**

Teaching
What direction or cue will you give?
How will you prompt the child's response?
Circle type of prompt(s) used:
Physical   Visual
Modeling   Verbal
Other: _____
Circle prompt fading procedure used:
Time delay   Most to least
Graduated guidance
Other: _____
What is the child's response?
What reinforcers are you using?
What is the correction procedure?
How will you collect data? *(circle answer)*
Percentage correct   Frequency
Duration   Permanent product
Other: _____

Sets

1. _____

_____

_____

_____

2. _____

_____

_____

_____

3. _____

_____

_____

_____

4. _____

_____

_____

_____

5. _____

_____

_____

_____

INSTRUCTIONAL PROGRAM SHEET: School Skills

Rides in School Bus, Car, or Other Transportation to and from School

Child: _____ Date initiated: _____ Date completed: _____

Objective: While transporting to and from school, the child rides in a school bus, car, or other means of transportation by staying in a car seat and remaining calm.

Mastery criterion:
- 5 days transporting to and from school, remaining in the car seat
- May have a couple prompts (e.g., visual and verbal) to use strategies to stay calm and in seat

Generalization:
People: At least two adults
Settings: To and from field trips, outings
Materials: Across vehicles (e.g., different buses, cars)

Things to consider: Child may have preferred objects on the ride to assist with self-regulation. Consider motivation systems for arrival to school and when arriving home from school.

Teaching sequence
1. Transports to school
2. Transports from school

PROGRAMMING LOG

	Acquisition		Generalization		Maintenance	
	Start date	End date	Start date	End date	Date/data	Date/data
1						
2						

LESSON PLAN: School Skills

Rides in School Bus, Car, or Other Transportation to and from School

Settings and materials	
Decontextualized	**Embedded**

Teaching
What direction or cue will you give?
How will you prompt the child's response?
Circle type of prompt(s) used:
Physical   Visual
Modeling   Verbal
Other: _____
Circle prompt fading procedure used:
Time delay   Most to least
Graduated guidance
Other: _____
What is the child's response?
What reinforcers are you using?
What is the correction procedure?
How will you collect data? *(circle answer)*
Percentage correct   Frequency
Duration   Permanent product
Other: _____

Sets

1. _____

_____

_____

_____

2. _____

_____

_____

_____

3. _____

_____

_____

_____

4. _____

_____

_____

_____

5. _____

_____

_____

_____

The DATA Model for Teaching Preschoolers with Autism by Ilene Schwartz, Julie Ashmun, Bonnie McBride, Crista Scott, and Susan Sandall. Copyright © 2017 by Paul H. Brookes Publishing Co., Inc. All rights reserved.

INSTRUCTIONAL PROGRAM SHEET: School Skills

Waits for Instruction to Begin

Child: _____ Date initiated: _____ Date completed: _____

Objective: Before a classroom activity, the child waits quietly and remains seated or standing until the teacher provides the instruction.

Mastery criterion:
- 90% or higher correct response for each set
- Minimum of 10 opportunities per day
- 2 consecutive teaching days

Generalization:
People: At least two adults
Settings: Across school locations
Materials: Across a variety of activities and materials

Things to consider: Child may need to learn to follow the direction to wait. If direction "Wait" is provided, this will need to be faded for independence of skill.

Teaching sequence
1. Waits for instruction during a 1:1 less preferred activity
2. Waits for instruction during a 1:1 more preferred activity
3. Waits for instruction during a small group activity
4. Waits for instruction during a large group activity
5. Waits for instruction across a total of five activities (may include previous sets)

PROGRAMMING LOG

	Acquisition		Generalization		Maintenance	
	Start date	End date	Start date	End date	Date/data	Date/data
1						
2						
3						
4						
5						

LESSON PLAN: School Skills

Waits for Instruction to Begin

Settings and materials	
Decontextualized	**Embedded**

Teaching
What direction or cue will you give?
How will you prompt the child's response?
Circle type of prompt(s) used:
Physical   Visual
Modeling   Verbal
Other: _____
Circle prompt fading procedure used:
Time delay   Most to least
Graduated guidance
Other: _____
What is the child's response?
What reinforcers are you using?
What is the correction procedure?
How will you collect data? *(circle answer)*
Percentage correct   Frequency
Duration   Permanent product
Other: _____

Sets

1. _____
   _____
   _____
   _____

2. _____
   _____
   _____
   _____

3. _____
   _____
   _____
   _____

4. _____
   _____
   _____

5. _____
   _____
   _____
   _____

INSTRUCTIONAL PROGRAM SHEET: School Skills

Works Independently on a Teacher Selected Activity

Child: _____ Date initiated: _____ Date completed: _____

Objective: When the teacher instructs the child to complete an activity, the child completes the activity calmly and in a timely manner.

Mastery criterion:
- 80% or higher correct response for each set
- Minimum of five opportunities per day
- 3 consecutive teaching days

Generalization:
People: At least two adults
Settings: Across school locations
Materials: Across a variety of materials and activities

Things to consider: Child completes one activity at a time, as instructed by the teacher. This activity should not be a preferred activity. Completing an activity may include a task analysis that is unique to the activity. Choose activities that are not too difficult for the child to complete. Child may need some assistance in learning how to complete the activity.

Teaching sequence
1. Completes one teacher selected activity
2. Completes a different teacher selected activity
3. Completes three different activities
4. Completes four different activities
5. Completes five different activities

PROGRAMMING LOG

	Acquisition		Generalization		Maintenance	
	Start date	End date	Start date	End date	Date/data	Date/data
1						
2						
3						
4						
5						

LESSON PLAN: School Skills

Works Independently on a Teacher Selected Activity

Settings and materials	
Decontextualized	**Embedded**

Teaching
What direction or cue will you give?
How will you prompt the child's response?
Circle type of prompt(s) used:

Physical	Visual
Modeling	Verbal
Other: _____	

Circle prompt fading procedure used:

Time delay	Most to least
Graduated guidance	
Other: _____	

What is the child's response?
What reinforcers are you using?
What is the correction procedure?
How will you collect data? *(circle answer)*

Percentage correct	Frequency
Duration	Permanent product
Other: _____	

Sets

1. _____

_____

_____

_____

2. _____

_____

_____

_____

3. _____

_____

_____

_____

4. _____

_____

_____

_____

5. _____

_____

_____

_____

INSTRUCTIONAL PROGRAM SHEET: School Skills

Begins and Completes Teacher Selected Activities

Child: _____ Date initiated: _____ Date completed: _____

Objective: When a teacher provides the instruction to complete a school activity that is not highly preferred by the child, he or she completes at least three different activities.

Mastery criterion:
- 80% or higher correct responding for each set
- Minimum of five opportunities per day
- 2 consecutive teaching days
- Minimum of three different activities each day

Generalization:
People: At least two adults
Settings: Across school locations
Materials: Across novel activities

Things to consider: Have the materials set up in bins or boxes for child to complete each activity. Also, consider having the child follow a picture schedule of the steps for the activity to complete.

Teaching sequence
1. Completes one activity
2. Completes two activities in succession
3. Completes three activities in succession

PROGRAMMING LOG

	Acquisition		Generalization		Maintenance	
	Start date	End date	Start date	End date	Date/data	Date/data
1						
2						
3						

The DATA Model for Teaching Preschoolers with Autism by Ilene Schwartz, Julie Ashmun, Bonnie McBride, Crista Scott, and Susan Sandall. Copyright © 2017 by Paul H. Brookes Publishing Co., Inc. All rights reserved.

LESSON PLAN: School Skills

Begins and Completes Teacher Selected Activities

Settings and materials	
Decontextualized	**Embedded**

Teaching
What direction or cue will you give?
How will you prompt the child's response?
Circle type of prompt(s) used:
Physical   Visual
Modeling   Verbal
Other: _____
Circle prompt fading procedure used:
Time delay   Most to least
Graduated guidance
Other: _____
What is the child's response?
What reinforcers are you using?
What is the correction procedure?
How will you collect data? *(circle answer)*
Percentage correct   Frequency
Duration   Permanent product
Other: _____

Sets

1. _____
_____
_____
_____

2. _____
_____
_____
_____

3. _____
_____
_____
_____

4. _____
_____
_____
_____

5. _____
_____
_____
_____

INSTRUCTIONAL PROGRAM SHEET: School Skills

Participates in a Group Activity

Child: _____ Date initiated: _____ Date completed: _____

Objective: During small and large group activities, the child participates by remaining with the group, responding to teacher questions and comments, and maintaining attention to the teacher and materials.

Mastery criterion:
- 80% or higher correct response for each set
- Minimum of three opportunities per day
- 3 consecutive teaching days

Generalization:
People: At least two adults
Settings: At least two settings
Materials: Across different activities and materials during group

Things to consider: Consider modifications and adaptations as needed for participation. For example, the child may need a physical adaptation to maintain a sitting position during sitting activities.

Teaching sequence
1. Participates by staying with the group for 2 minutes of the activity
2. Participates by staying with the group and maintaining attention to the teacher and materials for 2 minutes of the activity
3. Participates by staying with the group, maintaining attention to the teacher and materials, and responding to questions and comments for 3 minutes of activity
4. Participates by staying with the group, maintaining attention to the teacher and materials, and responding to questions and comments for 5 minutes of activity
5. Participates by staying with the group, maintaining attention to the teacher and materials, and responding to questions and comments for the duration of the activity or until appropriate to leave activity

PROGRAMMING LOG

	Acquisition		Generalization		Maintenance	
	Start date	End date	Start date	End date	Date/data	Date/data
1						
2						
3						
4						
5						

LESSON PLAN: School Skills

Participates in a Group Activity

Settings and materials	
Decontextualized	**Embedded**

Teaching
What direction or cue will you give?
How will you prompt the child's response?
Circle type of prompt(s) used:
Physical   Visual
Modeling   Verbal
Other: _____
Circle prompt fading procedure used:
Time delay   Most to least
Graduated guidance
Other: _____
What is the child's response?
What reinforcers are you using?
What is the correction procedure?
How will you collect data? *(circle answer)*
Percentage correct   Frequency
Duration   Permanent product
Other: _____

Sets

1. _____

2. _____

3. _____

4. _____

5. _____

INSTRUCTIONAL PROGRAM SHEET: Self-Advocacy

Requests a Break

Child: _____ Date initiated: _____ Date completed: _____

Objective: During an activity that is frustrating to the child or when the child is leaving an activity, the child requests a break from the activity either by verbally stating, "I need a break," or by exchanging a "break" picture symbol.

Mastery criterion:
- 80% or higher correct response for each set
- Minimum of five opportunities per day
- 3 consecutive teaching days

Generalization:
People: At least two adults
Settings: At least two settings
Materials: Across a variety of activities and materials

Things to consider: When a child requests a break, materials may be left out for the child to return to after the break for completion. Requesting a break is different from asking to be finished with an activity. When child requests a break, the activity stops and is returned to for completion. When a child requests to be finished, the activity is completed when the teacher determines it is completed.

Teaching sequence
1. Requests a break when working individually with a teacher
2. Requests a break when another child is present

PROGRAMMING LOG

	Acquisition		Generalization		Maintenance	
	Start date	End date	Start date	End date	Date/data	Date/data
1						
2						

LESSON PLAN: Self-Advocacy

Requests a Break

Settings and materials	
Decontextualized	**Embedded**

Teaching
What direction or cue will you give?
How will you prompt the child's response?
Circle type of prompt(s) used:
Physical   Visual
Modeling   Verbal
Other: _____
Circle prompt fading procedure used:
Time delay   Most to least
Graduated guidance
Other: _____
What is the child's response?
What reinforcers are you using?
What is the correction procedure?
How will you collect data? *(circle answer)*
Percentage correct   Frequency
Duration   Permanent product
Other: _____

Sets

1. _____
_____
_____
_____

2. _____
_____
_____
_____

3. _____
_____
_____
_____

4. _____
_____
_____
_____

5. _____
_____
_____
_____

INSTRUCTIONAL PROGRAM SHEET: Self-Advocacy

Protests

Child: _____ Date initiated: _____ Date completed: _____

Objective: When an adult or peer offers an undesirable item or activity, the child appropriately refuses the item or activity by using gestures (e.g., pushing away toy), using pictures (e.g., Picture Exchange Communication System [PECS] using the "no" symbol), or vocalization (e.g., "No," "I don't want that," or "No, thank you"). Appropriate protests or rejections do not include yelling, screaming, kicking, or pushing.

Mastery criterion:
- 90% or higher correct response for each set
- Minimum of 10 opportunities per day
- 2 consecutive teaching days

Generalization:
People: At least two adults and two peers
Settings: At least two settings
Materials: Across a variety of items/activities

Things to consider: Complete a reinforcer assessment to determine child's preferred and least preferred activities, items, or events. Be sure child will refuse objects before you start teaching this skill. Yelling and crying are not appropriate protests even when they are paired with a sign, vocalization, or picture.

Teaching sequence
1. Child pushes away item or drops an undesirable item
2. Child communicates "No, thank you" by saying "No," shaking head no, using a manual sign, or exchanging a picture symbol when presented with an undesirable item
3. Child communicates "No, thank you" by shaking head no, using a manual sign, or exchanging a picture symbol when presented with an undesirable activity
4. Child remains calm while communicating "No, thank you"

PROGRAMMING LOG

	Acquisition		Generalization		Maintenance	
	Start date	End date	Start date	End date	Date/data	Date/data
1						
2						
3						
4						

LESSON PLAN: Self-Advocacy

Protests

Settings and materials	
Decontextualized	**Embedded**

Teaching
What direction or cue will you give?
How will you prompt the child's response?
Circle type of prompt(s) used:
Physical   Visual Modeling   Verbal Other: _____
Circle prompt fading procedure used:
Time delay   Most to least Graduated guidance Other: _____
What is the child's response?
What reinforcers are you using?
What is the correction procedure?
How will you collect data? *(circle answer)*
Percentage correct   Frequency Duration   Permanent product Other: _____

Sets

1. _____

_____

_____

_____

2. _____

_____

_____

_____

3. _____

_____

_____

_____

4. _____

_____

_____

_____

5. _____

_____

_____

_____

INSTRUCTIONAL PROGRAM SHEET: Self-Advocacy

Requests Help

Child: _____ Date initiated: _____ Date completed: _____

Objective: When the child is in need of assistance, he or she requests help with a calm body from adults and peers by stating the need for help or using an augmentative communication system to request assistance.

Mastery criterion:
- 90% or higher correct response for each set
- Minimum of 10 opportunities per day
- 2 consecutive teaching days

Generalization:
People: At least two adults and two peers
Settings: At least two settings
Materials: Across a variety of materials

Things to consider: Opportunities may continually change as the child learns to complete tasks with the assistance provided. Be aware of these opportunities so the child is prompted to request help before exhibiting behaviors that indicate he or she is frustrated or upset, such as screaming or crying.

Teaching sequence
1. Requests help from an adult during one activity (e.g., help with coat during arrival and departure)
2. Requests help from a peer during the same activity
3. Requests help from an adult during another activity
4. Requests help from a peer during another activity
5. Requests help from adults during a variety of activities
6. Requests help from peers during a variety of activities

PROGRAMMING LOG

	Acquisition		Generalization		Maintenance	
	Start date	End date	Start date	End date	Date/data	Date/data
1						
2						
3						
4						
5						
6						

LESSON PLAN: Self-Advocacy

Requests Help

Settings and materials	
Decontextualized	**Embedded**

Teaching
What direction or cue will you give?
How will you prompt the child's response?
Circle type of prompt(s) used:
Physical   Visual
Modeling   Verbal
Other: _____
Circle prompt fading procedure used:
Time delay   Most to least
Graduated guidance
Other: _____
What is the child's response?
What reinforcers are you using?
What is the correction procedure?
How will you collect data? *(circle answer)*
Percentage correct   Frequency
Duration   Permanent product
Other: _____

Sets

1. _____
   _____
   _____
   _____

2. _____
   _____
   _____
   _____

3. _____
   _____
   _____
   _____

4. _____
   _____
   _____
   _____

5. _____
   _____
   _____
   _____

INSTRUCTIONAL PROGRAM SHEET: Self-Advocacy

Requests Clarification

Child: _____ Date initiated: _____ Date completed: _____

Objective: When the child is not following the directions or request, although he or she has demonstrated understanding of the directions previously, the child asks the adult or peer to repeat the directions or request (e.g., "What did you say?" or "What?") or tells him or her to "Say it again."

Mastery criterion:
- 90% or higher correct response for each set
- Minimum of 10 opportunities per day
- 2 consecutive teaching days

Generalization:
People: At least two adults and two peers
Settings: At least two settings
Materials: Across different activities

Things to consider: Provide opportunities by speaking softly and stating directions when there is a lot of stimulation and it is difficult to focus or hear the teacher. Some children will benefit from opportunities to practice, or role play, this skill in a highly structured setting with a teacher. Modeling is an effective prompt for many children.

Teaching sequence
1. Requests that an adult clarify what he or she said with one type of prompt
2. Requests that an adult clarify without prompting
3. Requests that a peer clarify

PROGRAMMING LOG

	Acquisition		Generalization		Maintenance	
	Start date	End date	Start date	End date	Date/data	Date/data
1						
2						
3						

LESSON PLAN: Self-Advocacy

Requests Clarification

Settings and materials	
Decontextualized	**Embedded**

Teaching
What direction or cue will you give?
How will you prompt the child's response?
Circle type of prompt(s) used:
Physical   Visual
Modeling   Verbal
Other: _____
Circle prompt fading procedure used:
Time delay   Most to least
Graduated guidance
Other: _____
What is the child's response?
What reinforcers are you using?
What is the correction procedure?
How will you collect data? *(circle answer)*
Percentage correct   Frequency
Duration   Permanent product
Other: _____

Sets

1. _____
_____
_____
_____

2. _____
_____
_____
_____

3. _____
_____
_____
_____

4. _____
_____
_____
_____

5. _____
_____
_____
_____

INSTRUCTIONAL PROGRAM SHEET: Self-Advocacy

Requests Accommodations

Child: _____ Date initiated: _____ Date completed: _____

Objective: During activities such as play or mealtime, child requests accommodations (e.g., a picture schedule, timer, or toy to keep attention while waiting) to be successful with the activity.

Mastery criterion:
- 80% or higher correct response for each set
- Minimum of five opportunities per day
- 3 consecutive teaching days

Generalization:
People: At least two adults and two peers
Settings: At least two settings
Materials: Across different activities and accommodations provided

Things to consider: Accommodations will vary and must be provided regularly so the child learns to identify that the accommodation is not available and will request it. Child may benefit from structured opportunities to practice this skill by a teacher "sabotaging" the environment and neglecting to put out the child's accommodation.

Teaching sequence
1. Child requests accommodation during one activity
2. Child requests accommodation across two activities
3. Child requests accommodations when needed

PROGRAMMING LOG

	Acquisition		Generalization		Maintenance	
	Start date	End date	Start date	End date	Date/data	Date/data
1						
2						
3						

LESSON PLAN: Self-Advocacy

Requests Accommodations

Settings and materials	
Decontextualized	**Embedded**

Teaching
What direction or cue will you give?
How will you prompt the child's response?
Circle type of prompt(s) used:
Physical   Visual
Modeling   Verbal
Other: _____
Circle prompt fading procedure used:
Time delay   Most to least
Graduated guidance
Other: _____
What is the child's response?
What reinforcers are you using?
What is the correction procedure?
How will you collect data? *(circle answer)*
Percentage correct   Frequency
Duration   Permanent product
Other: _____

Sets

1. _____

_____

_____

_____

2. _____

_____

_____

_____

3. _____

_____

_____

_____

4. _____

_____

_____

_____

5. _____

_____

_____

_____

INSTRUCTIONAL PROGRAM SHEET: Self-Advocacy

Identifies Likes and Dislikes

Child: _____ Date initiated: _____ Date completed: _____

Objective: When child is asked to identify what he or she likes or dislikes (e.g., "What's your favorite color?" or "What don't you like to eat?"), the child states the answer.

Mastery criterion:
- 90% or higher correct response for each set
- Minimum of 10 opportunities per day
- 2 consecutive teaching days
- At least five likes
- At least five dislikes

Generalization:
People: At least two adults and two peers
Settings: At least two settings
Materials: Across a variety of likes and dislikes and materials, if appropriate

Things to consider: Identify the child's likes and dislikes by talking with those that know him or her and observing the child. Also, consider teaching likes with which the child demonstrates strong interests.

Teaching sequence
1. Identifies likes (e.g., food, color, book, toy, animals) using one type of prompt (e.g., visual)
2. Identifies likes without prompts
3. Identifies dislikes using one type of prompt (e.g., visual)
4. Identifies dislikes without prompts

PROGRAMMING LOG

	Acquisition		Generalization		Maintenance	
	Start date	End date	Start date	End date	Date/data	Date/data
1						
2						
3						
4						

LESSON PLAN: Self-Advocacy

Identifies Likes and Dislikes

Settings and materials	
Decontextualized	**Embedded**

Teaching
What direction or cue will you give?
How will you prompt the child's response?
Circle type of prompt(s) used:
Physical   Visual
Modeling   Verbal
Other: _____
Circle prompt fading procedure used:
Time delay   Most to least
Graduated guidance
Other: _____
What is the child's response?
What reinforcers are you using?
What is the correction procedure?
How will you collect data? *(circle answer)*
Percentage correct   Frequency
Duration   Permanent product
Other: _____

Sets

1. _____

2. _____

3. _____

4. _____

5. _____

INSTRUCTIONAL PROGRAM SHEET: Self-Advocacy

States Identifying Information About Self

Child: _____   Date initiated: _____   Date completed: _____

Objective: When child is asked to identify information about him or herself (e.g., "What is your name?" or "How old are you?"), the child states the correct information.

Mastery criterion:
- 90% or higher correct response for each set
- Minimum of 10 opportunities per day
- 2 consecutive teaching days
- At least five statements of identification

Generalization:
People: At least two adults and two peers
Settings: At least two settings
Materials: Across different types of information

Things to consider: Confirm the child's identifying information by talking with family.

Skill sequence
1. States two pieces of identifying information (e.g., name, age)
2. States two new pieces of identifying information (e.g., pet, sibling)
3. States two new pieces of identifying information (e.g., parents, place child lives)

PROGRAMMING LOG

	Acquisition		Generalization		Maintenance	
	Start date	End date	Start date	End date	Date/data	Date/data
1						
2						
3						

LESSON PLAN: Self-Advocacy

States Identifying Information About Self

Settings and materials	
Decontextualized	**Embedded**

Teaching
What direction or cue will you give?
How will you prompt the child's response?
Circle type of prompt(s) used:
Physical   Visual
Modeling   Verbal
Other: _____
Circle prompt fading procedure used:
Time delay   Most to least
Graduated guidance
Other: _____
What is the child's response?
What reinforcers are you using?
What is the correction procedure?
How will you collect data? *(circle answer)*
Percentage correct   Frequency
Duration   Permanent product
Other: _____

Sets

1. _____

_____

_____

_____

2. _____

_____

_____

_____

3. _____

_____

_____

_____

4. _____

_____

_____

_____

5. _____

_____

_____

_____

INSTRUCTIONAL PROGRAM SHEET: Flexibility

Follows Classroom Routine and Schedule

Child: _____ Date initiated: _____ Date completed: _____

Objective: Throughout the school day, the child follows the schedule and classroom routines or follows the teacher's directions to transition from one activity to another with a calm body and without protest, and remaining with the group.

Mastery criterion:
- 90% or higher correct response for each set
- Minimum of 10 opportunities per day
- 2 consecutive teaching days

Generalization:
People: At least two adults
Settings: At least two locations in the school (i.e., outside, gym)
Materials: Across different posted schedules

Things to consider: Post a schedule so the child can reference it and be sure to direct child's attention to the schedule. Be consistent with the schedule and follow regular routines. Provide warnings for transitions.

Teaching sequence
1. Follows the schedule when referenced by an adult
2. Follows directions and references the schedule
3. Follows the routines and schedule

PROGRAMMING LOG

	Acquisition		Generalization		Maintenance	
	Start date	End date	Start date	End date	Date/data	Date/data
1						
2						
3						

LESSON PLAN: Flexibility

Follows Classroom Routine and Schedule

Settings and materials	
Decontextualized	**Embedded**

Teaching
What direction or cue will you give?
How will you prompt the child's response?
Circle type of prompt(s) used:
Physical   Visual
Modeling   Verbal
Other: _____
Circle prompt fading procedure used:
Time delay   Most to least
Graduated guidance
Other: _____
What is the child's response?
What reinforcers are you using?
What is the correction procedure?
How will you collect data? *(circle answer)*
Percentage correct   Frequency
Duration   Permanent product
Other: _____

Sets

1. _____
   _____
   _____
   _____

2. _____
   _____
   _____
   _____

3. _____
   _____
   _____
   _____

4. _____
   _____
   _____
   _____

5. _____
   _____
   _____
   _____

INSTRUCTIONAL PROGRAM SHEET: Flexibility

Follows Classroom Routine and Schedule—Example

Child: _____ Date initiated: _____ Date completed: _____

Objective: Throughout the school day, the child follows the schedule and classroom routines or follows the teacher's directions to transition from one activity to another with a calm body and without protest, and remaining with the group.

Mastery criterion:
- 90% or higher correct response for each set
- Minimum of 10 opportunities per day
- 2 consecutive teaching days

Generalization:
People: At least two adults
Settings: At least two locations in the school (i.e., outside, gym)
Materials: Across different posted schedules

Things to consider: Post a schedule so the child can reference it and be sure to direct child's attention to the schedule. Be consistent with the schedule and follow regular routines. Provide warnings for transitions.

Teaching sequence
1. Follows the schedule when referenced by an adult
2. Follows directions and references the schedule
3. Follows the routines and schedule

PROGRAMMING LOG

	Acquisition		Generalization		Maintenance	
	Start date	End date	Start date	End date	Date/data	Date/data
1	10/10/14	11/10/14	11/11/14	11/20/14		
2	11/11/14	1/20/15	1/21/15	1/30/15		
3	1/21/15	3/1/15	3/2/15	3/10/15	4/10/15; 100%	5/15/15; 100%

The DATA Model for Teaching Preschoolers with Autism by Ilene Schwartz, Julie Ashmun, Bonnie McBride, Crista Scott, and Susan Sandall. Copyright © 2017 by Paul H. Brookes Publishing Co., Inc. All rights reserved.

LESSON PLAN: Flexibility

Follows Classroom Routine and Schedule—Example

Settings and materials	
Decontextualized	**Embedded**
Work on skill in work area with individual schedule for individualized instruction	Provide instruction during preferred routines and activities

Teaching
What direction or cue will you give?
Sets 1 and 2: Teacher direction for next activity and "check schedule" Set 3: Teacher direction that is given to all children for transition
How will you prompt the child's response?
Circle type of prompt(s) used:
Physical   (Visual) (Modeling)   Verbal Other: _____
Circle prompt fading procedure used:
Time delay   Most to least (Graduated guidance) Other: _____
What is the child's response?
Follows directions, schedule or routine to transition to next activity
What reinforcers are you using?
Preferred activities and materials provided at beginning of next activity in schedule
What is the correction procedure?
Provide instruction again and provide prompt to move to next activity in schedule or routine
How will you collect data? *(circle answer)*
(Percentage correct)   Frequency Duration   Permanent product Other: _____

Sets

1. Follows schedule with visual support and when referenced by the adult; student has own schedule that resembles classroom schedule

2. Follows teacher directions for next activity and references either own schedule or classroom schedule when told to "check schedule"

3. Follows classroom routines and schedules when directed by teacher to the whole class to move to next activity on schedule

INSTRUCTIONAL PROGRAM SHEET: Flexibility

Accepts Interruptions or Unexpected Changes

Child: _____ Date initiated: _____ Date completed: _____

Objective: When an interruption or unexpected change occurs in the schedule or routine, the child may (verbally or nonverbally) appropriately express displeasure with the interruption or change but is able to accept it and move on.

Mastery criterion:
- 80% or higher correct response for each set
- Minimum of five opportunities per day
- 3 consecutive teaching days

Generalization:
People: At least two adults
Settings: At least two settings
Materials: Across preferred and nonpreferred activities and materials

Things to consider: Incorporate expected and unexpected change throughout schedule and routines. This goal may be taught along with self-regulation goals, such as Form 2.3 "Self-Regulates When Tense or Upset."

Teaching sequence
1. Accepts unexpected changes as posted on the schedule the day of the change
2. Accepts unexpected changes or interruptions in consistent routines
3. Accepts unexpected changes or interruptions as they occur

PROGRAMMING LOG

	Acquisition		Generalization		Maintenance	
	Start date	End date	Start date	End date	Date/data	Date/data
1						
2						
3						

LESSON PLAN: Flexibility

Accepts Interruptions or Unexpected Changes

Settings and materials	
Decontextualized	**Embedded**

Teaching

What direction or cue will you give?

How will you prompt the child's response?

Circle type of prompt(s) used:

Physical	Visual
Modeling	Verbal

Other: _____

Circle prompt fading procedure used:

Time delay	Most to least
Graduated guidance	

Other: _____

What is the child's response?

What reinforcers are you using?

What is the correction procedure?

How will you collect data? *(circle answer)*

Percentage correct	Frequency
Duration	Permanent product

Other: _____

Sets

1. _____

_____

_____

_____

2. _____

_____

_____

_____

3. _____

_____

_____

_____

4. _____

_____

_____

_____

5. _____

_____

_____

_____

INSTRUCTIONAL PROGRAM SHEET: Flexibility

Accepts Being Told "No" without Becoming Upset

Child: _____ Date initiated: _____ Date completed: _____

Objective: When the child makes a request and is told "no," the child accepts this decision without protest and with a calm body.

Mastery criterion:
- 90% or higher correct response for each set
- Minimum of 10 opportunities per day
- 2 consecutive teaching days

Generalization:
People: At least three adults
Settings: At least two settings
Materials: Across preferred and not preferred activities and materials

Things to consider: Conduct a reinforcer assessment to determine preferred and most preferred activities and items. This goal may be taught along with self-regulation goals such as "Self-Regulates When Tense or Upset." (Executive Functioning Form 2.3)

Teaching sequence
1. Accepts being told "no" for less preferred items and activities
2. Accepts being told "no" for preferred items and activities
3. Accepts being told "no" for most preferred items and activities

PROGRAMMING LOG

	Acquisition		Generalization		Maintenance	
	Start date	End date	Start date	End date	Date/data	Date/data
1						
2						
3						

LESSON PLAN: Flexibility

Accepts Being Told "No" without Becoming Upset

Settings and materials	
Decontextualized	Embedded

Teaching

What direction or cue will you give?

How will you prompt the child's response?

Circle type of prompt(s) used:

Physical   Visual

Modeling   Verbal

Other: _____

Circle prompt fading procedure used:

Time delay   Most to least

Graduated guidance

Other: _____

What is the child's response?

What reinforcers are you using?

What is the correction procedure?

How will you collect data? *(circle answer)*

Percentage correct   Frequency

Duration   Permanent product

Other: _____

Sets

1. _____

2. _____

3. _____

4. _____

5. _____

INSTRUCTIONAL PROGRAM SHEET: Flexibility

Relinquishes Preferred Toy, Food, or Materials

Child: _____ Date initiated: _____ Date completed: _____

Objective: When asked to give up a preferred item, the child relinquishes the item without protest or with appropriate protest (e.g., "I don't want to" or "Wait"). Child may receive adult reminder or support.

Mastery criterion:
- 90% or higher correct response for each set
- Minimum of 10 opportunities per day
- 2 consecutive teaching days

Generalization:
People: At least two adults
Settings: At least two settings
Materials: Across preferred items

Things to consider: Conduct a reinforce assessment to determine preferred and most preferred activities and items. This goal may be taught with self-regulation goals, such as "Self-Regulates When Tense or Upset." (Executive Functioning Form 2.3)

Teaching sequence
1. Relinquishes less preferred items and activities
2. Relinquishes preferred items and activities
3. Relinquishes most preferred items and activities

PROGRAMMING LOG

	Acquisition		Generalization		Maintenance	
	Start date	End date	Start date	End date	Date/data	Date/data
1						
2						
3						

The DATA Model for Teaching Preschoolers with Autism by Ilene Schwartz, Julie Ashmun, Bonnie McBride, Crista Scott, and Susan Sandall. Copyright © 2017 by Paul H. Brookes Publishing Co., Inc. All rights reserved.

LESSON PLAN: Flexibility

Relinquishes Preferred Toy, Food, or Materials

Settings and materials	
Decontextualized	**Embedded**

Teaching

What direction or cue will you give?

How will you prompt the child's response?

Circle type of prompt(s) used:

Physical	Visual
Modeling	Verbal

Other: _____

Circle prompt fading procedure used:

Time delay	Most to least
Graduated guidance	

Other: _____

What is the child's response?

What reinforcers are you using?

What is the correction procedure?

How will you collect data? *(circle answer)*

Percentage correct	Frequency
Duration	Permanent product

Other: _____

Sets

1. _____

2. _____

3. _____

4. _____

5. _____

INSTRUCTIONAL PROGRAM SHEET: Flexibility

Accepts that Things Don't Go as Expected

Child: _____ Date initiated: _____ Date completed: _____

Objective: During activities throughout the school day, child accepts being disappointed; for example, not winning a game, making an unintended mark on paper, or not getting the first turn, and remains calm. In these examples, the child may congratulate the winner, complete the art project, and may say, "That's okay, maybe next time."

Mastery criterion:
- 80% or higher correct response for each set
- Minimum of five opportunities per day
- 3 consecutive teaching days

Generalization:
People: At least two adults
Settings: At least two settings
Materials: Across preferred activities

Things to consider: This goal may be taught along with self-regulation goals such as "Self-Regulates When Tense or Upset." Consider an emotional regulation curriculum that teaches emotions on a scale such as 1–3 (e.g., 1 is calm, 2 is excited, 3 is frustrated or really excited) or a color scale (e.g., blue is calm, orange is slightly elevated emotions, red is angry), or using both numbers and colors. Once child recognizes emotions then, pair the self-soothe strategy with the emotion using the visual cue.

Teaching sequence
1. Little protest and disappointment demonstrated with one prompt (e.g., visual, verbal)
2. Demonstrates minimal disappointment
3. Remains calm and accepts that it does not go as expected

PROGRAMMING LOG

	Acquisition		Generalization		Maintenance	
	Start date	End date	Start date	End date	Date/data	Date/data
1						
2						
3						

LESSON PLAN: Flexibility

Accepts that Things Don't Go as Expected

Settings and materials	
Decontextualized	**Embedded**

Teaching
What direction or cue will you give?
How will you prompt the child's response?
Circle type of prompt(s) used:

Physical	Visual
Modeling	Verbal
Other: _____	

Circle prompt fading procedure used:

Time delay	Most to least
Graduated guidance	
Other: _____	

What is the child's response?
What reinforcers are you using?
What is the correction procedure?
How will you collect data? *(circle answer)*

Percentage correct	Frequency
Duration	Permanent product
Other: _____	

Sets

1. _____

_____

_____

_____

2. _____

_____

_____

_____

3. _____

_____

_____

_____

4. _____

_____

_____

_____

5. _____

_____

_____

_____

INSTRUCTIONAL PROGRAM SHEET: Self-Regulation

Waits for a Preferred Item or Activity

Child: _____   Date initiated: _____   Date completed: _____

Objective: When child requests an item or activity and is told to wait, he or she waits quietly and calmly for the item.

Mastery criterion:
- 90% or higher correct response for each set
- Minimum of 10 opportunities per day
- 2 consecutive teaching days

Generalization:
People: At least two adults and peers
Settings: At least two settings
Materials: Waits across activities and games

Things to consider: Teach child to look at a book or choose another activity while waiting. Consider amount of time that is developmentally appropriate for the child.

Teaching sequence
1. Waits up to 3 seconds
2. Waits up to 5 seconds
3. Waits up to 10 seconds
4. Waits up to 20 seconds
5. Waits up to 30 seconds or until turn naturally occurs

PROGRAMMING LOG

	Acquisition		Generalization		Maintenance	
	Start date	End date	Start date	End date	Date/data	Date/data
1						
2						
3						
4						
5						

LESSON PLAN: Self-Regulation

Waits for a Preferred Item or Activity

Settings and materials	
Decontextualized	**Embedded**

Teaching
What direction or cue will you give?
How will you prompt the child's response?
Circle type of prompt(s) used:
Physical   Visual
Modeling   Verbal
Other: _____
Circle prompt fading procedure used:
Time delay   Most to least
Graduated guidance
Other: _____
What is the child's response?
What reinforcers are you using?
What is the correction procedure?
How will you collect data? *(circle answer)*
Percentage correct   Frequency
Duration   Permanent product
Other: _____

Sets

1. _____

_____

_____

_____

2. _____

_____

_____

_____

3. _____

_____

_____

_____

4. _____

_____

_____

_____

5. _____

_____

_____

_____

INSTRUCTIONAL PROGRAM SHEET: Self-Regulation

Accepts Comfort from Others

Child: _____   Date initiated: _____   Date completed: _____

Objective: When child is upset or agitated, the child allows a caregiver, familiar adult, or peer to comfort him or her by giving a hug, pat on the back, redirecting the child, etc.

Mastery criterion:
- 80% or higher correct response for each set
- Minimum of five opportunities
- 4 consecutive teaching days

Generalization:
People: At least two adults and peers
Settings: At least two settings
Materials: Across a variety of activities

Things to consider: Child may need to be held tightly or softly depending on child's sensitivity to light or strong touch.

Teaching sequence
1. Accepts words, physical contact, or redirection as a means to comfort from one adult
2. Accepts words, physical contact, or redirection as a means to comfort from another adult
3. Accepts words, physical contact, or redirection as a means to comfort from a peer

PROGRAMMING LOG

	Acquisition		Generalization		Maintenance	
	Start date	End date	Start date	End date	Date/data	Date/data
1						
2						
3						

LESSON PLAN: Self-Regulation

Accepts Comfort from Others

Settings and materials	
Decontextualized	**Embedded**

Teaching
What direction or cue will you give?
How will you prompt the child's response?
Circle type of prompt(s) used:
Physical   Visual
Modeling   Verbal
Other: _____
Circle prompt fading procedure used:
Time delay   Most to least
Graduated guidance
Other: _____
What is the child's response?
What reinforcers are you using?
What is the correction procedure?
How will you collect data? *(circle answer)*
Percentage correct   Frequency
Duration   Permanent product
Other: _____

Sets

1. _____

_____

_____

_____

2. _____

_____

_____

_____

3. _____

_____

_____

_____

4. _____

_____

_____

_____

5. _____

_____

_____

_____

INSTRUCTIONAL PROGRAM SHEET: Self-Regulation

Self-Regulates When Tense or Upset

Child: _____ Date initiated: _____ Date completed: _____

Objective: When child is upset or agitated, child self-regulates by expressing his or her frustration in acceptable ways such as saying, "I'm mad," and asking to take a break with verbal or visual cues.

Mastery criterion:
- 80% or higher correct response for each set
- Minimum of five opportunities
- 4 consecutive teaching days
- Uses more than one way to manage frustration (expressively, takes a break, takes a deep breath)

Generalization:
People: At least two adults and peers
Settings: At least two settings
Materials: Across activities and visual cues

Things to consider: Teach strategies to self-soothe with story telling and role-play. Use verbal and visual cues to teach. Consider an emotional regulation curriculum that teaches emotions on a scale such as 1–3 (e.g., 1 is calm, 2 is excited, 3 is frustrated or really excited) or a color scale (e.g., blue is calm, orange is slightly elevated emotions, red is angry), or using both numbers and colors. Once child recognizes emotions, then pair the self-soothe strategy with the emotion using the visual cue.

Teaching sequence
1. Uses one self-soothe strategy with a verbal and visual cue
2. Uses another self-soothe strategy with a verbal and visual cue
3. Uses a total of three self-soothe strategies with verbal and visual cues
4. Uses a variety of self-soothe strategies with only one cue (fade verbal or visual cues from previous sets)

PROGRAMMING LOG

	Acquisition		Generalization		Maintenance	
	Start date	End date	Start date	End date	Date/data	Date/data
1						
2						
3						
4						

LESSON PLAN: Self-Regulation

Self-Regulates When Tense or Upset

Settings and materials	
Decontextualized	**Embedded**

Teaching

What direction or cue will you give?

How will you prompt the child's response?

Circle type of prompt(s) used:

Physical   Visual

Modeling   Verbal

Other: _____

Circle prompt fading procedure used:

Time delay   Most to least

Graduated guidance

Other: _____

What is the child's response?

What reinforcers are you using?

What is the correction procedure?

How will you collect data? *(circle answer)*

Percentage correct   Frequency

Duration   Permanent product

Other: _____

Sets

1. _____

2. _____

3. _____

4. _____

5. _____

INSTRUCTIONAL PROGRAM SHEET: Self-Regulation

Self-Regulates When Energy Level is High or Low

Child: _____ Date initiated: _____ Date completed: _____

Objective: When the child's energy level is too high or low, the child uses a strategy to regulate his or her energy level. Strategies may include deep breathing, squeezing a squishy ball, walking around the room or jumping on a trampoline.

Mastery criterion:
- 80% or higher correct response for each set
- Minimum of five opportunities
- 4 consecutive teaching days
- Uses more than one way to manage energy level (deep breathing, walking, jumping)

Generalization:
People: At least two adults and peers
Settings: At least two settings
Materials: Across a variety of activities

Things to consider: Consult an occupational therapist for recommendations for child. Consider an emotional regulation curriculum that teaches emotions on a scale such as 1–3 (e.g., 1 is calm, 2 is excited, 3 is frustrated or really excited) or a color scale (e.g., blue is calm, orange is slightly elevated emotions, red is angry), or using both numbers and colors. Once child recognizes emotions, then pair the self-soothe strategy with the emotion using the visual cue.

Teaching sequence
1. Uses one regulating strategy
2. Uses another regulating strategy
3. Uses at least three self-regulation strategies

PROGRAMMING LOG

	Acquisition		Generalization		Maintenance	
	Start date	End date	Start date	End date	Date/data	Date/data
1						
2						
3						

LESSON PLAN: Self-Regulation

Self-Regulates When Energy Level is High or Low

Settings and materials	
Decontextualized	**Embedded**

Teaching

What direction or cue will you give?

How will you prompt the child's response?

Circle type of prompt(s) used:

Physical   Visual

Modeling   Verbal

Other: _____

Circle prompt fading procedure used:

Time delay   Most to least

Graduated guidance

Other: _____

What is the child's response?

What reinforcers are you using?

What is the correction procedure?

How will you collect data? *(circle answer)*

Percentage correct   Frequency

Duration   Permanent product

Other: _____

Sets

1. _____

2. _____

3. _____

4. _____

5. _____

INSTRUCTIONAL PROGRAM SHEET: Persistence, Organization, and Time Management

Persists in Gaining a Person's Attention

Child: _____ Date initiated: _____ Date completed: _____

Objective: When the child makes a request, he or she gains a peer's or adult's attention by tapping the person or calling his or her name and then continues with tapping or calling name until person responds (can be up to 10 seconds).

Mastery criterion:
- 90% or higher correct response for each set
- Minimum of 10 opportunities per day
- 2 consecutive teaching days

Generalization:
People: At least two adults and peers
Settings: At least two settings
Materials: Across preferred items and activities

Things to consider: Turn away from child to indicate that you are not giving the child your attention so that he or she must get your attention. May need to teach child to expressively identify adults and peers.

Teaching sequence
1. Child taps adult next to him or her to gain attention
2. Child walks to adult and taps him or her to gain attention
3. Child taps a friend next to him or her to gain attention
4. Child walks to peer and taps him or her to gain attention
5. If verbal, child calls adult's name to gain attention
6. If verbal, child calls peer's name to gain attention

PROGRAMMING LOG

	Acquisition		Generalization		Maintenance	
	Start date	End date	Start date	End date	Date/data	Date/data
1						
2						
3						
4						
5						
6						

LESSON PLAN: Persistence, Organization, and Time Management

Persists in Gaining a Person's Attention

Settings and materials	
Decontextualized	**Embedded**

Teaching
What direction or cue will you give?
How will you prompt the child's response?
Circle type of prompt(s) used:
Physical   Visual
Modeling   Verbal
Other: _____
Circle prompt fading procedure used:
Time delay   Most to least
Graduated guidance
Other: _____
What is the child's response?
What reinforcers are you using?
What is the correction procedure?
How will you collect data? *(circle answer)*
Percentage correct   Frequency
Duration   Permanent product
Other: _____

Sets
1. _____
2. _____
3. _____
4. _____
5. _____

INSTRUCTIONAL PROGRAM SHEET: Persistence, Organization, and Time Management

Persists or Continues to Try When Something Is Difficult

Child: _____ Date initiated: _____ Date completed: _____

Objective: When the child is trying to complete a task, he or she continues to try or persist until completed or must ask for help.

Mastery criterion:
- 80% or higher correct response for each set
- Minimum of five opportunities per day
- 3 consecutive teaching days

Generalization:
People: At least two adults and peers
Settings: At least two settings
Materials: Across a variety of activities

Things to consider: Child must try and problem solve with different solutions before asking for help. At first give easier tasks, such as simple puzzles, for the child to complete. Make the activity more challenging as you progress through the teaching sequence.

Teaching sequence
1. Persists with a task for at least 10 seconds before asking for help
2. Persists with a more difficult task for at least 15 seconds before asking for help
3. Persists with a difficult task for at least 20 seconds before asking for help
4. Persists with a difficult task for at least 30 seconds before asking for help

PROGRAMMING LOG

	Acquisition		Generalization		Maintenance	
	Start date	End date	Start date	End date	Date/data	Date/data
1						
2						
3						
4						

LESSON PLAN: Persistence, Organization, and Time Management

Persists or Continues to Try When Something Is Difficult

Settings and materials

Decontextualized	Embedded

Teaching

What direction or cue will you give?

How will you prompt the child's response?

Circle type of prompt(s) used:

Physical   Visual

Modeling   Verbal

Other: _____

Circle prompt fading procedure used:

Time delay   Most to least

Graduated guidance

Other: _____

What is the child's response?

What reinforcers are you using?

What is the correction procedure?

How will you collect data? *(circle answer)*

Percentage correct   Frequency

Duration   Permanent product

Other: _____

Sets

1. _____
2. _____
3. _____
4. _____
5. _____

II. EXECUTIVE FUNCTIONING

INSTRUCTIONAL PROGRAM SHEET: Persistence, Organization, and Time Management

Follows a Sequence

Child: _____ Date initiated: _____ Date completed: _____

Objective: When given an activity that is at least a three-step sequence, the child completes the activity in order by following the directions or referencing the picture sequence.

Mastery criterion:
- 80% or higher correct response for each set
- Minimum of five opportunities per day
- 3 consecutive teaching days

Generalization:
People: At least two adults and peers
Settings: At least two settings
Materials: Across activities and picture sequences

Things to consider: Start with routines and tasks the child knows well and then present tasks that are more difficult and consist of more steps.

Teaching sequence
1. Completes a two-step sequence
2. Completes a three-step sequence
3. If appropriate, completes a four-step sequence

PROGRAMMING LOG

	Acquisition		Generalization		Maintenance	
	Start date	End date	Start date	End date	Date/data	Date/data
1						
2						
3						

The DATA Model for Teaching Preschoolers with Autism by Ilene Schwartz, Julie Ashmun, Bonnie McBride, Crista Scott, and Susan Sandall.

LESSON PLAN: Persistence, Organization, and Time Management

Finishes a Sequence

Settings and materials	
Decontextualized	**Embedded**

Teaching
What direction or cue will you give?
How will you prompt the child's response?
Circle type of prompt(s) used:
Physical   Visual
Modeling   Verbal
Other: _____
Circle prompt fading procedure used:
Time delay   Most to least
Graduated guidance
Other: _____
What is the child's response?
What reinforcers are you using?
What is the correction procedure?
How will you collect data? *(circle answer)*
Percentage correct   Frequency
Duration   Permanent product
Other: _____

Sets

1. _____

_____

_____

_____

2. _____

_____

_____

_____

3. _____

_____

_____

_____

4. _____

_____

_____

5. _____

_____

_____

_____

INSTRUCTIONAL PROGRAM SHEET: Persistence, Organization, and Time Management

Finishes an Activity in a Timely Manner

Child: _____ Date initiated: _____ Date completed: _____

Objective: The child completes an activity within an appropriate amount of time, cleans it up, and moves to the next activity, keeping pace with peers or group.

Mastery criterion:
- 80% or higher correct response for each set
- Minimum of five opportunities per day
- 3 consecutive teaching days

Generalization:
People: At least two adults and peers
Settings: At least two settings
Materials: Across at least five different activities

Things to consider: The length of time it takes other children of the same age in the classroom to complete the activity. Consider child's ability to do the activity before presenting the child with the task of completing it in a timely manner.

Teaching sequence
1. Completes task with assistance from an adult
2. Completes task with visual prompts (e.g., pictures, timers)
3. Completes task in a timely manner without assistance
4. Completes task in a timely manner without assistance and cleans up, if needed
5. Completes task in a timely manner, cleans up, and begins the next activity

PROGRAMMING LOG

	Acquisition		Generalization		Maintenance	
	Start date	End date	Start date	End date	Date/data	Date/data
1						
2						
3						
4						
5						

LESSON PLAN: Persistence, Organization, and Time Management

Finishes an Activity in a Timely Manner

Settings and materials	
Decontextualized	Embedded

Teaching
What direction or cue will you give?
How will you prompt the child's response?
Circle type of prompt(s) used:
Physical   Visual
Modeling   Verbal
Other: _____
Circle prompt fading procedure used:
Time delay   Most to least
Graduated guidance
Other: _____
What is the child's response?
What reinforcers are you using?
What is the correction procedure?
How will you collect data? *(circle answer)*
Percentage correct   Frequency
Duration   Permanent product
Other: _____

Sets

1. _____

_____

_____

_____

2. _____

_____

_____

_____

3. _____

_____

_____

_____

4. _____

_____

_____

_____

5. _____

_____

_____

_____

INSTRUCTIONAL PROGRAM SHEET: Problem Solving

Claims and Defends Objects

Child: _____ Date initiated: _____ Date completed: _____

Objective: When a peer or adult takes or attempts to take the child's item, the child calmly claims the item as his or her own either verbally, with pictures, or using gestures (e.g., sign for "my turn").

Mastery criterion:
- 90% or higher correct response for each set
- Minimum of 10 opportunities per day
- 2 consecutive teaching days

Generalization:
People: At least two adults and peers
Settings: At least two settings
Materials: Across at least five preferred items

Things to consider: Teach sharing by teaching the child to claim the item, then offer it when he or she is done with it.

Teaching sequence
1. Child claims object by holding it, stating "It's mine," using a gesture (e.g., "my turn") with adult assistance
2. Child claims object with no adult assistance

PROGRAMMING LOG

	Acquisition		Generalization		Maintenance	
	Start date	End date	Start date	End date	Date/data	Date/data
1						
2						

LESSON PLAN: Problem Solving

Claims and Defends Objects

Settings and materials	
Decontextualized	**Embedded**

Teaching
What direction or cue will you give?
How will you prompt the child's response?
Circle type of prompt(s) used:
Physical   Visual
Modeling   Verbal
Other: _____
Circle prompt fading procedure used:
Time delay   Most to least
Graduated guidance
Other: _____
What is the child's response?
What reinforcers are you using?
What is the correction procedure?
How will you collect data? *(circle answer)*
Percentage correct   Frequency
Duration   Permanent product
Other: _____

Sets

1. _____
   _____
   _____
   _____

2. _____
   _____
   _____
   _____

3. _____
   _____
   _____
   _____

4. _____
   _____
   _____
   _____

5. _____
   _____
   _____
   _____

INSTRUCTIONAL PROGRAM SHEET: Problem Solving

Identifies or Defines the Problem

Child: _____   Date initiated: _____   Date completed: _____

Objective: When a problem arises, such as two children want the same toy or a toy won't fit together, the child states the problem when asked what is wrong.

Mastery criterion:
- 80% or higher correct response for each set
- Minimum of five opportunities per day
- 3 consecutive teaching days

Generalization:
People: At least two adults and peers
Settings: At least two settings
Materials: Across at least five different activities or types of problem

Things to consider: Use story examples and role-play to teach a variety of problems that may arise. May use visual supports that provide a variety of choices to define the problem.

Teaching sequence
1. Defines at least one type of problem
2. Defines at least two types of problems
3. Defines a variety of problems

PROGRAMMING LOG

	Acquisition		Generalization		Maintenance	
	Start date	End date	Start date	End date	Date/data	Date/data
1						
2						
3						

LESSON PLAN: Problem Solving

Identifies or Defines the Problem

Settings and materials	
Decontextualized	**Embedded**

Teaching
What direction or cue will you give?
How will you prompt the child's response?
Circle type of prompt(s) used:
Physical   Visual
Modeling   Verbal
Other: _____
Circle prompt fading procedure used:
Time delay   Most to least
Graduated guidance
Other: _____
What is the child's response?
What reinforcers are you using?
What is the correction procedure?
How will you collect data? *(circle answer)*
Percentage correct   Frequency
Duration   Permanent product
Other: _____

Sets

1. _____
   _____
   _____
   _____

2. _____
   _____
   _____
   _____

3. _____
   _____
   _____
   _____

4. _____
   _____
   _____
   _____

5. _____
   _____
   _____
   _____

INSTRUCTIONAL PROGRAM SHEET: Problem Solving

Generates Solutions

Child: _____ Date initiated: _____ Date completed: _____

Objective: When a problem arises, the child suggests a solution to the problem. For example, if the child's paper rips, he or she suggests getting tape to fix it.

Mastery criterion:
- 80% or higher correct response for each set
- Minimum of five opportunities per day
- 3 consecutive teaching days

Generalization:
People: At least two adults and peers
Settings: At least two settings
Materials: Across a variety of possible solutions

Things to consider: Use story examples and role-play to teach appropriate solutions. Visual cues may be used to prompt solutions or if the child is nonverbal, to use as an expressive way to suggest a solution.

Teaching sequence
1. Suggests at least one type of solution to a problem
2. Suggests another type of solution to a problem
3. Suggests another type of solution to a problem
4. Suggests a variety of solutions across different types of problems

PROGRAMMING LOG

	Acquisition		Generalization		Maintenance	
	Start date	End date	Start date	End date	Date/data	Date/data
1						
2						
3						
4						

LESSON PLAN: Problem Solving

Generates Solutions

Settings and materials	
Decontextualized	**Embedded**

Teaching
What direction or cue will you give?
How will you prompt the child's response?
Circle type of prompt(s) used:

Physical	Visual
Modeling	Verbal
Other: _____	

Circle prompt fading procedure used:

Time delay	Most to least
Graduated guidance	
Other: _____	

What is the child's response?
What reinforcers are you using?
What is the correction procedure?
How will you collect data? *(circle answer)*

Percentage correct	Frequency
Duration	Permanent product
Other: _____	

Sets

1. _____

_____

_____

_____

2. _____

_____

_____

_____

3. _____

_____

_____

_____

4. _____

_____

_____

_____

5. _____

_____

_____

_____

INSTRUCTIONAL PROGRAM SHEET: Problem Solving

Carries Out Solutions

Child: _____   Date initiated: _____   Date completed: _____

Objective: When a problem arises, the child carries out a suggested solution, or negotiates or compromises with a peer to solve a problem.

Mastery criterion:
- 80% or higher correct response for each set
- Minimum of five opportunities per day
- 3 consecutive teaching days

Generalization:
People: At least two adults and peers
Settings: At least two settings
Materials: Across at least five different types of problems

Things to consider: Use story examples and role-play to teach appropriate negotiating or compromising. Consider using visual supports that include choices for solutions.

Teaching sequence
1. Carries out the solution told by the adult
2. Negotiates or compromises with a peer to solve a problem
3. Negotiates or compromises with a peer to solve a problem and follows through with all parts of the solution

PROGRAMMING LOG

	Acquisition		Generalization		Maintenance	
	Start date	End date	Start date	End date	Date/data	Date/data
1						
2						
3						

LESSON PLAN: Problem Solving

Carries Out Solutions

Settings and materials	
Decontextualized	**Embedded**

Teaching
What direction or cue will you give?
How will you prompt the child's response?
Circle type of prompt(s) used:
Physical   Visual
Modeling   Verbal
Other: _____
Circle prompt fading procedure used:
Time delay   Most to least
Graduated guidance
Other: _____
What is the child's response?
What reinforcers are you using?
What is the correction procedure?
How will you collect data? *(circle answer)*
Percentage correct   Frequency
Duration   Permanent product
Other: _____

Sets

1. _____
   _____
   _____
   _____

2. _____
   _____
   _____
   _____

3. _____
   _____
   _____
   _____

4. _____
   _____
   _____
   _____

5. _____
   _____
   _____
   _____

INSTRUCTIONAL PROGRAM SHEET: Emotional Knowledge

Identifies Simple Emotions

Child: _____ Date initiated: _____ Date completed: _____

Objective: When presented with different emotions in pictures or books and asked, "Which one is [happy]?" the child receptively identifies the correct picture of the stated emotion by pointing to it or giving or tapping the correct picture. If asked to identify the emotion expressively ("How does she feel?"), the child states the correct emotion depicted in the picture.

Mastery criterion:
- 90% or higher correct response for each set
- Minimum of 10 opportunities per day
- 2 consecutive teaching days
- At least four different emotions

Generalization:
People: At least two adults and peers
Settings: At least two settings
Materials: Across at least five novel pictures of each emotion in pictures or books

Things to consider: Consider using line drawings, as well as images and pictures in books. May need to teach one emotion at a time.

Teaching sequence
1. Two emotions receptively
2. Two different emotions receptively
3. Two emotions expressively
4. Two different emotions expressively

PROGRAMMING LOG

	Acquisition		Generalization		Maintenance	
	Start date	End date	Start date	End date	Date/data	Date/data
1						
2						
3						
4						

The DATA Model for Teaching Preschoolers with Autism by Ilene Schwartz, Julie Ashmun, Bonnie McBride, Crista Scott, and Susan Sandall. Copyright © 2017 by Paul H. Brookes Publishing Co., Inc. All rights reserved.

LESSON PLAN: Emotional Knowledge

Identifies Simple Emotions

Settings and materials	
Decontextualized	**Embedded**

Teaching
What direction or cue will you give?
How will you prompt the child's response?
Circle type of prompt(s) used:
Physical   Visual
Modeling   Verbal
Other: _____
Circle prompt fading procedure used:
Time delay   Most to least
Graduated guidance
Other: _____
What is the child's response?
What reinforcers are you using?
What is the correction procedure?
How will you collect data? *(circle answer)*
Percentage correct   Frequency
Duration   Permanent product
Other: _____

Sets

1. _____

   _____

   _____

   _____

2. _____

   _____

   _____

   _____

3. _____

   _____

   _____

   _____

4. _____

   _____

   _____

   _____

5. _____

   _____

   _____

   _____

INSTRUCTIONAL PROGRAM SHEET: Emotional Knowledge

Labels and Identifies Emotions in Self

Child: _____ Date initiated: _____ Date completed: _____

Objective: When a child is exhibiting an identifiable emotion and asked, "How do you feel," the child accurately identifies his or her emotion either expressively or by pointing to or tapping a picture of the emotion.

Mastery criterion:
- 80% or higher correct response for each set
- Minimum of five opportunities per day
- 3 consecutive teaching days
- At least four emotions

Generalization:
People: At least two adults and peers
Settings: At least two settings
Materials: Across a variety of materials and situations

Things to consider: Child must exhibit an emotion to identify if he or she is correctly identifying the emotion. Consider an emotional regulation curriculum that teaches emotions on a scale, such as 1–3 (e.g., 1 is calm, 2 is excited, 3 is frustrated or really excited) or a color scale (e.g., blue is calm, orange is slightly elevated emotions, red is angry), or using both numbers and colors. Once child recognizes emotions, then pair the self-soothe strategy with the emotion using the visual cue.

Teaching sequence
1. Two emotions
2. Two different emotions

PROGRAMMING LOG

	Acquisition		Generalization		Maintenance	
	Start date	End date	Start date	End date	Date/data	Date/data
1						

The DATA Model for Teaching Preschoolers with Autism by Ilene Schwartz, Julie Ashmun, Bonnie McBride, Crista Scott, and Susan Sandall. Copyright © 2017 by Paul H. Brookes Publishing Co., Inc. All rights reserved.

LESSON PLAN: Emotional Knowledge

Labels and Identifies Emotions in Self

Settings and materials	
Decontextualized	**Embedded**

Teaching
What direction or cue will you give?
How will you prompt the child's response?
Circle type of prompt(s) used:
Physical   Visual
Modeling   Verbal
Other: _____
Circle prompt fading procedure used:
Time delay   Most to least
Graduated guidance
Other: _____
What is the child's response?
What reinforcers are you using?
What is the correction procedure?
How will you collect data? *(circle answer)*
Percentage correct   Frequency
Duration   Permanent product
Other: _____

Sets

1. _____
   _____
   _____
   _____

2. _____
   _____
   _____
   _____

3. _____
   _____
   _____
   _____

4. _____
   _____
   _____
   _____

5. _____
   _____
   _____
   _____

INSTRUCTIONAL PROGRAM SHEET: Emotional Knowledge

Labels and Identifies Emotions in Others

Child: _____ Date initiated: _____ Date completed: _____

Objective: When a peer or adult is exhibiting an identifiable emotion and the child is asked, "How does he or she feel," the child accurately identifies the emotion either expressively or by pointing to or tapping a picture of the emotion.

Mastery criterion:
- 80% or higher correct response for each set
- Minimum of five opportunities per day
- 3 consecutive teaching days
- At least four different emotions

Generalization:
People: At least two adults and peers
Settings: At least two settings
Materials: Across a variety of materials and situations

Things to consider: The child must be able to label the emotion before identifying it in others.

Teaching sequence
1. Two emotions
2. Two other emotions

PROGRAMMING LOG

	Acquisition		Generalization		Maintenance	
	Start date	End date	Start date	End date	Date/data	Date/data
1						
2						

LESSON PLAN: Emotional Knowledge

Labels and Identifies Emotions in Others

Settings and materials	
Decontextualized	**Embedded**

Teaching

What direction or cue will you give?

How will you prompt the child's response?

Circle type of prompt(s) used:

Physical	Visual
Modeling	Verbal

Other: _____

Circle prompt fading procedure used:

Time delay	Most to least
Graduated guidance	

Other: _____

What is the child's response?

What reinforcers are you using?

What is the correction procedure?

How will you collect data? *(circle answer)*

Percentage correct	Frequency
Duration	Permanent product

Other: _____

Sets

1. _____
   _____
   _____
   _____

2. _____
   _____
   _____
   _____

3. _____
   _____
   _____
   _____

4. _____
   _____
   _____
   _____

5. _____
   _____
   _____
   _____

INSTRUCTIONAL PROGRAM SHEET: Emotional Knowledge

Justifies an Emotion

Child: _____ Date initiated: _____ Date completed: _____

Objective: When a peer or adult is demonstrating an emotion in vivo or in pictures, the child identifies the emotion and then accurately suggests a reason for that emotion when asked, "Why does he or she feel ____?"

Mastery criterion:
- 90% or higher correct response for each set
- Minimum of 10 opportunities per day
- 2 consecutive teaching days
- At least four different emotions

Generalization:
People: At least two adults and peers
Settings: At least two settings
Materials: Across a variety of pictures and in vivo examples

Things to consider: Use pictures that indicate a context for the emotion. If a child or adult is demonstrating an emotion in vivo, be sure the child recognizes the context for that emotion in order to justify the reason for the emotion.

Teaching sequence
1. Two emotions across at least six different contexts
2. Two emotions across at least six different contexts

PROGRAMMING LOG

	Acquisition		Generalization		Maintenance	
	Start date	End date	Start date	End date	Date/data	Date/data
1						
2						

The DATA Model for Teaching Preschoolers with Autism by Ilene Schwartz, Julie Ashmun, Bonnie McBride, Crista Scott, and Susan Sandall. Copyright © 2017 by Paul H. Brookes Publishing Co., Inc. All rights reserved.

LESSON PLAN: Emotional Knowledge

Justifies an Emotion

Settings and materials	
Decontextualized	**Embedded**

Teaching
What direction or cue will you give?
How will you prompt the child's response?
Circle type of prompt(s) used:
Physical   Visual
Modeling   Verbal
Other: _____
Circle prompt fading procedure used:
Time delay   Most to least
Graduated guidance
Other: _____
What is the child's response?
What reinforcers are you using?
What is the correction procedure?
How will you collect data? *(circle answer)*
Percentage correct   Frequency
Duration   Permanent product
Other: _____

Sets

1. _____

_____

_____

_____

2. _____

_____

_____

_____

3. _____

_____

_____

_____

4. _____

_____

_____

_____

5. _____

_____

_____

_____

INSTRUCTIONAL PROGRAM SHEET: Emotional Knowledge

Demonstrates Affection and Empathy Toward Peers

Child: _____ Date initiated: _____ Date completed: _____

Objective: When a peer is demonstrating an emotion, the child demonstrates affection and empathy toward the peer. For example, the child gives the peer a hug if the peer is happy or asks if the peer is okay if the peer is sad or hurt.

Mastery criterion:
- 80% or higher correct response for each set
- Minimum of five opportunities per day
- 3 consecutive teaching days
- Across at least two different emotions/situations

Generalization:
People: At least two adults and peers
Settings: At least two settings
Materials: Across a variety of contexts and emotional situations

Things to consider: If another child is reaching mastery of Item 2.2 (Accepts Comfort from Others), then pair this child with that peer for teaching. Teach how children may respond to another child's emotion with storytelling and role-play.

Teaching sequence
1. Responds to one type of emotion across one peer
2. Responds to another type of emotion across at least two peers

PROGRAMMING LOG

	Acquisition		Generalization		Maintenance	
	Start date	End date	Start date	End date	Date/data	Date/data
1						
2						

The DATA Model for Teaching Preschoolers with Autism by Ilene Schwartz, Julie Ashmun, Bonnie McBride, Crista Scott, and Susan Sandall. Copyright © 2017 by Paul H. Brookes Publishing Co., Inc. All rights reserved.

LESSON PLAN: Emotional Knowledge

Demonstrates Affection and Empathy Toward Peers

Settings and materials	
Decontextualized	**Embedded**

Teaching
What direction or cue will you give?
How will you prompt the child's response?
Circle type of prompt(s) used:
Physical   Visual
Modeling   Verbal
Other: _____
Circle prompt fading procedure used:
Time delay   Most to least
Graduated guidance
Other: _____
What is the child's response?
What reinforcers are you using?
What is the correction procedure?
How will you collect data? *(circle answer)*
Percentage correct   Frequency
Duration   Permanent product
Other: _____

Sets

1. _____
   _____
   _____
   _____

2. _____
   _____
   _____
   _____

3. _____
   _____
   _____
   _____

4. _____
   _____
   _____
   _____

5. _____
   _____
   _____
   _____

INSTRUCTIONAL PROGRAM SHEET: Imitation

Imitates Actions with Objects

Child: _____   Date initiated: _____   Date completed: _____

Objective: When presented with an object and told, "Do this," "Copy me," or "Do what I'm doing," the child imitates the adult's actions with the same objects.

Mastery criterion:
- 90% or higher correct response for each set
- 2 consecutive teaching days
- Minimum of 10 opportunities per day

Generalization:
People: At least two adults
Settings: At least two settings
Materials: At least five novel actions with novel toys

Things to consider: Child may be sensitive to noise-producing objects; consider using objects that are interesting or motivating to the child.

Teaching sequence
1. Actions you have seen the child perform with an object (i.e., in an unstructured setting, what actions have you seen the child make on objects?)
2. Imitates five adult actions with noise-producing objects (e.g., maracas, rhythm sticks, hammer on table)
3. Imitates five adult actions with toys (e.g., pushes car or train, feeds baby, stacks block)
4. Imitates five novel actions not used in previous sets

PROGRAMMING LOG

	Acquisition		Generalization		Maintenance	
	Start date	End date	Start date	End date	Date/data	Date/data
1						
2						
3						
4						

INSTRUCTIONAL PROGRAM SHEET: Imitation

Imitates Actions with Objects

Settings and materials	
Decontextualized	**Embedded**

Teaching

What direction or cue will you give?

How will you prompt the child's response?

Circle type of prompt(s) used:

Physical	Visual
Modeling	Verbal

Other: _____

Circle prompt fading procedure used:

Time delay	Most to least
Graduated guidance	

Other: _____

What is the child's response?

What reinforcers are you using?

What is the correction procedure?

How will you collect data? *(circle answer)*

Percentage correct	Frequency
Duration	Permanent product

Other: _____

Sets

1. _____

_____

_____

_____

2. _____

_____

_____

_____

3. _____

_____

_____

_____

4. _____

_____

_____

_____

5. _____

_____

_____

_____

INSTRUCTIONAL PROGRAM SHEET: Imitation

Imitates Actions with Objects—Example

Child: _____   Date initiated: _____   Date completed: _____

Objective: When presented with an object and told, "Do this," "Copy me," or "Do what I'm doing," the child imitates the adult's actions with the same objects.

Mastery criterion:
- 90% or higher correct response for each set
- Minimum of 10 opportunities per day
- 2 consecutive teaching days

Generalization:
People: At least two adults
Settings: At least two settings
Materials: At least five novel actions with novel toys

Things to consider: Child may be sensitive to noise-producing objects; consider using objects that are interesting or motivating to the child.

Teaching sequence
1. Actions you have seen the child perform with an object (i.e., in an unstructured setting, what actions have you seen the child make on objects?)
2. Imitates five adult actions with noise-producing objects (e.g., maracas, rhythm sticks, hammer on table)
3. Imitates five adult actions with toys (e.g., pushes car or train, feeds baby, stacks blocks)
4. Imitates five novel actions not used in previous sets

PROGRAMMING LOG

	Acquisition		Generalization		Maintenance	
	Start date	End date	Start date	End date	Date/data	Date/data
1	9/10/14	9/30/14	10/2/14	10/5/14	12/5/14; 100%	2/5/15; 100%
2	10/2/14	10/15/14	11/16/14	11/20/14	1/5/15; 100%	3/5/15; 100%
3	10/16/14	11/20/14	11/25/14	12/5/14	1/5/15; 100%	3/5/15; 80%
4	12/2/14	1/15/15	1/16/15	1/25/15	2/25/15; 80%	4/25/15; 100%

LESSON PLAN: Imitation

Imitates Actions with Objects

Settings and materials	
Decontextualized	**Embedded**
Work on skill in work area with objects for each set	Provide instruction during classroom activities, such as free play with objects the child has used in the decontextualized setting

Teaching
What direction or cue will you give?
"Do this" "Copy me" "Do what I'm/he/she's doing"
How will you prompt the child's response?
Circle type of prompt(s) used:

(Physical)	Visual
Modeling	Verbal
Other: _____	

Circle prompt fading procedure used:

Time delay	(Most to least)
Graduated guidance	
Other: _____	

What is the child's response?

Imitates the actions with the objects

What reinforcers are you using?

Praise and access to preferred item

What is the correction procedure?

Provide instruction with prompt for successful response

How will you collect data? *(circle answer)*

(Percentage correct)	Frequency
Duration	Permanent product
Other: _____	

Sets

1. Puts block in bucket
   Stirs spoon in bowl
   Puts cup to mouth
   Marks on paper
   Pushes car

2. Shakes maraca
   Hammers block
   Taps together rhythm sticks
   Pushes button on pop up toy
   Puts piece in noise producing toy (i.e., shape sorter)

3. Feeds baby
   Puts train on train track
   Pushes train on train track
   Puts figurine in play house or farm
   Stacks two identical blocks

4. Novel actions during play

INSTRUCTIONAL PROGRAM SHEET: Imitation

Imitates Large Motor Movements

Child: _____   Date initiated: _____   Date completed: _____

Objective: When an adult performs an action and says, "Do this," "Copy me," or "Do what I'm doing," the child imitates the adult's large motor movement.

Mastery criterion:
- 90% or higher correct response for each set
- Minimum of 10 opportunities per day
- 2 consecutive teaching days

Generalization:
People: At least two adults
Settings: At least two settings
Materials: At least five novel actions

Things to consider: For some children, it is helpful to use a mirror so that the child can see the adult and himself or herself performing the action.

Teaching sequence
1. Actions you have seen the child perform (e.g., clap hands, tap head)
2. Imitates five adult actions that are visible to the child (e.g., wave, clap hands, tap legs)
3. Imitates five adult actions that are not visible to the child (e.g., arms up, shake head "no," touch nose)
4. Imitates five novel actions not used in previous sets

PROGRAMMING LOG

	Acquisition		Generalization		Maintenance	
	Start date	End date	Start date	End date	Date/data	Date/data
1						
2						
3						
4						

LESSON PLAN: Imitation

Imitates Large Motor Movements

Settings and materials	
Decontextualized	**Embedded**

Teaching
What direction or cue will you give?
How will you prompt the child's response?
Circle type of prompt(s) used:
Physical   Visual
Modeling   Verbal
Other: _____
Circle prompt fading procedure used:
Time delay   Most to least
Graduated guidance
Other: _____
What is the child's response?
What reinforcers are you using?
What is the correction procedure?
How will you collect data? *(circle answer)*
Percentage correct   Frequency
Duration   Permanent product
Other: _____

Sets

1. _____

_____

_____

_____

2. _____

_____

_____

_____

3. _____

_____

_____

_____

4. _____

_____

_____

_____

5. _____

_____

_____

_____

INSTRUCTIONAL PROGRAM SHEET: Imitation

Imitates Fine Motor Movements

Child: _____ Date initiated: _____ Date completed: _____

Objective: When an adult performs an action and says, "Do this," "Copy me," or "Do what I'm doing," the child imitates the adult's fine motor movement.

Mastery criterion:
- 90% or higher correct response for each set
- Minimum of 10 opportunities per day
- 2 consecutive teaching days

Generalization:
People: At least two adults
Settings: At least two settings
Materials: At least five novel actions

Things to consider: Some children may have an aversion to touch certain textures. Use items that are interesting or motivating to the child.

Teaching sequence
1. Actions you have seen the child perform (e.g., using a pincer grasp, point)
2. Imitates five actions on objects (e.g., pinch, pull, twist)
3. Imitates five actions with hands (e.g., open and close hands, wiggle fingers, thumbs up)
4. Imitates five novel actions not used in previous sets

PROGRAMMING LOG

	Acquisition		Generalization		Maintenance	
	Start date	End date	Start date	End date	Date/data	Date/data
1						
2						
3						
4						

LESSON PLAN: Imitation

Imitates Fine Motor Movements

Settings and materials	
Decontextualized	**Embedded**

Teaching
What direction or cue will you give?
How will you prompt the child's response?
Circle type of prompt(s) used:

Physical   Visual

Modeling   Verbal

Other: _____

Circle prompt fading procedure used:

Time delay   Most to least

Graduated guidance

Other: _____

What is the child's response?
What reinforcers are you using?
What is the correction procedure?
How will you collect data? *(circle answer)*

Percentage correct   Frequency

Duration   Permanent product

Other: _____

Sets

1. _____
   _____
   _____
   _____

2. _____
   _____
   _____
   _____

3. _____
   _____
   _____
   _____

4. _____
   _____
   _____
   _____

5. _____
   _____
   _____
   _____

INSTRUCTIONAL PROGRAM SHEET: Imitation

Imitates Sounds and Words

Child: _____   Date initiated: _____   Date completed: _____

Objective: When told, "Say ____" or "Copy me," the child imitates the adult's sounds or words.

Mastery criterion:
- 90% or higher correct approximation of the sound or word
- Minimum of 10 opportunities per day
- 2 consecutive teaching days

Generalization:
People: At least two adults
Settings: At least two settings
Materials: At least five novel sounds/words

Things to consider: Consider the child's oral-motor ability and accept approximations; consult with a speech language pathologist.
Exercises or activities to increase vocalizations from the child include:
- When the child makes a speech sound, imitate him.
- When playing, make sounds associated with certain toys—slide a snake and say "ssss," roll a car and say "vroom, vroom," play with animals and make animal sounds, or push train and say "choo, choo."
- When singing a song or rhyme, pause and wait for the child to fill in the next word or sound.

Teaching sequence
1. Imitates a sound you have heard the child make
2. Imitates novel sounds
3. Imitates familiar words
4. Imitates novel words
5. Spontaneously imitates words or phrases

PROGRAMMING LOG

	Acquisition		Generalization		Maintenance	
	Start date	End date	Start date	End date	Date/data	Date/data
1						
2						
3						
4						
5						

LESSON PLAN: Imitation

Imitates Sounds and Words

Settings and materials	
Decontextualized	**Embedded**

Teaching
What direction or cue will you give?
How will you prompt the child's response?
Circle type of prompt(s) used:
Physical   Visual
Modeling   Verbal
Other: _____
Circle prompt fading procedure used:
Time delay   Most to least
Graduated guidance
Other: _____
What is the child's response?
What reinforcers are you using?
What is the correction procedure?
How will you collect data? *(circle answer)*
Percentage correct   Frequency
Duration   Permanent product
Other: _____

Sets

1. _____
   _____
   _____
   _____

2. _____
   _____
   _____
   _____

3. _____
   _____
   _____
   _____

4. _____
   _____
   _____
   _____

5. _____
   _____
   _____
   _____

INSTRUCTIONAL PROGRAM SHEET: Imitation

Imitates Multistep Sequences

Child: _____ Date initiated: _____ Date completed: _____

Objective: While an adult performs a sequence of actions in a group setting, the child imitates the multistep actions or phrases.

Mastery criterion:
- 80% or higher correct response for each set
- 2 consecutive teaching days
- Minimum of five opportunities per day
- At least five, three-step sequences

Generalization:
People: At least two adults
Settings: At least two settings
Materials: At least five novel sequences

Things to consider: Invite peers to join in the activity.

Teaching sequence
1. Imitates a three-step sequence of actions you have seen the child perform
2. Imitates a three-step sequence from familiar preschool songs (e.g., *Head, Shoulders, Knees, and Toes*)
3. Imitates a three-part phrase from a familiar rhyme, saying, or story (e.g., *Ready, set, go*)
4. Imitates at least five novel three-step sequences

PROGRAMMING LOG

	Acquisition		Generalization		Maintenance	
	Start date	End date	Start date	End date	Date/data	Date/data
1						
2						
3						
4						

LESSON PLAN: Imitation

Imitates Multistep Sequences

Settings and materials	
Decontextualized	**Embedded**

Teaching
What direction or cue will you give?
How will you prompt the child's response?
Circle type of prompt(s) used:
Physical   Visual
Modeling   Verbal
Other: _____
Circle prompt fading procedure used:
Time delay   Most to least
Graduated guidance
Other: _____
What is the child's response?
What reinforcers are you using?
What is the correction procedure?
How will you collect data? *(circle answer)*
Percentage correct   Frequency
Duration   Permanent product
Other: _____

Sets

1. _____
   _____
   _____
   _____

2. _____
   _____
   _____
   _____

3. _____
   _____
   _____
   _____

4. _____
   _____
   _____
   _____

5. _____
   _____
   _____
   _____

INSTRUCTIONAL PROGRAM SHEET: Matching and Categorizing

Matches Identical Objects

Child: _____   Date initiated: _____   Date completed: _____

Objective: When presented with an array of identical objects, given a corresponding object, and told "Put with same" or "Match," the child matches the identical objects.

Mastery criterion:
- 90% or higher correct response for each set
- Minimum of 10 opportunities per day
- At least eight sets of identical objects
- 2 consecutive teaching days

Generalization:
People: At least two adults
Settings: At least two settings
Materials: At least three novel objects

Things to consider: To begin, use toys that the child is interested in or that the child likes. However, do not use toys that are highly motivating as they can be too distracting. If needed, start first by teaching to match one object to one object, then add a distractor and increase the field of items to match to three.

Teaching sequence
1. Matches at least three identical objects that nest (e.g., cups, bowls, plates)
2. Matches at least three other identical objects (e.g., cars, blocks, balls)
3. Matches at least two other identical objects

PROGRAMMING LOG

	Acquisition		Generalization		Maintenance	
	Start date	End date	Start date	End date	Date/data	Date/data
1						
2						
3						

The DATA Model for Teaching Preschoolers with Autism by Ilene Schwartz, Julie Ashmun, Bonnie McBride, Crista Scott, and Susan Sandall. Copyright © 2017 by Paul H. Brookes Publishing Co., Inc. All rights reserved.

LESSON PLAN: Matching and Categorizing

Matches Identical Objects

Settings and materials	
Decontextualized	**Embedded**

Teaching

What direction or cue will you give?

How will you prompt the child's response?

Circle type of prompt(s) used:

Physical	Visual
Modeling	Verbal

Other: _____

Circle prompt fading procedure used:

Time delay	Most to least
Graduated guidance	

Other: _____

What is the child's response?

What reinforcers are you using?

What is the correction procedure?

How will you collect data? *(circle answer)*

Percentage correct	Frequency
Duration	Permanent product

Other: _____

Sets

1. _____

_____

_____

_____

2. _____

_____

_____

_____

3. _____

_____

_____

_____

4. _____

_____

_____

_____

5. _____

_____

_____

_____

INSTRUCTIONAL PROGRAM SHEET: Matching and Categorizing

Matches Identical Pictures

Child: _____ Date initiated: _____ Date completed: _____

Objective: When presented with an array of identical pictures, given a corresponding picture, and told "Put with same" or "Match," the child matches the pictures.

Mastery criterion:
- 90% or higher correct response for each set
- 2 consecutive teaching days
- Minimum of 10 opportunities per day
- At least eight sets of identical pictures

Generalization:
People: At least two adults
Settings: At least two settings
Materials: At least three novel pictures

Things to consider: To begin, use pictures of items that the child is interested in or that the child likes. However, do not use pictures that are highly motivating as they can be too distracting. If needed, start first by teaching to match one picture to one picture, then add a distractor and increase the field of items to match to three.

Teaching sequence
1. Matches at least three identical pictures from an array of three
2. Matches at least three identical pictures from an array of three
3. Matches at least three identical pictures from an array of three

PROGRAMMING LOG

	Acquisition		Generalization		Maintenance	
	Start date	End date	Start date	End date	Date/data	Date/data
1						
2						
3						

LESSON PLAN: Matching and Categorizing

Matches Identical Pictures

III. COGNITIVE

Settings and materials	
Decontextualized	Embedded

Teaching

What direction or cue will you give?

How will you prompt the child's response?

Circle type of prompt(s) used:

Physical   Visual

Modeling   Verbal

Other: _____

Circle prompt fading procedure used:

Time delay   Most to least

Graduated guidance

Other: _____

What is the child's response?

What reinforcers are you using?

What is the correction procedure?

How will you collect data? *(circle answer)*

Percentage correct   Frequency

Duration   Permanent product

Other: _____

Sets

1. _____

2. _____

3. _____

4. _____

5. _____

LESSON PLAN: Matching and Categorizing

Matches Identical Pictures

Settings and materials	
Decontextualized	Embedded

Teaching

What direction or cue will you give?

How will you prompt the child's response?

Circle type of prompt(s) used:

Physical   Visual

Modeling   Verbal

Other: _____

Circle prompt fading procedure used:

Time delay   Most to least

Graduated guidance

Other: _____

What is the child's response?

What reinforcers are you using?

What is the correction procedure?

How will you collect data? *(circle answer)*

Percentage correct   Frequency

Duration   Permanent product

Other: _____

Sets

1. _____

2. _____

3. _____

4. _____

5. _____

III. COGNITIVE

INSTRUCTIONAL PROGRAM SHEET: Matching and Categorizing

Matches Objects to Pictures

Child: _____ Date initiated: _____ Date completed: _____

Objective: When presented with an array of pictures, given an object that matches one of the pictures and told "Put with same" or "Match," the child matches the object to the identical picture.

Mastery criterion:
- 90% or higher correct response for each set
- 2 consecutive teaching days
- Minimum of 10 opportunities per day
- At least eight sets of objects to pictures

Generalization:
People: At least two adults
Settings: At least two settings
Materials: At least five novel identical objects and pictures

Things to consider: To begin, use items that the child is interested in, or that the child likes. However, do not use objects that are highly motivating as they can be too distracting. If needed, start first by teaching to match one object to a picture, then add a distractor and increase the field of items to three.

Teaching sequence
1. Matches at least three identical objects to pictures from an array of three
2. Matches at least three identical objects to pictures from an array of three
3. Matches at least three identical objects to pictures from an array of three

PROGRAMMING LOG

	Acquisition		Generalization		Maintenance	
	Start date	End date	Start date	End date	Date/data	Date/data
1						
2						
3						

The DATA Model for Teaching Preschoolers with Autism by Ilene Schwartz, Julie Ashmun, Bonnie McBride, Crista Scott, and Susan Sandall. Copyright © 2017 by Paul H. Brookes Publishing Co., Inc. All rights reserved.

LESSON PLAN: Matching and Categorizing

Matches Objects to Pictures

Settings and materials	
Decontextualized	**Embedded**

Teaching

What direction or cue will you give?

How will you prompt the child's response?

Circle type of prompt(s) used:

Physical   Visual

Modeling   Verbal

Other: _____

Circle prompt fading procedure used:

Time delay   Most to least

Graduated guidance

Other: _____

What is the child's response?

What reinforcers are you using?

What is the correction procedure?

How will you collect data? *(circle answer)*

Percentage correct   Frequency

Duration   Permanent product

Other: _____

Sets

1. _____

2. _____

3. _____

4. _____

5. _____

INSTRUCTIONAL PROGRAM SHEET: Matching and Categorizing

Matches Pictures to Objects

Child: _____ Date initiated: _____ Date completed: _____

Objective: When presented with an array of objects, given a corresponding picture, and told "Put with same" or "Match," the child matches the picture to the identical object.

Mastery criterion:
- ▪ 90% or higher correct response for each set
- ▪ 2 consecutive teaching days
- ▪ Minimum of 10 opportunities per day

Generalization:
People: At least two adults
Settings: At least two settings
Materials: At least five novel identical pictures and objects

Things to consider: To begin, use items that the child is interested in, or that the child likes. However, do not use objects that are highly motivating as they can be too distracting. If needed, start first by teaching to match one picture to an object, then add a distractor and increase the field of objects to three.

Teaching sequence
1. Matches at least three identical pictures to objects from an array of three
2. Matches at least three identical pictures to objects from an array of three
3. Matches at least three identical pictures to objects from an array of three

PROGRAMMING LOG

	Acquisition		Generalization		Maintenance	
	Start date	End date	Start date	End date	Date/data	Date/data
1						
2						
3						

LESSON PLAN: Matching and Categorizing

Matches Pictures to Objects

Settings and materials	
Decontextualized	**Embedded**

Teaching

What direction or cue will you give?

How will you prompt the child's response?

Circle type of prompt(s) used:

Physical	Visual
Modeling	Verbal

Other: _____

Circle prompt fading procedure used:

Time delay	Most to least
Graduated guidance	

Other: _____

What is the child's response?

What reinforcers are you using?

What is the correction procedure?

How will you collect data? *(circle answer)*

Percentage correct	Frequency
Duration	Permanent product

Other: _____

Sets

1. _____
_____
_____
_____

2. _____
_____
_____
_____

3. _____
_____
_____
_____

4. _____
_____
_____
_____

5. _____
_____
_____
_____

INSTRUCTIONAL PROGRAM SHEET: Matching and Categorizing

Matches Nonidentical Objects and Pictures

Child: _____ Date initiated: _____ Date completed: _____

Objective: When presented with an array of objects or pictures, given a picture or object that matches one from the array and told, "Put with same" or "Match," the child matches the nonidentical object or picture.

Mastery criterion:
- 90% or higher correct response for each set
- 2 consecutive teaching days
- Minimum of 10 opportunities per day
- At least eight sets of non-identical objects or pictures

Generalization:
People: At least two adults
Settings: At least two settings
Materials: At least three novel objects and three novel pictures

Things to consider: To begin, use items that the child is interested in, or that the child likes. However, do not use objects or pictures that are highly motivating as they can be too distracting. If needed, start first by teaching to match one picture to a picture or one object to an object, then add a distractor and increase the field of items to three.

Teaching sequence
1. Matches objects to objects (e.g., red car to blue car, yellow crayon to green crayon)
2. Matches pictures to pictures (e.g., tabby cat to black cat, tall water bottle to stout water bottle)

PROGRAMMING LOG

	Acquisition		Generalization		Maintenance	
	Start date	End date	Start date	End date	Date/data	Date/data
1						
2						

LESSON PLAN: Matching and Categorizing

Matches Nonidentical Objects and Pictures

Settings and materials	
Decontextualized	**Embedded**

Teaching
What direction or cue will you give?
How will you prompt the child's response?
Circle type of prompt(s) used:
Physical   Visual
Modeling   Verbal
Other: _____
Circle prompt fading procedure used:
Time delay   Most to least
Graduated guidance
Other: _____
What is the child's response?
What reinforcers are you using?
What is the correction procedure?
How will you collect data? *(circle answer)*
Percentage correct   Frequency
Duration   Permanent product
Other: _____

Sets

1. _____
   _____
   _____
   _____

2. _____
   _____
   _____
   _____

3. _____
   _____
   _____
   _____

4. _____
   _____
   _____
   _____

5. _____
   _____
   _____
   _____

INSTRUCTIONAL PROGRAM SHEET: Matching and Categorizing

Groups Objects According to Size, Shape, and Color

Child: _____ Date initiated: _____ Date completed: _____

Objective: When presented with an array of objects that can be grouped by size, shape or color, given a corresponding object, and told "Put with same" or "Match," the child groups, or matches, the objects according to size, shape, and color.

Mastery criterion:
- 90% or higher correct response for each set
- 2 consecutive teaching days
- Minimum of 10 opportunities per day
- At least three different sizes, six different shapes, and six different colors

Generalization:
People: At least two adults
Settings: At least two settings
Materials: At least five novel objects by size, shape, and color

Things to consider: Choose objects in which the attribute is salient. Consider using a visual prompt when initially teaching the skill. For example, when sorting by color, the child places the colored objects on colored pieces of paper.

Teaching sequence
1. Groups at least five items of each when given three different sizes (e.g., small, medium, and large)
2. Groups at least five items of each when given three different shapes (e.g., circle, triangle, square)
3. Groups at least five items of each when given three different shapes (e.g., rectangle, oval, diamond)
4. Groups at least five items of each when given three different colors (e.g., red, blue, yellow)
5. Groups at least five items of each when given three different colors (e.g. green, purple, orange)

PROGRAMMING LOG

	Acquisition		Generalization		Maintenance	
	Start date	End date	Start date	End date	Date/data	Date/data
1						
2						
3						
4						
5						

LESSON PLAN: Matching and Categorizing

Groups Objects According to Size, Shape, and Color

<table>
<tr><th colspan="2">Settings and materials</th></tr>
<tr><th>Decontextualized</th><th>Embedded</th></tr>
<tr><td></td><td></td></tr>
</table>

Teaching
What direction or cue will you give?
How will you prompt the child's response?
Circle type of prompt(s) used:

Physical	Visual
Modeling	Verbal
Other: _____	

Circle prompt fading procedure used:

Time delay	Most to least
Graduated guidance	
Other: _____	

What is the child's response?
What reinforcers are you using?
What is the correction procedure?
How will you collect data? *(circle answer)*

Percentage correct	Frequency
Duration	Permanent product
Other: _____	

Sets

1. _____

   _____

   _____

   _____

2. _____

   _____

   _____

   _____

3. _____

   _____

   _____

   _____

4. _____

   _____

   _____

   _____

5. _____

   _____

   _____

   _____

INSTRUCTIONAL PROGRAM SHEET: Matching and Categorizing

Groups Functionally Related Objects

Child: _____ Date initiated: _____ Date completed: _____

Objective: When presented with an array of pictures or objects that can be grouped by function, given a corresponding picture or object, and told "Put with same" or "Match," the child groups the functionally related items.

Mastery criterion:
- 90% or higher correct response for each set
- 2 consecutive teaching days
- Minimum of 10 opportunities per day
- At least 10 functionally related objects or pictures

Generalization:
People: At least two adults
Settings: At least two settings
Materials: At least three novel objects or pictures for each match/group

Things to consider: Choose objects that are of interest or familiar to the child.

Teaching sequence
1. Matches at least five groups of functionally related objects or pictures (e.g., paint brush to paint, bucket to shovel, toothbrush to toothpaste).
2. Groups at least five functionally related objects or pictures (e.g., paint brush, paint, water; toothbrush, toothpaste, faucet; bucket, shovel, sand)

PROGRAMMING LOG

	Acquisition		Generalization		Maintenance	
	Start date	End date	Start date	End date	Date/data	Date/data
1						
2						

The DATA Model for Teaching Preschoolers with Autism by Ilene Schwartz, Julie Ashmun, Bonnie McBride, Crista Scott, and Susan Sandall. Copyright © 2017 by Paul H. Brookes Publishing Co., Inc. All rights reserved.

LESSON PLAN: Matching and Categorizing

Groups Functionally Related Objects

Settings and materials	
Decontextualized	**Embedded**

Teaching
What direction or cue will you give?
How will you prompt the child's response?
Circle type of prompt(s) used:
Physical   Visual
Modeling   Verbal
Other: _____
Circle prompt fading procedure used:
Time delay   Most to least
Graduated guidance
Other: _____
What is the child's response?
What reinforcers are you using?
What is the correction procedure?
How will you collect data? *(circle answer)*
Percentage correct   Frequency
Duration   Permanent product
Other: _____

Sets

1. _____
_____
_____
_____

2. _____
_____
_____
_____

3. _____
_____
_____
_____

4. _____
_____
_____
_____

5. _____
_____
_____
_____

INSTRUCTIONAL PROGRAM SHEET: Matching and Categorizing

Categorizes Like Objects

Child: _____ Date initiated: _____ Date completed: _____

Objective: When presented with an array of pictures or objects that can be grouped by categories, given one corresponding picture or object, and told "Put with same" or "Match," the child groups, or categorizes the items.

Mastery criterion:
- 90% or higher correct response for each set
- 2 consecutive teaching days
- Minimum of 10 opportunities per day
- At least six different categories

Generalization:
People: At least two adults
Settings: At least two settings
Materials: At least three new items not previously taught for each category

Things to consider: To begin, use objects that the child is interested in, or that the child likes. However, do not use objects that are highly motivating as they can be too distracting. If needed, start first by teaching to match one object to one object, then add a distractor and increase the field of items to match to three.

Teaching sequence
1. Groups at least three objects or pictures together according to a broad-based category and across three categories (e.g., animals, food, clothing)
2. Groups at least three objects/pictures together according to a broad-based category and across three categories (e.g., vehicles, toys, furniture)

PROGRAMMING LOG

	Acquisition		Generalization		Maintenance	
	Start date	End date	Start date	End date	Date/data	Date/data
1						
2						

LESSON PLAN: Matching and Categorizing

Categorizes Like Objects

Settings and materials	
Decontextualized	**Embedded**

Teaching
What direction or cue will you give?
How will you prompt the child's response?
Circle type of prompt(s) used:

Physical	Visual
Modeling	Verbal
Other: _____	

Circle prompt fading procedure used:

Time delay	Most to least
Graduated guidance	
Other: _____	

What is the child's response?

What reinforcers are you using?

What is the correction procedure?

How will you collect data? *(circle answer)*

Percentage correct	Frequency
Duration	Permanent product
Other: _____	

Sets

1. _____

_____

_____

_____

2. _____

_____

_____

_____

3. _____

_____

_____

_____

4. _____

_____

_____

_____

5. _____

_____

_____

_____

INSTRUCTIONAL PROGRAM SHEET: Sequencing

Makes Simple Patterns

Child: _____ Date initiated: _____ Date completed: _____

Objective: When presented with materials that can be used to make simple ABAB patterns, the child creates patterns.

Mastery criterion:
- 80% or higher correct response for each set
- 3 consecutive teaching days
- Minimum of five opportunities per day
- At least six patterns

Generalization:
People: At least two adults
Settings: At least two settings
Materials: At least three sets of novel materials

Things to consider: Use objects that won't be too distracting, are easy to line up, and fit in the space you are teaching.

Teaching sequence
1. Reproduces (copies) ABAB pattern
2. Extends ABAB pattern (i.e., adds next ABAB to the pattern created by teacher)
3. Creates ABAB patterns

PROGRAMMING LOG

	Acquisition		Generalization		Maintenance	
	Start date	End date	Start date	End date	Date/data	Date/data
1						
2						
3						

LESSON PLAN: Sequencing

Makes Simple Patterns

Settings and materials	
Decontextualized	**Embedded**

Teaching
What direction or cue will you give?
How will you prompt the child's response?
Circle type of prompt(s) used:
Physical   Visual
Modeling   Verbal
Other: _____
Circle prompt fading procedure used:
Time delay   Most to least
Graduated guidance
Other: _____
What is the child's response?
What reinforcers are you using?
What is the correction procedure?
How will you collect data? *(circle answer)*
Percentage correct   Frequency
Duration   Permanent product
Other: _____

Sets

1. _____
_____
_____
_____

2. _____
_____
_____
_____

3. _____
_____
_____
_____

4. _____
_____
_____
_____

5. _____
_____
_____
_____

INSTRUCTIONAL PROGRAM SHEET: Sequencing

Places Objects from a Continuum in Order

Child: _____ Date initiated: _____ Date completed: _____

Objective: When presented with at least three items that can be put in sequential order, and told "Put these in order" or "Put these in order from ___ to ___," the child sequences the items.

Mastery criterion:
- 80% or higher correct response for each set
- 3 consecutive teaching days
- Minimum of five opportunities per day

Generalization:
People: At least two adults
Settings: At least two settings
Materials: At least three sets of novel materials

Things to consider: Use objects that won't be too distracting, that are easy to line up and which fit in the space you are teaching in.

Teaching sequence
1. Stacks nesting items
2. Orders items from biggest to smallest
3. Orders items from smallest to biggest
4. Orders items from longest to shortest
5. Orders items from shortest to longest
6. Orders items from part to whole (e.g., a series of pictures with parts of a house might start with one part of a house and each subsequent picture adds a part of the house until the last picture is the most whole, or complete image)

PROGRAMMING LOG

	Acquisition		Generalization		Maintenance	
	Start date	End date	Start date	End date	Date/data	Date/data
1						
2						
3						
4						
5						
6						

LESSON PLAN: Sequencing

Places Objects from a Continuum in Order

Settings and materials	
Decontextualized	**Embedded**

Teaching
What direction or cue will you give?
How will you prompt the child's response?
Circle type of prompt(s) used:
Physical   Visual
Modeling   Verbal
Other: _____
Circle prompt fading procedure used:
Time delay   Most to least
Graduated guidance
Other: _____
What is the child's response?
What reinforcers are you using?
What is the correction procedure?
How will you collect data? *(circle answer)*
Percentage correct   Frequency
Duration   Permanent product
Other: _____

Sets

1. _____

_____

_____

_____

2. _____

_____

_____

_____

3. _____

_____

_____

_____

4. _____

_____

_____

_____

5. _____

_____

_____

_____

INSTRUCTIONAL PROGRAM SHEET: Sequencing

Sequences Pictures to Tell a Story

Child: _____   Date initiated: _____   Date completed: _____

Objective: When presented with pictures that depict a sequence, and told, "Put these in order" or "Show me the story," the child orders the pictures from first to last.

Mastery criterion:
- 80% or higher correct response for each set
- 3 consecutive teaching days
- Minimum of five opportunities per day
- At least six sequences

Generalization:
People: At least two adults
Settings: At least two settings
Materials: At least three sets of novel sequences

Things to consider: Use pictures of stories or events in which the child has shown interest or is familiar.

Teaching sequence
1. Orders cause-and-effect pictures
2. Puts at least three pictures in order that depict a social sequence (e.g., washing hands, brushing teeth)
3. Puts at least three pictures in order that depict a story (e.g., person building a snowman, Goldilocks and the Three Bears)
4. Puts at least four pictures in order that depict a social sequence (can be same as above but add a new picture in the middle of the sequence)
5. Puts at least four pictures in order that depict a story (can be same as above but add a new picture in the middle of the sequence)
6. Continue to add up to five pictures, as is age appropriate.

PROGRAMMING LOG

	Acquisition		Generalization		Maintenance	
	Start date	End date	Start date	End date	Date/data	Date/data
1						
2						
3						
4						
5						
6						

LESSON PLAN: Sequencing

Sequences Pictures to Tell a Story

Settings and materials	
Decontextualized	**Embedded**

Teaching
What direction or cue will you give?
How will you prompt the child's response?
Circle type of prompt(s) used:
Physical   Visual
Modeling   Verbal
Other: _____
Circle prompt fading procedure used:
Time delay   Most to least
Graduated guidance
Other: _____
What is the child's response?
What reinforcers are you using?
What is the correction procedure?
How will you collect data? *(circle answer)*
Percentage correct   Frequency
Duration   Permanent product
Other: _____

Sets

1. _____

2. _____

3. _____

4. _____

5. _____

INSTRUCTIONAL PROGRAM SHEET: Sequencing

Recalls and Retells Past Events

Child: _____ Date initiated: _____ Date completed: _____

Objective: When asked, "Tell me what happened (during free choice)?" or "What did you do (when you visited Grandma)," the child recalls the event and tells about the event in the correct order.

Mastery criterion:
- 80% or higher correct response
- Minimum of five opportunities per day
- 3 consecutive teaching days

Generalization:
People: At least two adults
Settings: At least two settings
Materials: At least two new events with at least three details retold in order

Things to consider: It might be helpful to ask family members about recent events or other staff members at school so you have correct knowledge about recently occurring events in the child's life.

Teaching sequence
1. Recalls and retells at least three different events by stating one detail about each event that occurred recently (e.g., an item designed in an art project, the game played with a peer)
2. Recalls and retells at least three different events by stating two details about each event (e.g., going to the pumpkin patch: picking a pumpkin and going through a corn maze)
3. Recalls and retells at least three different events by stating at least three details about each event in the order they occurred. Events can range from the sequence of the daily routine (e.g., washing hands, eating snack, cleaning up snack) to a family vacation (e.g., driving to Grandma's house, swimming in her pool, going to Disneyland).

PROGRAMMING LOG

	Acquisition		Generalization		Maintenance	
	Start date	End date	Start date	End date	Date/data	Date/data
1						
2						
3						

LESSON PLAN: Sequencing

Recalls and Retells Past Events

Settings and materials	
Decontextualized	**Embedded**

Teaching
What direction or cue will you give?
How will you prompt the child's response?
Circle type of prompt(s) used:
Physical   Visual
Modeling   Verbal
Other: _____
Circle prompt fading procedure used:
Time delay   Most to least
Graduated guidance
Other: _____
What is the child's response?
What reinforcers are you using?
What is the correction procedure?
How will you collect data? *(circle answer)*
Percentage correct   Frequency
Duration   Permanent product
Other: _____

Sets

1. _____

   _____

   _____

   _____

2. _____

   _____

   _____

   _____

3. _____

   _____

   _____

   _____

4. _____

   _____

   _____

   _____

5. _____

   _____

   _____

   _____

INSTRUCTIONAL PROGRAM SHEET: Emergent Literacy

Makes Comments and Asks Questions While Looking at Picture Books

Child: _____ Date initiated: _____ Date completed: _____

Objective: While reading a picture book with an adult, the child makes comments and asks questions about the story.

Mastery criterion:
- Minimum of four comments or questions during one story
- 3 consecutive teaching days
- At least three different books

Generalization:
People: At least two adults
Settings: At least two settings
Materials: At least three different books

Things to consider: To start, use books that are interesting to the child. Consider teaching "Makes Comments" and "Asks a Variety of Questions" from the Communication, Initiating section of the checklist along with this goal.

Teaching sequence
1. Makes comments about story
2. Ask questions about story
3. Intermixes comments and questions during story

PROGRAMMING LOG

	Acquisition		Generalization		Maintenance	
	Start date	End date	Start date	End date	Date/data	Date/data
1						
2						
3						

The DATA Model for Teaching Preschoolers with Autism by Ilene Schwartz, Julie Ashmun, Bonnie McBride, Crista Scott, and Susan Sandall. Copyright © 2017 by Paul H. Brookes Publishing Co., Inc. All rights reserved.

LESSON PLAN: Emergent Literacy

Makes Comments and Asks Questions While Looking at Picture Books

Settings and materials	
Decontextualized	**Embedded**

Teaching
What direction or cue will you give?
How will you prompt the child's response?
Circle type of prompt(s) used:
Physical   Visual
Modeling   Verbal
Other: _____
Circle prompt fading procedure used:
Time delay   Most to least
Graduated guidance
Other: _____
What is the child's response?
What reinforcers are you using?
What is the correction procedure?
How will you collect data? *(circle answer)*
Percentage correct   Frequency
Duration   Permanent product
Other: _____

Sets

1. _____

_____

_____

_____

2. _____

_____

_____

_____

3. _____

_____

_____

_____

4. _____

_____

_____

_____

5. _____

_____

_____

_____

INSTRUCTIONAL PROGRAM SHEET: Emergent Literacy

Answers Factual Questions at the End of a Familiar Story

Child: _____   Date initiated: _____   Date completed: _____

Objective: After reading a book with an adult, the child answers factual questions about the main idea, main characters, or main events in the story.

Mastery criterion:
- 80% or higher correct response for each set
- Minimum of five opportunities per day
- 3 consecutive teaching days

Generalization:
People: At least two adults
Settings: At least two settings
Materials: At least three different stories

Things to consider: To start, use books that are interesting to the child. Consider reading books that are read to a large group during preschool.

Teaching sequence
1. Answers factual questions at the end of a page
2. Answers factual questions after two to three pages
3. Answers factual questions after four to five pages
4. Answers factual questions at the end of the story

PROGRAMMING LOG

	Acquisition		Generalization		Maintenance	
	Start date	End date	Start date	End date	Date/data	Date/data
1						
2						
3						
4						

The DATA Model for Teaching Preschoolers with Autism by Ilene Schwartz, Julie Ashmun, Bonnie McBride, Crista Scott, and Susan Sandall. Copyright © 2017 by Paul H. Brookes Publishing Co., Inc. All rights reserved.

LESSON PLAN: Emergent Literacy

Answers Factual Questions at the End of a Familiar Story

Settings and materials	
Decontextualized	Embedded

Teaching

What direction or cue will you give?

How will you prompt the child's response?

Circle type of prompt(s) used:

Physical   Visual

Modeling   Verbal

Other: _____

Circle prompt fading procedure used:

Time delay   Most to least

Graduated guidance

Other: _____

What is the child's response?

What reinforcers are you using?

What is the correction procedure?

How will you collect data? *(circle answer)*

Percentage correct   Frequency

Duration   Permanent product

Other: _____

Sets

1. _____

2. _____

3. _____

4. _____

5. _____

INSTRUCTIONAL PROGRAM SHEET: Emergent Literacy

Answers Questions Related to a Story that Require Inference

Child: _____ Date initiated: _____ Date completed: _____

Objective: When asked about a picture in a book, the child answers questions using inference. Examples include when the teacher asks why it's dark in the room in the story; the child sees the parent's hand on the light switch and says, "He turned the light off." The teacher asks why the child in the story is happy; the child looks at the picture and says, "He has a present."

Mastery criterion:
- 80% or higher correct response for each set
- 3 consecutive teaching days
- Minimum of five opportunities per day

Generalization:
People: At least two adults
Settings: At least two settings
Materials: At least five novel pictures in books

Things to consider: To start, use books that are interesting and familiar to the child.

Teaching sequence
1. Answers questions related to a story that require inference about simple *cause and effect*
2. Answers questions related to a story that require inference about *emotions*
3. Answers questions related to a story that require inference about *any topic*

PROGRAMMING LOG

	Acquisition		Generalization		Maintenance	
	Start date	End date	Start date	End date	Date/data	Date/data
1						
2						
3						

The DATA Model for Teaching Preschoolers with Autism by Ilene Schwartz, Julie Ashmun, Bonnie McBride, Crista Scott, and Susan Sandall. Copyright © 2017 by Paul H. Brookes Publishing Co., Inc. All rights reserved.

LESSON PLAN: Emergent Literacy

Answers Questions Related to a Story that Require Inference

Settings and materials	
Decontextualized	**Embedded**

Teaching
What direction or cue will you give?
How will you prompt the child's response?
Circle type of prompt(s) used:
Physical   Visual
Modeling   Verbal
Other: _____
Circle prompt fading procedure used:
Time delay   Most to least
Graduated guidance
Other: _____
What is the child's response?
What reinforcers are you using?
What is the correction procedure?
How will you collect data? *(circle answer)*
Percentage correct   Frequency
Duration   Permanent product
Other: _____

Sets

1. _____

_____

_____

_____

2. _____

_____

_____

_____

3. _____

_____

_____

_____

4. _____

_____

_____

5. _____

_____

_____

_____

INSTRUCTIONAL PROGRAM SHEET: Emergent Literacy

Makes Predictions When Reading a Story

Child: _____ Date initiated: _____ Date completed: _____

Objective: When asked about a picture in a book, or about the plot of a story, the child predicts what will happen next.

Mastery criterion:
- 80% or higher correct response for each set
- Minimum of five opportunities per day
- 3 consecutive teaching days

Generalization:
People: At least two adults
Settings: At least two settings
Materials: At least five novel pictures in a book

Things to consider: To start, use books that are interesting and familiar to the child.

Teaching sequence
1. Makes predictions about simple cause and effect
2. Makes predictions about emotions
3. Makes predictions about any topic related to the story

PROGRAMMING LOG

	Acquisition		Generalization		Maintenance	
	Start date	End date	Start date	End date	Date/data	Date/data
1						
2						
3						

LESSON PLAN: Emergent Literacy

Makes Predictions When Reading a Story

Settings and materials	
Decontextualized	**Embedded**

Teaching
What direction or cue will you give?
How will you prompt the child's response?
Circle type of prompt(s) used:
Physical   Visual
Modeling   Verbal
Other: _____
Circle prompt fading procedure used:
Time delay   Most to least
Graduated guidance
Other: _____
What is the child's response?
What reinforcers are you using?
What is the correction procedure?
How will you collect data? *(circle answer)*
Percentage correct   Frequency
Duration   Permanent product
Other: _____

Sets

1. _____
   _____
   _____
   _____

2. _____
   _____
   _____
   _____

3. _____
   _____
   _____
   _____

4. _____
   _____
   _____

5. _____
   _____
   _____
   _____

INSTRUCTIONAL PROGRAM SHEET: Emergent Literacy

Identifies Letters—Receptive

Child: _____   Date initiated: _____   Date completed: _____

Objective: When presented with at least three different letters and asked to identify one of them receptively (e.g., "show me ___," "where is ___," or "find the ___"), the child points to, touches, or picks up the correct letter.

Mastery criterion:
- 90% or higher correct response for each set
- Minimum of 10 opportunities per day
- 2 consecutive teaching days
- Identifies all capital letters

Generalization:
People: At least two adults
Settings: At least two settings
Materials: At least five novel pictures in a book

Things to consider: Consider letter picture cards that are simple and letters are all one color.

Teaching sequence
1. Identifies five letters (start with letters in the child's name)
2. Identifies 10 letters
3. Identifies 15 letters
4. Identifies 20 letters
5. Identifies all letters in the alphabet
6. Continue adding new sets of letter card, with generalization across a variety

PROGRAMMING LOG

	Acquisition		Generalization		Maintenance	
	Start date	End date	Start date	End date	Date/data	Date/data
1						
2						
3						
4						
5						
6						

LESSON PLAN: Emergent Literacy

Identifies Letters—Receptive

Settings and materials	
Decontextualized	**Embedded**

Teaching
What direction or cue will you give?
How will you prompt the child's response?
Circle type of prompt(s) used:
Physical   Visual
Modeling   Verbal
Other: _____
Circle prompt fading procedure used:
Time delay   Most to least
Graduated guidance
Other: _____
What is the child's response?
What reinforcers are you using?
What is the correction procedure?
How will you collect data? *(circle answer)*
Percentage correct   Frequency
Duration   Permanent product
Other: _____

Sets

1. _____
   _____
   _____
   _____

2. _____
   _____
   _____
   _____

3. _____
   _____
   _____
   _____

4. _____
   _____
   _____
   _____

5. _____
   _____
   _____
   _____

INSTRUCTIONAL PROGRAM SHEET: Emergent Literacy

Identifies Letters—Expressive

Child: _____   Date initiated: _____   Date completed: _____

Objective: When shown a letter and asked to identify it (e.g., "What letter is it?"), the child states the name of the letter either vocally or with an augmentative communication system.

Mastery criterion:
- 90% or higher correct response for each set
- 2 consecutive teaching days
- Minimum of 10 opportunities per day
- Identifies all capital letters

Generalization:
People: At least two adults
Settings: At least two settings
Materials: Across novel letter cards

Things to consider: Consider letter picture cards that are simple and letters are all one color.

Teaching sequence
1. Identifies five letters (start with letters in the child's name)
2. Identifies 10 letters
3. Identifies 15 letters
4. Identifies 20 letters
5. Identifies all letters in the alphabet
6. Continue adding new sets of letter cards, with generalization across a variety

PROGRAMMING LOG

	Acquisition		Generalization		Maintenance	
	Start date	End date	Start date	End date	Date/data	Date/data
1						
2						
3						
4						
5						
6						

LESSON PLAN: Emergent Literacy

Identifies Letters—Expressive

Settings and materials	
Decontextualized	**Embedded**

Teaching
What direction or cue will you give?
How will you prompt the child's response?
Circle type of prompt(s) used:
Physical   Visual
Modeling   Verbal
Other: _____
Circle prompt fading procedure used:
Time delay   Most to least
Graduated guidance
Other: _____
What is the child's response?
What reinforcers are you using?
What is the correction procedure?
How will you collect data? *(circle answer)*
Percentage correct   Frequency
Duration   Permanent product
Other: _____

Sets

1. _____
   _____
   _____
   _____

2. _____
   _____
   _____
   _____

3. _____
   _____
   _____
   _____

4. _____
   _____
   _____
   _____

5. _____
   _____
   _____
   _____

INSTRUCTIONAL PROGRAM SHEET: Emergent Math

Demonstrates Concept of One

Child: _____ Date initiated: _____ Date completed: _____

Objective: When presented with several like items and asked to indicate one, the child shows, gives, or assigns only one object.

Mastery criterion:
- 90% or higher correct response for each set
- 2 consecutive teaching days
- Minimum of 10 opportunities per day

Generalization:
People: At least two adults
Settings: At least two settings
Materials: Across novel items

Things to consider: Use objects that are of interest to the child. If instructing child to give you one item, be sure child is able to follow the direction "give." Child may indicate knowledge of concept by giving one item out of several to other children (e.g., markers) or placing one cup at each place for snack.

Teaching sequence
1. Gives object from a field of one
2. Gives one object from a field of two
3. Gives one object from a field of four
4. Gives one object from several offered (at least six)
5. Assigns one object from novel set of materials (e.g., box of crayons, bucket of cars, plate of cookies)

PROGRAMMING LOG

	Acquisition		Generalization		Maintenance	
	Start date	End date	Start date	End date	Date/data	Date/data
1						
2						
3						
4						
5						

LESSON PLAN: Emergent Math

Demonstrates Concept of One

Settings and materials	
Decontextualized	**Embedded**

Teaching
What direction or cue will you give?
How will you prompt the child's response?
Circle type of prompt(s) used:
Physical   Visual
Modeling   Verbal
Other: _____
Circle prompt fading procedure used:
Time delay   Most to least
Graduated guidance
Other: _____
What is the child's response?
What reinforcers are you using?
What is the correction procedure?
How will you collect data? *(circle answer)*
Percentage correct   Frequency
Duration   Permanent product
Other: _____

Sets

1. _____

   _____

   _____

   _____

2. _____

   _____

   _____

   _____

3. _____

   _____

   _____

   _____

4. _____

   _____

   _____

   _____

5. _____

   _____

   _____

   _____

INSTRUCTIONAL PROGRAM SHEET: Emergent Math

Counts Using 1:1 Correspondence

Child: _____ Date initiated: _____ Date completed: _____

Objective: When presented with at least 10 items and asked to count them (e.g., "Count the ___" or "How many ___ are there?"), the child counts by touching, pointing to, or moving 10 or more items, assigning numbers to each item in the correct order, and counting each item only once.

Mastery criterion:
- 90% or higher correct response for each set
- 2 consecutive teaching days
- Minimum of 10 opportunities per day

Generalization:
People: At least two adults
Settings: At least two settings
Materials: Across novel items

Things to consider: The child must be able to rote count and demonstrate an understanding of the concept of one. Use preferred materials. Is this a skill for which the child needs specialized instruction or will the child learn this skill in the general education setting with minimal modifications or embedded learning opportunities?

Teaching sequence
1. Counts up to three items
2. Counts up to six items
3. Counts up to 10 items
4. Counts at least 10 items using novel materials

PROGRAMMING LOG

	Acquisition		Generalization		Maintenance	
	Start date	End date	Start date	End date	Date/data	Date/data
1						
2						
3						
4						

LESSON PLAN: Emergent Math

Counts Using 1:1 Correspondence

Settings and materials	
Decontextualized	**Embedded**

Teaching

What direction or cue will you give?

How will you prompt the child's response?

Circle type of prompt(s) used:

Physical	Visual
Modeling	Verbal

Other: _____

Circle prompt fading procedure used:

Time delay	Most to least
Graduated guidance	

Other: _____

What is the child's response?

What reinforcers are you using?

What is the correction procedure?

How will you collect data? *(circle answer)*

Percentage correct	Frequency
Duration	Permanent product

Other: _____

Sets

1. _____

_____

_____

_____

2. _____

_____

_____

_____

3. _____

_____

_____

_____

4. _____

_____

_____

_____

5. _____

_____

_____

_____

INSTRUCTIONAL PROGRAM SHEET: Following Directions

Follows One-Step Directions without Contextual Cues

Child: _____   Date initiated: _____   Date completed: _____

Objective: When an adult instructs the child with a one-step direction such as sit down or get the ball, and does not provide contextual cues such as gestures or the item (ball), the child follows the direction.

Mastery criterion:
- 90% or higher correct response for each set
- Minimum of 10 opportunities per day
- 2 consecutive teaching days
- Follows at least five, one-step directions

Generalization:
People: At least two adults
Settings: At least two settings
Materials: Across a variety of materials needed for the directions

Things to consider: If asking the child to get an item (e.g., get the ball), the child must be able to identify the item. For children with motor or sensory challenges, consider ability to complete action. For example, a child may not give a high-five or clap hands if he or she is sensitive to the tap of another hand on his or her hand.

Teaching sequence
1. Follows at least four, one-step gross motor actions (e.g., stand up, sit down, give a high-five)
2. Follows one-step directions that involve another person or object (e.g., get the ball, give a friend a high-five)

PROGRAMMING LOG

	Acquisition		Generalization		Maintenance	
	Start date	End date	Start date	End date	Date/data	Date/data
1						
2						

The DATA Model for Teaching Preschoolers with Autism by Ilene Schwartz, Julie Ashmun, Bonnie McBride, Crista Scott, and Susan Sandall. Copyright © 2017 by Paul H. Brookes Publishing Co., Inc. All rights reserved.

LESSON PLAN: Following Directions

Follows One-Step Directions without Contextual Cues

Settings and materials	
Decontextualized	**Embedded**

Teaching
What direction or cue will you give?
How will you prompt the child's response?
Circle type of prompt(s) used:

Physical	Visual
Modeling	Verbal
Other: _____	

Circle prompt fading procedure used:

Time delay	Most to least
Graduated guidance	
Other: _____	

What is the child's response?
What reinforcers are you using?
What is the correction procedure?
How will you collect data? *(circle answer)*

Percentage correct	Frequency
Duration	Permanent product
Other: _____	

Sets

1. _____
   _____
   _____
   _____

2. _____
   _____
   _____
   _____

3. _____
   _____
   _____
   _____

4. _____
   _____
   _____
   _____

5. _____
   _____
   _____
   _____

INSTRUCTIONAL PROGRAM SHEET: Following Directions

Follows One-Step Directions without Contextual Cues—Example

Child: _____ Date initiated: _____ Date completed: _____

Objective: When an adult instructs the child with a one-step direction such as sit down or get the ball, and does not provide contextual cues such as gestures or the item (ball), the child follows the direction.

Mastery criterion:
- 90% or higher correct response for each set
- Minimum of 10 opportunities per day
- 2 consecutive teaching days
- Follows at least five, one-step directions

Generalization:
People: At least two adults
Settings: At least two settings
Materials: Across a variety of materials needed for the directions

Things to consider: If asking the child to get an item (e.g., get the ball), the child must be able to identify the item. For children with motor or sensory challenges, consider ability to complete action. For example, a child may not give a high-five or clap hands if he or she is sensitive to the tap of another hand on his or her hand.

Teaching sequence
1. Follows at least four, one-step gross motor actions (e.g., stand up, sit down, give a high-five)
2. Follows one-step directions that involve another person or object (e.g., get the ball, give a friend a high-five)

PROGRAMMING LOG

	Acquisition		Generalization		Maintenance	
	Start date	End date	Start date	End date	Date/data	Date/data
1	10/1/14	10/30/14	10/31/14	11/15/14	11/20/14; 80%	1/20/14; 100%
2	10/31/14	12/2/14	12/3/14	12/20/14	2/1/15; 100%	4/1/15; 80%

LESSON PLAN: Following Directions

Follows One-Step Directions without Contextual Cues—Example

Settings and materials	
Decontextualized	**Embedded**
Provide instruction during individualized work time in work area.	Provide instruction during classroom routines and activities.

Teaching
What direction or cue will you give?
Provide direction that is the one-step direction for the set.
How will you prompt the child's response?
Circle type of prompt(s) used:
Physical   Visual
(Modeling)   Verbal
Other: _____
Circle prompt fading procedure used:
(Time delay)   Most to least
Graduated guidance
Other: _____
What is the child's response?
Follows one-step direction within 4 seconds of direction
What reinforcers are you using?
Praise and preferred item
What is the correction procedure?
Provide direction again while performing the action (model prompt)—child is able to imitate and will follow the model.
How will you collect data? *(circle answer)*
(Percentage correct)   Frequency
Duration   Permanent product
Other: _____

Sets

1. Stand up
   Give a high-five
   Sit down
   Clap hands
   Get in line

2. Give Tasha the ball
   Give Teacher Caroline the paper
   Give Tasha a high-five
   Give the (toy) to Steven
   Get the (toy) from Teacher Henry

INSTRUCTIONAL PROGRAM SHEET: Following Directions

Follows One-Step Directions Related to Safety

Child: _____ Date initiated: _____ Date completed: _____

Objective: When an adult instructs the child with a one-step direction related to safety such as stop, wait, hold hands, and walk with me, the child follows the direction.

Mastery criterion:
- 90% or higher correct responding for each set
- Minimum of 10 opportunities per day
- 2 consecutive teaching days
- Follows at least four different one-step directions

Generalization:
People: At least two adults
Settings: At least two settings
Materials: Across a variety of materials

Things to consider: For children with motor or sensory challenges, consider ability to complete action. For example, a child may be sensitive to holding hands and will likely be upset by this. Consider ways to make this a positive experience.

Teaching sequence
1. Follows at least two, one-step directions related to safety (e.g., stop, walk with me)
2. Follows at least two, one-step directions related to safety (e.g., wait, hold hands)

PROGRAMMING LOG

	Acquisition		Generalization		Maintenance	
	Start date	End date	Start date	End date	Date/data	Date/data
1						
2						

LESSON PLAN: Following Directions

Follows One-Step Directions Related to Safety

Settings and materials	
Decontextualized	**Embedded**

Teaching
What direction or cue will you give?
How will you prompt the child's response?
Circle type of prompt(s) used:
Physical   Visual
Modeling   Verbal
Other: _____
Circle prompt fading procedure used:
Time delay   Most to least
Graduated guidance
Other: _____
What is the child's response?
What reinforcers are you using?
What is the correction procedure?
How will you collect data? *(circle answer)*
Percentage correct   Frequency
Duration   Permanent product
Other: _____

Sets

1. _____

2. _____

3. _____

4. _____

5. _____

INSTRUCTIONAL PROGRAM SHEET: Following Directions

Follows Directions to Give an Item to a Person

Child: _____   Date initiated: _____   Date completed: _____

Objective: When an adult instructs the child to give an item to another person and gives the child that item, the child follows the direction by finding the person and giving him or her the item.

Mastery criterion:
- 80% or higher correct response for each set
- Minimum of five opportunities per day
- 3 consecutive teaching days

Generalization:
People: At least two adults and two peers
Settings: At least two settings
Materials: Across a variety of materials needed for the directions

Things to consider: Child will need to learn the names of adults and peers to locate person to whom he or she should give the item.

Teaching sequence
1. Follows direction to give an item to an adult
2. Follows direction to give an item to another adult
3. Follows direction to give an item to a peer
4. Follows direction to give an item to another peer

PROGRAMMING LOG

	Acquisition		Generalization		Maintenance	
	Start date	End date	Start date	End date	Date/data	Date/data
1						
2						
3						
4						

LESSON PLAN: Following Directions

Follows Directions to Give an Item to a Person

Settings and materials	
Decontextualized	**Embedded**

Teaching
What direction or cue will you give?
How will you prompt the child's response?
Circle type of prompt(s) used:
Physical   Visual
Modeling   Verbal
Other: _____
Circle prompt fading procedure used:
Time delay   Most to least
Graduated guidance
Other: _____
What is the child's response?
What reinforcers are you using?
What is the correction procedure?
How will you collect data? *(circle answer)*
Percentage correct   Frequency
Duration   Permanent product
Other: _____

Sets

1. _____
_____
_____
_____

2. _____
_____
_____
_____

3. _____
_____
_____
_____

4. _____
_____
_____
_____

5. _____
_____
_____
_____

INSTRUCTIONAL PROGRAM SHEET: Following Directions

Follows Two-Step Directions without Contextual Cues

Child: _____ Date initiated: _____ Date completed: _____

Objective: When an adult or peer instructs the child with a two-step direction such as "Go get your doll, and put it in the crib," the child follows both directions in order without reminders or cues (i.e., the doll is not present in immediate environment).

Mastery criterion:
- 80% or higher correct response for each set
- Minimum of five opportunities per day
- 3 consecutive teaching days
- Follows at least five, two-step directions

Generalization:
People: At least two adults and peers
Settings: At least two settings
Materials: Across a variety of materials

Things to consider: If asking the child to get an item, the child must be able to identify the item (e.g., the doll and crib). For children with motor or sensory challenges, consider ability to complete action.

Teaching sequence
1. Follows at least three, two-step directions from an adult
2. Follows at least two, two-step directions from a peer during play

PROGRAMMING LOG

	Acquisition		Generalization		Maintenance	
	Start date	End date	Start date	End date	Date/data	Date/data
1						
2						

LESSON PLAN: Following Directions

Follows Two-Step Directions without Contextual Cues

Settings and materials	
Decontextualized	**Embedded**

Teaching
What direction or cue will you give?
How will you prompt the child's response?
Circle type of prompt(s) used:
Physical   Visual
Modeling   Verbal
Other: _____
Circle prompt fading procedure used:
Time delay   Most to least
Graduated guidance
Other: _____
What is the child's response?
What reinforcers are you using?
What is the correction procedure?
How will you collect data? *(circle answer)*
Percentage correct   Frequency
Duration   Permanent product
Other: _____

Sets

1. _____

   _____

   _____

   _____

2. _____

   _____

   _____

   _____

3. _____

   _____

   _____

   _____

4. _____

   _____

   _____

   _____

5. _____

   _____

   _____

   _____

INSTRUCTIONAL PROGRAM SHEET: Responding

Gestures or Vocalizes to Greet Others

Child: _____   Date initiated: _____   Date completed: _____

Objective: When an adult or peer greets the child, he or she responds with a greeting by waving or vocalizing.

Mastery criterion:
- 80% or higher correct response for each set
- Minimum of five opportunities per day
- 3 consecutive teaching days

Generalization:
People: At least two adults and two peers
Settings: At least two settings
Materials: Across materials, if needed

Things to consider: Child may use a gesture or some type of augmentative communication system.

Teaching sequence
1. Responds to greetings from adults
2. Responds to greetings from peers

PROGRAMMING LOG

	Acquisition		Generalization		Maintenance	
	Start date	End date	Start date	End date	Date/data	Date/data
1						
2						

LESSON PLAN: Responding

Gestures or Vocalizes to Greet Others

Settings and materials	
Decontextualized	**Embedded**

Teaching

What direction or cue will you give?

How will you prompt the child's response?

Circle type of prompt(s) used:

Physical   Visual

Modeling   Verbal

Other: _____

Circle prompt fading procedure used:

Time delay   Most to least

Graduated guidance

Other: _____

What is the child's response?

What reinforcers are you using?

What is the correction procedure?

How will you collect data? *(circle answer)*

Percentage correct   Frequency

Duration   Permanent product

Other: _____

Sets

1. _____

2. _____

3. _____

4. _____

5. _____

INSTRUCTIONAL PROGRAM SHEET: Responding

Chooses Items When Asked to Make a Choice

Child: _____ Date initiated: _____ Date completed: _____

Objective: When presented with two items and asked to choose one, the child indicates his or her preference by taking the item and acting upon it.

Mastery criterion:
- 90% or higher correct response for each set
- Minimum of 10 opportunities per day
- 2 consecutive teaching days

Generalization:
People: At least two adults
Settings: At least two settings
Materials: Across a variety of materials

Things to consider: Child may use a gesture (i.e., point) or some type of augmentative communication system to indicate choice. Preference assessment must be completed to determine child's choices.

Teaching sequence
1. Child responds with one preferred and one non-preferred item
2. Child responds with two preferred items (i.e., takes one item and acts upon it without getting upset that he or she does not have both items)

PROGRAMMING LOG

	Acquisition		Generalization		Maintenance	
	Start date	End date	Start date	End date	Date/data	Date/data
1						
2						

LESSON PLAN: Responding

Chooses Item When Asked to Make a Choice

Settings and materials	
Decontextualized	**Embedded**

Teaching
What direction or cue will you give?
How will you prompt the child's response?
Circle type of prompt(s) used:
Physical   Visual
Modeling   Verbal
Other: _____
Circle prompt fading procedure used:
Time delay   Most to least
Graduated guidance
Other: _____
What is the child's response?
What reinforcers are you using?
What is the correction procedure?
How will you collect data? *(circle answer)*
Percentage correct   Frequency
Duration   Permanent product
Other: _____

Sets

1. _____

   _____

   _____

   _____

2. _____

   _____

   _____

   _____

3. _____

   _____

   _____

   _____

4. _____

   _____

   _____

   _____

5. _____

   _____

   _____

   _____

INSTRUCTIONAL PROGRAM SHEET: Responding

Responds to "What Do You Want" When Items Are Not Present

Child: _____ Date initiated: _____ Date completed: _____

Objective: When asked "What do you want," and the item is not present for the child to see, he or she responds by naming the item he or she would like to have and interacts with it when received.

Mastery criterion:
- 90% or higher correct response for each set
- Minimum of 10 opportunities per day
- 2 consecutive teaching days

Generalization:
People: At least two adults
Settings: At least two settings
Materials: Across a variety of materials

Things to consider: Consider using visual prompts if child's primary mode of communication is verbal. Child must make requests for items in sight before requesting items out of sights. See Communication Goal, Initiating: Requests Items and Activities that Are in Sight (Communication Form 3.3).

Teaching sequence
1. Responds by requesting item that is in child's sight
2. Responds by requesting item seen within last 10 seconds
3. Responds by requesting item seen within last 30 seconds
4. Responds by requesting item seen over 1 minute ago
5. Responds by requesting item seen over 5 minutes ago
6. Responds by requesting a variety of items and acting upon them when given

PROGRAMMING LOG

	Acquisition		Generalization		Maintenance	
	Start date	End date	Start date	End date	Date/data	Date/data
1						
2						
3						
4						
5						
6						

LESSON PLAN: Responding

Responds to "What Do You Want" When Items Are Not Present

Settings and materials		Sets

Settings and materials	
Decontextualized	**Embedded**

Teaching
What direction or cue will you give?
How will you prompt the child's response?
Circle type of prompt(s) used:
Physical   Visual
Modeling   Verbal
Other: _____
Circle prompt fading procedure used:
Time delay   Most to least
Graduated guidance
Other: _____
What is the child's response?
What reinforcers are you using?
What is the correction procedure?
How will you collect data? *(circle answer)*
Percentage correct   Frequency
Duration   Permanent product
Other: _____

Sets

1. _____
   _____
   _____
   _____

2. _____
   _____
   _____
   _____

3. _____
   _____
   _____
   _____

4. _____
   _____
   _____

5. _____
   _____
   _____
   _____

INSTRUCTIONAL PROGRAM SHEET: Responding

Responds to a Variety of Questions

Child: _____   Date initiated: _____   Date completed: _____

Objective: When asked a variety of simple questions that begin with "what," "where," "who," "why," or "when," the child answers the question.

Mastery criterion:
- 90% or higher correct response for each type of question
- Minimum of 10 opportunities per day
- 2 consecutive teaching days
- Three different types of questions for each one listed in the objective

Generalization:
People: At least two adults
Settings: At least two settings
Materials: Across a variety of novel questions

Things to consider: Include preferred objects or pictures for the questions when available.

Teaching sequence
1. Responds to at least three different "what" questions
2. Responds to at least three different "where" questions
3. Responds to at least three different "who" questions
4. Responds to at least three different "why" questions
5. Responds to at least three different "when" questions

PROGRAMMING LOG

	Acquisition		Generalization		Maintenance	
	Start date	End date	Start date	End date	Date/data	Date/data
1						
2						
3						
4						
5						

LESSON PLAN: Responding

Responds to a Variety of Questions

Settings and materials	
Decontextualized	**Embedded**

Teaching
What direction or cue will you give?
How will you prompt the child's response?
Circle type of prompt(s) used:
Physical   Visual
Modeling   Verbal
Other: _____
Circle prompt fading procedure used:
Time delay   Most to least
Graduated guidance
Other: _____
What is the child's response?
What reinforcers are you using?
What is the correction procedure?
How will you collect data? *(circle answer)*
Percentage correct   Frequency
Duration   Permanent product
Other: _____

Sets

1. _____
2. _____
3. _____
4. _____
5. _____

INSTRUCTIONAL PROGRAM SHEET: Responding

Responds with Yes or No

Child: _____ Date initiated: _____ Date completed: _____

Objective: When asked a variety of simple questions with a "yes" or "no" answer, the child answers the question.

Mastery criterion:
- 90% or higher correct response for each type of question
- Minimum of 10 opportunities per day
- 2 consecutive teaching days

Generalization:
People: At least two adults
Settings: At least two settings
Materials: Across a variety of novel questions

Things to consider: Include preferred objects and pictures for "yes" answers and non-preferred objects and pictures for "no" answers. For identifying questions, such as, "Is this red?" be sure the child can identify colors.

Teaching sequence
1. Responds "yes" to preferred objects or pictures (e.g., "Do you want __?")
2. Responds "no" to non-preferred objects or pictures
3. Responds "yes" and "no" to a variety of preferred or non-preferred objects or pictures
4. Responds "yes" for the identity of an item (e.g., show a picture of a cat and ask, "Is this a cat?")
5. Responds "no" for the identify of an item
6. Responds "yes" and "no" to a variety of identifying questions (e.g., "Is this red?" or "Does this say 'meow'?")

PROGRAMMING LOG

	Acquisition		Generalization		Maintenance	
	Start date	End date	Start date	End date	Date/data	Date/data
1						
2						
3						
4						
5						
6						

LESSON PLAN: Responding

Responds to a Variety of Questions

Settings and materials	
Decontextualized	**Embedded**

Teaching
What direction or cue will you give?
How will you prompt the child's response?
Circle type of prompt(s) used:
Physical   Visual
Modeling   Verbal
Other: _____
Circle prompt fading procedure used:
Time delay   Most to least
Graduated guidance
Other: _____
What is the child's response?
What reinforcers are you using?
What is the correction procedure?
How will you collect data? *(circle answer)*
Percentage correct   Frequency
Duration   Permanent product
Other: _____

Sets

1. _____

2. _____

3. _____

4. _____

5. _____

INSTRUCTIONAL PROGRAM SHEET: Initiating

Uses Gestures to Initiate a Request

Child: _____   Date initiated: _____   Date completed: _____

Objective: When the child notices an item in sight that is desired, the child initiates a request for that item by pointing to it, then interacts with it when received.

Mastery criterion:
- 90% or higher correct response for each set
- Minimum of 10 opportunities per day
- 2 consecutive teaching days

Generalization:
People: At least two adults
Settings: At least two settings
Materials: Across a variety of preferred materials

Things to consider: Child may be sensitive to touch and, therefore, may be challenged with physical prompts when teaching to point at items. Consider having the child hold a small object with his or her other fingers when pointing to a more preferred object with pointing finger. Be sure to fade the small object as the child learns the pointing gesture.

Teaching sequence
1. Requests item that is directly in front of child (teacher may hold up item to be in child's line of vision)
2. Requests item that is at least 3 feet from child but still in sight
3. Requests item that is out of reach for child but still in sight

PROGRAMMING LOG

	Acquisition		Generalization		Maintenance	
	Start date	End date	Start date	End date	Date/data	Date/data
1						
2						
3						

LESSON PLAN: Initiating

Uses Gestures to Initiate a Request

Settings and materials	
Decontextualized	**Embedded**

Teaching
What direction or cue will you give?
How will you prompt the child's response?
Circle type of prompt(s) used:
Physical   Visual
Modeling   Verbal
Other: _____
Circle prompt fading procedure used:
Time delay   Most to least
Graduated guidance
Other: _____
What is the child's response?
What reinforcers are you using?
What is the correction procedure?
How will you collect data? *(circle answer)*
Percentage correct   Frequency
Duration   Permanent product
Other: _____

Sets

1. _____

_____

_____

_____

2. _____

_____

_____

_____

3. _____

_____

_____

_____

4. _____

_____

_____

_____

5. _____

_____

_____

_____

INSTRUCTIONAL PROGRAM SHEET: Initiating

Initiates with Words or Gestures to Greet Others

Child: _____   Date initiated: _____   Date completed: _____

Objective: When the child sees a familiar adult or peer, the child greets the adult or peer with either a gesture (e.g., wave) or verbally (e.g., says "Hi").

Mastery criterion:
- 80% or higher correct response for each set
- Minimum of five opportunities per day
- 3 consecutive teaching days

Generalization:
People: At least two adults and two peers
Settings: At least two settings
Materials: Across a variety of materials, if appropriate

Things to consider: Make sure the child has either the motor skills to gesture a greeting or has a method to expressively state a greeting. Teach this skill with preferred adults and peers and encourage the child to state the adult or peer's name with the greeting.

Teaching sequence
1. Child approaches, looks at familiar adult, and waves or says "Hi" to familiar adult
2. Child approaches, looks at familiar adult, and waves or says "Hi" to familiar adult
3. Child approaches, looks at familiar peer, and waves or says "Hi" to familiar peer
4. Child approaches, looks at familiar peer, and waves or says "Hi" to familiar peer

PROGRAMMING LOG

	Acquisition		Generalization		Maintenance	
	Start date	End date	Start date	End date	Date/data	Date/data
1						
2						
3						
4						

The DATA Model for Teaching Preschoolers with Autism by Ilene Schwartz, Julie Ashmun, Bonnie McBride, Crista Scott, and Susan Sandall. Copyright © 2017 by Paul H. Brookes Publishing Co., Inc. All rights reserved.

LESSON PLAN: Initiating

Initiates with Words or Gestures to Greet Others

Settings and materials	
Decontextualized	**Embedded**

Teaching
What direction or cue will you give?
How will you prompt the child's response?
Circle type of prompt(s) used:
Physical   Visual
Modeling   Verbal
Other: _____
Circle prompt fading procedure used:
Time delay   Most to least
Graduated guidance
Other: _____
What is the child's response?
What reinforcers are you using?
What is the correction procedure?
How will you collect data? *(circle answer)*
Percentage correct   Frequency
Duration   Permanent product
Other: _____

Sets

1. _____

_____

_____

_____

2. _____

_____

_____

_____

3. _____

_____

_____

_____

4. _____

_____

_____

5. _____

_____

_____

_____

INSTRUCTIONAL PROGRAM SHEET: Initiating

Requests Items and Activities that Are in Sight

Child: _____   Date initiated: _____   Date completed: _____

Objective: When the child notices an item or activity in sight that is desired, the child initiates a request for that item or activity, either verbally or with an augmentative communication system, and interacts with the item or activity when received.

Mastery criterion:
- 90% or higher correct response for each set
- Minimum of 10 opportunities per day
- 2 consecutive teaching days

Generalization:
People: At least two adults
Settings: At least two settings
Materials: Across a variety of preferred items and activities

Things to consider: Child must have a means of communicating. Examples include verbal communication, Picture Exchange Communication System, manual sign or American Sign Language, and a speech-generating device.

Teaching sequence
1. Requests item or activity that is directly in front of child (teacher may hold up item to be in child's line of vision)
2. Requests item or activity that is at least 3 feet from child but still in sight
3. Requests item or activity that is out of reach for child but still in sight

PROGRAMMING LOG

	Acquisition		Generalization		Maintenance	
	Start date	End date	Start date	End date	Date/data	Date/data
1						
2						
3						

LESSON PLAN: Initiating

Requests Items and Activities that Are in Sight

Settings and materials	
Decontextualized	**Embedded**

Teaching
What direction or cue will you give?
How will you prompt the child's response?
Circle type of prompt(s) used:
Physical   Visual
Modeling   Verbal
Other: _____
Circle prompt fading procedure used:
Time delay   Most to least
Graduated guidance
Other: _____
What is the child's response?
What reinforcers are you using?
What is the correction procedure?
How will you collect data? *(circle answer)*
Percentage correct   Frequency
Duration   Permanent product
Other: _____

Sets

1. _____

2. _____

3. _____

4. _____

5. _____

INSTRUCTIONAL PROGRAM SHEET: Initiating

Requests Items and Activities that Are Out of Sight

Child: _____ Date initiated: _____ Date completed: _____

Objective: When the child desires a preferred item that is not in the child's sight, the child initiates a request for that item either verbally or with an augmentative communication system and interacts with it when received.

Mastery criterion:
- 90% or higher correct response for each set
- Minimum of 10 opportunities per day
- 2 consecutive teaching days

Generalization:
People: At least two adults
Settings: At least two settings
Materials: Across a variety of preferred items and activities

Things to consider: Child must have a means of communicating. Examples include verbal communication, Picture Exchange Communication System, manual sign or American Sign Language, and a speech-generating device.

Teaching sequence
1. Requests item or activity seen within last 10 seconds
2. Requests item or activity seen within last 30 seconds
3. Requests item or activity seen over 1 minute ago
4. Requests item or activity seen over 5 minutes ago
5. Requests a variety of items/activities and acts upon them when given

PROGRAMMING LOG

	Acquisition		Generalization		Maintenance	
	Start date	End date	Start date	End date	Date/data	Date/data
1						
2						
3						
4						
5						

LESSON PLAN: Initiating

Requests Items and Activities that Are Out of Sight

Settings and materials		Sets
Decontextualized	**Embedded**	

Settings and materials
Teaching
What direction or cue will you give?
How will you prompt the child's response?
Circle type of prompt(s) used:
Physical   Visual
Modeling   Verbal
Other: _____
Circle prompt fading procedure used:
Time delay   Most to least
Graduated guidance
Other: _____
What is the child's response?
What reinforcers are you using?
What is the correction procedure?
How will you collect data? *(circle answer)*
Percentage correct   Frequency
Duration   Permanent product
Other: _____

Sets

1. _____

_____

_____

_____

2. _____

_____

_____

_____

3. _____

_____

_____

_____

4. _____

_____

_____

_____

5. _____

_____

_____

_____

INSTRUCTIONAL PROGRAM SHEET: Initiating

Requests the End of an Activity

Child: _____   Date initiated: _____   Date completed: _____

Objective: When the child desires the end of an activity, the child indicates this desire either verbally (e.g., "All done" or "I'm finished"), with an augmentative communication system or with sign language for "finished."

Mastery criterion:
- 90% or higher correct response for each set
- Minimum of 10 opportunities per day
- 2 consecutive teaching days

Generalization:
People: At least two adults
Settings: At least two settings
Materials: Across a variety of activities

Things to consider: Child must have a means of communicating. Examples include verbal communication, Picture Exchange Communication System, manual sign or American Sign Language, and a speech-generating device.

Teaching sequence
1. Requests the end of activity with prompting for at least one activity
2. Requests the end of an activity with no prompting for at least one activity
3. Requests the end of an activity across at least two activities
4. Requests the end of an activity across a variety of activities

PROGRAMMING LOG

	Acquisition		Generalization		Maintenance	
	Start date	End date	Start date	End date	Date/data	Date/data
1						
2						
3						
4						

LESSON PLAN: Initiating

Requests the End of an Activity

Settings and materials	
Decontextualized	**Embedded**

Teaching

What direction or cue will you give?

How will you prompt the child's response?

Circle type of prompt(s) used:

Physical	Visual
Modeling	Verbal

Other: _____

Circle prompt fading procedure used:

Time delay	Most to least
Graduated guidance	

Other: _____

What is the child's response?

What reinforcers are you using?

What is the correction procedure?

How will you collect data? *(circle answer)*

Percentage correct	Frequency
Duration	Permanent product

Other: _____

Sets

1. _____

2. _____

3. _____

4. _____

5. _____

INSTRUCTIONAL PROGRAM SHEET: Initiating

Makes Comments

Child: _____   Date initiated: _____   Date completed: _____

Objective: During activities, the child makes comments about his or her own actions or things he or she sees, such as "I'm drawing" and "It's blue" or "He's coloring," when noticing the action of a peer.

Mastery criterion:
- At least two comments during each activity
- Across five activities
- 2 consecutive teaching days

Generalization:
People: At least two adults
Settings: At least two settings
Materials: Across a variety of materials

Things to consider: Augmentative communication systems may be used for commenting. Use preferred materials so child is motivated to make comments.

Teaching sequence
1. Comments at least once during one activity
2. Comments at least twice during one activity
3. Comments at least twice during another activity
4. Comments at least twice during three activities
5. Comments at least twice during five activities

PROGRAMMING LOG

	Acquisition		Generalization		Maintenance	
	Start date	End date	Start date	End date	Date/data	Date/data
1						
2						
3						
4						
5						

LESSON PLAN: Initiating

Makes Comments

Settings and materials	
Decontextualized	Embedded

Teaching
What direction or cue will you give?
How will you prompt the child's response?
Circle type of prompt(s) used:
Physical   Visual
Modeling   Verbal
Other: _____
Circle prompt fading procedure used:
Time delay   Most to least
Graduated guidance
Other: _____
What is the child's response?
What reinforcers are you using?
What is the correction procedure?
How will you collect data? *(circle answer)*
Percentage correct   Frequency
Duration   Permanent product
Other: _____

Sets

1. _____

2. _____

3. _____

4. _____

5. _____

INSTRUCTIONAL PROGRAM SHEET: Initiating

Uses Sentence Stems to Comment and Request

Child: _____   Date initiated: _____   Date completed: _____

Objective: When the child is initiating a request or comment, the child uses sentence stems such as "I want ___," "It's a ___," "I see ___," and "I have ___" to make a complete sentence.

Mastery criterion:
- 90% or higher correct response for each set
- Minimum of 10 opportunities per day
- 2 consecutive teaching days

Generalization:
People: At least two adults
Settings: At least two settings
Materials: Across a variety of items or activities for a variety of sentences

Things to consider: Child must have a means of communicating. Examples include verbal communication, Picture Exchange Communication System, manual sign or American Sign Language, and a speech-generating device.

Teaching sequence
1. Requests with the sentence stem "I want ___" for a variety of comments
2. Comments with the sentence stem "It's a ___" for a variety of comments
3. Comments with the sentence stem "I see ___" for a variety of comments
4. Comments with the sentence stem "I have ___" for a variety of comments

PROGRAMMING LOG

	Acquisition		Generalization		Maintenance	
	Start date	End date	Start date	End date	Date/data	Date/data
1						
2						
3						
4						

LESSON PLAN: Initiating

Uses Sentence Stems to Comment and Request

Settings and materials	
Decontextualized	**Embedded**

Teaching
What direction or cue will you give?
How will you prompt the child's response?
Circle type of prompt(s) used:
Physical   Visual
Modeling   Verbal
Other: _____
Circle prompt fading procedure used:
Time delay   Most to least
Graduated guidance
Other: _____
What is the child's response?
What reinforcers are you using?
What is the correction procedure?
How will you collect data? *(circle answer)*
Percentage correct   Frequency
Duration   Permanent product
Other: _____

Sets

1. _____
   _____
   _____
   _____

2. _____
   _____
   _____
   _____

3. _____
   _____
   _____
   _____

4. _____
   _____
   _____
   _____

5. _____
   _____
   _____
   _____

INSTRUCTIONAL PROGRAM SHEET: Initiating

Asks a Variety of Questions to Gain Information

Child: _____ Date initiated: _____ Date completed: _____

Objective: When the child is seeking information, the child asks a question that begins with "what," "where," "who," "why," or "when" to gain the information.

Mastery criterion:
- Initiates at least 10 different questions
- Across five activities
- 2 consecutive teaching days
- Three different types of questions for each one listed in the objective

Generalization:
People: At least two adults
Settings: At least two settings
Materials: Across a variety of novel questions

Things to consider: Visual supports may be helpful in teaching this skill.

Teaching sequence
1. Asks at least three different "what" questions
2. Asks at least three different "where" questions
3. Asks at least three different "who" questions
4. Asks at least three different "why" questions
5. Asks at least three different "when" questions

PROGRAMMING LOG

	Acquisition		Generalization		Maintenance	
	Start date	End date	Start date	End date	Date/data	Date/data
1						
2						
3						
4						
5						

LESSON PLAN: Initiating

Asks a Variety of Questions to Gain Information

Settings and materials	
Decontextualized	**Embedded**

Teaching
What direction or cue will you give?
How will you prompt the child's response?
Circle type of prompt(s) used:
Physical   Visual
Modeling   Verbal
Other: _____
Circle prompt fading procedure used:
Time delay   Most to least
Graduated guidance
Other: _____
What is the child's response?
What reinforcers are you using?
What is the correction procedure?
How will you collect data? *(circle answer)*
Percentage correct   Frequency
Duration   Permanent product
Other: _____

Sets

1. _____

2. _____

3. _____

4. _____

5. _____

INSTRUCTIONAL PROGRAM SHEET: Comprehension and Expression of Words and Sentences

Identifies Common Nouns—Receptive

Child: _____ Date initiated: _____ Date completed: _____

Objective: When presented with at least three different pictures or objects from the environment and asked to identify one of them receptively (e.g., "Show me ___," "Where is ___," or "Find the ___"), the child points to, touches, or picks up the correct picture or object.

Mastery criterion:
- 90% or higher correct response for each set
- Minimum of 10 opportunities per day
- 2 consecutive teaching days
- Identifies at least 50 total pictures or objects

Generalization:
People: At least two adults
Settings: At least two settings
Materials: Across a variety of pictures or objects for each noun

Things to consider: Consider pictures that are simple, so the child can easily identify the item in the picture. Be careful of identifying information such as one picture with only a blue background from the array of pictures.

Teaching sequence
1. Identifies at least five common nouns in simple pictures
2. Identifies the five common nouns from previous set in other pictures
3. Identifies at least five common objects
4. Identifies the five common objects from previous set across different objects
5. Continue adding new sets of pictures and objects, with generalization across a variety, to total at least 50 items for the child's vocabulary building

PROGRAMMING LOG

	Acquisition		Generalization		Maintenance	
	Start date	End date	Start date	End date	Date/data	Date/data
1						
2						
3						
4						
5						

LESSON PLAN: Comprehension and Expression of Words and Sentences

Identifies Common Nouns—Receptive

Settings and materials	
Decontextualized	**Embedded**

Teaching
What direction or cue will you give?
How will you prompt the child's response?
Circle type of prompt(s) used:
Physical   Visual
Modeling   Verbal
Other: _____
Circle prompt fading procedure used:
Time delay   Most to least
Graduated guidance
Other: _____
What is the child's response?
What reinforcers are you using?
What is the correction procedure?
How will you collect data? *(circle answer)*
Percentage correct   Frequency
Duration   Permanent product
Other: _____

Sets

1. _____
   _____
   _____
   _____

2. _____
   _____
   _____
   _____

3. _____
   _____
   _____
   _____

4. _____
   _____
   _____
   _____

5. _____
   _____
   _____
   _____

INSTRUCTIONAL PROGRAM SHEET: Comprehension and Expression of Words and Sentences

Identifies Common Nouns—Expressive

Child: _____   Date initiated: _____   Date completed: _____

Objective: When shown a picture or object and asked what it is, or when noticing an item in the environment, the child states the name of the picture or object verbally or nonverbally (i.e., with an augmentative communication system).

Mastery criterion:
- 90% or higher correct response for each set
- Minimum of 10 opportunities per day
- 2 consecutive teaching days
- Identifies at least 50 total pictures or objects

Generalization:
People: At least two adults
Settings: At least two settings
Materials: Across a variety of pictures/objects for each noun

Things to consider: Consider pictures that are simple, so the child can easily identify the item in the picture. Consider teaching the words receptively before expressively.

Teaching sequence
1. Identifies at least five common nouns in simple pictures
2. Identifies the five common nouns from previous set in other pictures
3. Identifies at least five common objects
4. Identifies the five common objects from previous set across different objects
5. Continue adding new sets of pictures and objects, with generalization across a variety
6. Identifies at least 50 items to build vocabulary

PROGRAMMING LOG

	Acquisition		Generalization		Maintenance	
	Start date	End date	Start date	End date	Date/data	Date/data
1						
2						
3						
4						
5						

LESSON PLAN: Comprehension and Expression of Words and Sentences

Identifies Common Nouns—Expressive

Settings and materials	
Decontextualized	Embedded

Teaching
What direction or cue will you give?
How will you prompt the child's response?
Circle type of prompt(s) used:
Physical   Visual
Modeling   Verbal
Other: _____
Circle prompt fading procedure used:
Time delay   Most to least
Graduated guidance
Other: _____
What is the child's response?
What reinforcers are you using?
What is the correction procedure?
How will you collect data? *(circle answer)*
Percentage correct   Frequency
Duration   Permanent product
Other: _____

Sets

1. _____

_____

_____

_____

2. _____

_____

_____

_____

3. _____

_____

_____

_____

4. _____

_____

_____

_____

5. _____

_____

_____

_____

INSTRUCTIONAL PROGRAM SHEET: Comprehension and Expression of Words and Sentences

Identifies Actions—Receptive

Child: _____ Date initiated: _____ Date completed: _____

Objective: When presented with at least three different pictures of actions and asked to identify one of them receptively (e.g., "Show me ___," "Where is ___," or "Find the ___"), or when asked to identify the person engaging in the action (e.g., "Who is jumping?"), the child points to, touches, or picks up the correct picture or person engaging in the action.

Mastery criterion:
- 90% or higher correct response for each set
- Minimum of 10 opportunities per day
- 2 consecutive teaching days
- Identifies at least 15 actions

Generalization:
People: At least two adults
Settings: At least two settings
Materials: Across a variety of pictures for each action

Things to consider: Consider pictures that are simple, so the child can easily identify the action in the picture. Be careful of identifying information, such as one picture with only a blue background, from the array of pictures.

Teaching sequence
1. Identifies at least five actions in simple pictures
2. Identifies the five actions from previous set in other pictures
3. Identifies at least five live actions
4. Continue adding new sets of pictures and live actions, with generalization across a variety, to total at least 15 actions

PROGRAMMING LOG

	Acquisition		Generalization		Maintenance	
	Start date	End date	Start date	End date	Date/data	Date/data
1						
2						
3						
4						

LESSON PLAN: Comprehension and Expression of Words and Sentences

Identifies Actions—Receptive

Settings and materials	
Decontextualized	**Embedded**

Teaching
What direction or cue will you give?
How will you prompt the child's response?
Circle type of prompt(s) used:
Physical   Visual
Modeling   Verbal
Other: _____
Circle prompt fading procedure used:
Time delay   Most to least
Graduated guidance
Other: _____
What is the child's response?
What reinforcers are you using?
What is the correction procedure?
How will you collect data? *(circle answer)*
Percentage correct   Frequency
Duration   Permanent product
Other: _____

Sets

1. _____
   _____
   _____
   _____

2. _____
   _____
   _____
   _____

3. _____
   _____
   _____
   _____

4. _____
   _____
   _____
   _____

5. _____
   _____
   _____
   _____

INSTRUCTIONAL PROGRAM SHEET: Comprehension and Expression of Words and Sentences

Identifies Actions—Expressive

Child: _____ Date initiated: _____ Date completed: _____

Objective: When shown a picture of an action and asked what he or she is doing, or when noticing an action in the environment, the child states the action verbally or nonverbally (i.e., with an augmentative communication system).

Mastery criterion:
▧ 90% or higher correct response for each set
▧ Minimum of 10 opportunities per day
▧ 2 consecutive teaching days
▧ Identifies at least 15 actions (e.g., jumping, running, drawing)

Generalization:
People: At least two adults
Settings: At least two settings
Materials: Across a variety of pictures for each action

Things to consider: Consider pictures that are simple, so the child can easily identify the action in the picture. Consider teaching the actions receptively before expressively

Teaching sequence
1. Identifies at least five actions in simple pictures
2. Identifies the five actions from previous set in other pictures
3. Identifies at least five live actions
4. Continue adding new sets of pictures and live actions, with generalization across a variety, to total at least 15 actions

PROGRAMMING LOG

	Acquisition		Generalization		Maintenance	
	Start date	End date	Start date	End date	Date/data	Date/data
1						
2						
3						
4						

LESSON PLAN: Comprehension and Expression of Words and Sentences

Identifies Actions—Expressive

Settings and materials	
Decontextualized	**Embedded**

Teaching
What direction or cue will you give?
How will you prompt the child's response?
Circle type of prompt(s) used:
Physical Visual Modeling Verbal Other: _____
Circle prompt fading procedure used:
Time delay Most to least Graduated guidance Other: _____
What is the child's response?
What reinforcers are you using?
What is the correction procedure?
How will you collect data? *(circle answer)*
Percentage correct Frequency Duration Permanent product Other: _____

Sets

1. _____

_____

_____

_____

2. _____

_____

_____

_____

3. _____

_____

_____

_____

4. _____

_____

_____

_____

5. _____

_____

_____

_____

INSTRUCTIONAL PROGRAM SHEET: Comprehension and Expression of Words and Sentences

Uses Pronouns—Receptive

Child: _____   Date initiated: _____   Date completed: _____

Objective: When asked to identify an item or person by a pronoun (e.g., "Which one is your/my coat?" or "Show me your/his feet"), the child correctly identifies the item or person by pointing, tapping, or giving the item.

Mastery criterion:
- 90% or higher correct response for each set
- Minimum of 10 opportunities per day
- 2 consecutive teaching days

Generalization:
People: At least two adults
Settings: At least two settings
Materials: Across a variety of pronouns

Things to consider: When providing behavior-specific praise or an error correction, be sure to state the pronoun from the child's perspective (e.g., "This one is *your* coat" when identifying the coat you have, instead of stating "This one is *my* coat"). When identifying his or her or he or she, be sure the child can identify people by gender (female or male).

Teaching sequence
1. Identifies at least two pronouns
2. Identifies at least four pronouns
3. Identifies at least six pronouns
4. Identifies at least eight pronouns

PROGRAMMING LOG

	Acquisition		Generalization		Maintenance	
	Start date	End date	Start date	End date	Date/data	Date/data
1						
2						
3						
4						

The DATA Model for Teaching Preschoolers with Autism by Ilene Schwartz, Julie Ashmun, Bonnie McBride, Crista Scott, and Susan Sandall. Copyright © 2017 by Paul H. Brookes Publishing Co., Inc. All rights reserved.

LESSON PLAN: Comprehension and Expression of Words and Sentences

Uses Pronouns—Receptive

Settings and materials	
Decontextualized	**Embedded**

Teaching
What direction or cue will you give?
How will you prompt the child's response?
Circle type of prompt(s) used:
Physical   Visual
Modeling   Verbal
Other: _____
Circle prompt fading procedure used:
Time delay   Most to least
Graduated guidance
Other: _____
What is the child's response?
What reinforcers are you using?
What is the correction procedure?
How will you collect data? *(circle answer)*
Percentage correct   Frequency
Duration   Permanent product
Other: _____

Sets

1. _____
   _____
   _____
   _____

2. _____
   _____
   _____
   _____

3. _____
   _____
   _____
   _____

4. _____
   _____
   _____
   _____

5. _____
   _____
   _____
   _____

INSTRUCTIONAL PROGRAM SHEET: Comprehension and Expression of Words and Sentences

Uses Pronouns—Expressive

Child: _____   Date initiated: _____   Date completed: _____

Objective: When asked about possession of an item (e.g., "Whose coat is that?"), or when using a pronoun (e.g., "That is my/your coat" or "I have the ball"), the child correctly uses a pronoun.

Mastery criterion:
- 90% or higher correct response for each set
- Minimum of 10 opportunities per day
- 2 consecutive teaching days

Generalization:
People: At least two adults
Settings: At least two settings
Materials: Across a variety of pronouns

Things to consider: When providing behavior-specific praise or an error correction, be sure to state the pronoun from the child's perspective (e.g., "That's right. You said 'that is *your* coat,'" when he is identifying the coat you have, instead of stating "That's right. That is *my* coat."). When identifying his or her or he or she, be sure the child can identify people by gender (female or male). Consider teaching pronouns receptively before expressively.

Teaching sequence
1. Uses at least two pronouns
2. Uses at least four pronouns
3. Uses at least six pronouns
4. Uses at least eight pronouns

PROGRAMMING LOG

	Acquisition		Generalization		Maintenance	
	Start date	End date	Start date	End date	Date/data	Date/data
1						
2						
3						
4						

LESSON PLAN: Comprehension and Expression of Words and Sentences

Uses Pronouns—Expressive

Settings and materials	
Decontextualized	**Embedded**

Teaching

What direction or cue will you give?

How will you prompt the child's response?

Circle type of prompt(s) used:

Physical   Visual

Modeling   Verbal

Other: _____

Circle prompt fading procedure used:

Time delay   Most to least

Graduated guidance

Other: _____

What is the child's response?

What reinforcers are you using?

What is the correction procedure?

How will you collect data? *(circle answer)*

Percentage correct   Frequency

Duration   Permanent product

Other: _____

Sets

1. _____

2. _____

3. _____

4. _____

5. _____

INSTRUCTIONAL PROGRAM SHEET: Comprehension and Expression of Words and Sentences

Identifies Functions—Receptive

Child: _____ Date initiated: _____ Date completed: _____

Objective: When presented with at least three different pictures or objects from the environment and asked to identify one of them by its function receptively (e.g., "Show me the one you eat" or "Find the one you color with"), the child points to, touches, or picks up the correct picture or object.

Mastery criterion:
- 90% or higher correct response for each set
- Minimum of 10 opportunities per day
- 2 consecutive teaching days
- Identifies at least 10 functions across pictures or objects

Generalization:
People: At least two adults
Settings: At least two settings
Materials: Across a variety of pictures or objects for each function

Things to consider: Consider pictures that are simple, so the child can easily identify the item in the picture. Be careful of identifying information such as one picture with only a blue background from the array of pictures.

Teaching sequence
1. Identifies at least two functions of objects in pictures
2. Identifies the two functions from previous set in other pictures
3. Identifies at least two functions of objects in the environment
4. Identifies the two functions from previous set across different objects
5. Continue adding new sets of pictures and objects, with generalization across a variety, to total at least 10 functions

PROGRAMMING LOG

	Acquisition		Generalization		Maintenance	
	Start date	End date	Start date	End date	Date/data	Date/data
1						
2						
3						
4						
5						

LESSON PLAN: Comprehension and Expression of Words and Sentences

Identifies Functions—Receptive

Settings and materials	
Decontextualized	Embedded

Teaching
What direction or cue will you give?
How will you prompt the child's response?
Circle type of prompt(s) used:
Physical   Visual
Modeling   Verbal
Other: _____
Circle prompt fading procedure used:
Time delay   Most to least
Graduated guidance
Other: _____
What is the child's response?
What reinforcers are you using?
What is the correction procedure?
How will you collect data? *(circle answer)*
Percentage correct   Frequency
Duration   Permanent product
Other: _____

Sets

1. _____

_____

_____

_____

2. _____

_____

_____

_____

3. _____

_____

_____

_____

4. _____

_____

_____

_____

5. _____

_____

_____

_____

INSTRUCTIONAL PROGRAM SHEET: Comprehension and Expression of Words and Sentences

Identifies Functions—Expressive

Child: _____ Date initiated: _____ Date completed: _____

Objective: When shown a picture of an item or when shown an object and asked to identify its function (e.g., "What do you do with this?"), or when asked to fill in a statement to identify a function (e.g., "You eat with a __"), the child states the function of the item in the picture or the object verbally or nonverbally (i.e., with an augmentative communication system).

Mastery criterion:
- 90% or higher correct response for each set
- Minimum of 10 opportunities per day
- 2 consecutive teaching days
- Identifies at least 10 functions across pictures or objects

Generalization:
People: At least two adults
Settings: At least two settings
Materials: Across a variety of pictures/objects for each function

Things to consider: Consider pictures that are simple, so the child can easily identify the item in the picture. Consider teaching the functions receptively before expressively.

Teaching sequence
1. Identifies at least two functions of objects in pictures
2. Identifies the two functions from previous set in other pictures
3. Identifies at least two functions of objects in the environment
4. Identifies the two functions from previous set across different objects
5. Continue adding new sets of pictures and objects, with generalization across a variety, to total at least 10 functions

PROGRAMMING LOG

	Acquisition		Generalization		Maintenance	
	Start date	End date	Start date	End date	Date/data	Date/data
1						
2						
3						
4						
5						

LESSON PLAN: Comprehension and Expression of Words and Sentences

Identifies Functions—Expressive

Settings and materials	
Decontextualized	**Embedded**

Teaching
What direction or cue will you give?
How will you prompt the child's response?
Circle type of prompt(s) used:
Physical   Visual
Modeling   Verbal
Other: _____
Circle prompt fading procedure used:
Time delay   Most to least
Graduated guidance
Other: _____
What is the child's response?
What reinforcers are you using?
What is the correction procedure?
How will you collect data? *(circle answer)*
Percentage correct   Frequency
Duration   Permanent product
Other: _____

Sets

1. _____
   _____
   _____
   _____

2. _____
   _____
   _____
   _____

3. _____
   _____
   _____
   _____

4. _____
   _____
   _____
   _____

5. _____
   _____
   _____
   _____

INSTRUCTIONAL PROGRAM SHEET: Comprehension and Expression of Words and Sentences

Identifies Features—Receptive

Child: _____ Date initiated: _____ Date completed: _____

Objective: When presented with at least three different pictures or objects from the environment and asked to identify one of them by a feature of the object receptively (e.g., "Which one has a tail?" or "Find the one with a wheel"), the child points to, touches, or picks up the correct picture or object with the identifying feature.

Mastery criterion:
- 90% or higher correct response for each set
- Minimum of 10 opportunities per day
- 2 consecutive teaching days
- Identifies at least 10 features across pictures or objects

Generalization:
People: At least two adults
Settings: At least two settings
Materials: Across a variety of pictures/objects for each feature

Things to consider: Consider pictures that are simple, so the child can easily identify the item in the picture. Be careful of identifying information, such as one picture with only a blue background, from the array of pictures.

Teaching sequence
1. Identifies at least two features of objects in pictures
2. Identifies the two features from previous set in other pictures
3. Identifies at least two features of objects in the environment
4. Identifies the two features from previous set across different objects
5. Continue adding new sets of pictures and objects, with generalization across a variety, to total at least 10 features

PROGRAMMING LOG

	Acquisition		Generalization		Maintenance	
	Start date	End date	Start date	End date	Date/data	Date/data
1						
2						
3						
4						
5						

LESSON PLAN: Comprehension and Expression of Words and Sentences

Identifies Features—Receptive

Settings and materials	
Decontextualized	**Embedded**

Teaching
What direction or cue will you give?
How will you prompt the child's response?
Circle type of prompt(s) used:
Physical   Visual   Modeling   Verbal   Other: _____
Circle prompt fading procedure used:
Time delay   Most to least   Graduated guidance   Other: _____
What is the child's response?
What reinforcers are you using?
What is the correction procedure?
How will you collect data? *(circle answer)*
Percentage correct   Frequency   Duration   Permanent product   Other: _____

Sets

1. _____

   _____

   _____

   _____

2. _____

   _____

   _____

   _____

3. _____

   _____

   _____

   _____

4. _____

   _____

   _____

   _____

5. _____

   _____

   _____

   _____

INSTRUCTIONAL PROGRAM SHEET: Comprehension and Expression of Words and Sentences

Identifies Features—Expressive

Child: _____ Date initiated: _____ Date completed: _____

Objective: When shown a picture of an item or when shown an object and asked to identify it by a feature (e.g., "What does a dog have?") or when asked to fill in a statement to identify a feature (e.g., "A dog has a ___"), the child states a feature of the item in the picture or the object verbally or nonverbally (i.e., with an augmentative communication system).

Mastery criterion:
- 90% or higher correct response for each set
- Minimum of 10 opportunities per day
- 2 consecutive teaching days
- Identifies at least 10 features across pictures or objects

Generalization:
People: At least three adults
Settings: At least three settings
Materials: Across a variety of pictures or objects for each feature

Things to consider: Consider pictures that are simple, so the child can easily identify the item in the picture. Consider teaching features receptively before expressively.

Teaching sequence
1. Identifies at least two features of objects in pictures
2. Identifies the two features from previous set in other pictures
3. Identifies at least two features of objects in the environment
4. Identifies the two features from previous set across different objects
5. Continue adding new sets of pictures and objects, with generalization across a variety, to total at least 10 features

PROGRAMMING LOG

	Acquisition		Generalization		Maintenance	
	Start date	End date	Start date	End date	Date/data	Date/data
1						
2						
3						
4						
5						

LESSON PLAN: Comprehension and Expression of Words and Sentences

Identifies Features—Expressive

Settings and materials	
Decontextualized	**Embedded**

Teaching
What direction or cue will you give?
How will you prompt the child's response?
Circle type of prompt(s) used:

Physical	Visual
Modeling	Verbal
Other: _____	

Circle prompt fading procedure used:	
Time delay	Most to least
Graduated guidance	
Other: _____	

What is the child's response?
What reinforcers are you using?
What is the correction procedure?
How will you collect data? *(circle answer)*

Percentage correct	Frequency
Duration	Permanent product
Other: _____	

Sets

1. _____
   _____
   _____
   _____

2. _____
   _____
   _____
   _____

3. _____
   _____
   _____
   _____

4. _____
   _____
   _____
   _____

5. _____
   _____
   _____
   _____

INSTRUCTIONAL PROGRAM SHEET: Comprehension and Expression of Words and Sentences

Identifies Categories—Receptive

Child: _____ Date initiated: _____ Date completed: _____

Objective: When presented with at least three different pictures or objects from the environment and asked to identify one of them by a category receptively (e.g., "Which one is an animal?" or "Put with the animals"), the child points to, touches, or puts with the correct picture or object from the identifying category.

Mastery criterion:
- 90% or higher correct response for each set
- Minimum of 10 opportunities per day
- 2 consecutive teaching days
- Identifies at least five categories across pictures or objects

Generalization:
People: At least two adults
Settings: At least two settings
Materials: Across a variety of pictures or objects for each category

Things to consider: Consider pictures that are simple, so the child can easily identify the item in the picture. Be careful of identifying information such as one picture with only a blue background from the array of pictures.

Teaching sequence
1. Identifies at least two categories with objects in pictures
2. Identifies the two categories from previous set in other pictures
3. Identifies at least two categories of objects in the environment
4. Identifies the two categories from previous set across different objects
5. Identifies at least two categories with objects in pictures
6. Identifies the two categories from previous set in other pictures

PROGRAMMING LOG

	Acquisition		Generalization		Maintenance	
	Start date	End date	Start date	End date	Date/data	Date/data
1						
2						
3						
4						
5						
6						

LESSON PLAN: Comprehension and Expression of Words and Sentences

Identifies Categories—Receptive

Settings and materials	
Decontextualized	**Embedded**

Teaching

What direction or cue will you give?

How will you prompt the child's response?

Circle type of prompt(s) used:

Physical   Visual

Modeling   Verbal

Other: _____

Circle prompt fading procedure used:

Time delay   Most to least

Graduated guidance

Other: _____

What is the child's response?

What reinforcers are you using?

What is the correction procedure?

How will you collect data? *(circle answer)*

Percentage correct   Frequency

Duration   Permanent product

Other: _____

Sets

1. _____

   _____

   _____

   _____

2. _____

   _____

   _____

   _____

3. _____

   _____

   _____

   _____

4. _____

   _____

   _____

   _____

5. _____

   _____

   _____

   _____

INSTRUCTIONAL PROGRAM SHEET: Comprehension and Expression of Words and Sentences

Identifies Categories—Expressive

Child: _____ Date initiated: _____ Date completed: _____

Objective: When shown a picture of an item, or when shown an object and asked to identify its category (e.g., "What is a cat?"), or when asked to fill in a statement to identify a category (e.g., "A cat is a type of ___"), the child states the category of the item in the picture or the object verbally or nonverbally (i.e., with an augmentative communication system).

Mastery criterion:
- 90% or higher correct response for each set
- Minimum of 10 opportunities per day
- 2 consecutive teaching days
- Identifies at least five categories across pictures or objects

Generalization:
People: At least two adults
Settings: At least two settings
Materials: Across a variety of pictures or objects for each category

Things to consider: Consider pictures that are simple, so the child can easily identify the item in the picture. Consider teaching the categories receptively before expressively.

Teaching sequence
1. Identifies at least two categories with objects in pictures
2. Identifies the two categories from previous set in other pictures
3. Identifies at least two categories of objects in the environment
4. Identifies the two categories from previous set across different objects
5. Identifies at least two categories with objects in pictures
6. Identifies the two categories from previous set in other pictures

PROGRAMMING LOG

	Acquisition		Generalization		Maintenance	
	Start date	End date	Start date	End date	Date/data	Date/data
1						
2						
3						
4						
5						
6						

LESSON PLAN: Comprehension and Expression of Words and Sentences

Identifies Categories—Expressive

Settings and materials	
Decontextualized	**Embedded**

Teaching
What direction or cue will you give?
How will you prompt the child's response?
Circle type of prompt(s) used:
Physical   Visual
Modeling   Verbal
Other: _____
Circle prompt fading procedure used:
Time delay   Most to least
Graduated guidance
Other: _____
What is the child's response?
What reinforcers are you using?
What is the correction procedure?
How will you collect data? *(circle answer)*
Percentage correct   Frequency
Duration   Permanent product
Other: _____

Sets

1. _____
2. _____
3. _____
4. _____
5. _____

INSTRUCTIONAL PROGRAM SHEET: Comprehension and Expression of Words and Sentences

Identifies Attributes—Receptive

Child: _____ Date initiated: _____ Date completed: _____

Objective: When presented with materials that are varied by size, shape, or color and asked to identify one of them receptively based on its size, shape, or color (e.g., "Show me the big ball," "Find blue," or "Put it with circles"), the child identifies an item or an item in a picture based on the size, shape, or color by pointing to, tapping, or putting it with the correct item.

Mastery criterion:
- 90% or higher correct response for each set
- Minimum of 10 opportunities per day
- 2 consecutive teaching days
- Identifies at least four sizes, six shapes, and six colors

Generalization:
People: At least two adults
Settings: At least two settings
Materials: Across a variety of pictures or objects for each attribute

Things to consider: Materials for child to choose from must be varied across one attribute only (e.g., all materials are triangles, varying only by color; all blocks are orange squares, varying only by size). Consider having child sort by attribute before receptively identifying the items by attribute.

Teaching sequence
1. Identifies items by at least two different sizes (e.g., big, little)
2. Identifies items by at least two other sizes (e.g., huge, medium)
3. Identifies items by at least three shapes (e.g., circle, square, triangle)
4. Identifies items by at least three shapes (e.g., oval, rectangle, diamond)
5. Identifies items by at least three colors (e.g., blue, red, yellow)
6. Identifies items by at least three colors (e.g., purple, orange, green)

PROGRAMMING LOG

	Acquisition		Generalization		Maintenance	
	Start date	End date	Start date	End date	Date/data	Date/data
1						
2						
3						
4						
5						
6						

LESSON PLAN: Comprehension and Expression of Words and Sentences

Identifies Attributes—Receptive

Settings and materials	
Decontextualized	**Embedded**

Teaching

What direction or cue will you give?

How will you prompt the child's response?

Circle type of prompt(s) used:

Physical	Visual
Modeling	Verbal

Other: _____

Circle prompt fading procedure used:

Time delay	Most to least
Graduated guidance	

Other: _____

What is the child's response?

What reinforcers are you using?

What is the correction procedure?

How will you collect data? *(circle answer)*

Percentage correct	Frequency
Duration	Permanent product

Other: _____

Sets

1. _____

_____

_____

_____

2. _____

_____

_____

_____

3. _____

_____

_____

_____

4. _____

_____

_____

_____

5. _____

_____

_____

_____

INSTRUCTIONAL PROGRAM SHEET: Comprehension and Expression of Words and Sentences

Identifies Attributes—Expressive

Child: _____ Date initiated: _____ Date completed: _____

Objective: When presented with materials that are varied by size, shape, or color and asked to identify the item by its attribute (e.g., "Which one do you want?" or "What do you see?"), the child identifies the item by its size, shape, or color by requesting or commenting on the item.

Mastery criterion:
- 90% or higher correct response for each set
- Minimum of 10 opportunities per day
- 2 consecutive teaching days
- Identifies at least four sizes, six shapes, and six colors

Generalization:
People: At least two adults
Settings: At least two settings
Materials: Across a variety of pictures or objects for each attribute

Things to consider: Materials for child to choose from must be varied across one attribute only (e.g., all materials are triangles, varying only by color; all blocks are orange squares, varying only by size). Consider teaching receptively before expressively.

Teaching sequence
1. Identifies items by at least two different sizes (e.g., big, little)
2. Identifies items by at least two other sizes (e.g., huge, medium)
3. Identifies items by at least three shapes (e.g., circle, square, triangle)
4. Identifies items by at least three shapes (e.g., oval, rectangle, diamond)
5. Identifies items by at least three colors (e.g., blue, red, yellow)
6. Identifies items by at least three colors (e.g., purple, orange, green)

PROGRAMMING LOG

	Acquisition		Generalization		Maintenance	
	Start date	End date	Start date	End date	Date/data	Date/data
1						
2						
3						
4						
5						
6						

The DATA Model for Teaching Preschoolers with Autism by Ilene Schwartz, Julie Ashmun, Bonnie McBride, Crista Scott, and Susan Sandall. Copyright © 2017 by Paul H. Brookes Publishing Co., Inc. All rights reserved.

LESSON PLAN: Comprehension and Expression of Words and Sentences

Identifies Attributes—Expressive

Settings and materials		Sets
Decontextualized	**Embedded**	1. _____

Teaching

What direction or cue will you give?

How will you prompt the child's response?

Circle type of prompt(s) used:

Physical   Visual

Modeling   Verbal

Other: _____

Circle prompt fading procedure used:

Time delay   Most to least

Graduated guidance

Other: _____

What is the child's response?

What reinforcers are you using?

What is the correction procedure?

How will you collect data? *(circle answer)*

Percentage correct   Frequency

Duration   Permanent product

Other: _____

Sets

1. _____

2. _____

3. _____

4. _____

5. _____

INSTRUCTIONAL PROGRAM SHEET: Comprehension and Expression of Words and Sentences

Identifies Prepositions—Receptive

Child: _____ Date initiated: _____ Date completed: _____

Objective: When presented with materials and asked to put an item in a location or identify which item is in a location (e.g., "Put it under the chair" or "Which one is on the bridge?"), the child identifies the item by its location or puts the item in the correct location based on the preposition.

Mastery criterion:
- 90% or higher correct response for each set
- Minimum of 10 opportunities per day
- 2 consecutive teaching days
- Identifies at least six prepositions

Generalization:
People: At least two adults
Settings: At least two settings
Materials: Across a variety of materials

Things to consider: Use preferred materials for teaching.

Teaching sequence
1. Identifies two locations across materials
2. Identifies two locations across materials
3. Identifies two locations across materials

PROGRAMMING LOG

	Acquisition		Generalization		Maintenance	
	Start date	End date	Start date	End date	Date/data	Date/data
1						
2						
3						

The DATA Model for Teaching Preschoolers with Autism by Ilene Schwartz, Julie Ashmun, Bonnie McBride, Crista Scott, and Susan Sandall. Copyright © 2017 by Paul H. Brookes Publishing Co., Inc. All rights reserved.

LESSON PLAN: Comprehension and Expression of Words and Sentences

Identifies Prepositions—Receptive

Settings and materials	
Decontextualized	**Embedded**

Teaching
What direction or cue will you give?
How will you prompt the child's response?
Circle type of prompt(s) used:
Physical   Visual
Modeling   Verbal
Other: _____
Circle prompt fading procedure used:
Time delay   Most to least
Graduated guidance
Other: _____
What is the child's response?
What reinforcers are you using?
What is the correction procedure?
How will you collect data? *(circle answer)*
Percentage correct   Frequency
Duration   Permanent product
Other: _____

Sets

1. _____

   _____

   _____

   _____

2. _____

   _____

   _____

   _____

3. _____

   _____

   _____

   _____

4. _____

   _____

   _____

5. _____

   _____

   _____

   _____

INSTRUCTIONAL PROGRAM SHEET: Comprehension and Expression of Words and Sentences

Identifies Prepositions—Expressive

Child: _____   Date initiated: _____   Date completed: _____

Objective: When asked where an item is located (e.g., "Where is the block?" or "Where is the train?") or when indicating the location of an item, the child identifies the location of the item using a preposition (e.g. "It's *under* the table" or "It's *on* the bridge").

Mastery criterion:
- 90% or higher correct response for each set
- Minimum of 10 opportunities per day
- 2 consecutive teaching days
- Identifies at least six prepositions

Generalization:
People: At least two adults
Settings: At least two settings
Materials: Across a variety of materials

Things to consider: Use preferred materials for teaching. Consider teaching receptively before expressively.

Teaching sequence
1. Identifies two locations across materials
2. Identifies two locations across materials
3. Identifies two locations across materials

PROGRAMMING LOG

	Acquisition		Generalization		Maintenance	
	Start date	End date	Start date	End date	Date/data	Date/data
1						
2						
3						

LESSON PLAN: Comprehension and Expression of Words and Sentences

Identifies Prepositions—Expressive

Settings and materials	
Decontextualized	**Embedded**

Teaching
What direction or cue will you give?
How will you prompt the child's response?
Circle type of prompt(s) used:
Physical   Visual
Modeling   Verbal
Other: _____
Circle prompt fading procedure used:
Time delay   Most to least
Graduated guidance
Other: _____
What is the child's response?
What reinforcers are you using?
What is the correction procedure?
How will you collect data? *(circle answer)*
Percentage correct   Frequency
Duration   Permanent product
Other: _____

Sets

1. _____

   _____

   _____

   _____

2. _____

   _____

   _____

   _____

3. _____

   _____

   _____

   _____

4. _____

   _____

   _____

   _____

5. _____

   _____

   _____

   _____

INSTRUCTIONAL PROGRAM SHEET: Joint Attention

References Communicative Partner During Interaction

Child: _____ Date initiated: _____ Date completed: _____

Objective: When interacting with a familiar adult or peer, the child references the adult's or peer's face by looking toward the adult or peer (e.g., adult looks surprised and child reacts; child looks at peer when responding to a request).

Mastery criterion:
- 90% or higher correct response for each set
- Minimum of 10 opportunities per day
- 2 consecutive teaching days

Generalization:
People: At least two adults and peers
Settings: At least two settings
Materials: Across at least five different activities

Things to consider: Consider motivating games and materials to encourage eye contact.

Teaching sequence
1. Child references adult or peer with one prompt
2. Child references adult or peer

PROGRAMMING LOG

	Acquisition		Generalization		Maintenance	
	Start date	End date	Start date	End date	Date/data	Date/data
1						
2						

LESSON PLAN: Joint Attention

References Communicative Partner During Interaction

Settings and materials	
Decontextualized	**Embedded**

Teaching
What direction or cue will you give?
How will you prompt the child's response?
Circle type of prompt(s) used:
Physical   Visual
Modeling   Verbal
Other: _____
Circle prompt fading procedure used:
Time delay   Most to least
Graduated guidance
Other: _____
What is the child's response?
What reinforcers are you using?
What is the correction procedure?
How will you collect data? *(circle answer)*
Percentage correct   Frequency
Duration   Permanent product
Other: _____

Sets

1. _____
   _____
   _____
   _____

2. _____
   _____
   _____
   _____

3. _____
   _____
   _____
   _____

4. _____
   _____
   _____

5. _____
   _____
   _____
   _____

INSTRUCTIONAL PROGRAM SHEET: Joint Attention

References Communicative Partner During Interaction—Example

Child: _____ Date initiated: _____ Date completed: _____

Objective: When interacting with a familiar adult or peer, the child references the adult's or peer's face by looking toward the adult or peer (e.g., adult looks surprised and child reacts; child looks at peer when responding to a request).

Mastery criterion:
- 90% or higher correct response for each set
- Minimum of 10 opportunities per day
- 2 consecutive teaching days

Generalization:
People: At least two adults and peers
Settings: At least two settings
Materials: Across at least five different activities

Things to consider: Consider motivating games and materials to encourage eye contact.

Teaching sequence
1. Child references adult or peer with one prompt
2. Child references adult or peer

PROGRAMMING LOG

	Acquisition		Generalization		Maintenance	
	Start date	End date	Start date	End date	Date/data	Date/data
1	1/5/15	2/10/15	2/11/15	2/25/15		
2	2/11/15	3/20/15	3/21/15	3/25/15	4/25/15; 80%	6/5/15; 100%

LESSON PLAN: Joint Attention

References Communicative Partner During Interaction—Example

Settings and materials	
Decontextualized	**Embedded**
Use preferred materials close to adult's face to prompt child to reference adult during play activities in work area. Use exaggerated facial expressions.	Use preferred materials during play activities in the classroom if needed to get child's attention and to reference adult or peer.

Teaching
What direction or cue will you give?
No direction is provided. The stimulus (adult or peer interaction) is the cue.
How will you prompt the child's response?
Circle type of prompt(s) used:
Physical (Visual)
Modeling Verbal
Other: _____
Circle prompt fading procedure used:
(Time delay) Most to least
Graduated guidance
Other: _____
What is the child's response?
References (at least a glance) adult or peer's face
What reinforcers are you using?
Praise and preferred item provided upon reference
What is the correction procedure?
Present cue again (initiate interaction) and provide prompt (present preferred item for tracking to face). If incorrect again, move to another task.
How will you collect data? *(circle answer)*
(Percentage correct) Frequency
Duration Permanent product
Other: _____

Sets
1. Use preferred materials by moving them toward adult's face, teaching child to track to face Exaggerated facial expressions, with adults
2. Set one with a preferred peer
3. No prompts; references naturally

INSTRUCTIONAL PROGRAM SHEET: Joint Attention

Follows Pointing Gesture to Establish Joint Attention

Child: _____ Date initiated: _____ Date completed: _____

Objective: When an adult or peer points and looks toward an object, person, or event and comments on it, the child looks in the direction of a person's pointing gesture for at least 1 second.

Mastery criterion:
- 90% or higher correct response for each set
- Minimum of 10 opportunities per day
- 2 consecutive teaching days

Generalization:
People: At least two adults and peers
Settings: At least two settings
Materials: Across a variety of materials

Things to consider: Child can visibly see and track items. Child must have mobility to turn body and head in the direction of point.

Teaching sequence
1. Follows point to an object directly in front of child
2. Follows point to an object, person, or event within 3 feet of child
3. Follows point to an object, person, or event within 6 feet of child
4. Follows point to an object, person, or event across the room or further than 6 feet from child

PROGRAMMING LOG

	Acquisition		Generalization		Maintenance	
	Start date	End date	Start date	End date	Date/data	Date/data
1						
2						
3						
4						

LESSON PLAN: Joint Attention

Follows Pointing Gesture to Establish Joint Attention

Settings and materials	
Decontextualized	Embedded

Teaching
What direction or cue will you give?
How will you prompt the child's response?
Circle type of prompt(s) used:
Physical   Visual
Modeling   Verbal
Other: _____
Circle prompt fading procedure used:
Time delay   Most to least
Graduated guidance
Other: _____
What is the child's response?
What reinforcers are you using?
What is the correction procedure?
How will you collect data? *(circle answer)*
Percentage correct   Frequency
Duration   Permanent product
Other: _____

Sets

1. _____

_____

_____

_____

2. _____

_____

_____

_____

3. _____

_____

_____

_____

4. _____

_____

_____

5. _____

_____

_____

_____

INSTRUCTIONAL PROGRAM SHEET: Joint Attention

Follows Gaze to Establish Joint Attention

Child: _____ Date initiated: _____ Date completed: _____

Objective: When a person looks in the direction of an object, person, or event, the child looks in the general direction of the person's gaze within 5 seconds. Looking at the object includes orienting his or her head in the general direction of the person's gaze and looking at the object, person, or event for at least one second.

Mastery criterion:
- 90% or higher correct response for each set
- Minimum of 10 opportunities per day
- 2 consecutive teaching days

Generalization:
People: At least two adults and peers
Settings: At least two settings
Materials: Across a variety of materials

Things to consider: Child can visibly see and track items. Use exaggerated facial expressions and sounds to grab child's attention.

Teaching sequence
1. Object is directly in front of child and the instructor makes an exaggerated facial expression and points to item
2. Object is directly in front of child and the instructor makes an exaggerated facial expression (does not point)
3. Follows person's gaze to look at an object, person, or event no more than 3 feet away from child
4. Follows person's gaze to look at an object, person, or event no more than 6 feet away from child
5. Follows person's gaze to look at an object, person, or event across the room (i.e., more than 6 feet away from child)

PROGRAMMING LOG

	Acquisition		Generalization		Maintenance	
	Start date	End date	Start date	End date	Date/data	Date/data
1						
2						
3						
4						
5						

LESSON PLAN: Joint Attention

Follows Gaze to Establish Joint Attention

Settings and materials	
Decontextualized	**Embedded**

Teaching
What direction or cue will you give?
How will you prompt the child's response?
Circle type of prompt(s) used:
Physical   Visual
Modeling   Verbal
Other: _____
Circle prompt fading procedure used:
Time delay   Most to least
Graduated guidance
Other: _____
What is the child's response?
What reinforcers are you using?
What is the correction procedure?
How will you collect data? *(circle answer)*
Percentage correct   Frequency
Duration   Permanent product
Other: _____

Sets

1. _____

_____

_____

_____

2. _____

_____

_____

_____

3. _____

_____

_____

_____

4. _____

_____

_____

_____

5. _____

_____

_____

_____

INSTRUCTIONAL PROGRAM SHEET: Joint Attention

Initiates Gesture to Establish Joint Attention

Child: _____ Date initiated: _____ Date completed: _____

Objective: The child initiates a gesture (e.g., point) to comment on an object, person, or event.

Mastery criterion:
- 80% or higher correct response for each set
- Minimum of five opportunities per day
- 3 consecutive teaching days

Generalization:
People: At least two adults and peers
Settings: At least two settings
Materials: Across a variety of materials

Things to consider: Provide preferred materials to motivate child to initiate. Child can point to request items.

Teaching sequence
1. Initiates gesture/point to an object directly in front of child (e.g., book)
2. Initiates gesture/point to an object, person, or event within 3 feet of child (e.g., adult, peer)
3. Initiates gesture/point to an object, person, or event within 6 feet of child
4. Initiates gesture/point to an object, person, or event across the room or further than 6 feet from child

PROGRAMMING LOG

	Acquisition		Generalization		Maintenance	
	Start date	End date	Start date	End date	Date/data	Date/data
1						
2						
3						
4						

LESSON PLAN: Joint Attention

Initiates Gesture to Establish Joint Attention

Settings and materials	
Decontextualized	**Embedded**

Teaching
What direction or cue will you give?
How will you prompt the child's response?
Circle type of prompt(s) used:
Physical   Visual
Modeling   Verbal
Other: _____
Circle prompt fading procedure used:
Time delay   Most to least
Graduated guidance
Other: _____
What is the child's response?
What reinforcers are you using?
What is the correction procedure?
How will you collect data? *(circle answer)*
Percentage correct   Frequency
Duration   Permanent product
Other: _____

Sets

1. _____

2. _____

3. _____

4. _____

5. _____

INSTRUCTIONAL PROGRAM SHEET: Joint Attention

Initiates Gaze to Establish Joint Attention

Child: _____   Date initiated: _____   Date completed: _____

Objective: The child initiates gaze by looking at an object, person, or event for at least one second and then looking at the adult or peer. Looking at the object includes orienting his or her head in the general direction of the object, person, or event and then looking in the direction of the person to whom child is establishing joint attention.

Mastery criterion:

▨ 80% or higher correct response for each set
▨ Minimum of five opportunities per day
▨ 3 consecutive teaching days

Generalization:

People: At least two adults and peers
Settings: At least two settings
Materials: Across a variety of materials

Things to consider: Child can visibly see and track items. Child must have mobility to turn body and head in the direction of point.

Teaching sequence

1. Object, person, or event directly in front of child
2. Object, person, or event no more than 3 feet away from child
3. Object, person, or event no more than 6 feet away from child
4. Object, person, or event across the room (i.e., more than 6 feet away from child)

PROGRAMMING LOG

	Acquisition		Generalization		Maintenance	
	Start date	End date	Start date	End date	Date/data	Date/data
1						
2						
3						
4						

LESSON PLAN: Joint Attention

Initiates Gaze to Establish Joint Attention

Settings and materials	
Decontextualized	**Embedded**

Teaching
What direction or cue will you give?
How will you prompt the child's response?
Circle type of prompt(s) used:
Physical   Visual
Modeling   Verbal
Other: _____
Circle prompt fading procedure used:
Time delay   Most to least
Graduated guidance
Other: _____
What is the child's response?
What reinforcers are you using?
What is the correction procedure?
How will you collect data? *(circle answer)*
Percentage correct   Frequency
Duration   Permanent product
Other: _____

Sets

1. _____

   _____

   _____

   _____

2. _____

   _____

   _____

   _____

3. _____

   _____

   _____

   _____

4. _____

   _____

   _____

   _____

5. _____

   _____

   _____

   _____

INSTRUCTIONAL PROGRAM SHEET: Joint Attention

Maintains a Social–Communicative Interaction

Child: _____ Date initiated: _____ Date completed: _____

Objective: When interacting with a familiar adult, the child maintains a social–communicative interaction for at least two sequences of turn taking.

Mastery criterion:
- 80% or higher correct affective response for each set
- Minimum of five opportunities per day
- 3 consecutive teaching days

Generalization:
People: At least two adults and peers
Settings: At least two settings
Materials: Across a variety of interactions

Things to consider: Interactions may range from peek-a-boo to a conversation.

Teaching sequence
1. Responds to adult initiation of social interaction by taking one turn
2. Responds to adult initiation of social interaction by taking two turns
3. Initiates familiar interactions with adults
4. Initiates familiar interactions with peers
5. Initiates novel interactions with adults and peers

PROGRAMMING LOG

	Acquisition		Generalization		Maintenance	
	Start date	End date	Start date	End date	Date/data	Date/data
1						
2						
3						
4						
5						

LESSON PLAN: Joint Attention

Maintains a Social–Communicative Interaction

V. SOCIAL

Settings and materials	
Decontextualized	Embedded

Teaching
What direction or cue will you give?
How will you prompt the child's response?
Circle type of prompt(s) used:
Physical Visual
Modeling Verbal
Other: _____
Circle prompt fading procedure used:
Time delay Most to least
Graduated guidance
Other: _____
What is the child's response?
What reinforcers are you using?
What is the correction procedure?
How will you collect data? *(circle answer)*
Percentage correct Frequency
Duration Permanent product
Other: _____

Sets

1. _____
_____
_____
_____

2. _____
_____
_____
_____

3. _____
_____
_____
_____

4. _____
_____
_____
_____

5. _____
_____
_____
_____

INSTRUCTIONAL PROGRAM SHEET: Pragmatic Rules

Maintains Appropriate Proximity to Conversation Partner

Child: _____ Date initiated: _____ Date completed: _____

Objective: When the child is conversing with an adult or peer, the child maintains appropriate proximity by standing at just the right distance from the adult or peer without touching him or her.

Mastery criterion:
- 80% or higher correct response for each set
- Minimum of five opportunities per day
- 3 consecutive teaching days

Generalization:
People: At least two adults and two peers
Settings: At least two settings
Materials: Across a variety of materials

Things to consider: Child may need a visual boundary when teaching. Consider the child's sensory challenges.

Teaching sequence
1. Maintains proximity when peer or adult approaches child and starts conversation with two or fewer prompts
2. Maintains proximity when peer or adult approaches child and starts conversation without prompts
3. Maintains proximity when child initiates conversation with a peer or adult with two or fewer prompts
4. Maintains proximity when child initiates conversation with a peer or adult without prompts

PROGRAMMING LOG

	Acquisition		Generalization		Maintenance	
	Start date	End date	Start date	End date	Date/data	Date/data
1						
2						
3						
4						

LESSON PLAN: Pragmatic Rules

Maintains Appropriate Proximity to Conversation Partner

Settings and materials	
Decontextualized	**Embedded**

Teaching
What direction or cue will you give?
How will you prompt the child's response?
Circle type of prompt(s) used:
Physical   Visual
Modeling   Verbal
Other: _____
Circle prompt fading procedure used:
Time delay   Most to least
Graduated guidance
Other: _____
What is the child's response?
What reinforcers are you using?
What is the correction procedure?
How will you collect data? *(circle answer)*
Percentage correct   Frequency
Duration   Permanent product
Other: _____

Sets

1. _____

_____

_____

_____

2. _____

_____

_____

_____

3. _____

_____

_____

_____

4. _____

_____

_____

5. _____

_____

_____

_____

INSTRUCTIONAL PROGRAM SHEET: Pragmatic Rules

Orients Body Toward Speaker

Child: _____   Date initiated: _____   Date completed: _____

Objective: When the child is conversing with or listening to an adult or peer, the child turns his or her body to face the other person talking.

Mastery criterion:
- 90% or higher correct response for each set
- Minimum of 10 opportunities per day
- 2 consecutive teaching days

Generalization:
People: At least two adults and two peers
Settings: At least two settings
Materials: Across a variety of materials

Things to consider: Child may not look directly at the person, but turns body toward person. Consider sensory challenges.

Teaching sequence
1. Turns toward speaker who is next to child
2. Turns toward speaker who is at least 3 feet from child
3. Turns toward speaker across the room (at least 6 feet from child)

PROGRAMMING LOG

	Acquisition		Generalization		Maintenance	
	Start date	End date	Start date	End date	Date/data	Date/data
1						
2						
3						

The DATA Model for Teaching Preschoolers with Autism by Ilene Schwartz, Julie Ashmun, Bonnie McBride, Crista Scott, and Susan Sandall.

LESSON PLAN: Pragmatic Rules

Orients Body Toward Speaker

Settings and materials	
Decontextualized	**Embedded**

Teaching
What direction or cue will you give?
How will you prompt the child's response?
Circle type of prompt(s) used:
Physical   Visual
Modeling   Verbal
Other: _____
Circle prompt fading procedure used:
Time delay   Most to least
Graduated guidance
Other: _____
What is the child's response?
What reinforcers are you using?
What is the correction procedure?
How will you collect data? *(circle answer)*
Percentage correct   Frequency
Duration   Permanent product
Other: _____

Sets

1. _____

_____

_____

_____

2. _____

_____

_____

_____

3. _____

_____

_____

_____

4. _____

_____

_____

_____

5. _____

_____

_____

_____

INSTRUCTIONAL PROGRAM SHEET: Pragmatic Rules

Maintains Eye Contact

Child: _____ Date initiated: _____ Date completed: _____

Objective: When the child is conversing with an adult or peer, the child looks in the direction of the other person talking and glances at them at least once during the conversation.

Mastery criterion:
- 90% or higher correct response for each set
- Minimum of 10 opportunities per day
- 2 consecutive teaching days

Generalization:
People: At least two adults and two peers
Settings: At least two settings
Materials: Across a variety of materials

Things to consider: Child does not need to look directly at the person for a sustained period of time. Consider sensory challenges. Prerequisite skill is to orient body toward the speaker.

Teaching sequence
1. Looks toward person directly in front of child during conversation
2. Looks toward person next to child during conversation (i.e., must turn head to look at person)

PROGRAMMING LOG

	Acquisition		Generalization		Maintenance	
	Start date	End date	Start date	End date	Date/data	Date/data
1						
2						

The DATA Model for Teaching Preschoolers with Autism by Ilene Schwartz, Julie Ashmun, Bonnie McBride, Crista Scott, and Susan Sandall. Copyright © 2017 by Paul H. Brookes Publishing Co., Inc. All rights reserved.

LESSON PLAN: Pragmatic Rules

Maintains Eye Contact

Settings and materials	
Decontextualized	**Embedded**

Teaching
What direction or cue will you give?
How will you prompt the child's response?
Circle type of prompt(s) used:
Physical   Visual
Modeling   Verbal
Other: _____
Circle prompt fading procedure used:
Time delay   Most to least
Graduated guidance
Other: _____
What is the child's response?
What reinforcers are you using?
What is the correction procedure?
How will you collect data? *(circle answer)*
Percentage correct   Frequency
Duration   Permanent product
Other: _____

Sets

1. _____
   _____
   _____
   _____

2. _____
   _____
   _____
   _____

3. _____
   _____
   _____
   _____

4. _____
   _____
   _____

5. _____
   _____
   _____
   _____

INSTRUCTIONAL PROGRAM SHEET: Pragmatic Rules

Voice Volume Appropriate to Setting

Child: _____ Date initiated: _____ Date completed: _____

Objective: When the child is talking, his or her voice volume will be just right for the setting (e.g., quiet during quiet time in the classroom, loud when outside).

Mastery criterion:
- 90% or higher correct response for each set
- Minimum of 10 opportunities per day
- 2 consecutive teaching days

Generalization:
People: At least two adults and two peers
Settings: At least two settings
Materials: Across a variety of materials

Things to consider: A voice volume meter (e.g., 1 = quiet, 3 = loud) may be helpful for teaching.

Teaching sequence
1. Talks with a whisper when told to talk quietly
2. Talks loudly or yells when told to be loud
3. Talks in a "just right" voice when told to do so
4. Identifies locations in which to be quiet (e.g., library, when people are sleeping)
5. Identifies locations in which to be loud (e.g., outside, at a stadium)
6. Identifies locations in which to talk with a regular, speaking volume, "just right" (e.g., in the classroom during discussion, at mealtimes)
7. Moderates voice level under all three types of conditions (e.g., quiet, just right, loud)

PROGRAMMING LOG

	Acquisition		Generalization		Maintenance	
	Start date	End date	Start date	End date	Date/data	Date/data
1						
2						
3						
4						
5						
6						
7						

LESSON PLAN: Pragmatic Rules

Voice Volume Appropriate to Setting

Settings and materials	
Decontextualized	**Embedded**

Teaching

What direction or cue will you give?

How will you prompt the child's response?

Circle type of prompt(s) used:

Physical	Visual
Modeling	Verbal

Other: _____

Circle prompt fading procedure used:

Time delay	Most to least
Graduated guidance	

Other: _____

What is the child's response?

What reinforcers are you using?

What is the correction procedure?

How will you collect data? *(circle answer)*

Percentage correct	Frequency
Duration	Permanent product

Other: _____

Sets

1. _____

_____

_____

_____

2. _____

_____

_____

_____

3. _____

_____

_____

_____

4. _____

_____

_____

_____

5. _____

_____

_____

_____

INSTRUCTIONAL PROGRAM SHEET: Pragmatic Rules

Responds to Common Facial Expressions and Gestures

Child: _____ Date initiated: _____ Date completed: _____

Objective: During a social–communicative interaction with an adult or peer, the child will respond appropriately to the adult or peer's facial expressions and gestures (e.g., adult shakes head "no," child does not engage in the behavior).

Mastery criterion:
- 90% or higher correct response for each set
- Minimum of 10 opportunities per day
- 2 consecutive teaching days

Generalization:
People: At least two adults and two peers
Settings: At least two settings
Materials: Across a variety of materials

Things to consider: Child must be able to orient body and look toward speaker to identify and follow facial expressions and gestures. A variety of gestures may be taught that mean: yes, no, I don't know, sit down, stand up, that's smelly, I don't feel well, stop, come here, wait a minute, and go ahead.

Teaching sequence
1. Identifies at least five types of gestures by demonstrating the gesture when asked to do so (e.g., "Show me how to say 'I don't know'") or expressively identifies the gesture (e.g., when adult or peer shrugs shoulders and asks the child "What does that mean?" the child responds "I don't know.")
2. Identifies at least five more gestures
3. Responds appropriately to gestures taught in set one and two
4. Responds appropriately to at least three facial expressions (e.g., if a peer looks surprised, the child says "What happened?" or if the adult looks disgusted, the child may say "Oh no" or may stop his or her behavior)
5. Responds appropriately to at least three more facial expressions (e.g., tired, angry, sad)

PROGRAMMING LOG

	Acquisition		Generalization		Maintenance	
	Start date	End date	Start date	End date	Date/data	Date/data
1						
2						
3						
4						
5						

LESSON PLAN: Pragmatic Rules

Responds to Common Facial Expressions and Gestures

Settings and materials	
Decontextualized	**Embedded**

Teaching
What direction or cue will you give?
How will you prompt the child's response?
Circle type of prompt(s) used:
Physical   Visual
Modeling   Verbal
Other: _____
Circle prompt fading procedure used:
Time delay   Most to least
Graduated guidance
Other: _____
What is the child's response?
What reinforcers are you using?
What is the correction procedure?
How will you collect data? *(circle answer)*
Percentage correct   Frequency
Duration   Permanent product
Other: _____

Sets

1. _____

_____

_____

_____

2. _____

_____

_____

_____

3. _____

_____

_____

_____

4. _____

_____

_____

_____

5. _____

_____

_____

_____

INSTRUCTIONAL PROGRAM SHEET: Pragmatic Rules

Appropriately Interjects

Child: _____   Date initiated: _____   Date completed: _____

Objective: During a conversation, the child waits for a pause, then says, "Excuse me," "Guess what?" or "Do you know what I did?" to interject or join the conversation.

Mastery criterion:
- 90% or higher correct response for each set
- Minimum of 10 opportunities per day
- 2 consecutive teaching days

Generalization:
People: At least two adults and two peers
Settings: At least two settings
Materials: Across a variety of materials

Things to consider: For verbal and nonverbal child, he or she may use a picture to exchange the communicative attempt to interject. This program may be taught after Persists in Gaining a Person's Attention." (Executive Functioning Form 3.1)

Teaching sequence
1. Says "Excuse me" or "Guess what?" to an adult who is turned away from child, but not engaged in a conversation
2. Says "Excuse me" or "Guess what?" to an adult who is having a conversation
3. Waits for a pause of at least 2 seconds, then says "Excuse me" or "Guess what?" to adults
4. Waits for a pause of at least 2 seconds, then says "Excuse me" or "Guess what?" to peers

PROGRAMMING LOG

	Acquisition		Generalization		Maintenance	
	Start date	End date	Start date	End date	Date/data	Date/data
1						
2						
3						
4						

LESSON PLAN: Pragmatic Rules

Appropriately Interjects

Settings and materials	
Decontextualized	**Embedded**

Teaching

What direction or cue will you give?

How will you prompt the child's response?

Circle type of prompt(s) used:

Physical	Visual
Modeling	Verbal

Other: _____

Circle prompt fading procedure used:

Time delay	Most to least
Graduated guidance	

Other: _____

What is the child's response?

What reinforcers are you using?

What is the correction procedure?

How will you collect data? *(circle answer)*

Percentage correct	Frequency
Duration	Permanent product

Other: _____

Sets

1. _____

   _____

   _____

   _____

2. _____

   _____

   _____

   _____

3. _____

   _____

   _____

   _____

4. _____

   _____

   _____

   _____

5. _____

   _____

   _____

   _____

INSTRUCTIONAL PROGRAM SHEET: Pragmatic Rules

Ends the Conversation Appropriately

Child: _____   Date initiated: _____   Date completed: _____

Objective: At the end of a conversation, the child ends it appropriately with a closing comment such as, "I have to go now" or "See you later."

Mastery criterion:
- 90% or higher correct response for each set
- Minimum of 10 opportunities per day
- 2 consecutive teaching days

Generalization:
People: At least two adults and two peers
Settings: At least two settings
Materials: Across a variety of materials

Things to consider: Child must be able to have an exchange of at least two turns to have a conversation before ending it.

Teaching sequence
1. States a closing comment during role play, a scenario directed by an adult
2. Ends the conversation with an adult, appropriately
3. Ends the conversation with a peer, appropriately

PROGRAMMING LOG

	Acquisition		Generalization		Maintenance	
	Start date	End date	Start date	End date	Date/data	Date/data
1						
2						
3						

LESSON PLAN: Pragmatic Rules

Ends the Conversation Appropriately

Settings and materials	
Decontextualized	**Embedded**

Teaching
What direction or cue will you give?
How will you prompt the child's response?
Circle type of prompt(s) used:

Physical	Visual
Modeling	Verbal
Other: _____	

Circle prompt fading procedure used:

Time delay	Most to least
Graduated guidance	
Other: _____	

What is the child's response?
What reinforcers are you using?
What is the correction procedure?
How will you collect data? *(circle answer)*

Percentage correct	Frequency
Duration	Permanent product
Other: _____	

Sets

1. _____

_____

_____

_____

2. _____

_____

_____

_____

3. _____

_____

_____

_____

4. _____

_____

_____

_____

5. _____

_____

_____

_____

INSTRUCTIONAL PROGRAM SHEET: Interaction with Peers

Maintains Proximity to Peers

Child: _____   Date initiated: _____   Date completed: _____

Objective: When told, "It's time to play with (peer)," the child maintains proximity (i.e., within 3 feet) to the peer during play until the natural end of the activity.

Mastery criterion:
- 80% or higher correct response for each set
- Minimum of five opportunities per day
- 3 consecutive teaching days

Generalization:
People: At least three peers
Settings: At least two settings
Materials: Across a variety of materials

Things to consider: Preferred peers; allow child to access preferred items while in proximity to peer; sensory issues. Gradually increase time and number of peers while decreasing distance between child and peers.

Teaching sequence
1. Child remains in an area when peer approaches (e.g., child stays at the sensory table when a peer joins them)
2. Child joins peer in an area (e.g., child enters the block area when peers are playing in blocks)
3. Maintains proximity to peers during a preferred activity (e.g., art, play court, blocks)
4. Maintains proximity to peers during any activity appropriate for more than one child

PROGRAMMING LOG

	Acquisition		Generalization		Maintenance	
	Start date	End date	Start date	End date	Date/data	Date/data
1						
2						
3						
4						

LESSON PLAN: Interaction with Peers

Maintains Proximity to Peers

Settings and materials	
Decontextualized	**Embedded**

Teaching
What direction or cue will you give?
How will you prompt the child's response?
Circle type of prompt(s) used:
Physical   Visual
Modeling   Verbal
Other: _____
Circle prompt fading procedure used:
Time delay   Most to least
Graduated guidance
Other: _____
What is the child's response?
What reinforcers are you using?
What is the correction procedure?
How will you collect data? *(circle answer)*
Percentage correct   Frequency
Duration   Permanent product
Other: _____

Sets

1. _____
_____
_____
_____

2. _____
_____
_____
_____

3. _____
_____
_____
_____

4. _____
_____
_____
_____

5. _____
_____
_____
_____

INSTRUCTIONAL PROGRAM SHEET: Interaction with Peers

Imitates Peers

Child: _____ Date initiated: _____ Date completed: _____

Objective: When peers are following directions and playing appropriately, the child imitates the actions of the peers. For example, when peer is clapping hands in circle, child imitates actions, or when peer is pushing trains on the train tracks, the child gets a train and imitates the peer's actions.

Mastery criterion:
- 90% or higher correct response for each set
- Minimum of 10 opportunities per day
- 2 consecutive teaching days

Generalization:
People: At least three peers
Settings: At least two settings
Materials: Across a variety of materials

Things to consider: Preferred peers who are engaging in appropriate behaviors.

Teaching sequence
1. Child imitates a peer's motor actions when told to "Copy, (peer's name)" or "Do what (he or she) is doing"
2. Child imitates a peer's actions with toys when provided with similar materials and told to "Copy, (peer's name)" or "Do what (he or she) is doing"
3. Child imitates a peer's actions during large group activities with one prompt
4. Child imitates a peer's actions during large group activities with no prompts
5. Child imitates a peer's actions during play with a set of toys with one prompt
6. Child imitates a peer's actions during play with a set of toys with no prompts

PROGRAMMING LOG

	Acquisition		Generalization		Maintenance	
	Start date	End date	Start date	End date	Date/data	Date/data
1						
2						
3						
4						
5						
6						

LESSON PLAN: Interaction with Peers

Imitates Peers

Settings and materials	
Decontextualized	**Embedded**

Teaching
What direction or cue will you give?
How will you prompt the child's response?
Circle type of prompt(s) used:
Physical   Visual
Modeling   Verbal
Other: _____
Circle prompt fading procedure used:
Time delay   Most to least
Graduated guidance
Other: _____
What is the child's response?
What reinforcers are you using?
What is the correction procedure?
How will you collect data? *(circle answer)*
Percentage correct   Frequency
Duration   Permanent product
Other: _____

Sets

1. _____

2. _____

3. _____

4. _____

5. _____

INSTRUCTIONAL PROGRAM SHEET: Interaction with Peers

Takes Turns with Peers

Child: _____ Date initiated: _____ Date completed: _____

Objective: When an adult directs the child to take a turn, the child follows the direction by offering a toy to a friend, waiting, and then taking the toy again when it is his or her turn.

Mastery criterion:
- 90% or higher correct response for each set
- Minimum of 10 opportunities per day
- 2 consecutive teaching days

Generalization:
People: At least three peers
Settings: At least two settings
Materials: Across a variety of materials

Things to consider: Begin with preferred peers and simple turn taking such as rolling a ball back and forth.

Teaching sequence
1. Takes turn in back and forth activities such as rolling a ball back and forth or pushing a toy back and forth
2. Takes a turn with a less preferred object
3. Takes a turn with a more preferred object
4. Takes a turn across a variety of materials

PROGRAMMING LOG

	Acquisition		Generalization		Maintenance	
	Start date	End date	Start date	End date	Date/data	Date/data
1						
2						
3						
4						

LESSON PLAN: Interaction with Peers

Takes Turns with Peers

Settings and materials	
Decontextualized	**Embedded**

Teaching
What direction or cue will you give?
How will you prompt the child's response?
Circle type of prompt(s) used:
Physical   Visual
Modeling   Verbal
Other: _____
Circle prompt fading procedure used:
Time delay   Most to least
Graduated guidance
Other: _____
What is the child's response?
What reinforcers are you using?
What is the correction procedure?
How will you collect data? *(circle answer)*
Percentage correct   Frequency
Duration   Permanent product
Other: _____

Sets

1. _____
   _____
   _____
   _____

2. _____
   _____
   _____
   _____

3. _____
   _____
   _____
   _____

4. _____
   _____
   _____
   _____

5. _____
   _____
   _____
   _____

INSTRUCTIONAL PROGRAM SHEET: Interaction with Peers

Responds to Interactions from Peers

Child: _____   Date initiated: _____   Date completed: _____

Objective: When a peer initiates an interaction such as offers an item or asks a question, the child responds to the peer by taking the item or answering the question.

Mastery criterion:
- 80% or higher correct response for each set
- Minimum of five opportunities per day
- 3 consecutive teaching days

Generalization:
People: At least three peers
Settings: At least two settings
Materials: Across a variety of materials

Things to consider: Begin with prompting preferred peers to initiate the interaction

Teaching sequence
1. Takes an item offered by a peer
2. Responds to a question from a peer
3. Responds to a comment from a peer

PROGRAMMING LOG

	Acquisition		Generalization		Maintenance	
	Start date	End date	Start date	End date	Date/data	Date/data
1						
2						
3						

LESSON PLAN: Interaction with Peers

Responds to Interactions from Peers

Settings and materials	
Decontextualized	**Embedded**

Teaching
What direction or cue will you give?
How will you prompt the child's response?
Circle type of prompt(s) used:
Physical   Visual
Modeling   Verbal
Other: _____
Circle prompt fading procedure used:
Time delay   Most to least
Graduated guidance
Other: _____
What is the child's response?
What reinforcers are you using?
What is the correction procedure?
How will you collect data? *(circle answer)*
Percentage correct   Frequency
Duration   Permanent product
Other: _____

Sets

1. _____
_____
_____
_____

2. _____
_____
_____
_____

3. _____
_____
_____
_____

4. _____
_____
_____
_____

5. _____
_____
_____
_____

INSTRUCTIONAL PROGRAM SHEET: Interaction with Peers

Initiates Interactions Toward Peers

Child: _____ Date initiated: _____ Date completed: _____

Objective: In the presence of a peer, the child initiates an interaction towards the peer by offering items, making requests or commenting.

Mastery criterion:
- ■ 90% or higher correct response for each set
- ■ Minimum of 10 opportunities per day
- ■ 2 consecutive teaching days

Generalization:
People: At least three peers
Settings: At least two settings
Materials: Across a variety of materials

Things to consider: Visual prompts to suggest sharing, commenting, or to invite peer to play are helpful supports for teaching this skill. Provide peer with child's preferred item to set up opportunity for request.

Teaching sequence
1. Requests items from peers with a prompt
2. Requests items from peers
3. Gives peer an item with a prompt
4. Offers items to peers
5. Initiates a variety of interactions with peers

PROGRAMMING LOG

	Acquisition		Generalization		Maintenance	
	Start date	End date	Start date	End date	Date/data	Date/data
1						
2						
3						
4						
5						

LESSON PLAN: Interaction with Peers

Initiates Interactions Toward Peers

Settings and materials	
Decontextualized	**Embedded**

Teaching
What direction or cue will you give?
How will you prompt the child's response?
Circle type of prompt(s) used:
Physical   Visual
Modeling   Verbal
Other: _____
Circle prompt fading procedure used:
Time delay   Most to least
Graduated guidance
Other: _____
What is the child's response?
What reinforcers are you using?
What is the correction procedure?
How will you collect data? *(circle answer)*
Percentage correct   Frequency
Duration   Permanent product
Other: _____

Sets

1. _____
   _____
   _____
   _____

2. _____
   _____
   _____
   _____

3. _____
   _____
   _____
   _____

4. _____
   _____
   _____
   _____

5. _____
   _____
   _____
   _____

INSTRUCTIONAL PROGRAM SHEET: Interaction with Peers

Takes Turns During Unstructured Activities

Child: _____   Date initiated: _____   Date completed: _____

Objective: During unstructured activities, such as art or free play, the child waits for a turn and provides opportunities for peers to have a turn by offering items or asking the peer if he or she wants a turn.

Mastery criterion:
- 80% or higher correct response for each set
- Minimum of five opportunities per day
- 3 consecutive teaching days

Generalization:
People: At least three peers
Settings: At least two settings
Materials: Across a variety of materials and activities

Things to consider: Provide activities with which the child prefers to participate and has the skills to participate. Consider teaching "Takes Turns with Peers" (Social Programming Form 3.3) before teaching this skill.

Teaching sequence
1. Asks for a turn with one prompt (e.g., visual or verbal reminder)
2. Asks for a turn with no prompts
3. Waits for a turn (may find another item to play with while waiting)
4. Offers a turn with one prompt (i.e., visual or verbal reminder)
5. Offers a turn with no prompts
6. Takes at least three turns during unstructured activities with a variety of materials

PROGRAMMING LOG

	Acquisition		Generalization		Maintenance	
	Start date	End date	Start date	End date	Date/data	Date/data
1						
2						
3						
4						
5						
6						

The DATA Model for Teaching Preschoolers with Autism by Ilene Schwartz, Julie Ashmun, Bonnie McBride, Crista Scott, and Susan Sandall. Copyright © 2017 by Paul H. Brookes Publishing Co., Inc. All rights reserved.

LESSON PLAN: Interaction with Peers

Takes Turns During Unstructured Activities

Settings and materials	
Decontextualized	**Embedded**

Teaching
What direction or cue will you give?
How will you prompt the child's response?
Circle type of prompt(s) used:
Physical   Visual
Modeling   Verbal
Other: _____
Circle prompt fading procedure used:
Time delay   Most to least
Graduated guidance
Other: _____
What is the child's response?
What reinforcers are you using?
What is the correction procedure?
How will you collect data? *(circle answer)*
Percentage correct   Frequency
Duration   Permanent product
Other: _____

Sets

1. _____
   _____
   _____
   _____

2. _____
   _____
   _____
   _____

3. _____
   _____
   _____
   _____

4. _____
   _____
   _____
   _____

5. _____
   _____
   _____
   _____

INSTRUCTIONAL PROGRAM SHEET: Interaction with Peers

Demonstrates Acceptable Ways of Joining an Activity

Child: _____   Date initiated: _____   Date completed: _____

Objective: During play activities, the child joins the activity by asking to join, offering a toy or idea, or asking a question about the activity.

Mastery criterion:
- 80% or higher correct response for each set
- Minimum of five opportunities per day
- 3 consecutive teaching days

Generalization:
People: At least three peers
Settings: At least two settings
Materials: Across a variety of materials and activities

Things to consider: Provide activities with which the child prefers to participate and has the skills to participate. Consider teaching "Organizes Play by Suggesting Play Plans" (Play Programming Form 3.4) along with this skill.

Teaching sequence
1. Asks for a turn or to join play with one type of prompt (e.g., visual)
2. Asks for a turn or to join play with no prompts
3. Offers a toy or an idea for the activity with one type of prompt (e.g., visual)
4. Offers a toy or an idea for the activity with no prompts
5. Appropriately joins a variety of activities with at least two different methods to join (e.g., asks, offers)

PROGRAMMING LOG

	Acquisition		Generalization		Maintenance	
	Start date	End date	Start date	End date	Date/data	Date/data
1						
2						
3						
4						
5						

The DATA Model for Teaching Preschoolers with Autism by Ilene Schwartz, Julie Ashmun, Bonnie McBride, Crista Scott, and Susan Sandall. Copyright © 2017 by Paul H. Brookes Publishing Co., Inc. All rights reserved.

LESSON PLAN: Interaction with Peers

Demonstrates Acceptable Ways of Joining an Activity

V. SOCIAL

Settings and materials	
Decontextualized	Embedded

Teaching

What direction or cue will you give?

How will you prompt the child's response?

Circle type of prompt(s) used:

Physical   Visual

Modeling   Verbal

Other: _____

Circle prompt fading procedure used:

Time delay   Most to least

Graduated guidance

Other: _____

What is the child's response?

What reinforcers are you using?

What is the correction procedure?

How will you collect data? *(circle answer)*

Percentage correct   Frequency

Duration   Permanent product

Other: _____

Sets

1. _____

2. _____

3. _____

4. _____

5. _____

INSTRUCTIONAL PROGRAM SHEET: Interaction with Peers

Maintains a Conversation

Child: _____   Date initiated: _____   Date completed: _____

Objective: When interacting with a familiar peer, the child maintains a social–communicative interaction that is on-topic for at least three turns by asking an initial question, making on-topic comments, and asking follow-up questions.

Mastery criterion:
- 80% or higher correct response for each set
- Minimum of five opportunities per day
- Minimum of five topics
- 3 consecutive teaching days

Generalization:
People: At least three peers
Settings: At least two settings
Materials: Across a variety of materials

Things to consider: Set up opportunities during regular routines with child's preferred materials and with familiar or preferred peers (e.g., conversation during snack, conversation about play actions or themes).

Teaching sequence
1. Maintains two on-topic turns in the interaction (e.g., responds to peer with a comment, asks peer a question)
2. Maintains three on-topic turns in the interaction (e.g., initiates with a question, make a comment, asks another question)
3. Maintains three on-topic turns in the social–communicative interaction with two different peers
4. Maintains three on-topic turns in the social–communicative interaction with two different peers, across three different topics
5. Maintains three on-topic turns in the social–communicative interaction with three different peers, across materials and setting

PROGRAMMING LOG

	Acquisition		Generalization		Maintenance	
	Start date	End date	Start date	End date	Date/data	Date/data
1						
2						
3						
4						
5						

LESSON PLAN: Interaction with Peers

Maintains a Conversation

Settings and materials	
Decontextualized	**Embedded**

Teaching
What direction or cue will you give?
How will you prompt the child's response?
Circle type of prompt(s) used:
Physical   Visual
Modeling   Verbal
Other: _____
Circle prompt fading procedure used:
Time delay   Most to least
Graduated guidance
Other: _____
What is the child's response?
What reinforcers are you using?
What is the correction procedure?
How will you collect data? *(circle answer)*
Percentage correct   Frequency
Duration   Permanent product
Other: _____

Sets

1. _____
_____
_____
_____

2. _____
_____
_____
_____

3. _____
_____
_____
_____

4. _____
_____
_____
_____

5. _____
_____
_____
_____

INSTRUCTIONAL PROGRAM SHEET: Interaction with Peers

Gives Assistance to Peers

Child: _____   Date initiated: _____   Date completed: _____

Objective: In the presence of a peer who needs assistance, the child offers or tries to help him or her.

Mastery criterion:
- 80% or higher correct response for each set
- Minimum of five opportunities per day
- 3 consecutive teaching days

Generalization:
People: At least three peers
Settings: At least two settings
Materials: Across a variety of materials

Things to consider: Set up opportunities during regular routines (e.g., assisting to pour milk at snack, assisting with coats and backpacks during transitions).

Teaching sequence
1. Assists peer with adult support
2. Offers to help and assists a peer with a prompt
3. Offers to help and assists a peer with no prompts

PROGRAMMING LOG

	Acquisition		Generalization		Maintenance	
	Start date	End date	Start date	End date	Date/data	Date/data
1						
2						
3						

Gives Assistance to Peers

Settings and materials	
Decontextualized	**Embedded**

Teaching
What direction or cue will you give?
How will you prompt the child's response?
Circle type of prompt(s) used:
Physical   Visual
Modeling   Verbal
Other: _____
Circle prompt fading procedure used:
Time delay   Most to least
Graduated guidance
Other: _____
What is the child's response?
What reinforcers are you using?
What is the correction procedure?
How will you collect data? *(circle answer)*
Percentage correct   Frequency
Duration   Permanent product
Other: _____

Sets

1. _____
   _____
   _____
   _____

2. _____
   _____
   _____
   _____

3. _____
   _____
   _____
   _____

4. _____
   _____
   _____

5. _____
   _____
   _____
   _____

INSTRUCTIONAL PROGRAM SHEET: Play Fundamentals

Activates Cause and Effect Toys

Child: _____ Date initiated: _____ Date completed: _____

Objective: In the presence of a cause and effect toy such as a jack-in-the-box or a see-n-say, the child activates the toy.

Mastery criterion:
- 90% or higher correct response for each set
- Minimum of 10 opportunities per day
- 2 consecutive teaching days

Generalization:
People: At least two adults and peers
Settings: At least two settings
Materials: Across at least three novel toys

Things to consider: Teach with simple and preferred cause and effect toys, toys that may light up or make sounds.

Teaching sequence
1. Activates one cause and effect toy
2. Activates another toy
3. Activates another toy
4. Activates another toy
5. Activates another toy

PROGRAMMING LOG

	Acquisition		Generalization		Maintenance	
	Start date	End date	Start date	End date	Date/data	Date/data
1						
2						
3						
4						
5						

LESSON PLAN: Play Fundamentals

Activates Cause and Effect Toys

Settings and materials	
Decontextualized	**Embedded**

Teaching
What direction or cue will you give?
How will you prompt the child's response?
Circle type of prompt(s) used:
Physical   Visual
Modeling   Verbal
Other: _____
Circle prompt fading procedure used:
Time delay   Most to least
Graduated guidance
Other: _____
What is the child's response?
What reinforcers are you using?
What is the correction procedure?
How will you collect data? *(circle answer)*
Percentage correct   Frequency
Duration   Permanent product
Other: _____

Sets

1. _____
_____
_____
_____

2. _____
_____
_____
_____

3. _____
_____
_____
_____

4. _____
_____
_____
_____

5. _____
_____
_____
_____

INSTRUCTIONAL PROGRAM SHEET: Play Fundamentals

Activates Cause and Effect Toys—Example

Child: _____ Date initiated: _____ Date completed: _____

Objective: In the presence of a cause and effect toy such as a jack-in-the-box or a see-n-say, the child activates the toy.

Mastery criterion:
- 90% or higher correct response for each set
- Minimum of 10 opportunities per day
- 2 consecutive teaching days

Generalization:
People: At least two adults and peers
Settings: At least two settings
Materials: Across at least three novel toys

Things to consider: Teach with simple and preferred cause and effect toys, toys that may light up or make sounds.

Teaching sequence
1. Activates one cause and effect toy
2. Activates another toy
3. Activates another toy
4. Activates another toy
5. Activates another toy.

PROGRAMMING LOG

	Acquisition		Generalization		Maintenance	
	Start date	End date	Start date	End date	Date/data	Date/data
1	1/5/15	1/15/15	1/16/15; across people, setting	1/25/15; across people, setting	2/25/15; 80%	4/25/15; 100%
2	1/16/15	2/2/15	2/3/15; across people, setting	2/10/15; across people, setting	3/10/15	5/10/15
3	2/3/15	2/16/15	2/17/15; across people, setting	2/25/15; across people, setting	3/25/15	5/25/15
4	2/18/15	3/5/15	3/6/15; across people, setting	3/10/15; across people, setting	4/10/15	6/10/15
5	3/6/15	3/20/15	3/21/15; across people, setting & novel toys	3/25/15; across people, setting & novel toys	4/26/15	6/15/15

LESSON PLAN: Play Fundamentals

Activates Cause and Effect Toys—Example

Settings and materials	
Decontextualized	**Embedded**
Activates toy at table in work area during individualized instruction. See sets for toy to activate.	Activates toy from previous sets during free playtime.

Teaching
What direction or cue will you give?
Direction may be given during teaching of first few sets, then no direction. Cue to activate toy is the toy itself.
How will you prompt the child's response?
Circle type of prompt(s) used:
(Physical)   Visual Modeling   (Verbal) Other: _____
Circle prompt fading procedure used:
Time delay   (Most to least) Graduated guidance Other: _____
What is the child's response?
Activates toy (e.g., pushes button)
What reinforcers are you using?
Praise and use preferred toys so the activation is reinforcing to child (i.e., natural reinforcer).
What is the correction procedure?
Provide verbal direction and physical prompt for child to be successful.
How will you collect data? *(circle answer)*
(Percentage correct)   Frequency Duration   Permanent product Other: _____

Sets
1. Activates musical toy
2. Activates pop-up toy
3. Activates spinning toy
4. Activates ball toy (puts ball in hole and watches it fall through toy)
5. Activates See-n-Say

INSTRUCTIONAL PROGRAM SHEET: Play Fundamentals

Uses Play Materials Appropriately

Child: _____ Date initiated: _____ Date completed: _____

Objective: In the presence of toys or told "time to play," the child initiates and makes at least one action upon close-ended toys (i.e., clear beginning and end) in a functional manner.

Mastery criterion:
- 90% or higher correct response for each set
- Minimum of 10 opportunities per day
- 2 consecutive teaching days

Generalization:
People: At least two adults and peers
Settings: At least two settings
Materials: Across at least three novel toys

Things to consider: Functionally or socially appropriate actions are those for which the object was intended or designed (e.g., child puts peg in peg board, child holds play telephone to ear). Some toys may stimulate the child. Consider toys that are not as stimulating. This program may be taught with "Imitates Actions with Objects" to teach the child functionally appropriate actions to conduct with the toys. Count each action with the toy as an opportunity.

Teaching sequence
1. Plays with one, close-ended toy (e.g., puzzle, peg board, shape sorter)
2. Plays with another close-ended toy
3. Plays with another toy
4. Plays with another toy
5. Plays with another toy

PROGRAMMING LOG

	Acquisition		Generalization		Maintenance	
	Start date	End date	Start date	End date	Date/data	Date/data
1						
2						
3						
4						
5						

LESSON PLAN: Play Fundamentals

Uses Play Materials Appropriately

Settings and materials	
Decontextualized	**Embedded**

Teaching
What direction or cue will you give?
How will you prompt the child's response?
Circle type of prompt(s) used:
Physical   Visual
Modeling   Verbal
Other: _____
Circle prompt fading procedure used:
Time delay   Most to least
Graduated guidance
Other: _____
What is the child's response?
What reinforcers are you using?
What is the correction procedure?
How will you collect data? *(circle answer)*
Percentage correct   Frequency
Duration   Permanent product
Other: _____

Sets
1. _____
2. _____
3. _____
4. _____
5. _____

INSTRUCTIONAL PROGRAM SHEET: Play Fundamentals

Functional Play with Toys Related to a Theme

Child: _____ Date initiated: _____ Date completed: _____

Objective: In the presence of a set of toys or told "Time to play," the child initiates and plays with open-ended toys (i.e., toys that can be played with in a variety of ways) in a functional manner.

Mastery criterion:
- 90% or higher correct response for each set
- Minimum of 10 opportunities per day
- 2 consecutive teaching days

Generalization:
People: At least two adults and peers
Settings: At least two settings
Materials: Across at least three novel sets of toys

Things to consider: Functional or socially appropriate actions are those for which the objects were intended or designed such as feeds baby, brushes baby's teeth, and puts the baby to bed. Child only needs to demonstrate each functional play action; the actions do not need to be in order or sustained. This program may be taught with "Imitates Actions with Objects" to teach the child functionally appropriate actions to conduct with the toys. Count each action with the toy as an opportunity.

Teaching sequence
1. Plays with one set of open-ended toys
2. Plays with another set of toys
3. Plays with another set of toys
4. Plays with another set of toys
5. Plays with another set of toys

PROGRAMMING LOG

	Acquisition		Generalization		Maintenance	
	Start date	End date	Start date	End date	Date/data	Date/data
1						
2						
3						
4						
5						

LESSON PLAN: Play Fundamentals

Functional Play with Toys Related to a Theme

Settings and materials	
Decontextualized	**Embedded**

Teaching
What direction or cue will you give?
How will you prompt the child's response?
Circle type of prompt(s) used:
Physical   Visual
Modeling   Verbal
Other: _____
Circle prompt fading procedure used:
Time delay   Most to least
Graduated guidance
Other: _____
What is the child's response?
What reinforcers are you using?
What is the correction procedure?
How will you collect data? *(circle answer)*
Percentage correct   Frequency
Duration   Permanent product
Other: _____

Sets

1. _____
   _____
   _____
   _____

2. _____
   _____
   _____
   _____

3. _____
   _____
   _____
   _____

4. _____
   _____
   _____

5. _____
   _____
   _____
   _____

INSTRUCTIONAL PROGRAM SHEET: Play Fundamentals

Representational Actions with Objects

Child: _____ Date initiated: _____ Date completed: _____

Objective: In the presence of toys or asked, "What can this be?" the child uses the object to represent another (e.g., a block is used as a car).

Mastery criterion:
- 90% or higher correct response for each set
- Minimum of 10 opportunities per day
- 2 consecutive teaching days

Generalization:
People: At least two adults and peers
Settings: At least two settings
Materials: Across at least three novel representations for five objects

Things to consider: Child must be able to make functional actions with toys.

Teaching sequence
1. Uses objects similar to the real object (e.g., pretends a red ball is an apple)
2. Substitutes objects for other objects (e.g., a block for an orange, a box for a hat, a stick to stir food)
3. Creates multiple uses for one object (e.g., a box is a car, a hat, a shoe)

PROGRAMMING LOG

	Acquisition		Generalization		Maintenance	
	Start date	End date	Start date	End date	Date/data	Date/data
1						
2						
3						

LESSON PLAN: Play Fundamentals

Representational Actions with Objects

Settings and materials	
Decontextualized	**Embedded**

Teaching
What direction or cue will you give?
How will you prompt the child's response?
Circle type of prompt(s) used:
Physical   Visual
Modeling   Verbal
Other: _____
Circle prompt fading procedure used:
Time delay   Most to least
Graduated guidance
Other: _____
What is the child's response?
What reinforcers are you using?
What is the correction procedure?
How will you collect data? *(circle answer)*
Percentage correct   Frequency
Duration   Permanent product
Other: _____

Sets

1. _____

_____

_____

_____

2. _____

_____

_____

_____

3. _____

_____

_____

_____

4. _____

_____

_____

_____

5. _____

_____

_____

_____

INSTRUCTIONAL PROGRAM SHEET: Play Fundamentals

Sequence of Play Actions Related to a Play Theme

Child: _____ Date initiated: _____ Date completed: _____

Objective: In the presence of a set of toys or told "Time to play," the child initiates and plays with open-ended toys (i.e., toys that can be played with in a variety of ways) by sequencing actions to build a play theme.

Mastery criterion:
- At least three sequenced actions
- Across five different play themes (sets of toys)
- 2 consecutive teaching days for each set of toys

Generalization:
People: At least two adults and peers
Settings: At least two settings
Materials: Across a variety of materials

Things to consider: Use a visual prompt for sequences of play actions.

Teaching sequence
1. Sequenced play with one set of toys
2. Sequenced play with another set of toys
3. Sequenced play with a third set of toys
4. Sequenced play with a fourth set of toys
5. Sequenced play with a fifth set of toys

PROGRAMMING LOG

	Acquisition		Generalization		Maintenance	
	Start date	End date	Start date	End date	Date/data	Date/data
1						
2						
3						
4						
5						

LESSON PLAN: Play Fundamentals

Sequence of Play Actions Related to a Play Theme

Settings and materials	
Decontextualized	**Embedded**

Teaching
What direction or cue will you give?
How will you prompt the child's response?
Circle type of prompt(s) used:
Physical   Visual
Modeling   Verbal
Other: _____
Circle prompt fading procedure used:
Time delay   Most to least
Graduated guidance
Other: _____
What is the child's response?
What reinforcers are you using?
What is the correction procedure?
How will you collect data? *(circle answer)*
Percentage correct   Frequency
Duration   Permanent product
Other: _____

Sets

1. _____

_____

_____

_____

2. _____

_____

_____

_____

3. _____

_____

_____

_____

4. _____

_____

_____

_____

5. _____

_____

_____

_____

INSTRUCTIONAL PROGRAM SHEET: Play Fundamentals

Narrates Play

Child: _____ Date initiated: _____ Date completed: _____

Objective: During play, child narrates play actions by commenting on his or her actions or that of peers.

Mastery criterion:
- At least three narrations or comments during each play period
- Across five play periods
- 2 consecutive teaching days

Generalization:
People: At least two adults and peers
Settings: At least two settings
Materials: Across a variety of materials

Things to consider: Augmentative communication systems may be used in place of verbal narration.

Teaching sequence
1. Narrates at least one action during play periods
2. Narrates at least two actions during play periods
3. Narrates at least three actions during play periods

PROGRAMMING LOG

	Acquisition		Generalization		Maintenance	
	Start date	End date	Start date	End date	Date/data	Date/data
1						
2						
3						

Narrates Play

Settings and materials	
Decontextualized	**Embedded**

Teaching
What direction or cue will you give?
How will you prompt the child's response?
Circle type of prompt(s) used:
Physical   Visual
Modeling   Verbal
Other: _____
Circle prompt fading procedure used:
Time delay   Most to least
Graduated guidance
Other: _____
What is the child's response?
What reinforcers are you using?
What is the correction procedure?
How will you collect data? *(circle answer)*
Percentage correct   Frequency
Duration   Permanent product
Other: _____

Sets

1. _____

2. _____

3. _____

4. _____

5. _____

INSTRUCTIONAL PROGRAM SHEET: Independent Play

Entertains Self by Playing with Toys Appropriately

Child: _____ Date initiated: _____ Date completed: _____

Objective: In the presence of toys or when told, "Time to play," the child plays for at least 5 minutes independently.

Mastery criterion:
- Four out of four opportunities
- Across 2 days

Generalization:
People: At least two adults
Settings: At least two settings
Materials: Across a variety of play materials

Things to consider: Begin with preferred items. May need to teach the child other play skills such as "Uses Play Materials Appropriately" for the child to be successful with playing independently for 5 minutes.

Teaching sequence
1. Plays for 1 minute with toys
2. Plays for 2 minutes with toys
3. Plays for 3 minutes with toys
4. Plays for 4 minutes with toys
5. Plays for 5 minutes with toys

PROGRAMMING LOG

	Acquisition		Generalization		Maintenance	
	Start date	End date	Start date	End date	Date/data	Date/data
1						
2						
3						
4						
5						

LESSON PLAN: Independent Play

Entertains Self by Playing with Toys Appropriately

Settings and materials	
Decontextualized	**Embedded**

Teaching
What direction or cue will you give?
How will you prompt the child's response?
Circle type of prompt(s) used:
Physical   Visual
Modeling   Verbal
Other: _____
Circle prompt fading procedure used:
Time delay   Most to least
Graduated guidance
Other: _____
What is the child's response?
What reinforcers are you using?
What is the correction procedure?
How will you collect data? *(circle answer)*
Percentage correct   Frequency
Duration   Permanent product
Other: _____

Sets

1. _____
   _____
   _____
   _____

2. _____
   _____
   _____
   _____

3. _____
   _____
   _____
   _____

4. _____
   _____
   _____

5. _____
   _____
   _____
   _____

INSTRUCTIONAL PROGRAM SHEET: Independent Play

Completes a Puzzle

Child: _____ Date initiated: _____ Date completed: _____

Objective: When presented with a puzzle, the child completes it by getting the pieces out of the box and putting the puzzle together.

Mastery criterion:
- 80% or higher correct response for each set
- Minimum of five opportunities
- Across 4 days

Generalization:
People: At least two adults
Settings: At least two settings
Materials: Across a variety of puzzles

Things to consider: Consider the child's developmental level in deciding how many steps of the sequence below to complete. Begin with preferred puzzles. Consider the child's fine motor ability for picking up the pieces.

Teaching sequence
1. Inset, non-interlocking puzzles (at least 5 pieces)
2. Inset, interlocking puzzles (at least 9 pieces)
3. Inset, interlocking puzzles (at least 15 pieces
4. Interlocking puzzles (at least 12 pieces)
5. Interlocking puzzles (at least 20 pieces)

PROGRAMMING LOG

	Acquisition		Generalization		Maintenance	
	Start date	End date	Start date	End date	Date/data	Date/data
1						
2						
3						
4						
5						

LESSON PLAN: Independent Play

Completes a Puzzle

Settings and materials	
Decontextualized	**Embedded**

Teaching

What direction or cue will you give?

How will you prompt the child's response?

Circle type of prompt(s) used:

Physical   Visual

Modeling   Verbal

Other: _____

Circle prompt fading procedure used:

Time delay   Most to least

Graduated guidance

Other: _____

What is the child's response?

What reinforcers are you using?

What is the correction procedure?

How will you collect data? *(circle answer)*

Percentage correct   Frequency

Duration   Permanent product

Other: _____

Sets

1. _____
_____
_____
_____

2. _____
_____
_____
_____

3. _____
_____
_____
_____

4. _____
_____
_____
_____

5. _____
_____
_____
_____

INSTRUCTIONAL PROGRAM SHEET: Independent Play

Colors or Draws

Child: _____ Date initiated: _____ Date completed: _____

Objective: When presented with coloring or drawing materials, the child colors or draws independently.

Mastery criterion:
- 80% or higher correct response for each set
- Minimum of five opportunities per day
- 3 consecutive teaching days
- Three different sets of materials (e.g., crayons, markers, paint)

Generalization:
People: At least two adults
Settings: At least two settings
Materials: Across a variety of coloring and drawing materials

Things to consider: Child may scribble, draw circles and lines, or draw simple shapes or designs (e.g., a happy face) considering his or her developmental age. Consider the child's developmental level in deciding how many steps of the sequence below to complete. Child may need to learn how to use materials through imitation before considering independence for this activity. Also, review "Uses Classroom Materials."

Teaching sequence
1. Scribbles on paper
2. Colors within lines
3. Draws circles
4. Draws lines (e.g., horizontal, vertical, diagonal)
5. Draws simple shapes (e.g., happy face, sun)
6. Draws more complex shapes (e.g., house, tree)

PROGRAMMING LOG

	Acquisition		Generalization		Maintenance	
	Start date	End date	Start date	End date	Date/data	Date/data
1						
2						
3						
4						
5						
6						

The DATA Model for Teaching Preschoolers with Autism by Ilene Schwartz, Julie Ashmun, Bonnie McBride, Crista Scott, and Susan Sandall. Copyright © 2017 by Paul H. Brookes Publishing Co., Inc. All rights reserved.

LESSON PLAN: Independent Play

Colors or Draws

Settings and materials	
Decontextualized	**Embedded**

Teaching
What direction or cue will you give?
How will you prompt the child's response?
Circle type of prompt(s) used:
Physical   Visual
Modeling   Verbal
Other: _____
Circle prompt fading procedure used:
Time delay   Most to least
Graduated guidance
Other: _____
What is the child's response?
What reinforcers are you using?
What is the correction procedure?
How will you collect data? *(circle answer)*
Percentage correct   Frequency
Duration   Permanent product
Other: _____

Sets

1. _____

2. _____

3. _____

4. _____

5. _____

INSTRUCTIONAL PROGRAM SHEET: Independent Play

Begins and Completes at Least Three Activities

Child: _____ Date initiated: _____ Date completed: _____

Objective: In the presence of toys the child knows how to play with or when told, "Time to play," the child chooses an activity, begins to play, and completes play (to the natural end of the activity) with at least three activities consecutively.

Mastery criterion:
- 80% or higher correct response
- Begins and completes three activities consecutively each day
- 3 consecutive teaching days
- Across open and close-ended activities

Generalization:
People: At least two adults
Settings: At least two settings
Materials: Across a variety of materials

Things to consider: Use toys with which the child knows how to play. Visual prompts and a timer may be helpful.

Teaching sequence
1. Plays with one activity at table or on floor (materials are next to child)
2. Plays with two activities (materials are next to child)
3. Plays with three activities (materials are next to child)
4. Plays with three activities in which child needs to move to get materials

PROGRAMMING LOG

	Acquisition		Generalization		Maintenance	
	Start date	End date	Start date	End date	Date/data	Date/data
1						
2						
3						
4						

LESSON PLAN: Independent Play

Begins and Completes at Least Three Activities

Settings and materials	
Decontextualized	**Embedded**

Teaching

What direction or cue will you give?

How will you prompt the child's response?

Circle type of prompt(s) used:

Physical   Visual

Modeling   Verbal

Other: _____

Circle prompt fading procedure used:

Time delay   Most to least

Graduated guidance

Other: _____

What is the child's response?

What reinforcers are you using?

What is the correction procedure?

How will you collect data? *(circle answer)*

Percentage correct   Frequency

Duration   Permanent product

Other: _____

Sets

1. _____

2. _____

3. _____

4. _____

5. _____

INSTRUCTIONAL PROGRAM SHEET: Interactive Play

Engages in Parallel Play

Child: _____ Date initiated: _____ Date completed: _____

Objective: In the presence of peers playing or when told "It's time to play with a friend (friend's name)," the child plays alongside or near the other child(ren), with similar materials, for the duration or until the natural end of the activity.

Mastery criterion:
- 80% or higher correct response for each set
- Minimum of five opportunities per day
- 3 consecutive teaching days

Generalization:
People: At least three peers
Settings: At least two settings
Materials: Across a variety of materials

Things to consider: Offer child preferred materials to play with while teaching this skill. Consider teaching skill in a preferred area of the classroom (i.e., blocks, games).

Teaching sequence
1. Plays in the same area of the classroom (blocks, books, dramatic play, etc.) as peers
2. Plays at the same table with similar materials as peers (e.g., does art at the art table with peers)
3. Plays next to peers with similar materials (i.e., within 3 feet of peers)

PROGRAMMING LOG

	Acquisition		Generalization		Maintenance	
	Start date	End date	Start date	End date	Date/data	Date/data
1						
2						
3						

The DATA Model for Teaching Preschoolers with Autism by Ilene Schwartz, Julie Ashmun, Bonnie McBride, Crista Scott, and Susan Sandall. Copyright © 2017 by Paul H. Brookes Publishing Co., Inc. All rights reserved.

LESSON PLAN: Interactive Play

Engages in Parallel Play

Settings and materials	
Decontextualized	**Embedded**

Teaching
What direction or cue will you give?
How will you prompt the child's response?
Circle type of prompt(s) used:
Physical   Visual
Modeling   Verbal
Other: _____
Circle prompt fading procedure used:
Time delay   Most to least
Graduated guidance
Other: _____
What is the child's response?
What reinforcers are you using?
What is the correction procedure?
How will you collect data? *(circle answer)*
Percentage correct   Frequency
Duration   Permanent product
Other: _____

Sets

1. _____

_____

_____

_____

2. _____

_____

_____

_____

3. _____

_____

_____

_____

4. _____

_____

_____

_____

5. _____

_____

_____

_____

INSTRUCTIONAL PROGRAM SHEET: Interactive Play

Engages in Associative Play

Child: _____ Date initiated: _____ Date completed: _____

Objective: In the presence of peers playing or when told, "It's time to play with a friend (/friend's name)," the child plays with the same materials as other child(ren) for the duration or until the natural end of the activity. Child(ren) may have different agendas or goals about play.

Mastery criterion:
- 80% or higher correct response for each set
- Minimum of five opportunities per day
- 3 consecutive teaching days

Generalization:
People: At least three peers
Settings: At least two settings
Materials: Across a variety of materials

Things to consider: This is not a cooperative play goal. The children only need to play with the same materials.

Teaching sequence
1. Plays in the same area of the classroom with the same materials (e.g., blocks, books, dramatic play, etc.) as peers
2. Plays at the same table with the same materials as peers (e.g., draws pictures by using one set of markers)
3. Plays next to peers with the same materials (i.e., within 3 feet of peers)

PROGRAMMING LOG

	Acquisition		Generalization		Maintenance	
	Start date	End date	Start date	End date	Date/data	Date/data
1						
2						
3						

LESSON PLAN: Interactive Play

Engages in Associative Play

Settings and materials	
Decontextualized	**Embedded**

Teaching
What direction or cue will you give?
How will you prompt the child's response?
Circle type of prompt(s) used:
Physical   Visual
Modeling   Verbal
Other: _____
Circle prompt fading procedure used:
Time delay   Most to least
Graduated guidance
Other: _____
What is the child's response?
What reinforcers are you using?
What is the correction procedure?
How will you collect data? *(circle answer)*
Percentage correct   Frequency
Duration   Permanent product
Other: _____

Sets

1. _____
_____
_____
_____

2. _____
_____
_____
_____

3. _____
_____
_____
_____

4. _____
_____
_____

5. _____
_____
_____
_____

INSTRUCTIONAL PROGRAM SHEET: Interactive Play

Makes Comments About Play to Peers

Child: _____ Date initiated: _____ Date completed: _____

Objective: During play with peers, the child makes comments about his or her own play to the peer by looking toward peer.

Mastery criterion:
- At least three comments during each play period
- Across five play periods
- 2 consecutive teaching days

Generalization:
People: At least three peers
Settings: At least two settings
Materials: Across a variety of materials

Things to consider: Augmentative communication systems may be used in place of verbal comments. Use preferred materials so child is motivated to comment to peer(s). Also, review "Narrates Play" before teaching this skill.

Teaching sequence
1. Comments at least once during play periods
2. Comments at least once and looks toward peer(s) during play periods
3. Comments at least twice and looks toward peer(s) during play periods
4. Comments at least three times and looks toward peer(s) for each comment during play periods

PROGRAMMING LOG

	Acquisition		Generalization		Maintenance	
	Start date	End date	Start date	End date	Date/data	Date/data
1						
2						
3						
4						

LESSON PLAN: Interactive Play

Makes Comments About Play to Peers

Settings and materials	
Decontextualized	**Embedded**

Teaching
What direction or cue will you give?
How will you prompt the child's response?
Circle type of prompt(s) used:
Physical   Visual
Modeling   Verbal
Other: _____
Circle prompt fading procedure used:
Time delay   Most to least
Graduated guidance
Other: _____
What is the child's response?
What reinforcers are you using?
What is the correction procedure?
How will you collect data? *(circle answer)*
Percentage correct   Frequency
Duration   Permanent product
Other: _____

Sets

1. _____

   _____

   _____

   _____

2. _____

   _____

   _____

   _____

3. _____

   _____

   _____

   _____

4. _____

   _____

   _____

   _____

5. _____

   _____

   _____

   _____

INSTRUCTIONAL PROGRAM SHEET: Interactive Play

Organizes Play by Suggesting Play Plans

Child: _____ Date initiated: _____ Date completed: _____

Objective: During play with peers, the child suggests play plans (e.g., let's build a bridge and put the train on it) to peers.

Mastery criterion:
- At least three play plans each day
- Across at least three sets of play materials
- 2 consecutive teaching days

Generalization:
People: At least three peers
Settings: At least two settings
Materials: Across a variety of materials

Things to consider: Augmentative communication systems may be used. Use preferred materials so child is motivated to suggest plans to peer(s).

Teaching sequence
1. Suggests play plans with one type of prompt (i.e., visual) across three sets of play materials
2. Suggests play plans with no prompts across one set of play materials
3. Suggests play plans with no prompts across two sets of play materials
4. Suggests play plans with no prompts across three sets of play materials

PROGRAMMING LOG

	Acquisition		Generalization		Maintenance	
	Start date	End date	Start date	End date	Date/data	Date/data
1						
2						
3						
4						

The DATA Model for Teaching Preschoolers with Autism by Ilene Schwartz, Julie Ashmun, Bonnie McBride, Crista Scott, and Susan Sandall. Copyright © 2017 by Paul H. Brookes Publishing Co., Inc. All rights reserved.

LESSON PLAN: Interactive Play

Organizes Play by Suggesting Play Plans

Settings and materials	
Decontextualized	**Embedded**

Teaching
What direction or cue will you give?
How will you prompt the child's response?
Circle type of prompt(s) used:
Physical   Visual
Modeling   Verbal
Other: _____
Circle prompt fading procedure used:
Time delay   Most to least
Graduated guidance
Other: _____
What is the child's response?
What reinforcers are you using?
What is the correction procedure?
How will you collect data? *(circle answer)*
Percentage correct   Frequency
Duration   Permanent product
Other: _____

Sets

1. _____
_____
_____
_____

2. _____
_____
_____
_____

3. _____
_____
_____
_____

4. _____
_____
_____
_____

5. _____
_____
_____
_____

INSTRUCTIONAL PROGRAM SHEET: Interactive Play

Follows a Peer's Play Idea

Child: _____ Date initiated: _____ Date completed: _____

Objective: During play with peers, the child listens to and follows a peer's play idea (e.g., peer suggests making a train track, the child joins the peer in making the track).

Mastery criterion:
- 80% or higher correct response for each set
- Minimum of five opportunities per day
- 3 consecutive teaching days

Generalization:
People: At least three peers
Settings: At least two settings
Materials: Across a variety of materials

Things to consider: Child must be able to understand and act upon the materials in the way the peer suggests. Consider peer models that will suggest ideas and that the child prefers to play with.

Teaching sequence
1. Follows play idea with one type of prompt (i.e., verbal) with one peer
2. Follows play idea with no prompts with one peer
3. Follows play ideas from another peer
4. Follows play ideas from three peers

PROGRAMMING LOG

	Acquisition		Generalization		Maintenance	
	Start date	End date	Start date	End date	Date/data	Date/data
1						
2						
3						
4						

LESSON PLAN: Interactive Play

Follows a Peer's Play Idea

Settings and materials	
Decontextualized	**Embedded**

Teaching
What direction or cue will you give?
How will you prompt the child's response?
Circle type of prompt(s) used:
Physical   Visual
Modeling   Verbal
Other: _____
Circle prompt fading procedure used:
Time delay   Most to least
Graduated guidance
Other: _____
What is the child's response?
What reinforcers are you using?
What is the correction procedure?
How will you collect data? *(circle answer)*
Percentage correct   Frequency
Duration   Permanent product
Other: _____

Sets

1. _____
_____
_____
_____

2. _____
_____
_____
_____

3. _____
_____
_____
_____

4. _____
_____
_____

5. _____
_____
_____
_____

INSTRUCTIONAL PROGRAM SHEET: Interactive Play

Plays Cooperatively

Child: _____ Date initiated: _____ Date completed: _____

Objective: During play with peers, the child listens to peers and offers ideas in order to play cooperatively with peers until the natural end of the play. Playing cooperatively includes taking on a pretend role during dramatic play and leading the play by offering play suggestions to peers.

Mastery criterion:

- ▧ Across four roles or play ideas
- ▧ Across 4 consecutive teaching days

Generalization:
People: At least three peers
Settings: At least two settings
Materials: Across a variety of materials

Things to consider: Create situations for this type of play by making materials available. Consider having some real objects and no objects available in play scheme.

Teaching sequence

1. Enacts roles with peers and acts out play idea provided by an adult (e.g., adults says, "Let's play the three little pigs," and child and peer act out at least three steps of the storyline)
2. Enacts roles and acts out play with minimal adult support (less than 50% of support from an adult)
3. Child plays cooperatively with peer(s) with no adult support

PROGRAMMING LOG

	Acquisition		Generalization		Maintenance	
	Start date	End date	Start date	End date	Date/data	Date/data
1						
2						
3						

LESSON PLAN: Interactive Play

Plays Cooperatively

Settings and materials	
Decontextualized	**Embedded**

Teaching

What direction or cue will you give?

How will you prompt the child's response?

Circle type of prompt(s) used:

Physical   Visual

Modeling   Verbal

Other: _____

Circle prompt fading procedure used:

Time delay   Most to least

Graduated guidance

Other: _____

What is the child's response?

What reinforcers are you using?

What is the correction procedure?

How will you collect data? *(circle answer)*

Percentage correct   Frequency

Duration   Permanent product

Other: _____

Sets

1. _____

   _____

   _____

   _____

2. _____

   _____

   _____

   _____

3. _____

   _____

   _____

   _____

4. _____

   _____

   _____

   _____

5. _____

   _____

   _____

   _____

INSTRUCTIONAL PROGRAM SHEET: Interactive Play

Plays Games with Rules

Child: _____ Date initiated: _____ Date completed: _____

Objective: When it's time to play a game (social or board), as indicated by teacher direction or peer invitation, the child plays the game by conforming to game rules and maintaining participation until the natural completion of the game.

Mastery criterion:
- 80% or higher correct response
- Minimum of five opportunities per day
- 3 consecutive teaching days

Mastery criterion for social games:
- Participation in social games with only one adult prompt
- 3 consecutive teaching days

Generalization:
People: At least three peers
Settings: At least two settings
Materials: Across a variety of board games and social games

Things to consider: Start with simple games. If possible, use motivating characters, toys or activities.

Teaching sequence
1. Waits turn with a simple game with one peer
2. Waits turn with a simple game with two peers
3. Plays game with at least two peers by following sequence of turns and rules with no more than four adult prompts
4. Plays game with at least two peers by following sequence of turns and rules with one or fewer adult prompts

PROGRAMMING LOG

	Acquisition		Generalization		Maintenance	
	Start date	End date	Start date	End date	Date/data	Date/data
1						
2						
3						
4						

LESSON PLAN: Interactive Play

Plays Games with Rules

Settings and materials	
Decontextualized	**Embedded**

Teaching
What direction or cue will you give?
How will you prompt the child's response?
Circle type of prompt(s) used:
Physical   Visual
Modeling   Verbal
Other: _____
Circle prompt fading procedure used:
Time delay   Most to least
Graduated guidance
Other: _____
What is the child's response?
What reinforcers are you using?
What is the correction procedure?
How will you collect data? *(circle answer)*
Percentage correct   Frequency
Duration   Permanent product
Other: _____

Sets

1. _____

   _____

   _____

   _____

2. _____

   _____

   _____

   _____

3. _____

   _____

   _____

   _____

4. _____

   _____

   _____

   _____

5. _____

   _____

   _____

   _____

Glossary

ABA   *See* applied behavior analysis.

antecedent   A stimulus that occurs before a response. This can be an instruction, an event (someone entering a room or a peer asking a question), an environmental cue (the lights go off), etc.

applied behavior analysis (ABA)   The application of behavioral principles to change (i.e., increase or decrease the frequency of) socially important behaviors. Described by Baer, Wolf, and Risley in the article "Some Current Dimensions of Applied Behavior Analysis" (1968).

autism   Autism/autism spectrum disorder is a lifelong developmental disability characterized by qualitative impairments in social-communicative behaviors and restricted or repetitive range of behaviors. There is no known cure for autism, but early intensive behavioral interventions (like Project DATA) have been shown to be extremely effective in the treatment of autism.

behavioral momentum   An instructional strategy in which an adult makes requests that are generally easy for the child (i.e., high probability responses) followed by a more difficult or challenging request (i.e., low probability response). The probability of the child's response to the more difficult request is increased once the child is already responding to high probability requests.

communicative temptations   An environmental arrangement that increases the motivation for a child to use words, gestures, or symbols to communicate. For example, if a child's favorite toy is visible but out of reach, it is a communicative temptation to increase the likelihood that the child will request the toy.

consequence   A stimulus that immediately follows a response. A consequence can occur naturally (e.g., spilled milk when you knock over a cup) or can be planned (e.g., presentation of a preferred toy contingent upon a target behavior).

contingency   The relationship between a specific behavior and its consequence. Contingencies act to shape behavior and can increase the likelihood that behaviors occur more frequently (i.e., when consequences are reinforcers) or occur less frequently (e.g., when consequences are punishers).

data-based decision making   An evaluation strategy that uses student performance data to determine changes that need to be made in a child's program.

data   Information that is collected and analyzed (e.g., the number of toilet accidents a child has during the day) to determine child progress and to guide decisions about the child's program.

decontextualized teaching or testing   Instruction or assessment activities that occur in a specialized instructional setting or designated instructional time.

differential reinforcement   Reinforcement of a behavior other than the target behavior. This type of reinforcement is generally used to increase appropriate alternatives to a challenging behavior while the challenging target behavior is on extinction. For example, a child may receive reinforcement for raising his hand during circle, rather than calling out.

direct testing   The process of gathering assessment information by creating specific opportunities to assess a child's ability to demonstrate target skills or behaviors.

discrete trial   An instructional strategy that breaks complex skills into small parts to teach and requires that all parts of the skills are learned to mastery. Discrete trials are methods for delivery instruction that include five components: instruction, prompt (if necessary) response, consequence, and intertrial interval. A discrete trial is also sometimes called a teaching loop in special education.

discriminative stimulus (S^D) A stimulus that indicates that reinforcement is available for a specific behavior. For example, when a teacher says, "Stand up," it indicates that reinforcement is available when the child stands up. That same behavior may not be reinforced under other stimulus conditions (e.g., when the teacher is reading a story).

embedded instruction Short, planned instructional episodes that occur within the ongoing classroom activities and routines.

evidence-based strategies Instructional and behavior change strategies that have been demonstrated to be effective by a collection of research by multiple investigators, across multiple settings, with multiple participants.

extended, intensive instruction The component of Project DATA during which children receive intensive instruction based on their individual needs. This part of the program supplements children's participation in a high-quality integrated preschool program.

extinction A behavior reduction strategy that involves removing reinforcement (e.g., attention) from a behavior that was previously reinforced. When extinction is used, children often demonstrate an extinction burst, a short but potential increase in the target behavior, before the behavior decreases.

generalization To demonstrate a learned skill or behavior in a variety of settings, with a variety of materials, and with a variety of people.

inclusion Programs that include children with and without disabilities across all settings and provide the services and supports necessary to promote active participation of all.

instruction The first component of a discrete trial. An instruction is a clear, short directive telling a student what observable, measurable behavior is expected.

instructional programs A systematic plan that describes and defines what behavior is going to be taught, what strategies will be used to teach the behavior, and what the criteria for acquisition and generalization will be. An instructional program must include an objective, a criteria for acquisition and generalization, steps in the instructional process, and a description of what instructional strategies will be used to teach the skills.

integrated early childhood experience An early childhood program that includes children with and without disabilities across all environments and activities and provides the instruction and support necessary so that all children participate and learn.

intertrial interval The brief pause between the end of one discrete trial and the beginning of the next.

natural reinforcement An activity or item that is used as a reinforcer that is part of the ongoing activity or routine. For example, if a child wants to go outside and the teacher is blocking the door, when the child says, "Open," opening the door and providing the child access to the outside is a natural reinforcer.

negative punishment The removal of a stimulus (e.g., access to a preferred toy) that decreases the likelihood of the behavior happening again.

negative reinforcement The removal of a stimulus that increases the likelihood of that behavior happening again.

planned ignoring A behavior reduction strategy in which attention is removed from a child for a short and prespecified amount of time, contingent on a target behavior (e.g., hitting). The child is not removed from the setting.

positive punishment   The addition of a stimulus following a behavior that decreases the likelihood of that behavior happening again.

positive reinforcement   The addition of a stimulus following a behavior that increases the likelihood of that behavior happening again.

preference assessment   An assessment process to rate children's current preference for different items and activities. This is used to identify stimuli that are more likely to function as reinforcers (remember, a reinforcer increases the likelihood of a behavior happening again). This is completed with observation, interview, or direct testing.

prompt fading   The systematic process of decreasing the salience of a prompt, while maintaining correct responding on the part of the child. There are two primary strategies for decreasing prompts: 1) increasing the amount of time between the instruction and the prompt (e.g., time delay), and 2) decreasing the intrusiveness of the prompt (e.g., decreasing the type of physical prompting from hand over hand to a touch at the elbow).

prompts   Any assistance that occurs before a response to provide support for a correct response. Prompts may be verbal, pictures, gestural, physical, environmental, model, or a combination of these.

punishment   A consequence that decreases the likelihood of a behavior happening again.

reinforcement   A consequene that increases the likelihood of a behavior happening again. Reinforcers may include activities, people, food, and items.

schedule of reinforcement   The amount of reinforcement that is provided by the environment (e.g., teacher, parent, or natural environment) for a target behavior. Schedules of reinforcement can be manipulated (e.g., strengthened or thinned) to assist in the acquisition of a behavior and in making that behavior more durable.

s^D: *See* discriminative stimulus.

stimulus   Anything that evokes a specific behavior. A discriminative stimulus is a stimulus in the presence of which a particular behavior is reinforced.

target behavior   The behavior to be changed by the intervention strategy or instructional program.

teaching loop   A way to frame an instructional interaction that includes getting the child's attention, providing an instruction, providing an opportunity for the child to respond, and providing a consequence that is appropriate to the child's response. The content and pacing of future teaching loops are based on child performance in previous teaching loops.

technical support for families   Information that is provided to families that addresses the special needs and circumstances of raising a child with autism spectrum disorder. This may include information about the diagnosis, evidence-based instructional strategies, effective parenting strategies, and recommended practices in school-based interventions.

three-term contingency   The interdependency among antecedents, behaviors, and consequences. For example, a behavior is more likely to be reinforced when it occurs during certain antecedent conditions (e.g., teacher asks a question—antecedent, child raises their hand—behavior, teacher calls on child—consequence.

time out (from positive reinforcement)   A behavior reduction strategy in which positive reinforcement (e.g., attention) is withheld from a child contingent on a target behavior.

References

Alberto, P.A., & Troutman, A.C. (2012). *Applied behavior analysis for teachers.* (9th Ed.). Pearson Higher Ed: Upper Saddle River, NJ.

Allen, K.E., Benning, P.M., & Drummond, W.T. (1972). Integration of normal and handicapped children in a behavior modification preschool: A case study. In G. Semb (Ed.), *Behavior analysis and education* (pp. 127–141). Lawrence, KS: University of Kansas.

American Psychiatric Association. (2013). Diagnostic and statistical manual of mental disorders (5th Ed.). Washington, DC.

Baer, D.M., Wolf, M.M., & Risley, T.R. (1968). Some current dimensions of applied behavior analysis. *Journal of Applied Behavior Analysis, 1,* 91–97.

Bailey, D.B., & Wolery, M. (1992). *Teaching infants and preschoolers with disabilities* (2nd Ed.). Englewood Cliffs, NJ: Prentice Hall.

Baker, B.L., & Brightman, A.J. (2003). *Steps to Independence: Teaching Everyday Skills to Children with Special Needs, Fourth Edition.* Baltimore, MD: Paul H. Brookes Publishing Co.

Barton, E.E., & Smith, B.J. (2015). *The Preschool Inclusion Toolbox: How to Build and Lead a High-Quality Program.* Baltimore, MD: Paul H. Brookes Publishing Co.

Berke, K., Bickert, T., & Heroman, C. (2010). *Teaching Strategies Gold: Birth through kindergarten assessment toolkit.* Washington, DC: Teaching Strategies, Inc.

Billingsley, F., Gallucci, C., Peck, C.A., Schwartz, I.S., & Staub, D. (1996). "But those kids can't even do math": An alternative conceptualization outcome for inclusive education. *Special Education Leadership Review, 3*(1), 43–55.

Bredekamp, S., & Copple, C. (eds.). (1997). *Developmentally appropriate practice in early childhood programs* (rev. ed.). Washington, DC: National Association for the Education of Young Children.

Bricker, D., Capt, B., Pretti-Frontczak, K., Waddell, M. (2002). *Assessment, Evaluation, and Programming System for Infants and Children, Second Edition.* Baltimore, MD: Paul H. Brookes Publishing Co.

Carr, Edward G. (2007). The expanding vision of positive behavior support: Research perspectives on happiness, helpfulness, hopefulness. *Journal of Positive Behavior Interventions, 9*(1), (pp. 3–14).

Cooper, J.O., Heron, T.E., & Heward, W.L. (2007). *Applied Behavior Analysis* (2nd Ed.). Upper Saddle River, NJ: Merrill.

Dawson, G., & Osterling, J. (1997). Early intervention in autism: Effectiveness and common elements of current approaches. In Guralnick (Ed.) *The effectiveness of early intervention: Second generation research* (pp. 307–326). Baltimore, MD: Paul H. Brookes Publishing Co.

Dunlap, G., Wilson, K., Strain, P., & Lee, J.K. (2013). *Prevent-Teach-Reinforce for Young Children: The Early Childhood Model of Individualized Positive Behavior Support.* Baltimore, MD: Paul H. Brookes Publishing Co.

Dunn, L.M., & Dunn, L.M. (1997). *Peabody Picture Vocabulary Test*, 3rd edition. Circle Pines, MN: American Guidance Service.

Gauvreau, A.N., & Schwartz, I.S. (2013). Using visual supports to promote appropriate behavior in young children with autism and related disorders. *Young Exceptional Children Monograph Series, 15,* 29–44.

Greenwood, C.R., Delquadri, J., & Hall, R.V. (1984). Opportunity to respond and student academic performance. *Focus on behavior analysis in education, 58–88.*

Grisham-Brown, J., & Pretti-Frontczak, K. (2011). *Assessing Young Children in Inclusive Settings: The Blended Practices Approach.* Baltimore, MD: Paul H. Brookes Publishing Co.

Hemmeter, M.L., & Fox, L. (2009). The Teaching Pyramid: A model for the implementation of classroom practices within a program-wide approach to behavior support. *NHSA DIALOG, 12*(2), 133–147.

Johnson-Martin, N., Attermeier, S., Hacker, B. (1990). *The Carolina Curriculum for Preschoolers with Special Needs.* Baltimore, MD: Paul H. Brookes Publishing Co.

Koegel, R.L., Russo, D.C., & Rincover, A. (1977). Assessing and training teachers in the generalized use of behavior modification with autistic children. *Journal of Applied Behavior Analysis, 10,* 197–205.

Leon-Guerrero, R.M., Matsumoto, C., & Martin, J. (2011). *Show ME the Data!: Databased Instructional Decisions Made Simple and Easy.* Shawnee Mission, KS: AAPC.

Mayer, G.R., Sulzer-Azaroff, B., & Wallace, M. (2014). *Behavior analysis for lasting change.* Cornwall-on-Hudson, NY: Sloane Publishing.

Merrell, K.W. (2003). *Preschool and Kindergarten Behavior Scales, 2nd edition.* Austin, TX: PRO-ED.

Meyer, D.J., & Vadasey, P.F. (2007). *Sibshops: Workshops for Siblings of Children with Special Needs.* Baltimore, MD: Paul H. Brookes Publishing Co.

McLean, M., Hemmeter, M.L., & Snyder, P. (2013). *Essential elements for assessing infants and preschoolers with special needs.* Boston, MA: Pearson.

National Research Council. (2001). Educating children with autism. Washington, DC: National Academy.

Sandall, S.R., & Schwartz, I.S. (2008). *Trainer's Guide to Building Blocks for Teaching Preschoolers with Special Needs* (2nd Ed.). Baltimore, MD: Paul H. Brookes Publishing Co.

Sandall, S.R., Schwartz, I.S., & Lacroix, B. (2004). Interventionists' perspectives about data collection in integrated early childhood classrooms. *Journal of Early Intervention, 26*(3), 161–174.

Schwartz, I.S. (1987). A review of techniques for naturalistic language training. *Child Language Teaching and Therapy, 3,* 267–276.

Schwartz, I.S., & Davis, C.A. (2006). Early Intervention for Children with Autism Spectrum Disorder. IMPACT—Supporting Success in School and Beyond for Students with Autism Spectrum Disorders. University of Minnesota, Institute on Community Integration.

Schwartz, I.S., Sandall, S.R., & Gauvreau, A.N. (2013). Planning to individualize: Meeting the needs of all children using activity matrices. *Teaching Young Children, 7*(2), 21–23.

Schwartz, I.S., Sandall, S.R., McBride, B.J., & Boulware, G.L. (2004). Project DATA (developmentally appropriate treatment for autism): An inclusive, school-based approach to educating children with autism. *Topics in Early Childhood Special Education, 24,* 156–168.

Schwartz, I.S., Thomas, C.J., McBride, B., & Sandall, S.R. (2013). A school-based preschool program for children with ASD: A quasi-experimental assessment of child change in Project DATA. *School Mental Health.* doi: 10.1007/s12310-013-9103-7

Smith, L.E., Greenberg, J.S., & Seltzer, M.M. (2012). Social support and well-being at mid-life among mothers of adolescents and adults with autism spectrum disorders. *Journal of Autism and Developmental Disorders, 42*(9), 1818–1826.

Smith, L.E., Hong, J., Seltzer, M.M., Greenberg, J.S., Almeida, D.M., & Bishop, S.L. (2010). Daily experiences among mothers of adolescents and adults with autism spectrum disorder. *Journal of Autism and Developmental Disorders, 40*(2), 167–178.

Strain, P.S., Schwartz, I.S., & Barton, E. (2011). Providing Interventions for Young Children with ASD: What We Still Need to Accomplish. *Topics in Early Childhood Special Education, 33,* 321–332. *doi: 10.1177/1053815111429970.*

VORT Corporation. (1999). *HELP for Preschoolers: Assessment and curriculum guide.* Palo Alto, CA: VORT.

Wolery, M., Bailey, D.B., & Sugai, G.M. (1988). *Effective teaching: Principles and procedures of applied behavior analysis with exceptional students.* Boston, MA: Pearson.

Wong, C., Odom, S.L., Hume, K.A., Cox, A.W., Fettig, A., Kucharczyk, S., & Schultz, T.R. (2015). Evidence-based practices for children, youth, and young adults with autism spectrum disorder: A comprehensive review. *Journal of Autism and Developmental Disorders,* 1–16.

APPENDIX A

The DATA Model Skills Checklist

The DATA Model Skills Checklist

Child's name:	Date of birth:
Parent(s)/guardian(s):	
First administration date:	Staff member(s) completing form:
Second administration date:	Staff member(s) completing form:
Child's preferred items and activities:	
Child's primary mode of communication:	

Directions:

1. This checklist is intended to be filled out at least twice during the school year. For each administration, use a different colored pen to differentiate between the two administration dates. For example, for the first administration use a blue pen, and for the second administration, use a red pen.

2. Several items are directly tested; others are observed and scored during classroom routines and activities. Adult instructions are provided for items to be directly tested. Scoring is as follows:

   2 = Consistently/always meets criterion

   1 = Inconsistently/sometimes meets criterion

   0 = Does not/never meet(s) criterion

3. After completing the checklist, put a * next to items that are priorities for learning, then fill out the *Priority skills* section at the end of this checklist with those items.

NOTES _____

_____

_____

_____

_____

_____

_____

_____

A. ADAPTIVE

1.	Mealtime	Scoring	Comments	*
1.1	Drinks from open cup *Brings open cup to mouth and returns cup to surface without spilling*	0　1　2		
1.2	Eats with fork or spoon *Spears or scoops food and brings to mouth with minimal spilling*	0　1　2		
1.3	Eats a variety of food *Discuss importance, level of priority with family before making an intervention plan*	0　1　2		
1.4	Remains at table during meals *Remains at table until asked to leave, adult excuses child, or until the natural end of the mealtime*	0　1　2		
2.	**Personal hygiene**	**Scoring**	**Comments**	*
2.1	Toilet trained—urine *Demonstrates bladder control, using the toilet to void. Adult may provide some assistance for clothing and occasional reminders are acceptable, as developmentally appropriate.*	0　1　2		
2.2	Toilet trained—bowel *Demonstrates bowel control, using the toilet to void. Adult may provide some assistance with clothing and occasional reminders are acceptable, as developmentally appropriate.*	0　1　2		
2.3	Washes and dries hands *Child is able to complete all steps of hand washing routine independently. Occasional reminders are acceptable as appropriate to age.*	0　1　2		
3.	**School skills**	**Scoring**	**Comments**	*
3.1	Manages personal belongings *When given a direction to get their own materials (e.g., lunchbox, backpack, coat) or during a transition in the schedule, the child is able to get and put away personal belongings needed for the activity.*	0　1　2		
3.2	Uses classroom materials *When given classroom materials such as scissors, markers, paper, etc., child is able to use materials appropriately. For example, child picks up scissors and attempts to cut with scissors.*	0　1　2		
3.3	Completes transitions between activities *When an activity is finished, child is able to clean up if needed, get materials for next activity, and line up and remain with group completing the transition.*	0　1　2		
3.4	Walks with peers in small or large groups across a variety of school settings *Walks in school building, school grounds, and in the community staying in pace with an adult. Child does not run off or need hand held for entire duration of walking activity.*	0　1　2		
3.5	Rides in school bus, car, or other transportation to and from school *Child is able to sit and remain in car seat or other appropriate seating with absence of protest for duration of trip.*	0　1　2		

3.	School skills *(continued)*	Scoring			Comments	*
3.6	Waits for instruction to begin (individual, small group, large group) *Child is able to wait quietly and remain seated or standing until the teacher provides the direction for the activity.*	0	1	2		
3.7	Works independently on a teacher selected activity *Child is able to sit and attend to a nonpreferred activity until completion.*	0	1	2		
3.8	Begins and completes at least three different teacher selected activities *Teacher prepares activities and child will complete them with only a few reminders or directions.*	0	1	2		
3.9	Participates in a group activity for:	0	1	2		
	■ 5 minutes	0	1	2		
	■ 10 minutes	0	1	2		
	■ 15 minutes	0	1	2		
	Participation includes attending to materials and teacher, acting on the materials if required, remaining with the group until natural end of activity. Group activities may include but are not limited to both small and large group, transitions with the group, and lunch or snack.					
4.	**Self-Advocacy**	Scoring			Comments	*
4.1	Requests a break when needed *Child makes request for a break before leaving area or room.*	0	1	2		
4.2	Protests *During a nonpreferred activity or offered a less preferred item, the child will communicate, "No," "No thank you," "I don't want that," or "I'm done," either verbally or nonverbally.*	0	1	2		
4.3	Requests help from adults and peers when needed *When child needs help, he or she will do so with a calm body.*	0	1	2		
4.4	Requests clarification when needed *Child may ask the adult to repeat the direction, state that he or she doesn't know what to do, etc.*	0	1	2		
4.5	Asks for accommodations *For example, may ask to see pictures or a schedule, may ask for another minute to finish activity.*	0	1	2		
4.6	Identify likes and dislikes *Child will state at least four different items he/she likes and four different items he/she dislikes, such as food, toys, color.*	0	1	2		
4.7	States identifying information about self *When asked identifying information such as "What is your name?" or "How old are you?" child will respond correctly across at least four different identifying items.*	0	1	2		

A. ADAPTIVE *(continued)*

5.	Behaviors that interfere with participation and learning			
The purpose of this section is to identify behaviors that have been resistant to ongoing classroom instruction and behavioral support. The purpose is not to identify all behaviors the child may demonstrate, only those that are chronic and interfere with instruction.

Example: Screaming	(Yes)	No	Context: **Child screams when asked to do a nonpreferred activity. This only happens with one of the teachers in the classroom.**
Aggression	Yes	No	Context:
Self-injurious behavior	Yes	No	Context:
Property destruction	Yes	No	Context:
Running away	Yes	No	Context:
Self-stimulatory behavior	Yes	No	Context:
Screaming	Yes	No	Context:
Noncompliance	Yes	No	Context:
Other	Yes	No	Context:
Other	Yes	No	Context:
Other	Yes	No	Context:

Summary notes for adaptive

The DATA Model for Teaching Preschoolers with Autism by Ilene Schwartz, Julie Ashmun, Bonnie McBride, Crista Scott, and Susan Sandall. Copyright © 2017 by Paul H. Brookes Publishing Co., Inc. All rights reserved.

1.	Flexibility	Scoring			Comments	*
1.1	Follows classroom routine and schedule	0	1	2		
	Child references posted schedule in classroom or follows teacher's directions to transition to another activity with a calm body.					
1.2	Accepts interruptions or unexpected change	0	1	2		
	Child may verbally or nonverbally, appropriately express displeasure with change, but is able to accept change or interruptions and move on.					
1.3	Accepts being told "no" without becoming upset or angry	0	1	2		
	When the child is told that he or she cannot have the object or activity, child accepts this response without becoming upset as age appropriate.					
1.4	Relinquishes preferred toy, food, or materials to an adult or peer when asked	0	1	2		
	Child may receive adult reminder or support, but will relinquish item without protest or with appropriate protest (e.g., "I don't want to." or "wait.").					
1.5	Accepts that things don't go as expected	0	1	2		
	During a group game the child does not have the first turn, does not protest, and will participate in the game.					
	If a child does not finish first in the game, they do not protest, may say, "That's okay . . . maybe next time" or congratulate the winner.					
	If a child is drawing a picture and makes an unintended mark, the child does not rip up his or her paper.					
2.	**Self-Regulation: Self and emotional control**	Scoring			Comments	*
2.1	Waits for a preferred item or activity	0	1	2		
	When child is told to wait, he or she will wait quietly and calmly for the item.					
2.2	Accepts comfort from others if upset or agitated	0	1	2		
	Allows caregiver or familiar adult to give them a hug or peers to pat their back.					
2.3	Self-regulates when tense or upset with verbal or visual cue	0	1	2		
	For example, calms self by counting to 10, taking a breath, taking a break, etc.					
2.4	Self-regulates when energy level is high or low with verbal or visual cue	0	1	2		
	If energy level is high, the child may count to 10 or squeeze a squishy ball. If energy level is low, the child may walk around the room or jump on a trampoline.					
3.	**Persistence, organization, and time management**	Scoring			Comments	*
3.1	Persists in gaining a person's attention	0	1	2		
	Child will call a person's name or tap that person until the person acknowledges the child.					
3.2	Persists, or continues to try, when something is difficult	0	1	2		
	The child is trying to put a toy together, and the pieces don't fit, but they persist in trying to put the pieces together.					

3. Persistence, organization, and time management (*continued*)	Scoring	Comments	*
3.3 Follows a sequence of at least three steps in an activity *For example, when given verbal or visual steps in a sequence, child will complete the activity in order by following the direction or referencing the picture sequence.*	0 1 2		
3.4 Finishes an activity within a timely manner, cleans up, and moves to the next activity *Consider developmentally appropriate time which may be indicated by the child completing the activity when other children of the same age in the classroom complete the activity.*	0 1 2		
4. Problem solving	**Scoring**	**Comments**	*
4.1 Claims and defends possessions *For example, if a peer takes the child's trading cards, the child will try to hold on to them or say, "That's mine."*	0 1 2		
4.2 Identifies or defines the problem *If two children want the same toy, the child will communicate that the problem is two children want one toy.*	0 1 2		
4.3 Generates solutions *If an art project rips, the child may suggest getting tape to fix it or make a new one.*	0 1 2		
4.4 Carries out solutions by negotiating or compromising *Two children want the same toy and the child suggests they take turns, do eeney-meaney-miney-mo or set a timer to show when a turn is over.*	0 1 2		
5. Emotional knowledge	**Scoring**	**Comments**	*
5.1 Identifies simple emotions in pictures and books *When presented with different emotions in pictures or books and asked, "Which one is happy," child will point to, give, or tap the picture. If asked, "How does she feel," child will state, "She is happy."*	0 1 2		.
5.2 Labels and identifies emotions in self *If their toy breaks, and the child is sad, they can label that emotion accurately when asked, "How do you feel?"*	0 1 2		
5.3 Labels and identifies emotions in others *If a peer is angry, the child will be able to say, "He is mad."*	0 1 2		
5.4 Justifies an emotion once identified/labeled *If a girl is crying the child can say she is crying because she fell down and is hurt.*	0 1 2		
5.5 Demonstrates affection and empathy toward peers *Gives hugs or handshakes to peers and asks if a peer is okay when appropriate.*	0 1 2		
Summary notes for executive functioning			

1.	Imitation	Scoring			Comments	*
1.1	Imitates actions with objects	0	1	2		
	Imitates five common actions and five novel actions with objects (e.g., place block on block, shake maraca, push car, pull toy, squeeze toy, scribble, drink from a cup, feed a doll)					
1.2	Imitates large motor movements	0	1	2		
	Imitates five actions that are visible to the child (that the child can see themselves perform such as wave, clap hands, and tap legs) and five that are not (e.g., arms up, shake head no, arms out to side, cover face such as peek-a-boo, touch nose, turn around)					
1.3	Imitates fine motor movements	0	1	2		
	Imitates three different actions (e.g., open and close hands, extend index finger as in a point, wiggle fingers, thumbs up, squeeze clay or squeaky toy, pinch clothespin)					
1.4	Imitates words	0	1	2		
	Child imitates frequently used, novel, and developmentally appropriate sounds and words.					
1.5	Imitates multistep sequences	0	1	2		
	Imitates multistep actions or phrases while following along with teacher in a group setting (e.g., repeat after me songs or rhymes, action songs)					
2.	Matching and categorizing	Scoring			Comments	*
2.1	Matches identical objects	0	1	2		
	Matches six different objects from an array of at least three					
2.2	Matches identical pictures	0	1	2		
	Matches six different pictures or photos from an array of at least three					
2.3	Matches objects to pictures	0	1	2		
	Matches six different objects to pictures from an array of at least three					
2.4	Matches pictures to objects	0	1	2		
	Matches three different pictures to objects from an array of at least three					
2.5	Matches nonidentical objects/pictures	0	1	2		
	Matches six different objects/pictures from at least three different categories (e.g., cars, foods, blocks) from an array of at least three					
2.6	Groups objects according to:					
	■ Size	0	1	2		
	■ Shape	0	1	2		
	■ Color	0	1	2		
	Groups at least three objects for each attribute—size, shape, and color					
2.7	Groups functionally related objects	0	1	2		
	Puts together at least three objects that are functionally related across six different groups (for painting—child gathers paint, brush, paper; to play in a sandbox child gets bucket, shovel, and sifter)					

2. Matching and categorizing (*continued*)	Scoring	Comments	*
2.8 Categorizes like objects *Puts together at least three objects in a group according to a broad-based category (e.g., food, clothing, animals; child gathers all toy animals together, puts play dishes and utensil on table, gathers clothing in order to play dress-up). Must group items for at least six different categories*	0 1 2		

3. Sequencing	Scoring	Comments	*
3.1 Makes simple patterns *Child replicates, extends, and creates simple a–b–a–b patterns (e.g., makes a pattern of train, car, train, car, or with colored Legos does red, yellow, red, yellow).*	0 1 2		
3.2 Places objects from a continuum in order ■ Size ■ Part to whole *When given at least three objects to place in a series, child orders the items with at least three different examples.*	0 1 2 0 1 2		
3.3 Sequences pictures to tell a story *Child sequences at least four pictures in the correct order across at least four different types of sequences (e.g., washing hands, making a sandwich).*	0 1 2		
3.4 Recalls and retells past events *Child recalls at least three events and tells about each event in the correct order.*	0 1 2		

4. Emergent literacy	Scoring	Comments	*
4.1 Makes comments and asks questions while looking at picture books *Child uses gesture and/or words to share or obtain information about pictures and text in books (e.g., child points to red balloon; says, "Look at balloon"; or asks, "Where's the mouse?"*	0 1 2		
4.2 Answers factual questions at the end of a familiar story *At the end of the story, child can answer factual questions about the main idea, main characters, or main events in the story.*	0 1 2		
4.3 Answers questions related to a story that requires inference *Child is able to "read" information from a picture and tell adult why he or she thinks as he or she does. For example, a teacher asks why the child in the picture is sad, the child looks at the picture of a child with a scraped knee and says, "He hurt his knee."*	0 1 2		
4.4 Makes predictions when reading a story *Child makes predictions about what will happen in the story. For example, a teacher asks, "I wonder what will happen to Sam?" and the child predicts what will happen to Sam.*	0 1 2		
4.5 Identifies letters—receptively *Child identifies all the letters in the alphabet, receptively.*	0 1 2		
4.6 Identifies letters—expressively *Child identifies all the letters in the alphabet, expressively.*	0 1 2		

5.	Emergent math	Scoring	Comments	*
5.1	Demonstrates concept of one *When given several items, child gives or assigns one item when asked to do so. For example, child gives one cup to each student during snack, or child gives one cup to you when asked to do so.*	0 1 2		
5.2	Counting objects with one-to-one correspondence *Child counts at least ten items.*	0 1 2		

Summary notes for cognitive

The DATA Model for Teaching Preschoolers with Autism by Ilene Schwartz, Julie Ashmun, Bonnie McBride, Crista Scott, and Susan Sandall. Copyright © 2017 by Paul H. Brookes Publishing Co., Inc. All rights reserved.

D. COMMUNICATION

1.	Following directions	Scoring			Comments	*
1.1	Follows one-step directions without contextual cues	0	1	2		
	For example, adult tells the child, "Get the ball" when it is not immediately present; child gets the ball. Child must be able to follow at least five different simple directions.					
1.2	Follows one-step directions related to safety	0	1	2		
	For example: hold hands, stop, wait, hands down, walk with me. Child must be able to follow at least four different directions.					
1.3	Follows directions to give an item to a person	0	1	2		
	When given an item, the child will follow the direction, such as "Go give Jeremy the ball."					
1.4	Follows two-step directions without contextual cues	0	1	2		
	When doll is not present in immediate environment and an adult or peer tells the child, "Go get your doll and put it on the table," child will follow both directions in order without reminders. Child must be able to follow at least four different two-step directions.					
2.	Responding	Scoring			Comments	*
2.1	Gestures or vocalizes to greet others	0	1	2		
	Child waves arm or vocalizes when greeting and when leaving others.					
2.2	Chooses item when asked to make a choice	0	1	2		
	Present two items and ask child to choose. Child must indicate preferred choice by then taking the item and acting upon it.					
2.3	Responds to question "What do you want?" when items are not present	0	1	2		
	Child is not able to see preferred items but will request them when asked.					
2.4	Responds to a variety of questions					
	■ What	0	1	2		
	■ Where	0	1	2		
	■ Who	0	1	2		
	■ Why	0	1	2		
	■ When	0	1	2		
	Child must be able to respond to three different types of questions for each one listed above.	0	1	2		
2.5	Responds with a yes or no answer					
	■ When asked, "Do you want _____?"	0	1	2		
	■ When asked, "Is this a cow?"	0	1	2		
	Child must be able to answer both yes and no.					

3.	Initiating	Scoring			Comments	*
3.1	Uses gestures to initiate a request *For example, pointing to items out of reach*	0	1	2		
3.2	Initiates with words or gestures to greet others *For example, child waves or says "Hi."*	0	1	2		
3.3	Requests items or activities that are in sight *Child must request a variety of preferred items when child can see the items.*	0	1	2		
3.4	Requests items or activities that are out of sight *Child must request a variety of preferred items that are not visible to the child.*	0	1	2		
3.5	Requests the end of an activity *Child will ask to be "All done" or "Finished" after working with an activity.*	0	1	2		
3.6	Makes comments *During activities, child makes simple comments such as "I'm drawing" during an art activity or "Baby crying" during play.*	0	1	2		
3.7	Uses sentence stems, such as "I want _____," "It's a _____," "I see _____," and "I have _____" to comment and request *Child says a variety of sentences with each sentence stem.*	0	1	2		
3.8	Asks a variety of questions to gain more information					
	■ What (e.g., what is that)	0	1	2		
	■ Where (e.g., where are the markers)	0	1	2		
	■ Who (e.g., who is that)	0	1	2		
	■ Why (e.g., why is she crying)	0	1	2		
	■ When (e.g., when are we going)	0	1	2		
	Child must be able to initiate three different types of questions for each one listed above.					

4.	Comprehension and expression of words and sentences	Receptive			Expressive			Comments	*
4.1	Identifies at least 50 common nouns in pictures and the environment *For example, child points to a ball or truck in pictures from an array of at least three. Child names objects in pictures spontaneously or when asked.*	0	1	2	0	1	2		
4.2	Identifies at least 15 actions in pictures and the environment *For example, when looking at a book or pictures out on table, teacher says, "Who is jumping?" or "Show me reading" and child indicates correct answer. When a teacher asks, "What is he or she doing?" child names action.*	0	1	2	0	1	2		
4.3	Uses pronouns *Child must use a variety of pronouns that may include me, mine, I, you, my, and this.*	0	1	2	0	1	2		

D. COMMUNICATION *(continued)*

4.	Comprehension and expression of words and sentences *(continued)*	Receptive	Expressive	Comments	*
4.4	Identifies at least 10 functions across a variety of common objects or pictures *For example, teacher puts out three different objects or pictures and asks, "Which one do you eat?" "Which one do you play with?" "Which one do you read?" Child fills in the blank when asked, "You eat with a _____?"*	0 1 2	0 1 2		
4.5	Identifies at least 10 features across a variety of common objects or pictures *For example, teacher puts out three different objects or pictures and asks questions such as, "Which one has a tail?" and "Which one has wheels?" Child fills in the blank when a teacher says, "A bird has a _____."*	0 1 2	0 1 2		
4.6	Identifies at least five categories across a variety of common objects or pictures within each category *For example, teacher puts out objects or pictures and asks questions such as, "Which one is an animal?" "Which one is a food?" Child fills in the blank when a teacher says, "This is a kind of _____."*	0 1 2	0 1 2		
4.7	Identifies and uses a variety of attributes				
	■ Colors	0 1 2	0 1 2		
	■ Sizes	0 1 2	0 1 2		
	■ Shapes	0 1 2	0 1 2		
	■ _____	0 1 2	0 1 2		
	For example, teacher puts out several blocks, different only by color and asks "Give me the green block." When requesting an item, child uses modifiers, such as "I want the big block."				
4.8	Identifies and uses prepositions *For example, teacher asks the child "Which car is under the bridge?" or "Give me the car that is on the bridge?" Additionally, teacher may request "Where is the train?" and the child responds "Under the bridge." Child must identify a variety of prepositions.*	0 1 2	0 1 2		
Summary notes for communication					

1.	Joint attention	Scoring			Comments	*
1.1	References communicative partner during a social-communicative interaction *For example, adult looks surprised and child reacts. Child looks at peer when responding to a request.*	0	1	2		
1.2	Follows pointing gesture to establish joint attention *Child looks in the direction of a person's pointing gesture while that person looks at an object, person, or event and comments on it. Child's glance must be longer than 1 second.*	0	1	2		
1.3	Follows gaze to establish joint attention *Child looks in direction of person's gaze while person looks at object, person, or event. Child's glance must be longer than 1 second.*	0	1	2		
1.4	Initiates gestures to establish joint attention *For example, points to a picture when looking at a book; child points to other children playing.*	0	1	2		
1.5	Initiates gaze to establish joint attention *For example, looks at a child crying and then looks at adult.*	0	1	2		
1.6	Maintains a social-communicative interaction with an adult for two exchanges *Consider developmentally appropriate interactions. Interactions may range from peek-a-boo to a conversation.*	0	1	2		
2.	**Pragmatic rules**	**Scoring**			**Comments**	*
2.1	Maintains appropriate proximity to conversation partner *The child does not stand too close or touch other person.*	0	1	2		
2.2	Orients body towards speaker *During a conversation, the child turns their body to the other person.*	0	1	2		
2.3	Maintains eye contact *During a conversation, the child looks in the direction of the other person.*	0	1	2		
2.4	Uses voice volume appropriate to setting *When inside a building, does not talk loudly.*	0	1	2		
2.5	Responds appropriately to common facial expressions and gestures (e.g., head nod and shake) *For example, if adult shakes head to indicate no, the child responds accordingly.*	0	1	2		
2.6	Appropriately interjects *During a conversation, the child waits for a pause and then says "Excuse me," "Guess what," or "Do you know what I did?"*					
2.7	Ends the conversation appropriately *When the conversation is over the child says, "I have to go now" or "See you later."*	0	1	2		

3.	Interactions with peers	Scoring			Comments	*
3.1	Maintains proximity to peers *Child stays within three feet of peers when playing in an unstructured setting.*	0	1	2		
3.2	Imitates peers *For example, when peer is clapping hands in circle, child imitates actions, when peer says, "hip, hip, hooray,, child says, or approximates, the same.*	0	1	2		
3.3	Takes turns with peers *For example, rolling ball back and forth, taking turns with toys. Child will follow direction of an adult to take a turn by offering toy to friend, waiting, and then taking toy again when it is his or her turn.*	0	1	2		
3.4	Responds to interactions from peers *For example, physically accepts toy from peer, answers question.*	0	1	2		
3.5	Initiates interactions towards peers *For example, offers a toy, spontaneously requests an object*	0	1	2		
3.6	Takes turns during unstructured activities *When playing with art materials that are limited, the child will wait for a turn for the scissors.* *When playing grocery store in dramatic play, the child will wait for turn to be the cashier and will provide opportunity for another child to be cashier.*	0	1	2		
3.7	Demonstrates acceptable ways of joining an activity *Observes peers at playing with blocks and asks to join in "Can I play?" or offers a block to put on the structure they are building.*	0	1	2		
3.8	Maintains a conversation with a peer *Child continues a communicative interaction with a peer by asking questions and making comments for at least three turns.*	0	1	2		
3.9	Gives assistance to peers *If a peer is trying to get a toy to work, the child will try to help them.*	0	1	2		
Summary notes for social						

1.	Play fundamentals	Scoring			Comments	*
1.1	Activates cause and effect toys *Cause and effect toys may include jack-in-the-box, wind-up radio, See-N-Say*	0	1	2		
1.2	Uses play materials appropriately *Child acts on objects using functionally or socially appropriate actions. Functionally or socially appropriate actions are those for which the object was intended or designed (e.g., child holds play telephone to ear, puts comb to head and attempts to comb hair, puts glasses on eyes).*	0	1	2		
1.3	Demonstrates functional play with toys related to play theme *For example, feeds baby, brushes baby's teeth, and puts the baby to bed. Child only needs to demonstrate each functional play action; the actions do not need to be in order or sustained.*	0	1	2		
1.4	Uses representational actions with objects *For example, child uses a box as a hat, a spoon as a telephone, a stick to stir food.*	0	1	2		
1.5	Completes a sequence of pretend play actions related to play theme *With dramatic play materials, child may prepare food with the kitchen set, set the table, and place the food on the table. Child must be able to play with a variety of toys across sequences of play themes.*	0	1	2		
1.6	Narrates play *Child describes or states what he or she is doing with play materials.*	0	1	2		
2.	**Independent play**	**Scoring**			**Comments**	*
2.1	Entertains self by playing appropriately with toys for at least 5 minutes *Child can choose toy or be given toys.*	0	1	2		
2.2	Completes puzzles *Child completes puzzles as developmentally appropriate. Consider inset, inset interlocking, and jigsaw puzzles.*	0	1	2		
2.3	Colors or draws *Child uses drawing or writing materials as developmentally appropriate. Consider scribbling, circles, lines, and drawing simple shapes and designs (e.g., a happy face).*	0	1	2		
2.4	Begins and completes at least three different age appropriate activities independently *For example, child chooses a book, looks at it, puts it away.*	0	1	2		
3.	**Interactive play**	**Scoring**			**Comments**	*
3.1	Engages in parallel play *Child plays with farm materials near peer playing with animals. Child plays with dollhouse materials while peer plays with dollhouse.*	0	1	2		
3.2	Engages in associative play *Child plays with same materials, but child(ren) may have different agendas or goals about play. Children do not have to carry out same activity, but are playing on same toys. Children not working toward same goals as in cooperative play.*	0	1	2		

3.	Interactive play *(continued)*	Scoring			Comments	*
3.3	Makes comments about own play to peers *When drawing will remark to a peer, "I am drawing a train" or when building playing with plastic animals will comment, "The shark is swimming in the ocean."*	0	1	2		
3.4	Organizes play by suggesting a play plan *Might suggest, "Let's make a train track and then drive the trains."*	0	1	2		
3.5	Follow a peer's play idea *If peer suggests making a train track and driving trains, the child will join the play to make a track.*	0	1	2		
3.6	Plays cooperatively *Take on pretend role during dramatic play, lead the play by offering play suggestions to peers, and follow game with rules.*	0	1	2		
3.7	Plays games with rules until end of game *Child plays at least three different games, including board games, with only minimal adult supervision.*	0	1	2		
Summary notes for play						

Adaptive

1.

2.

3.

Executive Functioning

1.

2.

3.

Cognitive

1.

2.

3.

Communication

1.

2.

3.

Social

1.

2.

3.

Play

1.

2.

3.

APPENDIX B

DATA Model Skills Checklist: Curriculum Crosswalk

This document is a crosswalk of the DATA Model Skills Checklist with the Assessment, Evaluation, Programming System (AEPS). The crosswalk with the AEPS includes both the birth to 3 and the 3 to 6 assessments.

As stated in Chapter 5, many comprehensive curriculum-referenced assessments provide a picture of child behavior, but often this level of assessment is not sufficient for children with autism spectrum disorders (ASD). Many of the components of the DATA Model Skills Checklist are cross-referenced with the AEPS components because of the broad picture of child development skills these assessments provide. Although many skills are cross-referenced, it is recommended to assess the discrete skill more thoroughly using this checklist to support the child's learning while addressing the core deficits of ASD.

A. ADAPTIVE

1.	Mealtime	AEPS
1.1	Drinks from open cup	0–3 Adaptive A 3—Drinks from cup or glass
		3–6 Adaptive A 1.2—Takes in proper amount of liquid and returns cup to surface
1.2	Eats with fork or spoon	0–3 Adaptive A 4—Eats with fork or spoon
		3–6 Adaptive A 1.5—Eats with utensils
1.3	Eats a variety of food	3–6 Adaptive A 1.3, 1.4—Eats a variety of food textures; Selects and eats a variety of food types
1.4	Remains at table during meals	0–3 Social B 2.0—Participates in established social routines
		3–6 Social C 2.2—Follows established rules at home and in classroom
2.	**Personal hygiene**	**AEPS**
2.1	Toilet trained—urine	0–3 Adaptive B 1.0—Initiates toileting
		3–6 Adaptive B 1.0—Carries out all toileting functions
2.2	Toilet trained—bowel	0–3 Adaptive B 1.0—Initiates toileting
		3–6 Adaptive B 1.0—Carries out all toileting functions
2.3	Washes and dries hands	0–3 Adaptive B 2.0—Washes and dries hands
		3–6 Adaptive B 1.0—Carries out all toileting functions
3.	**School skills**	**AEPS**
3.1	Manages personal belongings	
3.2	Uses classroom materials	3–6 Social B 2.1 and 3.1—Interacts appropriately with materials during small and large group activities
3.3	Completes transitions between activities	0–3 Social B 2.0—Participates in established social routines
3.4	Walks with peers in small or large groups across a variety of school settings	0–3 Social B 2.0—Participates in established social routines
3.5	Rides in school bus, car, or other transportation to and from school	0–3 Social B 2.0—Participates in established social routines
3.6	Waits for instruction to begin (individual, small group, large group)	
3.7	Works independently on a teacher selected activity	3–6 Social B 1.0—Initiates and completes age-appropriate activities
3.8	Begins and completes at least 3 different teacher selected activities	
3.9	Participates in a group activity for:	3–6 Social B 2.0 and 3.0—Watches, listens, and participates during small and large group activities (AEPS does not include time criteria)
	▪ 5 minutes	
	▪ 10 minutes	
	▪ 15 minutes	

4.	**Self-Advocacy**	**AEPS**	
4.1	Requests a break when needed		
4.2	Protests	0–3 Social-Communication B 1.4—Uses gestures or vocalizations to protest actions or reject objects or people	
4.3	Requests help from adults and peers when needed		
4.4	Requests clarification when needed	3–6 Social-Communication A 2.3—Asks questions for clarification	
4.5	Asks for accommodations		
4.6	Identify likes and dislikes	3–6 Social D 1.0—Communicates personal likes and dislikes	
4.7	States identifying information about self	3–6 Social D 3.0—Relates identifying information about self and others	
5.	**Behaviors that interfere with participation and learning**		

The purpose of this section is to identify behaviors that have been resistant to ongoing classroom instruction and behavioral support. The purpose is not to identify all behaviors the child may demonstrate, only those that are chronic and interfere with instruction.

	Yes	No
Example: Screaming	Yes	No
Aggression	Yes	No
Self-injurious behavior	Yes	No
Property destruction	Yes	No
Running away	Yes	No
Self-stimulatory behavior	Yes	No
Screaming	Yes	No
Noncompliance	Yes	No
Other	Yes	No
Other	Yes	No
Other	Yes	No

1.	Flexibility	AEPS
1.1	Follows classroom routine and schedule	0–3 Social B 2.0—Participates in established social routines 3–6 Social C 2.2—Follows established rules at home and in classroom
1.2	Accepts interruptions or unexpected change	
1.3	Accepts being told "no" without becoming upset or angry	
1.4	Relinquishes preferred toy, food, or materials to an adult or peer when asked	
1.5	Accepts that things don't go as expected	
2.	**Self-regulation: Self and emotional control**	**AEPS**
2.1	Waits for a preferred item or activity	
2.2	Accepts comfort from others if upset or agitated	0–3 Social A 2.3—Uses familiar adults for comfort, closeness, or physical contact
2.3	Self-regulates when tense or upset with verbal or visual cue	0–3 Social B 1.2—Uses appropriate strategies to self-soothe
2.4	Self-regulates when energy level is high or low with verbal or visual cue	0–3 Social B 1.2—Uses appropriate strategies to self-soothe
3.	**Persistence, organization, and time management**	**AEPS**
3.1	Persists in gaining a person's attention	
3.2	Persists, or continues to try, when something is difficult	
3.3	Follows a sequence of at least 3 steps in an activity	3–6 Cognitive C 1.0—Follows directions of three or more related steps that are not routinely given
3.4	Finishes an activity within a timely manner, cleans up, and moves to the next activity	
4.	**Problem solving**	**AEPS**
4.1	Claims and defends possessions	3–6 Social A 3.3—Claims and defends possessions
4.2	Identifies or defines the problem	3–6 Cognitive E 1.2—Identifies means to goal
4.3	Generates solutions	3–6 Cognitive E 1.1—Suggests acceptable solutions to problems
4.4	Carries out solutions by negotiating or compromising	3–6 Social A 3.0—Resolves conflicts by selecting effective strategy

B. EXECUTIVE FUNCTIONING *(continued)*

5.	Emotional knowledge	AEPS
5.1	Identifies simple emotions in pictures and books	
5.2	Labels and identifies emotions in self	3–6 Social-Communication A 1.3—Uses words, phrases, or sentences to label own or others' affect emotions 3–6 Social D 2.2—Identifies own affect and emotions
5.3	Labels and identifies emotions in others	3–6 Social-Communication A 1.3—Uses words, phrases, or sentences to label own or others' affect and emotions 3–6 Social D 2.1—Identifies affect and emotions of others
5.4	Justifies an emotion once identified or labeled	3–6 Cognitive E 2.1—Gives reason for inference
5.5	Demonstrates affection and empathy toward peers	3–6 Social A 1.1—Responds to others in distress or need 3–6 Social D 2.0—Understands how own behaviors, thoughts, and feelings relate to consequences for others

C. COGNITIVE

1.	Imitation	AEPS
1.1	Imitates actions with objects	
1.2	Imitates large motor movements	0–3 Cognitive D 1.0—Imitates motor action that is not commonly used
1.3	Imitates fine motor movements	
1.4	Imitates words	0–3 Cognitive D 2.0—Imitates words that are not frequently used
1.5	Imitates multistep sequences	
2.	**Matching and categorizing**	**AEPS**
2.1	Matches identical objects	0–3 Cognitive G 1.3—Matches pictures or objects
2.2	Matches identical pictures	0–3 Cognitive G 1.3—Matches pictures or objects
2.3	Matches objects to pictures	0–3 Cognitive G 1.3—Matches picture or objects
2.4	Matches pictures to objects	0–3 Cognitive G 1.3—Matches pictures or objects
2.5	Matches nonidentical objects and pictures	0–3 Cognitive G 1.3—Matches pictures or objects
2.6	Groups objects according to: ■ Size ■ Shape ■ Color	0–3 Cognitive G 1.2—Groups objects according to size, shape, or color 3–6 Cognitive B 1.3—Groups objects on the basis of physical attribute
2.7	Groups functionally related objects	0–3 Cognitive G 1.1—Groups functionally related objects 3–6 Cognitive B 1.2—Groups objects on the basis of function
2.8	Categorizes like objects	0–3 Cognitive G 1.0—Categorizes like objects 3–6 Cognitive B 1.1—Groups objects, people, or events on the basis of category
3.	**Sequencing**	**AEPS**
3.1	Makes simple patterns	
3.2	Places objects from a continuum in order ■ Size ■ Part to whole	3–6 Cognitive C 2.0—Places objects in series according to length or size
3.3	Sequences pictures to tell a story	3–6 Cognitive C 3.1—Completes sequence of familiar story or event
3.4	Recalls and retells past events	3–6 Cognitive D 1.0—Recalls events that occurred on same day, without contextual cues
4.	**Emergent literacy**	**AEPS**
4.1	Makes comments and asks questions while looking at picture books	0–3 Cognitive G 4.2—Makes comments and asks questions while looking at picture books
4.2	Answers factual questions at the end of a familiar story	3–6 Social-Communication A 2.4—Responds to contingent questions
4.3	Answers questions related to a story that requires inference	3–6 Cognitive E 2.3—Gives possible cause for some event

4.	Emergent literacy (continued)	AEPS
4.4	Makes predictions when reading a story	3–6 Cognitive E 2.2—Makes prediction about future or hypothetical events
4.5	Identifies letters—receptively	3–6 Cognitive H 3.1—Identifies letter names
4.6	Identifies letters—expressively	3–6 Cognitive H 3.1—Identifies letter names
5.	**Emergent math**	**AEPS**
5.1	Demonstrates concept of one	0–3 Cognitive G 2.0—Demonstrates functional use of one-to-one correspondence
5.2	Counting objects with one-to-one correspondence	3–6 Cognitive G 1.1—Counts at least 10 objects

D. COMMUNICATION

1.	Following directions	AEPS
1.1	Follows one-step directions without contextual cues	0–3 Social-Communication C 2.2—Carries out one-step direction without contextual cues
1.2	Follows one-step directions related to safety	
1.3	Follows directions to give an item to a person	
1.4	Follows two-step directions without contextual cues	0–3 Social-Communication C 2.0—Carries out two-step directions without contextual cues
2.	**Responding**	**AEPS**
2.1	Gestures or vocalizes to greet others	0–3 Social-Communication B 1.3—Gestures or vocalizes to greet others 3–6 Social A 1.5—Responds to affective initiations from others
2.2	Chooses item when asked to make a choice	3–6 Social D 1.2—Selects activities or objects
2.3	Responds to question "What do you want?" when items are not present	3–6 Social-Communication A 2.4—Responds to contingent questions
2.4	Responds to a variety of questions ■ What ■ Where ■ Who ■ Why ■ When	3–6 Social-Communication A 2.4—Responds to contingent questions
2.5	Responds with a yes or no answer ■ When asked, "Do you want ___?" ■ When asked, "Is this a cow?"	3–6 Social-Communication A 2.4—Responds to contingent questions
3.	**Initiating**	**AEPS**
3.1	Uses gestures to initiate a request	
3.2	Initiates with words or gestures to greet others	0–3 Social-Communication B 1.3—Gestures or vocalizes to greet others 3–6 Social A 1.4—Initiates greetings to others who are familiar
3.3	Requests items and activities that are in sight	3–6 Social-Communication A 1.5—Uses words, phrases, or sentences to make commands to and requests of others
3.4	Requests items and activities that are out of sight	3–6 Social-Communication A 1.5—Uses words, phrases, or sentences to make commands to and requests of others
3.5	Requests the end of an activity	
3.6	Makes comments	3–6 Social-Communication A 1.7—Uses words, phrases, or sentences to inform
3.7	Uses sentence stems such as "I want _____," "It's a _____," "I see _____," and "I have _____" to comment and request	3–6 Social-Communication A 1.5—Uses words, phrases, or sentences to make commands to and requests of others 3–6 Social-Communication A 1.7 Uses words, phrases, or sentences to inform

3.	Initiating *(continued)*	AEPS
3.8	Asks a variety of questions to gain more information ▪ What ▪ Where ▪ Who ▪ Why ▪ When	3–6 Social-Communication B 3.0—Asks questions
4.	**Comprehension and expression of words and sentences**	**AEPS**
4.1	Identifies at least 50 common nouns in pictures and the environment	0–3 Social-Communication C 1.0 (receptively, criteria is 20)—Locates objects, people, or events without contextual cues 0–3 Social-Communication D 1.4 (expressively, criteria is 15)—Uses 15 object or event labels
4.2	Identifies at least 15 actions in pictures and the environment	0–3 Social-communication D 1.2 (expressively, criteria is 5)—Uses five action words
4.3	Uses pronouns	0–3 Social-Communication D 1.3 (expressively, criteria is 2)—Uses two pronouns 3–6 Social-Communication B 4.0 (expressively)—Uses pronouns
4.4	Identifies at least 10 functions across a variety of common objects or pictures	
4.5	Identifies at least 10 features across a variety of common objects or pictures	
4.6	Identifies at least five categories across a variety of common objects or pictures within each category	
4.7	Identifies and uses a variety of attributes ▪ Colors ▪ Sizes ▪ Shapes ▪ _____	0–3 Social-communication D 1.1 (expressive)—Uses five descriptive words 3–6 Cognitive A 1.0—Demonstrates understanding of color, shape, and size concepts 3–6 Cognitive A 2.0—Demonstrates understanding of qualitative and quantitative concepts 3–6 Social-Communication B 5.0 (expressive)—Uses descriptive words
4.8	Identifies and uses prepositions	3–6 Cognitive A. 3.1—Demonstrates understanding of 12 different spatial relations concepts 3–6 Social-communication B 5.4 (expressive)—Uses prepositions

1.	Joint attention	AEPS
1.1	References communicative partner during a social-communicative interaction	0–3 Social-Communication A 1.0—Turns and looks toward person speaking 3–6 Social-Communication A 3.2
1.2	Follows pointing gesture to establish joint attention	0–3 Social-Communication A 2.1—Follows person's pointing gesture to establish joint attention
1.3	Follows gaze to establish joint attention	0–3 Social-Communication A 2.0—Follows person's gaze to establish joint attention
1.4	Initiates gestures to establish joint attention	0–3 Social-Communication B 1.2—Points to an object, person, or event
1.5	Initiates gaze to establish joint attention	
1.6	Maintains a social-communicative interaction with an adult for two exchanges	0–3 Social A 2.0—Initiates and maintains interaction with familiar adult
2.	**Pragmatic rules**	**AEPS**
2.1	Maintains appropriate proximity to conversation partner	3–6 Social-Communication A 3.2—Uses socially appropriate physical orientation
2.2	Orients body towards speaker	3–6 Social-Communication A 3.2—Uses socially appropriate physical orientation
2.3	Maintains eye contact	0–3 Social-Communication A 1.0—Turns and looks toward person speaking 3– Social-Communication A 3.2—Uses socially appropriate physical orientation
2.4	Uses voice volume appropriate to setting	3–6 Social-Communication A 3.1—Varies voice to impart meaning
2.5	Responds appropriately to common facial expressions and gestures (e.g., head nod and shake)	0–3 Social A 1.0 (expressions)—Responds appropriately to familiar adult's affect
2.6	Appropriately interjects	
2.7	Ends the conversation appropriately	
3.	**Interactions with peers**	**AEPS**
3.1	Maintains proximity to peers	0–3 Social C 1.3—Plays near one or two peers 3–6 Social A 1.2—Establishes and maintains proximity to peers
3.2	Imitates peer	
3.3	Takes turns with peers	3–6 Social A 1.3—Takes turns with others
3.4	Responds to interactions from peers	0–3 Social C 1.2—Responds appropriately to peer's social behavior 3–6 Social A 1.5—Responds to affective initiations from others

3.	Interactions with peers (*continued*)	AEPS
3.5	Initiates interactions towards peers	0–3 Social C 1.1—Initiates social behavior toward peer
		3–6 Social A 1.0—Interacts with others as play partners
3.6	Takes turns during unstructured activities	3–6 Social A 1.3—Takes turns with others
3.7	Demonstrates acceptable ways of joining an activity	3–6 Social A 2.1—Joins others in cooperative activity
3.8	Maintains a conversation with a peer	0–3 Social C 2.0—Initiates and maintains communicative exchange with peer
3.8	Gives assistance to peers	3–6 Social A 1.1—Responds to others in distress or need

1.	Play fundamentals	AEPS
1.1	Activates cause and effect toys	0–3 Cognitive C 1.0—Correctly activates mechanical toy
1.2	Uses play materials appropriately	0–3 Cognitive F 1.2—Uses functionally appropriate actions with objects
		0–3 Cognitive F 1.3—Uses simple motor actions on different objects
1.3	Demonstrates functional play with toys related to play theme	0–3 Cognitive F 1.2—Uses functionally appropriate actions with objects
1.4	Uses representational actions with objects	0–3 Cognitive F 1.1—Uses representational actions with objects
		3–6 Cognitive F 1.3—Uses imaginary props
1.5	Completes a sequence of pretend play actions related to play theme	3–6 Cognitive F 1.2—Plans and acts out recognizable event, theme, or storyline
1.6	Narrates play	
2.	**Independent play**	**AEPS**
2.1	Entertains self by playing appropriately with toys for at least 5 minutes	0–3 Social C 1.5—Entertains self by playing appropriately with toys
2.2	Completes puzzles	
2.3	Colors or draws	
2.4	Begins and completes at least three different age appropriate activities independently	3–6 Social B 1.0—Initiates and completes age-appropriate activities
3.	**Interactive play**	**AEPS**
3.1	Engages in parallel play	
3.2	Engages in associative play	
3.3	Makes comments about own play to peers	0–3 Social C 2.1—Initiates communication with peer
3.4	Organizes play by suggesting a play plan	3–6 Cognitive F 1.2—Plans and acts out recognizable event, theme, or storyline
		3–6 Cognitive F 1.1—Enacts roles or identities
3.5	Follows a peer's play idea	
3.6	Plays cooperatively	3–6 Cognitive F 1.0—Engages in cooperative, imaginary play
		3–6 Social A 2.2—Maintains cooperative participation with others
3.7	Plays games with rules until end of game	3–6 Cognitive F 2.0—Engages in games with rules

APPENDIX C

DATA Model Skills Checklist: Materials List

We recommend creating a materials kit, or two, for your classroom that includes the items named below so they are easily accessible during assessment periods. In addition, some checklist items call for materials specific to the child you are working with. Please adapt the list as needed for your program.

ADAPTIVE

- Observe or test these skills during routine activities when necessary materials are available.

EXECUTIVE FUNCTIONING

- No specific materials are needed for sections 1 through 4. Consider having child's preferred items available for observation during routines and activities.

Emotional Knowledge

- Picture books with children expressing a variety of emotions
- Flash cards or pictures of children expressing a variety of emotions

COGNITIVE

Imitation

- At least five pairs of toys that match

Matching and Categorizing

- At least six pairs of identical objects
- At least six pairs of identical pictures or photos
- At least six objects with matching pictures
- At least six pairs of nonidentical, but similar objects
- At least three different items for each physical attribute (size, shape, color)

- At least six different categories of functionally related objects (paint/paper/paintbrush)
- At least six different categories based on a broad category (food, animals)

Sequencing

- At least 3 sets of about 10 small items to replicate or extend a pattern (counting bears, crayons, Legos)
- At least three sets of objects or pictures that vary or progress by size or length (small red ball, medium-size red ball, and large red ball; house image put in order from part to whole)
- At least four sets of four pictures that depict a logical sequence of events (washing hands, cleaning up)

Emergent literacy

- Picture books that tell a story
- Picture cards and objects—capital letters of the alphabet

Emergent math

- At least 10 similar items that can be counted using one-to-one correspondence

COMMUNICATION

- No specific materials are needed for sections 1 through 3. Consider having child's preferred items available for observation during routines and activities.

Comprehension and expression of words and sentences

Some of the materials in this section can serve multiple purposes. Also, each set below must include multiple exemplars. For example, for pictures of common nouns, the criteria is that the child identifies 50, therefore this set list includes 100 pictures and 25 objects so that multiple exemplars are available.

- 100 pictures of common nouns
- 25 common objects
- 30 pictures with actions
- 20 objects or pictures with clear functions (something you eat, read, play with)
- 20 objects or pictures with clear features (has wheels, a tail)
- 20 objects or pictures with clear categories (food, animal)
- 20 objects or pictures with clear attributes (color, size, shape)

SOCIAL

■ No materials needed for sections 1 and 2

Interactions with Peers

■ Materials of interest to the child for imitating and taking turns

PLAY

Play Fundamentals

■ Three different cause-and-effect toys

■ Five objects to play with functionally (busy balls, shape sorter, potato head)

■ Five objects to use for representational actions (box as a hat, spoon as a telephone)

■ Three sets of objects for sequenced pretend play (baby, toothbrush, bottle, blanket, brush)

Independent Play

■ Toys of interest to child being assessed

■ Puzzles (inset, interlocking, jigsaw)

■ Paper, writing utensil (marker, crayon)

Interactive Play

■ Materials of interest to child being assessed. It may be best to observe or test these in the child's preschool classroom environment.

■ Three board games

APPENDIX D

Frequently Asked Questions

What is Project DATA?

Project DATA (Developmentally Appropriate Treatment for Autism) is a school-based early intensive behavioral intervention (EIBI) program for young children with Autism Spectrum Disorder (ASD). The project was developed in 1997 with support from a model demonstration grant from the U.S. Department of Education with strong in-kind support from the Seattle Public School District. Currently, Project DATA is funded by a combination of school district money and private donations. See Chapter 1 for an in-depth description of the model.

How is Project DATA different from other Early Intensive Behavior Intervention programs for young children with ASD?

Project DATA is a school-based, inclusive program. Inclusion (meaningful participation in groups of children with and without disabilities) is a central tenet of Project DATA. Beginning on the first day of Project DATA, children with ASD spend time in inclusive preschool classrooms. In these classrooms they have the opportunities and the necessary amount of adult guidance to interact successfully with their typically developing peers. This continued interaction with typically developing children is central to helping children with ASD develop and demonstrate valued social-communicative skills. Families report that the opportunities to meet families of other children with ASD and families of typically developing children enable them to build inclusive social networks and create opportunities for their children to interact with peers outside of school.

What research supports the instructional strategies used in Project DATA?

All instructional strategies used in Project DATA have been validated empirically in the behavioral and educational research literature. Some of these instructional strategies include incidental teaching, discrete trial training, the Picture Exchange Communication System (PECS), visual support strategies, and effective prompting strategies (e.g., time delay, most-to-least prompting, graduated guidance). Data are collected daily on child performance to determine the effectiveness of all programs to teach new behaviors and decrease challenging behaviors. In addition, in 2013, our team published a retrospective record review of Project DATA participants that demonstrated significant improvement across all developmental domains for the children in the program (Schwartz, Thomas, et al.).

Why 20 hours a week?

We provide school-based programming for 20 hours per week for two reasons. First, 20 hours is within the range of hours provided by programs that have documented positive outcomes for young children with ASD. Second, the schedule of the extended day program is an ecologically valid model. That is, with this model, school districts and other programs will be able to replicate and reasonably sustain this model of services.

What is your teacher-student ratio?

We have a minimum of one adult to two children during the extended day portion of the Project DATA model. Children work in different sized groups and individually with adults. Group assignments are made on an individual basis for all children.

Whom does the program serve?

Project DATA was developed to serve young children with ASD, or who are at risk for a diagnosis of ASD, and are receiving special education services in public schools. In the model Project DATA site, all children who participate in the program are referred by the local school district.

In addition to the children in the classroom, family members receive services from Project DATA. These include parent information and support services, as well as home or center visits. See Chapter 9 for a detailed description of how Project DATA works with families.

What are staff qualifications?

In the model Project DATA classroom at University of Washington (UW), the head teachers of Project DATA classrooms supervise teaching assistants and educational assistants. Therefore, these head teachers are master's-level teachers with training in autism, applied behavior analysis, and early childhood special education. The teaching assistants are graduate students in the special education program at UW. Educational assistants range from certified teachers and graduate students to people with experience working with children but no formal training in education. Additionally, Ph.D.-level consultants provide training, family support, and consultation.

In communities that have implemented Project DATA, the head teachers come with a variety of qualifications including certified special education teachers, BCBAs, and speech language pathologists. The most important qualification is the ability to work with other adults to provide individualized, high-quality programming to young children with ASD.

How does Project DATA staff decide what behaviors and skills to teach children with ASD?

Project DATA teachers utilize broad-based curriculum-based measurements (CBM) and the DATA Model Skills Checklist to identify behaviors and skills to teach children in the program. Project DATA teachers also use other sources of information such as an IEP, other assessments that have already been conducted, and the Project DATA Family Interview Survey.

What plan do you have for training staff? Who does the training?

Staff receive training in basic behavioral principles, effective instructional strategies including discrete trial training and naturalistic intervention strategies, program development, data collection and analysis, and the fundamentals of generalization before they begin working with children. Senior project staff conduct all staff training. All staff members meet regularly with their supervisors to review child progress and everyone receives ongoing coaching to improve their teaching and collaboration skills.

As a teacher, can I implement Project DATA on my own?

Teachers may use the DATA Model Skills Checklist to inform instruction and may use the instructional programming sheets to support teaching children with ASD. To make this program successful, however, full administrative support is important for making necessary changes, such as providing more trained paraprofessionals and lengthening the school day for the children in the program. See Chapter 10 for more information about implementing Project DATA in your community.

Do I need to collect data every day?

Yes. Daily data collection is essential in providing the information to conduct data-based decision making. This type of decision making relies on frequent and accurate information about child behavior and performance on instructional programs.

What resources are available for professional development to teachers and school districts who would like to implement Project DATA?

Professional development is available with the UW's Haring Center, PDU (Professional Development Unit). Contact the Haring Center PDU at (206) 543-4011 or pdutrain@uw.edu.

Index

Page numbers followed by *f* and *t* indicate figures and tables, respectively.

ABA, *see* Applied behavior analysis
Acquisition, as learning stage, 54
Activity matrix, for including children with a, 12–13, 13*f*
Adaptive instructional program forms, 118–165
Adaptive skills checklist, materials list for, 451
Administrator, qualifications and responsibilities for, 111
AEPS, *see* Assessment, Evaluation, and Programming System, 2nd edition
Antecedents of challenging behaviors, changing
  applied behavior analysis in, 19–24
  controlling access to preferred activities in, 23–24
  improving clarity of environment in, 21–22
  improving quality of environment in, 22–23
  increasing clarity of expectations in, 20–21
Applied behavior analysis (ABA)
  basic principles of, 19–28
  changing antecedents in, 19–24
ASD, *see* Autism spectrum disorder
Assessment, Evaluation, and Programming System, 2nd edition (AEPS), 5, 46, 50, 439
  DATA Model Skills Checklist, Curriculum Crosswalk, 439–450
  in support for DATA Model, 5
Assessment in early childhood classrooms, 43–50
  DATA Model Skills Checklist in, 45–48, *see also* DATA Model Skills Checklist
  information from, translating into programs of instruction, 48–50
Attention, joint, instructional program forms for, 332–345
Autism spectrum disorder (ASD)
  children with
    as children first, 3–4
    families of, 95–106, *see also* Family(ies)
    high-quality inclusive early childhood program for, characteristics of, 9–17
    core deficits of, inclusion and, 10–11

Behavioral objective, writing, 52–53
Behaviors, challenging, *see* Challenging behaviors
Binders, instructional, 62, 63*f*–66*f*, 67
Building Blocks for Teaching Preschoolers with Special Needs, Second Edition (Sandall & Schwartz), 10
  see also Building Blocks Framework
Building Blocks Framework, for including children with autism spectrum disorder, 11–15
  activity matrix in, 12–13, 13*f*
  addressing challenging behavior in, 15–16

embedded learning opportunities (ELOs) in, 14–15
well-designed classroom environment in, 11–12

Categorizing
  instructional program forms for, 234–239
  skills checklist for, materials list for, 451–452
Chaining, to facilitate learning, 40
Challenging behaviors
  antecedents of, changing, 19–24, *see also* Antecedents of challenging behaviors, changing
  consequences of, changing, 24–28
    negative reinforcement in, 25–26
    positive reinforcement in, 24–25, 25*t*
    punishment in, 27–28
  in inclusive programs, addressing, 15–16
  motivations for, 15
Child performance data, summarizing, 89, 90*f*–92*f*
Child response, in discrete trials, 34
Childhood Autism Rating Scale (CARS), in support for DATA Model, 5
Choice making as teaching strategy, 39
Classroom assistant, qualifications and responsibilities for, 111
Classroom environment, well-designed, for including children with autism spectrum disorder (ASD), 11–12
Cognitive instructional program forms, 212–263
Cognitive skills checklist, materials list for, 451–452
Collaboration, in Project DATA Model, 8
Communication
  across classroom and extended day program, 76–78, 77*f*
  instructional program forms for, 264–331
  skills checklist for, materials list for, 452
Comprehension and expression of words and sentences
  instructional program forms for, 300–331
  skills checklist for, materials list for, 452
Consequence(s)
  of challenging behaviors, changing, 24–28
  in discrete trials, 34–36
Coordination, in Project DATA Model, 8
Coordinator/administrator, qualifications and responsibilities for, 111
Curriculum, quality-of-life influenced, in Project DATA Model, 8
Curriculum crosswalk, skills checklist for preschool aged children with autism as, 439

Curriculum planning, 43–50
    assessment of current performance level in,
        43–50 *see also* Assessment, in early
        childhood classrooms
    skills selection in, 43
    translating assessment information into,
        48–50

Daily data sheet, 83, 86*f*
    task analysis, 83, 87*f*
Daily program checklist, 64*f*
Data
    child performance, summarizing, 89, 90*f*–92*f*
    collection of
        daily, rationale for, 456
        reasons for, 79–80
    decisions based on, making, 89, 92–93
    duration, 80–81
    frequency, 80
    level of independence, 81
    permanent product, 81
    rate, 81
    school placement, supporting DATA model, 4
    time sampling, 81–82
    types of, 80–82
Data-based decision making, 78–93
DATA Model, *see* Project DATA Model
DATA Model Skills Checklist, 45–48
    guidelines for completing, 46, 48
    implementing, 46
    sections of, 45–46
    selected items from, 47*f*
Data sheet(s)
    creating, selecting, and using, 82–89, 84*f*–88*f*
    daily, 83, 86*f*
    task analysis daily, 83, 87*f*
    trials daily, 83, 84*f*
    trials daily with graphing, 83, 85*f*
    weekly, 88*f,* 89
Decontextualized *versus* embedded teaching, to
    facilitate learning, 40–41, 70–71
Developmentally Appropriate Treatment for Autism,
    see Project DATA Model
Directions, following, instructional program forms
    for, 264–273
Discrete trials, to facilitate learning, 29–37, 70–71
    child response in, 34
    components of, 29–30, 30*f*
    consequence in, 34–36
    instruction in, 30–32
    intertrial interval in, 36
    prompt in, 32–34
    recommended practices in using, 36–37, 38*f*
Discriminative stimulus (S^D), instruction and, 31
Duration data, 80–81

Education classes, for families in Project DATA
    program, 97

Embedded learning opportunities (ELOs), for
    including children with autism spectrum
    disorder (ASD), 14–15
Embedded teaching, decontextualized teaching
    versus, 40–41, 70–71
Emergent literacy
    instructional program forms for, 248–259
    skills checklist for, materials list for, 452
Emergent math
    instructional program forms for, 260–263
    skills checklist for, materials list for, 452
Emotional knowledge
    instructional program forms for, 202–211
    skills checklist for, materials list for, 451
Environment
    arranging to reduce clutter and improve function, 22
    clarity of, improving, in changing antecedents of
        challenging behaviors, 21–22
    classroom, well-designed, for including children
        with autism spectrum disorder (ASD), 11–12
    physical, for extended day program, 73, 75
    quality of, improving, in changing antecedents of
        challenging behaviors, 22–23
Executive functioning instructional program forms,
    166–211
Executive functioning skills checklist, materials list
    for, 451
Expectations, clarity of, increasing, in changing
    antecedents of challenging behaviors, 20–21
Expression and comprehension of words and
    sentences
    instructional program forms for, 330–331
    skills checklist for, materials list for, 452
Extended day program, 71–76
    class composition of, 72–73
    classroom and, staff communication across,
        76–78, 77*f*
    goal of, 72
    instructional grouping in, 75–76
    instructional strategies for, selecting, 67
    physical environment of, 73, 75
    schedule for, 73, 74*f*
    staffing of, 72–73
    time allotment for, rationale for, 455

Failure, student, as instructional failure, 4
Family(ies)
    social support for, 7–8, 103–106
    technical support for, in Project DATA Model, 7–8,
        95–103
Family Interview Survey form, 97, 98*f*–102*f*
Flexibility, instructional program forms for, 166–177
Fluency, as learning stage, 54
Following directions, instructional program forms
    for, 264–273
Frequency data, 80

Generalization, as learning stage, 54

Head teacher, qualifications and responsibilities for, 111

Home Visit Notes form, 103, 104f–105f

Home visits, in parent support program, 97, 103, 104f–105f

Hygiene, personal, instructional program forms for, 128–133

Imitation
  instructional program forms for, 212–223
  skills checklist for, materials list for, 451

Implementation checklist for Project DATA, 111, 112f
  in program planning, 113
  in program quality evaluation, 113–114
  in sustainability evaluation, 114

Implementing Project DATA Model, 109–115
  checklist for, 111, 112f
  inclusive early childhood program identification in, 110
  partner identification in, 109
  program planning in, 113
  quality self-assessment in, 113–114
  schedule in, 110
  staffing in, 110–111
  sustainability evaluation in, 114
  team leader identification in, 110

Incidental teaching as teaching strategy, 40

Inclusion, core deficits of autism spectrum disorder and, 10–11

Inclusive early childhood program
  high-quality, for children with autism spectrum disorder, 9–17
  in implementing Project DATA, 110

Independent play
  instructional program forms for, 392–399
  skills checklist for, materials list for, 453

Individual program review sheet, 66f

Initiating, instructional program forms for, 284–299

Instruction
  in discrete trial, 30–32
  embedded, for including children with autism spectrum disorder, 14–15
  extended, intensive, in Project DATA Model, 7
  high-quality, guidelines for, 31–32
  S^D and, 31

Instructional failure, student failure as, 4

Instructional grouping, for extended day program, 75–76

Instructional program(s)
  blank, with lesson plan form, 58f–59f
  instructional information in, organizing, 62, 63f–66f, 67
  purpose of, 51
  sample of skill sequence in, 57f
  sample of task analysis in, 56f
  using, to guide lesson planning and teaching, 60–67

writing, 51–55, 56f–59f
  behavioral objective in, 52–53
  learning stages in, 54–55
  mastery criteria in, appropriate, selecting, 53–55
  teaching sequence or task analysis development in, 55

Instructional programs, Project DATA forms
  adaptive, 118–165
  cognitive, 212–263
  communication, 264–331
  executive functioning, 166–211
  play, 378–420
  social, 332–377

Instructional strategies to facilitate learning, 29–41
  discrete trials as, 29–37, see also Discrete trials to facilitate learning

Instructions, improved, in increasing clarity of expectations, 20

Integrated early childhood experience, in Project DATA Model, 6–7

Interaction with peers
  instructional program forms for, 260–277
  skills checklist for, materials list for, 453

Interactive play
  instructional program forms for, 400–413
  skills checklist for, materials list for, 453

Intertrial interval, in discrete trials, 36

Joint attention, instructional program forms for, 332–345

Knowledge, emotional
  instructional program forms for, 202–211
  skills checklist for, materials list for, 451

Learning
  instructional strategies to facilitate, 29–41
    chaining as, 40
    decontextualized versus embedded teaching as, 40–41
    discrete trials as, 29–37, see also Discrete trials to facilitate learning
    naturalistic teaching strategies as, 37, 39–40
    shaping as, 40
  stages of, 54–55

Lesson plan, sample of, 61f

Lesson planning, instructional program guiding, 60–62, 61f

Level of independence data, 81

Literacy, emergent
  instructional program forms for, 248–255
  skills checklist for, materials list for, 452

Maintenance, as learning stage, 54–55

Maintenance and generalization tracking form, 65f

Matching
    instructional program forms for, 224–233
    skills checklist for, materials list for, 451–452
Materials list, DATA Model Skills Checklist,
        451–453
Math, emergent
    instructional program forms for, 260–263
    skills checklist for, materials list for, 452
Mealtime, instructional program forms for, 118–127
Modeling, 33
Model–question as teaching strategy, 39

Natural reinforcers, for embedded learning
        opportunities (ELOs), 14
Naturalistic teaching strategies, to facilitate
        learning, 37, 39–40
Negative reinforcement, in changing consequences
        of challenging behaviors, 25–26

Organization, instructional program forms for,
        190–191

Partners, community, for Project DATA Model in
        community, identifying, 109
PBIS, see Positive behavior intervention and support
Peabody Picture Vocabulary Test, 3rd edition
        (PPVT-III)
    in support for DATA Model, 5
Peers, interaction with
    instructional program forms for, 360–377
    skills checklist for, materials list for, 453
Permanent product data, 81
Persistence, instructional program forms for, 186–189
Personal hygiene, instructional program forms for,
        128–133
Physical prompt, 33
PKBS-2, see Preschool and Kindergarten Behavior
        Scale, 2nd Edition, in support of DATA Model
Play
    fundamentals of
        instructional program forms for, 378–391
        skills checklist for, materials list for, 453
    independent
        instructional program forms for, 392–399
        skills checklist for, materials list for, 453
    instructional program forms for, 378–413
    interactive
        instructional program forms for, 400–413
        skills checklist for, materials list for, 453
    skills checklist for, materials list for, 453
Positive behavior intervention and support (PBIS)
    for preventing challenging behaviors, 16
Positive reinforcement, in changing consequences of
        challenging behaviors, 24–25, 25t
PPVT-III, see Peabody Picture Vocabulary Test
Pragmatic rules, instructional program forms for,
        346–359

Preschool and Kindergarten Behavior Scale, 2nd
        Edition (PKBS-2), in support for DATA
        Model, 5
Preschool Inclusion Toolbox: How to Build and
        Lead a High Quality Program (Barton &
        Smith), 110
Problem solving, instructional program forms for,
        194–201
Project DATA head teacher, qualifications and
        responsibilities for, 111
Project DATA Model
    behaviors and skills targeted in, selection of, 456
    changing antecedents of challenging behaviors in,
        19–24
    children served by, 456
    collaboration and coordination in, 8
    compared with other Early Intensive Behavior
        Intervention programs, 455
    core beliefs of, 3–4
    core components of, 6–8, 6f
    data-based decision making in, 78–93
    description of, 455
    extended, intensive instruction in, 7, 71–76, see
        also Extended day program
    implementing in your community, 109–115, see
        also Implementing Project DATA Model
    instructional components in, 69–70
    instructional programs for, 117–420, see also
        Instructional programs, Project DATA
    instructional strategies to facilitate learning in,
        29–41, see also Instructional strategies to
        facilitate learning
    integrated early childhood experience in, 6–7
    introducing, 3–8
    professional development resources for, 456
    quality-of-life curriculum in, 8
    research support for, 4–5
    research supporting, 455
    skills checklist of, 421–438, see also Skills,
        checklist, Project DATA
    social support to families and, 7–8, 103, 106
    staff qualifications for, 456
    teacher-student ratio for, 455
    teaching style for, 69–78, see also Teaching
        Project DATA Style
    technical and social support for families in, 7–8
    technical support to families and, 7–8, 95–103,
        104f–105f
    transition support in, 106–107
    use of, by individual teacher, 456
    what to teach in, determining, 43–50, see also
        Curriculum planning
    working collaboratively with other providers in,
        106
Prompt fading in discrete trials, 32–33
Prompts
    in discrete trials, 32–34
    improved, in increasing clarity of expectations,
        20–21
    types of, 33–34

Punishment, in changing consequences of challenging behaviors, 27–28

Quality-of-life influenced curriculum, in Project DATA Model, 8

Rate data, 81
Reading, emergent, instructional program forms for, 256–259
Reinforcement schedules
    continuous, 26
    intermittent, 26–27, 27t
Reinforcers
    in changing consequences of challenging behaviors, 24–27
    natural, for embedded learning opportunities (ELOs), 14
    potential, increasing salience of, 23–24
Research support, for DATA Model, 4–5
Responding, instructional program forms for, 274–283
Rules, pragmatic, instructional program forms for, 346–359

Schedule(s)
    for extended day program, 73, 74f
    in implementing Project DATA, 110
    for improving clarity of environment, 22
School placement data, supporting DATA Model, 4
School skills, instructional program forms for, 134–151
S^D (discriminative stimulus), instruction and, 31
Self-advocacy, instructional program forms for, 152–165
Self-regulation, instructional program forms for, 178–185
Sentences and words, comprehension and expression of
    instructional program forms for, 330–331
    skills checklist for, materials list for, 452
Sequencing
    instructional program forms for, 240–247
    skills checklist for, materials list for, 452
Shaping, to facilitate learning, 40
Skills checklist, DATA Model, 421–438
    materials list for, 451–453
    for preschool aged children with autism, 439–450

Social instructional program forms, 332–377
Social skills checklist, materials list for, 453
Social support, for families, 7–8, 103, 106
    in Project DATA Model, 7–8
Staff, for Project DATA
    qualifications for, 456
    training of, 456
Staffing
    for extended day program, 72–73
    in implementing Project DATA, 110–111
Student failure, as instructional failure, 4

Task analysis, development of, in writing instructional program, 55, 56f
Task analysis daily data sheet, 83, 87f
Teaching, instructional program guiding, 60–67
Teaching Project DATA Style, 69–78
    defining, 69–71
Teaching sequence, development of, in writing instructional program, 55
Team leader in implementing Project DATA, 110
Technical support, for families, 7–8, 95–103, 104f–105f
    in Project DATA Model, 7–8
Time delay as teaching strategy, 39–40
Time management, instructional program forms for, 192–193
Time sampling data, 81–82
Transition support, 106–107
Trial daily data sheet, with graphing, 83, 85f
Trials daily data sheet, 83, 84f

Verbal prompt, 34
Visual prompt, 33
Visual supports
    in classroom environment for including children with autism spectrum disorder, 12
    for improving clarity of environment, 21–22
    in Teaching Project DATA Style, 71

Weekly data sheet, 88f, 89
Words and sentences, comprehension and expression of
    instructional program forms for, 330–331
    skills checklist for, materials list for, 452